The Governing of Britain 1688–1848

In this fascinating and compelling book, Peter Jupp examines how the scope and purpose of the government was radically reshaped during the eighteenth century, and shows how the power and influence of central government was fundamentally altered during a period of tumultuous change. In this groundbreaking study, Jupp throws fresh light on debates surrounding the 'long eighteenth century', providing the first analysis of its kind of the expanding role of the executive, the public sphere and popular politics.

The legacy of the English Revolution was fundamental to the shift that took place from monarchical to ministerial government from the seventeenth century onwards. The diminishing of royal power was accompanied by the growth of a civil service and, more importantly, by changes to the structure and activities of Parliament. During this period, Parliament met more frequently and for longer periods of time, resulting in an increase in the amount of legislation passed. There were more general elections – crucially, more of these than ever before were contested elections. Moreover, political parties became established as fundamental to parliamentary and constitutional politics, and in turn, these changes encouraged the growth of new forms of political activity amongst the middle and lower classes. The era saw a dramatic increase in provincial clubs and societies, a proliferation of pressure groups and lobby interests and a growing body of publishers and writers commenting on parliamentary affairs.

Providing new insights into how Parliament became central to the process of governing and how it evolved as a crucial link between the landed elite and the rest of society, this analysis of government in Britain, spanning three centuries, is an essential guide to a formative era in political life.

Peter Jupp is Emeritus Professor of History at Queen's University, Belfast. He is co-editor, with Eoin Magennis, of *Crowds in Ireland, c.1720–1920* (2000), and author of *British Politics on the Eve of Reform* (1998).

The Governing of Britain, 1688–1848

The executive, Parliament and the people

Peter Jupp

Routledge
Taylor & Francis Group

LONDON AND NEW YORK

First published 2006
by Routledge
2 Park Square, Milton Park, Abingdon, Oxon OX14 4RN

Simultaneously published in the USA and Canada
by Routledge
270 Madison Ave, New York, NY 10016

Routledge is an imprint of the Taylor & Francis Group, an informa business

Typeset in Galliard by
Newgen Imaging Systems (P) Ltd, Chennai, India
Printed and bound in Great Britain by
MPG Books Ltd, Bodmin

British Library Cataloguing in Publication Data
A catalogue record for this book is available from the British Library

Library of Congress Cataloging in Publication Data
Jupp, Peter.
    The governing of Britain, 1688–1848: the executive, Parliament,
and the people / by Peter Jupp.
        p. cm.
    Includes bibliographical references and index.
        1. Great Britain – Politics and government – 18th century.
    2. Great Britain – Politics and government – 19th century.
    3. Great Britain. Parliament – History – 18th century. 4. Great Britain.
    Parliament – History – 19th century. 5. Monarchy – Great Britain –
    History – 18th century. 6. Monarchy – Great Britain – History –
    19th century. I. Title.
    DA480.J87 2006
    320.44109'03–dc22   2005035653

ISBN10: 0–415–22948–0 (hbk)
ISBN10: 0–415–22949–9 (pbk)
ISBN10: 0–203–96932–4 (ebk)

ISBN13: 978–0–415–22948–7 (hbk)
ISBN13: 978–0–415–22949–4 (pbk)
ISBN13: 978–0–203–96932–8 (ebk)

Contents

Tables

Preface and acknowledgements

The purpose of this book is to provide readers with an assessment of the changes that took place in the ways Britain was governed by the executive and Parliament during a period when, as it happens, her position as an international power was transformed. At the time of the 'Glorious Revolution', England stood, after France and the Hapsburg empire, in the second rank of European powers. By 1848, however, what had become the United Kingdom of Great Britain and Ireland was unquestionably the world's dominant territorial, commercial and industrial power.

Apart from curiosity, the reasons for attempting an assessment lie in the changes that have taken place in the research and teaching of British history. In the 1960s, executive (or 'central') government was a major topic of research in British history and the backbone of most university and school courses. Since then, however, the subject matter of research has broadened very considerably, not least in the political history of this period. Thus, although research on the conduct and policies of governments has continued, it has been put into the shade by the attention paid to other themes. These include, in the rough chronological order in which they have attracted historians, the social profile of MPs and the histories of parliamentary constituencies; the rise, fall and reconstitution of parliamentary parties; popular or 'non elite' politics; the functional and ideological features of the development of the English/British state and the ideological and cultural (particularly the religious) contexts of political behaviour at all levels of society (particularly of the governing class). More recently, the processes leading to parliamentary legislation have also become a major research topic.

This broadening of the subject matter of research has been accompanied by two other developments. One has been the proliferation of the concepts used by historians to characterise specific periods of political history and to illustrate what they regard as their critical features. In this particular period two books have been particularly influential. The first in order of its publication in 1985 is J. C. D. Clark's *English Society, 1688–1832*. Here he formulates the concept of a 'long eighteenth century' during which England was an 'ancien-regime' state 'dominated politically, culturally and ideologically by the three pillars of an early-modern social order: monarchy, aristocracy, church'. The second, published four years later, was John Brewer's *The Sinews of Power*. In this he argues that the increase in Britain's military involvement in Europe after 1688 and the accompanying increases in government borrowing, taxation and bureaucracy created a 'fiscal-military state'. This, he says, 'was the single most important transformation in English government' between the Tudors and the 1830s and made a major contribution to Britain's growth as a world power.

The second development, at least in Britain, has been the contraction of the time that students can devote to particular periods of history and a broadening of the range of subjects of all kinds – political, social, cultural – that they can study. The result in many institutions is that students are encouraged to study a variety of topics during, and for, comparatively short periods of time. The consequence, in the case of political history, is that an increasing number of students lack an adequate knowledge of the principal developments in the subject over long periods of time. The key point in this regard, is that without such knowledge, it is very difficult to comprehend fully the thinking that influenced politicians at any point in time either in this period or in the next hundred years or so – no matter what their place in society. This is due to the fact that for most politicians interpretations of key political events and personalities in the past contributed substantially to the formulation of their political views and standpoints.

Taken together, these developments led to the conclusion that an assessment of executive and parliamentary government in the light of historiography since the 1960s would not only be an interesting exercise in its own right but would also be useful to students and the general reader. Amongst other things, it might serve to reintegrate the practice of executive government into political history. The unusually long time-span of 1688–1848 was chosen partly because it coincides with the transformation of Britain's status as a world power and partly to see whether the concept of 'a long eighteenth century' is as applicable to the processes of government as it might be to the mental outlook of the landed classes. It soon became clear, however, that it would be impracticable to deal with each of the issues selected for assessment over the period as a whole. The book therefore has two parts, with 1760 being the dividing line between them. Apart from being close to the middle of the period as a whole, the 1760s were marked by a new monarch, the disintegration of the two major parties of the earlier period, the foundation of the 'second' British empire, and the beginnings of a new form of radical politics.

The issues examined are the same in both parts of the book. The first chapters in each case (1 and 5) begin with introductions describing key developments in the periods concerned before assessing the changes in the framework of the executive – that is, the monarch, the first ministers, the cabinets and the various departments of state. The second (2 and 6) then turn to the scope, purpose and achievements of the executive – that is the range of issues they dealt with, the thinking that lay behind policy, and their respective contributions to political stability, domestic security and the growth of Britain as a world power. In the third chapters (3 and 7), the focus is on Parliament: its functions and the extent to which these affected the conduct of the executive and represented the interests of the population at large. Finally, in the fourth chapters (4 and 8), an assessment is made of the principal elements of public opinion and the degree to which these were linked to the processes of parliamentary and executive government.

The completion of this book owes a great deal to others. The writing of an interpretative synthesis had long been an ambition but the particular focus of this book was suggested to me by Norman Gash in the course of conversation about my *British Politics on the Eve of Reform*. This was followed by an invitation from Routledge to write a general history and I am grateful to them for allowing me to follow Professor Gash's suggestion rather than tackle the rather different project they then had in mind.

Research on the topic has been conducted over four decades: partly in the course of work on other subjects and partly for teaching purposes. I therefore owe a considerable debt to colleagues and students, particularly to past and current research students, especially those who took an MA in British political history which I taught with Dr Ian Packer. The book would not have been finished, however, without two recent periods of research leave funded by Queen's University, Belfast and the Arts and Humanities Research Council; and made possible by the generosity of colleagues in what was then the School of History. I would therefore like to record my gratitude to all concerned.

Finally, I owe a very particular debt to those who read a draft of the book. Two of these, one of whom was Professor Eric Evans, the other being anonymous, did so on behalf of the publishers. Two others, Professor David Hayton and Ms Joanna Innes, did so at my request. All four reports were immensely helpful and led to the correcting of errors of both fact and interpretation and various additional lines of enquiry. I am grateful to all of them, and particularly to David Hayton and Joanna Innes for various other forms of advice and encouragement. They are all absolved, however, from any responsibility for the final text.

Abbreviations

I have been as sparing as possible in the citation of sources and have applied the following rules. The full titles and dates of books are given when first referred to together with their place of publication if it is other than London. Subsequent references provide short titles only. In the case of articles, full details are provided with the first reference but short titles thereafter, although in this case I have also provided the source in order to obviate looking back through the endnotes to find it.

Throughout I have adopted the following abbreviations:

BIHR   *Bulletin of the Institute of Historical Research*
BL   *British Library*
CJ   *Commons Journal*
EconHR   *Economic History Review*
EHR   *English Historical Review*
HJ   *The Historical Journal*
HR   *Historical Research*
IHS   *Irish Historical Studies*
JBS   *Journal of British Studies*
JICH   *Journal of Imperial and Commonwealth History*
PH   *Parliamentary History*
PP   *Parliamentary Papers*
P&P   *Past and Present*
TRHS   *Transactions of the Royal Historical Society*

The titles of other journals are given in full.

Part I

1688–1760

1 The framework of the executive

Introduction

During this period there were a number of crucial developments that set the context for the chapters that follow. One was the flight of James II, his deposition, and the establishment by Parliament of the monarchy of King William and Queen Mary. Here began the development of the mixed system of government that is the theme of the first three chapters. This, however, did not take place in a vacuum. It was strongly influenced by a number of other key developments, four of which are touched on here. One was the growth of England's power within the British archipelago. A second was Britain's growth as a world power. A third was Britain's ability to fund long periods of warfare that was itself due, in part at least, to the rapid expansion of her trade and commerce. Finally, although the propertied elite soon acquired a strong dominance of the principal institutions of government, this was accompanied by a gradual, if uneven, growth in various forms of 'non-elite' or popular political activity.

The first of these, the growth of England's power within the British archipelago, was largely due to the new means established to govern both Ireland and Scotland.[1] In Ireland's case, James II's decision to land at Kinsale in March 1689 and to take arms against William of Orange and his supporters led first, to his defeat by King William, 1690–1, and second, to the confiscation of about one million acres possessed by his largely Catholic followers. This was followed in October 1792 by King William and Queen Mary being recognised as rulers by the Irish Parliament and by steps being taken to prevent Catholics from worshipping, owning property and educating their children. In due course, the Irish Parliament came to represent only the Protestant and Anglican minority, its administration being conducted normally by Irish 'undertakers' on behalf of the British executive – a fallback being found in an act passed in 1719 which declared that the British Parliament had the right to make laws for Ireland, if it so chose. As for Scotland, a solution to management had been found in the Act of Union of 1707 that abolished the Scottish Parliament and required sixteen elected peers to be sent to the House of Lords in London and for forty five MPs to sit in the Commons. It was also decided that there would be a common flag, the 'Union Jack', as well as a common coinage between the two kingdoms and a freedom of trade across the borders and within the colonies. Taken together, these measures gave the executive more direct responsibility for governing both kingdoms.

Britain's status as a European power also increased substantially. This was due in part to the wealth and resources that accrued from her colonial possessions: in India, where there were bases in Madras and Calcutta that were managed after 1709 by a United (East India) Company; in north America, where British colonies stretched from Maine to South Carolina; and elsewhere – a British settlement on the Gold Coast of Africa being founded in 1750. It was largely due, however, to Britain's capacity to take part successfully in continental wars. Between 1689 and 1763, she was engaged in five. In the first, the 'Nine Years War', 1688–97, she was in partnership principally with the Habsburg Empire (Austria–Hungary), the United Provinces (Holland) and Spain against France. Four years later she was engaged with the same partners and opponents in the war of the 'Spanish Succession', 1701–13. There then followed the war of the 'Quadruple Alliance', 1718–20, in which she was joined by France, Holland and ultimately, the Emperor to resist Spanish ambitions in France and Italy. These were succeeded by the wars of Jenkins' Ear (against Spain, 1739–41) and of the Austrian Succession, 1739–48, when Britain joined with France and Holland as a result of Maria Theresia's succession to the Empire and Frederick the Great's invasion of Silesia on behalf of Prussia. Finally, Britain was allied with Prussia against France and Spain in the 'Seven Years War' of 1756–63. Altogether, Britain was engaged in major European wars for 42 of these 76 years – a tangible reason why war, the raising of troops, and their funding were such critical aspects of the politics of this period.

In all these cases, Britain was on the winning side, but before the Seven Years War, none provided more important tangible gains than that of the Spanish Succession that was brought to a conclusion by the Peace of Utrecht (1713). In that France ceded the whole of Hudson Bay and all her settlements in Newfoundland as well as Nova Scotia, the only exception being the island of Cape Breton. In addition, she also ceded St Kitts (which had been captured in 1702) and agreed to recognise the Protestant succession and not to aid the Catholic or Jacobite cause. As for the other adversary, Spain, she ceded Gibraltar and Minorca, both of which had been captured in 1704 and 1708, and gave up the Assiento which had given her the monopoly of supplying slaves to her colonies in south America. Taken together, these added substantially to Britain's overseas possessions and gave her some vital strategic interests.

Britain's capacity to engage so successfully in these wars was, from various perspectives, remarkable. The population of England and Wales was small by comparison with that of France or the Habsburg Empire and has been estimated at under 6 millions at the start of this period, less than a third of that her principal rival. Further, it rose to only about 6.7 millions by 1761. Those of Scotland and Ireland were even smaller (*c*.1 and 2.8 millions, respectively) and although these apparently rose at a faster rate than that of England, were together less than 5 millions by 1761. However, England, and to a much lesser degree her satellite kingdoms, benefited from two other factors. The first was the possession of a vibrant urban population that helped to fuel the growth of international trade and commerce was the another striking feature of the period. In England, just over 770,000 lived in towns of some size, of which London (550,000) was the largest, the next in population being, in order, Norwich, Bristol, Newcastle and Exeter. In Scotland, Edinburgh (35,000) and Glasgow (12,000) were the most sizeable but Dublin would have dwarfed them both. By 1760, on the other hand, the size of the population of the leading English towns exceeded 1 million with Birmingham, Liverpool and Manchester having grown larger than Exeter. This development helps to explain the doubling (or near doubling respectively) of the value of exports and imports between 1700 and 1760.

The second factor was the ability to borrow money, which together with taxes, was able to fund expenditure. As we might expect, real expenditure usually exceeded agreed income during wartime, the deficit being made up by borrowing at fixed rates of interest from the public. In 1691 the newly established 'national debt' stood at a mere £3.1 millions. By 1759, it had risen to £91.1 millions. The capacity to borrow, however, would have been far less if lenders had not been convinced that their money would receive regular dividends and might eventually be paid back in full. This depended on healthy tax receipts and it was these that the government was able to achieve. Government income therefore rose substantially during this period and most of that increase was achieved by shifting the burden of taxation from the land and assessed taxes on the gentry to indirect taxation on (largely) internal trade. In 1690, 42% of tax income came from land and assessed direct taxes and 58% from indirect taxes, 60% of which was in the form of excise duties. By 1750, just 28% came from direct taxes and 72% from indirect, the same proportion of which was accounted for by taxes on internal trade. Here was the link between the growth of commerce and trade in the towns and the high credit standing of the government.

The most serious internal threats to British stability took the form of the Jacobite rebellions in favour of the Stuart cause in 1715 and 1745, both of which were easily defeated. In other respects, however, the internal dangers for the new regimes were comparatively modest. Anglicanism was by far the dominant faith in England, where Catholics and Protestant Dissenters probably numbered less than 100,000 in 1760. The Anglican Church was comparatively weaker in Wales but was sustained in Ireland by the 'penal laws' against Catholics and Dissenters and the support of the Irish Parliament. In Scotland, King William's landing in 1688 led to the immediate restoration of the presbyterian form of the Church of Scotland, with episcopal clergy being removed. Episcopalianism, however, survived in some parts of the country, although this was persecuted following the '45 and was a constant source of friction within the Church.

Yet religion, usually in the form of anti-Catholic or anti-Dissent feeling, its ramifications in elections, as well as food scarcity, generated a steady stream of popular riots – another feature of this period. In all, there were nine periods when these spread further than a few centres. These were as follows: (1) September–December 1688, when there were attacks on Catholic property, principally in London, but also in Bristol, York, Newcastle and Edinburgh; (2) 1693–5, when food riots took place in the Severn and Thames valleys, Northants, Essex and Suffolk; (3) in 1710, when pro-Sacheverell and anti-Dissent disturbances occurred in more than twenty-five towns in England; (4) in June–August 1715, when there were attacks upon dissenting meeting houses in more than thirty towns in England; (5) from March to April 1734, when widespread election riots took place, principally against the Excise Bill; (6) from April to January 1740–1, the occasion of extensive food riots in England and Wales; (7) from April to October 1746, when there were attacks on Catholic chapels in Liverpool, Bath, Sunderland and Manchester; (8) between August and December 1756–7, when there were over 140 food riots in England and Wales and finally (9) between August and September 1757, the time of widespread riots against the Militia Act in at least eight English counties.

The means by which either the executive or Parliament could contain such unrest were limited. The executive possessed troops but no police and the use of troops to suppress anything other than outright rebellion was problematic because of the sensitivities of local authorities. Both institutions therefore had to tread carefully, making use of harsh legal punishments that might be exercised with discretion at the local level. These included the Riot Act of 1715 which sought to dispel crowds quickly; the Transportation Act of 1718 which made transportation to the American colonies an option for those convicted of serious crimes; and the 'Black Act' of 1723 which added poaching to the list of the 'Bloody Code' – a lengthy list of capital offences. It is also notable that various acts allowed Westminster and adjacent parish householders to pay for their own 'watch' by constables and that a Bow Street Police Office was established in 1739.

So far, the evidence we have surveyed suggests that the governments of this period would have been largely occupied in diplomacy, the waging and funding of war, the maintenance of the Protestant constitution, the development of the internal and external empire, and the keeping of the peace with the very limited means at their disposal. But this was also a period rich in intellectual and artistic developments which all helped to give life to other aspects of politics. Locke, Newton, Halley, Berkeley, Dryden, Vanbrugh, Defoe and Clarendon all published major works between 1688 and 1709. Purcell was an active composer then and Wren's St Paul's Cathedral was opened formally in 1697. These luminaries were followed by Handel who settled in London in 1712, Francis Hutcheson, Hume, Burnet, Addison,

Pope, Steele, Swift and Fielding. Thomas Arne's 'Rule Britannia' was sung publicly for the first time in 1740 and in 1752 the Gregorian Calendar was introduced by removing eleven days from the calendar (3–13 September) and starting the new one on 1 January, thereby bringing Britain in line with continental Europe. The extent to which the ideas introduced by these writers challenged politicians is a moot point but of one point we can be certain – that they did influence the burgeoning metropolitan and urban culture that was fed by an increasing number of newspapers and pamphlets. Of these, one of the most influential was Lord Bolingbroke's *The Craftsman*, launched in 1726 and available until 1750.

The monarchy

The deposition of James II in 1688 and the terms on which the Crown was settled on William of Orange and the House of Hanover by the proper-tied elite between 1689 and 1701 – the 'Revolution' and the 'Revolution settlement' – imposed severe limitations on the exercise of royal authority. The deposition itself, which took place following the birth of a son to King James in June, set to one side the principle of strict hereditary succession. This was followed by a series of parliamentary measures that defined the limitations, the most important of which were the Bill of Rights (1689) the Coronation Oath Act (1689) and the Act of Settlement (1701). Taken together, they established the following key limitations:

1 the monarch had to be Protestant (Bill of Rights) and an Anglican (Act of Settlement);
2 monarchs could not dispense with or suspend laws without parliamentary consent (Bill of Rights);
3 parliaments had to be held frequently (Bill of Rights) – a demand that was swiftly translated into 'annually' by Parliament's refusal to provide the executive with revenue for more than a year at a time;
4 parliaments should last no more than three years and elections for a new one should take place within three years of the dissolution of the last (Triennial Act, 1694);
5 monarchs could not leave the kingdom without parliamentary consent and foreign-born monarchs could not engage the 'nation' in a war for the defence of their homeland without such consent (Act of Settlement);
6 government should be conducted with the consent of the Privy Council (Act of Settlement);
7 a standing army could not be kept in times of peace without parliamentary consent (Bill of Rights).

Appearances, however, can be deceptive. The vast majority of the elite that was responsible for these laws had no wish to reduce the monarchy to a cipher. Rather, their intention was to take practical steps to curb the arbitrary, and from their point of view, revolutionary, actions of James II, and, as events unfolded, to guard against similar actions by his successors. Thus, although these measures undoubtedly placed severe limitations on the unfettered exercise of kingship, British monarchs still possessed considerable power and influence. They remained the acknowledged heads of state and in practical terms this meant that they were the heads of the various branches of the state – the established church, the judiciary, the army, the navy and the executive. They also had extensive means of translating this nominal power into real influence. Royal approval, for example, was required for all the senior, and many of the middle-ranking, appointments in the church, the judiciary and the armed forces. In addition, in a society where high rank bestowed political influence to which lesser rank was often a stepping stone, it was the monarch who had the final say on the creation of peers, baronets and knights.

Although the destruction of much of the Palace of Westminster by fire in 1698 brought about the physical separation of the Court and the government departments, with the Court being moved to St James's, Kensington or to Hampton Court, the power of the monarchy within the executive remained extensive. Two factors provided the context for this. The first was that it was the monarch's income, generated partly from hereditary possessions but largely from a Civil List consisting of the hereditary revenues from the customs, excise and postal taxes granted by Parliament, that paid for all the expenses of government with the exception of those of the armed forces.[2] Royal and state expenditure were therefore inextricably mixed. The second was that apart from the Treasury, the royal Household or Court was by far the largest employer of all the other branches of the executive and contained members at the highest level who occupied places in the cabinet and held seats in both houses of Parliament. This meant that the Court itself was a significant branch of government.

Ultimately, however, the influence of the Crown in the executive rested on what were known as its 'prerogatives' or exclusive rights. The principal one stemmed from the fact that all ministers (or the heads of departments) were first and foremost ministers of the Crown. The monarch could therefore appoint them or dismiss them at will – a prerogative that was exercised as late as November 1834 when William IV dispensed with the services of Lord Melbourne's internally divided administration. A second was that the approval of the monarch was required before any ministerial decisions could take effect or any bills approved by both houses of Parliament could become an act. The monarch therefore possessed an effective veto on measures – a prerogative that George III exercised in various ways on three occasions between 1783 and 1807.[3] Finally, royal approval of the dissolution of Parliament was required before it could take effect. The timing of general elections within the framework of the law determining the duration of individual Parliaments was therefore left, ultimately, to royal discretion. The significance of this increased over time. Thus, as the influence that ministers could bring to bear on the results of elections grew after 1714, no government lost an election between then and 1835 and most increased their majorities. Royal approval of a general election therefore became tantamount to approving the continuation of the party in power.

From a legalistic point of view, then, the Revolution settlement abolished some of the powers of the Crown but left other, important, ones intact. The crucial development, however, was not so much a matter of law as practical politics. As noted above, Parliament quickly seized the opportunity afforded by the Revolution to grant supplies for limited periods of time. In view of the fact that Britain was then engaged in what was to be a prolonged and expensive war with France, this made it essential for the monarch, in his capacity as head of the executive, to convene Parliament on an annual basis. This resulted in the monarch having to rely for ministers on those who could command a majority in Parliament as opposed simply to those with whom his own preference lay. Moreover, not only was there fierce warfare in the Commons between the sometimes evenly matched parties of Whigs and Tories during William and Anne's reigns but general elections were frequent, there being ten between 1690 and 1713. The ability of the monarch to choose ministers freely was therefore circumscribed from the outset by the state of parliamentary politics – a state that happened to be highly volatile. Overall, the settlement and its practical effects resulted in a constitutional arrangement best described as a 'limited monarchy'. The monarchy's power had been reduced but what remained was still substantial. It could only exercise it, however, in partnership with willing allies in Parliament. As Richard Pares put it many years ago, the monarch was expected to govern in some sense and if he did not do so it was because of personal shortcomings not because his subjects claimed that he should confine himself to 'reigning without ruling'.[4]

What role, then, did the monarchy play in the executive arm of government during this period? As suggested above, a crucial consideration when attempting to answer this question is the personality and character of the monarchs concerned, William III (1688–1702), Anne (1702–14), George I (1714–27) and George II (1727–60). In this respect, the first point to make is that all of them were relatively stable individuals who took their responsibilities seriously, albeit to lesser or greater degrees. Given the vagaries of hereditary succession and the fact that two of the monarchs (William III and George I) were strangers to the country that they were to reign over, this was an outcome of some significance. Their abilities, temperaments and interests, however, were very different. William III was certainly the most determined and authoritative of the four. When he signified his readiness to accept the throne at the age of 37, he was one of Europe's leading soldiers, diplomats and administrators, having relieved the Dutch state from French occupation and built it up into a formidable power. Indeed, he had become so accustomed to ruling his homeland without restraint that he failed to grasp that the Revolution had trimmed monarchical power. He therefore carried out his duties in England in the manner of a chief executive, devising what were, in effect, his own foreign and financial policies in collaboration with individual departmental heads. Reserved, reclusive, and often absent on military operations, he regarded the extremes of party warfare in the Commons as an irritant that were best dealt with by relying, as he evidently put it, 'upon the bottome [*sic*] of the trimmers' – the moderates of both parties who were ready to work together.[5]

Although Anne succeeded at approximately the same age as William (she was 37 when she was crowned in 1702) their gender was not the only point of contrast between them. Although William was a Stuart on his mother's side, he was both Dutch and a Calvinist. Anne, on the other hand, was 'entirely English'[6] and a devout Anglican. However, the advantages gained by these attributes were counterbalanced by other differences. Whereas William had been highly experienced in matters of state and physically fit at the time of his accession, Anne succeeded in poor health and had been denied the opportunity of gaining any training in her role by both her father, James II, and her late brother-in-law. Thus, although she was as determined as William to maintain the power and influence of the monarchy and worked assiduously to do so, the combination of her lack of experience, her more modest intelligence, her poor health, and the disadvantages of her gender, meant that she was less equipped to resist the further encroachments on her role that the Act of Settlement promised. In particular, she relied more on her ministers in the devising of policy than had been her predecessor's habit.[7]

In the cases of the first two Hanoverians, historians now take a more favourable view of their abilities and devotion to duty than once was the case. George I had prepared himself for his new responsibilities while Elector of Hanover before his accession at the age of 44 and brought to them a reputation as a sound and unflappable soldier-administrator who took an interest in new thinking on the functions of kingship. When King, he was initially hampered by his poor command of English and distracted by what were held to be his disproportionate interest in the affairs of Hanover, his affair with Melusina von der Schulenberg (later, Duchess of Kendal), and his first love – the army. However, the record shows that even during those years (1714–20) he attended to state business regularly when in England which he left for five occasions during his reign; and that once he was persuaded to relegate Hanoverian interests in his list of priorities and to dispense with the services of his German advisers, this continued to be the case until his death.[8]

There has also been some reassessment of George II. Admittedly, this has not extended to his personality and character. He therefore remains much as contemporaries found him: a conceited, hot-tempered man with no intellectual interests whose consuming passions were his wife, his mistresses, Hanover (which he contrived to visit every alternate summer), and the perfidy of the English. In England, he said on one occasion, 'he was obliged to enrich people for being rascals and buy them not to cut his throat'. The House of Commons, he said on another, was full of 'king killers or republicans'.[9]

His political role, on the other hand, is now seen as becoming more assertive than it was once thought to be. Prior to his accession in 1727 at the age of 43, he had initiated a long Hanoverian tradition of heirs to the throne associating themselves with Opposition politics by becoming the nominal head of Walpole's Opposition Whigs. This was followed, 1727–42, by a period when he was content for the most part to place his confidence in two far superior politicians, his wife, Queen Caroline, and his first minister, Walpole. Thereafter, however, despite his innate lack of self-confidence and advancing years, he played a more assertive role, surviving, as one has historian has put it, 'an armed rebellion, two threats of invasion, and at least three serious parliamentary crises'. When he died in 1760, there was those like Horace Walpole who felt he had gained respect for having weathered these storms.[10]

If all the monarchs of this period were able and ready in various degrees to rule as well as reign, what can be said of the means available to them to do so? In the case of two leading sources of royal power – the royal Household or Court and patronage – the story is one of a gradual decline. At the start of the period, for example, the royal Household not only possessed a much larger staff than most of the individual departments of state, but the inner conclave – the Court – was the very centre of government. During the course of the next thirty years, however, the size of the Household remained static – there were $c.950$ in that of George I – while the staff of the civil and military bureaucracy increased exponentially in response to the demands of war.[11] This development was accompanied by a decline in the political importance of the Court. There were several reasons for this. One was the physical separation of the government offices and the Court caused by the fire that destroyed the Palace of Westminster in 1698. Another was the neglect of the Court by William III and the sombre atmosphere created by Anne. And a third was the development of alternative and more desirable meeting places for both the political and cultural elites. William's and Anne's reigns coincided with the development of fierce parliamentary warfare between the two parliamentary parties and a proliferation in London of places where they might meet in the shape of aristocratic town houses, taverns, coffee houses and political clubs. As one historian of the later-Stuart Court puts it, Queen Anne's drawing rooms were full but chiefly of 'either diehard Tories or political neutrals with little parliamentary interest, financial clout, or social prestige'.[12]

The declining influence of the Household in general and the Court in particular was reflected in the particular influence of the senior household officials. The most senior, such as the head of the Household, the Lord Chamberlain, were usually members of the cabinet council but a larger number held seats in both houses of Parliament. In Anne's reign there was in each parliamentary session an average of 11 in the Lords and 14 in the Commons. However, although the senior members retained their importance at a cabinet level, their more numerous colleagues in Parliament had neither the strength in numbers or the inclination to make the 'court interest' the driving force of their politics. According to their historian, they were 'a fairly lackadaisical bunch' for whom membership of the Household made little difference to their political conduct.[13]

During the early Hanoverian period, there was little change to the influence of the Court and the Household officials. In the case of the Court, it had ceased to be the nerve centre of the day-to-day politics of the governing class but the power of the Crown and the presence of royal officials in cabinet councils ensured that it continued to be an important forum for discussion and intrigue on the part of its senior and most influential members. The varied quality of Court life in the mid-eighteenth century – turning on serious matters of state at one moment to trivialities the next – is vividly captured by Lord Chesterfield:

> there is a sort of chit-chat, or small talk, which is the general run of conversation at courts, and in most mixed companies. It is a sort of middling conversation, neither silly nor edifying; but, however, very necessary for you to be master of. It turns upon the public events of Europe, and then is at its best; very often upon the number, the goodness, or badness, the discipline, or the clothing of the troops of different princes; sometimes upon the families, the marriages, the relations of princes, and considerable people; and sometimes … the magnificence of public entertainments, balls, masquerades etc.[14]

Similarly, there was no significant change in the influence of the Household officials in Parliament although their number did increase. Thus, the 11 who sat in the Commons in 1715, which was slightly lower than the average for the previous two decades, grew to 24 in 1727 and when the number of those belonging to Household of the Prince of Wales in the 1750s are included, some 40. In the Lords the number also rose from an average of 11 before 1714 to 27 in 1720–1. However, it appears that even these larger numbers were insufficient to create a Court interest that could be of serious account on its own.[15]

On the other hand, the stasis in the influence of the Court and the Household officials co-existed with a declining influence in other areas. Household officials, for example, continued to be members of the cabinet council – the larger of the executive bodies spawned by the Privy Council – but were usually absent from the smaller, inner cabinet of about five or six ministers that steadily became the engine of executive government after 1714. Moreover, there also seems to have been a decline in the personal control that the Crown could exercise over patronage. In William's and even Anne's time this had been extensive but under the first two Georges, the Whigs and particularly Walpole made increasing claims upon it in order to sustain their regime.[16] Thus, although both kings were fully supportive of the Whig hegemony and the means required to support it, their personal control of patronage in all but military matters – a subject dear to their hearts – fell away.

The decline in royal influence by means of the Household and patronage co-existed with a similar decline in the particular influence that the monarch could bring to bear on who would be in office and what their policies might be. However, it would be too simplistic to ascribe the latter to the former. In the last resort, the royal prerogatives determining the right to appoint and dismiss ministers and to veto unpalatable policies were not only decisive but were widely held to be so by all shades of political opinion. Thus, although the ability to influence events through the Court or by patronage were of some account, the questions of who would govern on behalf of the Crown and how they would govern would ultimately turn on the disposition of a particular monarch in relation to specific political situations. It is to these issues that we now turn.

In the case of the choice of those who filled the leading offices of state, the decisive turning point took place between 1714 and 1716. Following his accession, George I replaced a predominately Tory government with Whigs, who then inflicted a crushing defeat on their adversaries at the general election in the first months of 1715. The Jacobite rebellion took place later in the year and in 1716, the duration of Parliaments was extended to seven years and the Tories were excluded from high (although not all) political offices until the late 1750s on the grounds of their identification with the Jacobite cause. Hitherto, William and Anne had been driven by their hatred of the English party system to try and establish 'mixed' administrations containing members of both parties or neutrals which would be managed on their behalf by a single minister or undertaker, who was usually the head of the Treasury. In William's case, he was in effect his own first minister as a result of his practice of seeing each of his ministers individually, including the senior Treasury minister, and issuing instructions to them on matters of policy and patronage – although, perhaps in deference to the Treasury Lord's status, he normally worked through the latter's suggested agenda.[17] However, such was the extent of party warfare and the fluctuating fortunes of the parties in the Commons, that he changed the dominant political complexion of his ministers repeatedly. Initially, he tried to maintain an even balance between the parties but following the appointment of Lord Godolphin as First Lord of the Treasury in November 1690, he gave the majority of posts to Tories. The pendulum then swung backwards and forwards. By 1694 Whigs predominated but Godolphin retained his place; and in 1699–1700 with Godolphin once again at the Treasury (he had been dismissed in 1696), Tories were favoured.

In Anne's case, however, although the intention was identical – she once referred to the English parties as her 'bug-bears' – the outcome was different. Unlike her brother-in-law, she had no previous experience of administration and ministry-making. Thus, although she was determined to maintain her influence on policy, in practice she relied more heavily than William on her principal ministers, Marlborough, Godolphin and Harley. Further, the winding up during the first two months of Anne's reign of the Commission that had been responsible for the Treasury during her predecessor's led to a decline in royal supervision of its business. Whereas William had attended, on average, 19 meetings of the Commission every year, Anne attended only 22 of the reconstituted Treasury Board during the whole of her reign.[18] In view of the fact that this was a period when the bureaucracy, of which the Treasury was the leading element, grew substantially, this was a significant weakening of the royal supervision of government.

She was also forced to recognise that the results of elections could determine the political colour of her ministry. Initially, she too favoured mixed administrations, albeit of a predominantly Tory hue given her high-Church sympathies, and exercised her prerogative decisively on occasions. For example, she insisted successfully on Normanby's inclusion in her first ministry and Dartmouth's appointment as Secretary of State in 1710; and was equally successful in resisting Godolphin's attempt to make himself master of senior appointments in February 1708 and opposing Nottingham's appointment on three occasions in 1710 and 1711.[19] However, her preference for a mixture, if not a balance, of parties could not withstand the landslide Tory victory at the 1710 election caused by the outcry against the prosecution of the high-Church cleric, Dr Sacheverell. Even her first minister, Harley, was taken aback with the result that she was obliged to allow him to form an exclusively Tory administration which lasted until her death.

Under the first two Georges, however, the Whigs were allowed to establish a monopoly of high office. Initially, this had not been George I's intention. He had hoped for a moderate ministry that excluded the extremists of both parties and intended in any case to rely heavily on the advice of colleagues in the Hanoverian Court.[20] He was soon disappointed. The 1715 general election results, the Jacobite rebellion, and the dismissal in 1715–16 of the Earl of Nottingham and other Tories ready to accept the new dynasty, left the Whigs as the only reliable candidates for senior political office. In addition, Whig resistance to his pro-Hanover foreign policy in 1716–17 and the growing hostility to his reliance on German advisers meant that he was forced to abandon them after 1719 as far as British affairs were concerned.[21] Thereafter, the Whigs were the first Hanoverians' inevitable source of ministers, although even then George I sought to balance the various factions into which they fell. It would be wrong to conclude, however, that the masters had become servants. Both kings were broadly in sympathy with what became the doctrine of the Whigs in power and therefore saw the relationship as one of mutual convenience. Neither were afraid to go their own ways by seeking to make appointments of their own choosing or by exploring the possibilities of favouring Tory appointments – thereby indicating that they were ultimately the maker and breaker of governments and keeping the Whigs on their toes. Hardly any of these initiatives, however, bore fruit. In the case of individuals, George II failed in his attempts to make Spencer Compton his first minister in 1727, failed to retain Lord Carteret as a minister in 1744, and failed again to have Henry Fox succeed Pelham in that position in 1753. His only 'success' was to have Compton, now Lord Wilmington, succeed Walpole in

1742 but the general astonishment with which this appointment was received was still reverberating when Wilmington died a few months later, in 1743. As for giving office to some Tories, this was considered in 1717, 1721, 1725, 1727, 1744 and 1746, but the fact that nothing came of this indicates the practical limitations on their freedom of manoeuvre. Perhaps the best illustration of the balance of power that emerged in this period between the King, the leading politicians and the Commons is the events of February 1746. George II wished to retain Lord Carteret as his unofficial adviser but Pelham and his colleagues resigned in protest and the Commons made it clear that they would not provide Carteret and his friends with a majority should they be put in their place. The King therefore gave way and restored Pelham to office even though it is likely that if he had turned to any Whig leaders other than Carteret and Pelham, the Commons would have acquiesced.

A similar story emerges from a consideration of the royal influence on policy. In general terms, the Revolution Settlement had undoubtedly imposed constraints on the room for manoeuvre. The necessity of there being annual Parliaments enhanced the importance of the monarch and ministers executing policy by statute – legislation approved by Parliament – rather than by any other device. Further, in the one area where legislation was not required – declarations of war and peace and the making of treaties with foreign courts – there were two specific constraints. The first was contained in the Act of Settlement where it was stipulated that a monarch could not make war in defence of foreign dominions without parliamentary consent – a device specifically designed to check excessive Hanoverian concern with their homeland. The second arose from the greater control that the Commons acquired over money bills. Thus, if a treaty involved subsidies to foreign powers or an additional financial commitment in terms of military support, it was inevitably subject to parliamentary scrutiny. The upshot was that it quickly became normal for the monarch and his ministers to seek parliamentary approval of treaties they had negotiated, whether or not they had financial implications.[22]

It was within this context that a predominantly royal form of government gave way during William's and Anne's reigns to one in which royal and ministerial influence were more evenly balanced. In William's case, his prolonged absences at war until 1695 meant that although he retained full control over military and diplomatic policies, some of the key means of raising the revenue to finance them were more the initiatives of his ministers. Moreover, although he was able to devote himself more thoroughly to the full range of policy after his return, it would appear that the trend continued, with the remaining coping stones of the 'financial revolution' being put in place principally by his First Lord after 1697, Charles Montagu. Further, the trend was replicated on the negative side of the equation. Thus, William vetoed bills on five occasions between 1692 and 1696 but following serious protests from the backbenches did not do so again.[23]

The gradual slippage from royal to a combination of royal and ministerial government continued in Anne's reign. This was not for want of endeavour on her part. She had daily conferences with ministers, presided over the weekly and sometimes twice-weekly cabinet meetings which made the final decisions on policy, and otherwise oversaw appointments in every department of state. Furthermore, her views were undoubtedly influential on some key matters of policy: most notably, the Union with Scotland; Marlborough's military and diplomatic strategies; Oxford's (Harley's) successful post-1710 peace policy; and the Hanoverian succession.[24] On the other hand, her views were never decisive. Broadly speaking, they were in line with those of her ministers. A sign of the times was that Anne only used her veto once – against the Scottish Militia Bill in March 1708 – the last time this particular royal prerogative was used directly against a bill although, as has been stated earlier, George III contrived on several occasions to make successful use of it indirectly.[25]

The drift towards a more ministerial and less royal form of government continued in the early Hanoverian period, although it is important not to overestimate its extent. George I, for example, was more assiduous in the formal requirements of kingship than was once thought to have been the case. Initially, he consulted closely with his German advisers, principally on foreign policy, but he was persuaded by his English ministers to bring this to an end in 1719. However, even before this occurred, he had continued Anne's practice of presiding over regular meetings of the cabinet council and this was to be his custom for the rest of his reign. The only significant difference between his practice and hers was that George relied more on private meetings with individual ministers in his 'closet' (or private rooms) at Court. On the other hand, it was during his reign that the importance of the cabinet council to decision-making declined and that of the smaller, inner, cabinet composed chiefly of departmental heads, increased. The fact that the former invariably met in his presence whereas the latter did not, meant that the distance between the King and the nerve-centre of government grew.

However, as mentioned above, it is important not to exaggerate the distance or to think that it effected all areas of policy. The King could and did summon individual ministers for private discussion and ministers, for their part, could, and did take up, their right of personal access to the King. It is therefore better to think of a scenario in which the King found it sensible for his senior colleagues to discuss matters privately as opposed to one in which they did so in order to strengthen their authority against his. As so often happened in the Hanoverian era, everything turned on the disposition of the monarch. George I's role in policy-making illustrates the point. His principal interest was foreign policy and historians are agreed that it is here that he played an important role. Initially, the pro-Hanoverian thrust of his own policy alienated his ministers, but from 1719 he acted in collaboration with his principal foreign secretaries, Stanhope and Townshend, in devising a strategy which suited Hanoverian and British interests, the most notable example of which on the British side of the equation was the Quadruple Alliance of 1720 with Spain, Holland and Sardinia. He was far less actively involved, however, in domestic policy. It is important to set this in its proper perspective. The king may have been more interested in foreign affairs but this did not mean he was uninterested in their domestic counterpart or that he had fewer means to influence it. He was fully committed, for example, to the unsuccessful pro-toleration campaign to repeal the Occasional Conformity and Schism acts masterminded by Lord Sunderland, 1716–19, and was equally supportive of the economic and financial reforms devised by Walpole in the 1720s. The fact that he did not play an important role in the shaping of domestic policies was more the result of his approval of those of his ministers and his increasing weariness with state business than any real diminution of his means to influence events.[26]

George II's role is more difficult to assess as no thorough study of him has yet to appear. However, the evidence that does exist suggests that he had the ability and the inclination to play a more prominent role than his father. Possessed of a good command of English, a photographic memory and consequently a fondness for detail, his principal deficiencies as the head of the executive lay in his extra-mural pursuits, his irascibility and a lack of self-confidence. Even so, he, like his father, took a special interest in foreign policy, particularly that likely to have a bearing on the fortunes of his beloved Hanover. Generally speaking, most of his own ideas coincided with those of his ministers, but there were cases when he took a line of his own. Between 1728 and 1730, for example, he persuaded Townshend to give British support to Wittelsbach pretensions to the Imperial Crown which would have soured relations with Austria permanently had they come to fruition; and in 1741 he committed Hanover to support a French claimant to the same dignity without consulting his British ministers. Overall, it has been said that until the appointment of Pitt as Secretary of State in 1757, there was only one occasion when a minister successfully pursued a policy that was contrary to the King's wishes.[27]

In the case of domestic matters, his role was conditioned by the fact that his reign coincided with Walpole's regime, the Jacobite rebellion of 1745, and more generally, the apogee of the Whig hegemony. This coincidence might suggest that the king was much more dependent on the Whigs as far as domestic issues are concerned than his father had been – a point that his being forced to accept terms requested by Pelham and the 'Old Corps' on their taking office in 1746 seems to underline. The burden of evidence, however, points to a different conclusion. It therefore seems that on most issues George II was well aware of his ministers' intentions and more to the point, usually approved of them. His personal initiatives may have been few in number – his encouragement to Pelham in 1751 to introduce a programme of reform following the end of the war of the Austrian succession, being a rare example – but that does not mean he was a lackey.[28]

The role of the monarchy as the head of the executive therefore changed over time. The Revolution of 1688 and the statutes that followed reduced the powers of the Crown but still left sufficient intact for the monarch to be able to have a decisive say in who governed and how they governed. During this period, however, successive monarchs allowed the initiative for overall policy to slip into the hands of their ministers. As we have seen, this was due partly to their personalities and interests and partly to the fact that they usually agreed with ministerial policy. But it was also due to their readiness to work with sources of authority and responsibility that were new to the executive – first ministers, cabinets and a much expanded bureaucracy. It is to these that we now turn.

First and prime ministers

It is one of the oddities of British political history that although the term 'prime minister' had been applied to an individual as early as 1678, it did not come into official use until 1878 when Disraeli was so designated as a signatory to the Treaty of Berlin; and was 'not known to the law' until 1905 when Edward VII issued a warrant giving the prime minister precedence in ceremonials after the Archbishop of York.[29] The fundamental reason for this reticence in the eighteenth and well into the nineteenth centuries was the reluctance to challenge the role of the monarch as the head of the executive. Thus, while it seemed appropriate to call upon the Lord Treasurer or *First Lord* of the Treasury to take the lead amongst ministers in view of the Treasury's dominance of other departments of state, referring to him as prime minister seemed to devalue the role of the monarch as well as his senior colleagues. This is the reason why the term was often used to describe a first minister who was assuming a power beyond his proper sphere of authority. As the Elder Pitt put it in October 1761 when justifying his decision to resign as Secretary of State as a result of his colleagues' opposition to his proposal for a declaration of war against Spain: if he had stayed and insisted upon his point of view, he would have been taking upon himself the title 'Prime Minister' – 'an abomination in a free country'. In reference to the matter two months later, George Grenville agreed, describing it publicly as 'an odious title'.[30] It is also the reason why it is an error to assume that all first ministers had, and saw themselves as having, equivalent degrees of authority and to judge them accordingly. To do so would be anachronistic.

 That said, one of the most important developments in this period was the establishment of a convention that government would be conducted in the monarch's name by a group of ministers who would have an acknowledged head. Further, that such a head would normally occupy the position of First Lord of the Treasury and certainly be capable of commanding a majority in Lords and Commons. The reasons for this are obvious enough. The prolonged wars of the period, particularly 1688–1713, led to a huge increase in public debt and public revenue, a substantial growth of the fiscal and military bureaucracy, and with that, a consequent rise in the power of the Treasury. In addition, the establishment of annual sessions of Parliament and the intensification of party politics made it essential that the head be capable of attracting majority support. The desirability of a first minister with these particular qualifications was therefore driven by forces and circumstances beyond the monarch's immediate control.

The development, however, was neither immediate nor continuous. Prior to 1714, William III's determination to devise policy himself and his and Queen Anne's preferences for mixed administrations meant that until 1708 there was no single minister at the head of his colleagues in anything but a nominal sense. Instead there were either 'dummy' heads such as Lord Carmarthen, 1690–3, collectives such as the 'Junto', *c.*1693–1700, and 1701–2, or 'duumvirs' such as Godolphin and Marlborough, 1702–8. It was only Godolphin, 1708–9, and more particularly, Robert Harley, 1710–14, who were first ministers in the sense that they were both first in the counsels of the Crown and the acknowledged heads of their colleagues. Both were also heads of the Treasury.

In the early Hanoverian period, the proscription of Tories from high office narrowed the choice of ministers to Whigs but fierce competition between the four leading figures, Robert Walpole and Lords Stanhope, Sunderland, and Townshend, ensured that there was no undisputed first minister until after Walpole was appointed First Lord and Chancellor of the Exchequer in 1721. As we shall see, Walpole set new yardsticks of what could be expected of the position during his long tenure of the posts until 1742, but the position of first and sole minister was by no means set in stone. Lord Wilmington, who succeeded him briefly as First Lord (1742–3) was an acknowledged stopgap and although Henry Pelham (1743–54) was first minister in the mode of Walpole, his successor, the Duke of Newcastle, was obliged to form a junction with William Pitt in July 1757. This followed an interlude, October 1756–July 1757, when Newcastle had resigned as First Lord and been replaced by the Duke of Devonshire who tried and failed to form an administration. George II's reign therefore came to an end with his ministers headed by a 'duumvirate' of Newcastle and Pitt, much like the duumvirate of Stanhope and Sunderland in his father's, 1717–21, or that of Godolphin and Marlborough in Queen Anne's.

But, how far did any of these 'first' ministers – Godolphin, Harley, Walpole, Pelham and, briefly, Newcastle – deserve the opprobrious term 'prime' minister that was hurled at some of them? On this issue, reference to the definition of modern prime ministers is useful. These hold that office without any need for royal approval but simply by virtue of being the head of the party with a majority of followers in the House of Commons. They control large swathes of the political system, appoint their own ministerial colleagues and are the final arbiters on policy. The position of the first ministers of this period was very different. All of them, for example, required the support of the Crown in order to become first minister and to retain the position. Admittedly, the choice of alternatives available to the Crown was sometimes severely limited due to the configuration of parties in the Commons. This might be said of Harley's position in 1710 and that of

Walpole, Pelham and Newcastle after 1714. In Harley's case, however, it is very unlikely that even with the support of the massive Tory majority behind him after the 1710 election, he ever saw himself as more than the Queen's servant who had undertaken to conduct business on her behalf. Further, in the case of Walpole and his successors, two episodes underline the interdependence between the monarch and his first minister rather than the dependence of the one on the other. In 1733–4, when Walpole's power was supposedly at its zenith, it was George II's support which rescued him from defeat in the Commons on his Excise Bill and which helped to secure him victory in the 1734 election that followed.[31] Further, although Pelham's threat of resignation in 1746 that obliged the King to agree to sever his private consultations with his first minister's rival, Lord Carteret, is rightly regarded as a significant assertion of ministerial power, it was not a case of the King seeking to remove his minister. On the contrary, George II was content to see Pelham continue.

With regard to parties, the chief point of contrast between then and now is that virtually all members of both parties then acknowledged that it was the monarch's right to choose his or her ministers. Thus, although the state of parties in the Commons determined the range of choice available to the Crown, it was accepted on all sides that the monarch made first ministers not the parties. The clearest demonstration of this was George I's establishment of a largely Whig administration following his accession in 1714, despite the fact that there was a Tory majority in the Commons.

There were other differences. Prime ministers now have virtual control of all the main areas of patronage that are still available but the situation was different then. As we have seen, William and Anne kept a close supervisory eye on the patronage of all the principal departments and the first two Hanoverians were particularly jealous of military patronage and to some extent the ecclesiastical variety too. First ministers of this period usually possessed the whip hand within the Treasury but although Walpole came closest to making the attempt, no first minister could ever claim to have engrossed the patronage of all the principal departments.[32]

Similarly, they never had complete responsibility for, or authority over, their principal colleagues. As we have observed, the cabinet council throughout this period contained representatives of the royal Household as well as the Lord Chancellor, and, on occasion, the Archbishop of Canterbury – each of whom was regarded as confidants of the monarch in both their special areas of responsibility and on other issues. In addition, both the cabinet council and the smaller, inner cabinet that developed in this period contained, in the two Secretaries of State for the northern and southern departments, members who were regarded specifically as royal representatives. The two departments concerned had a miscellaneous variety of responsibilities but this included foreign and colonial policies – those in which the monarchs of this period took a special interest and, more to the point, those that were specifically conducted in their name. This meant that within each ministry there were three ministers of potentially equal influence with the monarch and it was this which gave rise to duumvirates and triumvirates. As we have seen, these configurations declined in frequency but it appears that Walpole was the only first minister of this period to have established a clear superiority over the Secretaries – and then only after Townshend's resignation in 1730 – and that none were conceded the right to determine the holders of the senior offices.[33]

There were also limitations to their ability to influence the overall policy of governments. To some extent these were embedded in the conventions of office holding. Each senior minister had specific responsibilities and an equal right to discuss them personally with the monarch. This encouraged them to think of their departments as their own bailiwicks and to resist the encroachments of others. In the case of the First Lord, his specific responsibilities were to raise the money necessary to pay for the state's civilian and military operations and to ensure they were accepted by Parliament as a result of his powers of persuasion and management. However, it was not conceded at this stage that this gave him the right to determine foreign or colonial policies. Moreover, there were more practical constraints. Most First Lords were more interested in some aspects of policy than others. Godolphin, for example, was primarily interested in Treasury matters and was instrumental in bringing about the 'Financial' revolution;[34] Pelham told Bubb Dodington in 1752 that although 'he had a great regard for all Europe', he 'did not trouble himself much about it' and that 'the bottom of his politicks' was his concern 'to keep things on a right foot at home'.[35] Further, as Pelham probably realised, the routine tasks of the position were such that it would take a man of extraordinary capacity to be able to deal with those and, at the same time, have superintendence of all areas of policy. Thus as J. H. Plumb and others have stressed, the routine workload of first ministers, if carried out in full, was immense. The weekly duties when Parliament was in session included: the reading of all the dispatches flowing in from the embassies and foreign courts; the perusal of reports from agents within the three kingdoms; formal meetings with members of the Privy Council, the outer and inner cabinets and the Treasury Board; conferences with individual ministers; the delivery of speeches and the encouragement of supporters in Parliament; and, of course, daily audiences with the monarch. Moreover, all this had to be accomplished with no more than a secretary or two, the first minister having no equivalent of a private office. In extraordinary hands, here were the means to influence policy on a broad front. In lesser hands, it is easy to see how the burdens of routine administration could easily stifle any such inclination.[36]

On the other hand, historians are agreed that to a lesser or greater degree, Godolphin, Harley, Walpole and Pelham were able to conduct their business in ways that have more in common with those of a modern prime minister – hence the contemporary use of the term. Walpole was the chief exemplar. He therefore insisted on remaining in the Commons throughout his twenty years as First Lord, rather than following custom and taking a seat in the Lords at some stage. This served to underline the view that he owed his position as much to his command of the Commons as to the will of the Crown. It also established a tradition that was followed by all subsequent first ministers who did not already occupy places in the Lords on their appointment. In addition, he took much greater steps to establish his own personal authority. These included: more extensive influence over the press; attempts to control all the patronage of the Crown; a preference for working with a small inner cabinet of a handful of members, as opposed to the larger cabinet council; the supervision of all areas of policy after Townshend's resignation in 1730 removed a powerful competitor in the foreign department; and much greater control over the voting behaviour of all the office holders as well as the independent supporters of the government. Given the length of Walpole's tenure of the office, a new generation of politicians became accustomed to a style and form of management that made a deep, if not necessarily appealing, impression.[37]

Further, the numerous duties of the office and the particular ways Walpole executed them provided him with the opportunity to give an overall coherence to government policies – another anticipated, if not always realised, function of modern prime ministers. This, if it were taken, would provoke the question of whose government it was: the king's or Walpole's. Although this question was raised by his opponents, Walpole never forgot who his master was. On the other hand, there is a consensus amongst historians that there was something more to his policies than a series of pragmatic and unrelated reactions to a range of disparate problems. Professor Plumb, writing in the late 1950s, puts it no higher than the objectives of peace, prosperity and a contented King and Parliament.[38] Since then, however, studies of particular areas of policy such as finance and the economy, have led others to suggest that Walpole had something close to a coherent strategy for achieving those ends. Professor Dickson made this claim with regard to financial policy in 1967 and the view that it probably applied more generally has since entered authoritative textbooks.[39] Further, similar claims have been made for Pelham, Walpole's eventual successor.[40] This is a matter which will be investigated more fully in the next chapter, but the relevant point here is that on this issue as on others, Walpole, and to a lesser extent, Pelham, developed the role of first minister beyond the limits practised by their predecessors, Godolphin and Harley.

Cabinets

This period also saw the emergence of a small group of office holders who met regularly to discuss policy and to advise the monarch. The terminology is important. Hereditary rulers had customarily consulted with a small number of advisers, most of whom held offices of one kind or another. What happened in this case was that it became customary for a small group of specific office holders to meet regularly with or without the monarch present.

This in itself was not an entirely new development. Prior to the Revolution, the Privy Council was the institution to which most past and present senior office holders belonged but this had become too large and too diverse a body to be an effective instrument of government. As a result, it had become customary for the monarch to be advised by a sub-committee of the Council, known as the 'foreign committee' because overseas affairs were its principal business.[41] Following the Revolution, however, there appears to have been some redefinition of this system. Thus, although William III continued the practice of meeting the Privy Council and individual departmental heads on a regular weekly basis, he augmented this with meetings of a select number of Council members who held specific offices on Sundays after dinner. These became known as a 'cabinet council', thereby indicating that the number was small enough to meet in a 'cabinet' or a private room. In addition, he also allowed meetings 'on particular occasions... [of] ... the great officers of the Crown' solely on their own, naming them in May–June 1694 as the Lord Chancellor, the Lord President of the Privy Council, the Lord Privy Seal and the two Secretaries of State.[42]

The development of an outer cabinet with the monarch present and an inner cabinet consisting solely of ministers took stronger root in Queen Anne's reign. The Privy Council continued to be the body with overall responsibility for sub-committees such as the cabinet council, but its own role became increasingly nominal. This coincided with the Queen continuing the practice of meeting with the cabinet council and having some issues discussed in advance or subsequently by an inner group, designated on some occasions as 'Lords of the Committee'. This would consult, if necessary, with ministers and individuals outside the cabinet council and then report back to it so that a final decision could be taken by the 'Queen in council'.

By that stage, the office holders who could normally claim a place in the outer cabinet council had become reasonably well established and represented all the key branches of the state. The royal Household was represented by the Lord Chamberlain (the head of the Household), the Lord Steward and on a more occasional basis, the Master of the Horse; the nominal heads of the civilian and effective heads of the legal and ecclesiastical departments by the Lord President of the (Privy) Council*, the Lord Privy Seal*, the Lord Keeper or Chancellor* and occasionally the Archbishop of Canterbury; and the heads of the civilian and military departments by the Lord Treasurer or First Lord of the Treasury* (and occasionally the Chancellor of the Exchequer if the posts were held by different men), the three Secretaries of State* (one being for Scotland), the Lord Lieutenant of Ireland* and the Commander-in-Chief* of the armed forces. Needless to say, the presence of some post-holders was probably regarded as more essential than that of others: these have been asterisked. Moreover, it also appears that attendance levels differed. The usual attendance at the cabinet council, which met in a royal residence, was about 9 out of the total of 12–14, while that at the inner cabinet or 'Lords of the Committee', which met in Whitehall, was four or five. There may have been several reasons for this: the fact that the Queen was present at the one but not the other; the considerable number of cabinet meetings, which may have deterred those with little to say – there were 64 in 1705 and 62 between June 1710 and June 1711; and the likelihood that only those immediately concerned with the subjects referred to it needed to attend the meetings of the inner cabinet.[43]

This system continued in George I's reign but had been modified significantly by the end of his son's. The crucial issue was the relative importance of the two bodies. During William and Anne's reigns the initiative lay with the cabinet council. However, during the latter stages of George I's reign and throughout George II's, this fell steadily into the hands of the smaller, inner cabinet. In 1739–41 this consisted of the First Lord of the Treasury, the two Secretaries of State, the Lord Chancellor and the Lord President of the Council, although it was not unusual for others to be added when circumstances required. In 1760, for example, the number had increased to 9 or 10. Overall, whereas the inner cabinet of Queen Anne's time had been a body which prepared matters for discussion by the cabinet council, its equivalent in the early Hanoverian period increasingly made decisions that were reported to that council for formal consideration but essentially, for ratification. This is why it was also called the 'efficient' cabinet.

The principal reasons for what amounts to the beginnings of the modern cabinet are to be found in the personalities and the practicalities involved. George I afterwards, and George II in general, were content to see this process take place, partly because it reduced the demands on them and partly because they were usually in agreement with the thinking of the inner group. The personal aspect of what turned out to be a major political development is illustrated by the fact that when they went to Hanover, the Lords Justices who deputised for them were drawn from the cabinet council, thereby providing the inner group with a greater opportunity to become the effective ministers. It also suited the longest serving first ministers, Walpole and Pelham, especially during the frequent periods of war or internal unrest, when swift responses were most effectively carried out by a small, as opposed to a larger and more unwieldy, group. Here, in fact, was the key. After 1714, the pressures generated by diplomacy, war, the Jacobite threat, the funding of government debt and parliamentary management required swifter, more co-ordinated, and crucially, more confidential, responses than a cabinet council that had grown to 15–17 by 1740 and nearly 20 by 1760 could easily supply. The development of an inner cabinet could therefore be regarded as a practical necessity.

On the other hand, it was a development that carried with it an implicit threat to the role of the King and that of the 'King in Council'. In 1738 William Pulteney captured the sense of unease with which some viewed it: 'We have in this kingdom several councils; we have a privy council, a cabinet council; and for all I know a more secret and less numerous council still, by which the other two are directed'.[44] The difficulties were overcome, however, by the inner cabinet respecting the constitutional proprieties of the 'King in Council' having supreme executive authority but otherwise making the key decisions itself. Thus, by 1760 the existence of an inner cabinet taking the lead in the shaping and co-ordinating of policy was not only a recognised fact of political life but also regarded as essential, particularly in war time. This explains why the Duke of Newcastle was able to draw up a memorandum for consideration by the ten-strong 'Committee of the Cabinet Council' in 1757 with no misgivings that he was doing anything unusual or improper.[45]

But what subjects did cabinets of either kind discuss? The principal ones were diplomacy and military operations. These were the primary responsibilities of the monarch and ones in which all of them took a keen personal interest, although Anne's was limited by her lack of earlier experience. Any other matter could be discussed but it seems that as the bureaucracy grew in size, the inner cabinet dealt only with those of a pressing nature that were related to these primary concerns. Thus, by the end of George II's reign it was customary for the inner cabinet to discuss diplomacy, military and naval operations, army recruitment, and the state of the fleet, but not to deal routinely with either the equipping of the armed forces or their administration. In addition, it was rare for the cabinet to discuss colonial or Treasury matters on any regular basis. The tradition established by the 'foreign committee' of the Privy Council before the Revolution was therefore still largely in tact.[46]

There was also some continuity in procedure. It has been established that in Anne's reign, the inner cabinet or 'Lords of the Committee', but not the Cabinet Council, routinely summoned other ministers or officials to attend its meetings at the Cockpit in Whitehall for questioning on specific issues. This was still the practice in 1740. Thus, at a meeting at the Cockpit on 22 May, the Lords of the Admiralty attended a meeting of the inner cabinet to describe the state of the navy in view of the war with Spain. Their report was so alarming that one of the six who are mentioned as being present concluded that if a battle between the fleets took place 'we should certainly be outnumbered, and consequently lucky if we were not overpowered'.[47] As far as we can tell, the practice of the inner cabinet occasionally inviting other ministers or officials to attend its meetings continued for the rest of this period.

Although the choice of subjects that were regularly discussed was obviously dictated by what was thought to be the most important functions of government, consideration of those that were regarded as less important casts some useful light on contemporary perceptions of the various branches of the executive. Colonial affairs, for example, were regarded as the particular preserve of the monarch and not sufficiently important to deserve frequent discussion at this level – at least, until 1756. Thus, the President of the Board of Trade, the body responsible for colonial administration, did not sit in the cabinet.[48] The relatively minor role of Treasury business is, however, more difficult to explain. Regular royal participation in Treasury business seems to have ceased during Anne's reign and although the First Lord was usually the principal member of the cabinet, it is notable that when the First Lord was not also Chancellor of the Exchequer, the last post was not normally represented in the cabinet.[49] This suggests that Treasury business was seen as too specialised for frequent discussion and this, if true, underlines the departmentalised, as opposed to the centralised, structure of the executive as a whole. The development of an inner cabinet may have given some central direction to foreign and military affairs but the other functions of government were carried out almost independently of each other.

The departments of state

England and Wales were administered centrally by six different types of 'department of state' as they were referred to in contemporary directories. These were as follows: (1) royal, consisting of the royal households and the officers of state most closely connected to the monarch such as the secretaries of state; (2) naval; (3) military; (4) legal; (5) revenue and (6) ecclesiastical. Each one of these had numerous sub-departments and offices. In addition, Ireland and Scotland had their own departments and some, but not all, replicated the functions of those in London.

   As noted above, the leading instrument of government at the start of this period – the cabinet council – represented all these different types of departments and included a minister for Scotland and the Lord Lieutenant of Ireland. In due course, however, the combination of the frequent wars of this period and the strains of funding them with parliamentary approval led to some departments becoming much more important and influential than the others. Thus, although the size and activities of the royal, ecclesiastical and legal departments did not decline, they were overtaken by the growth in that of the revenue and the naval and military departments. The development was only partially represented by the membership of the increasingly influential inner cabinet where the presence the Lord President and the Lord Chancellor guaranteed continuity with the past, but there was little doubt by the 1720s that the dominant offices were those of the two Secretaries of State (foreign policy and local government) and the revenue and military departments. The Secretaries' offices in London were small but they had a large number of officials who reported to them in the form of county administrators and overseas representatives. The revenue and military departments were much larger and each one contained subsidiary offices. The revenue embraced the Treasury and about twenty other offices including, Customs, Excise and the Post Office. The naval department consisted of the Admiralty, Pay and Navy offices; and the military department, of the War Office and those of the Paymaster-General and the Master-General of the Ordnance. Further, both departments had numerous outstations dotted around the country. Taken together, it was the personnel of these offices who had the greatest impact on policy and who are the focus of this section.

The most notable developments took place between 1688 and 1714 in response to the demands of war. New posts and offices were established, some existing offices were re-organised, and a substantial increase took place in the numbers employed in others. In the case of new offices, the Board of Stamps was created in 1694 and this was followed in 1696 by the establishment of an Inspector-General of Imports and Exports, a Register of Shipping and a Board of Trade and Plantations. The latter was established as a committee of the Privy Council and had a wide brief that included, largely of its own volition, the collection of information on the state of the poor. As for the increase in numbers, a guide is provided by the growth of the military. Thus, the number of British troops rose to 28,000 at the height of the wars while recruits to the navy climbed from 22,000 to 48,500 – in total, about 15% of men of serviceable age according to one calculation.[50] Recruitment on this 'unprecedented' scale not only required some expansion in the military departments concerned, it also had to be paid for by borrowing and taxation. This explains the increases in the principal tax offices – Customs and Excise. The number of employees in the former rose by 33% between 1690 and 1716 (from 1313 to 1750); and no less than 129% in the latter (from 1211 to 2778).[51] Although it is notoriously difficult to provide accurate figures for the total number of government employees at this time, those available for all the offices in England with the exception of the army suggest an increase of about 130% between 1690/1692 and 1716, by which time they were just over 6,000; and by a much more modest 21% by 1755 after which they accelerated again in response to the Seven Years War.[52]

These developments were accompanied by a growing bureaucratic culture. At first glance, this seems surprising. Before 1714, efforts were made, especially during Anne's reign, to develop a non-political civil service, but afterwards, the Whigs made appointments on a ruthlessly partisan basis.[53] The reason why partisanship did not hinder bureaucratisation to any significant extent can be found in the conventions adopted in the Treasury. By 1714, these included a guarantee to officials that they had security of tenure regardless of their politics. Thus, although the Whigs filled vacancies with their own supporters, they were unable to make a clean sweep. The bureaucracy that had been established in the Treasury before 1714 – by which time it has been described as 'an embryo hierarchy of capable public servants, advancing by merit as well as seniority' – therefore continued into the Hanoverian era.[54] The same happened in other offices, leading, by the 1760s, to the situation in which political patronage was essential to an application for a post but could not ensure its success.[55]

Similar developments, it has been argued, took place in many of the other offices, both old and new. Applicants for clerkships or analogous posts were set examinations and offered training on appointment. Payment came in the form of salaries (rather than fees for specific duties) followed by retirement pensions. Salary scales were related to performance and seniority, and routine duties were defined. It was recognised that officials would continue to regard their posts as a form of private property but an attempt was made by these various devices to encourage the notion that they were also held for the public good. Although these terms and conditions did not apply to all posts, the consensus is that their example played a part in creating, generally, 'High standards of public service' within the bureaucracy.[56]

How far bureaucratisation led to greater efficiency is a difficult question to answer. In some offices, such as the outstanding case of the Excise Office, it certainly did but in others it depended more on the capacities of the ministers in charge and their permanent officials. Notable examples of very capable ministers are William Blathwayt, Secretary at War, 1683–1704, William Lowndes and John Scrope, successive secretaries to the Treasury, 1695–1724 and 1724–52, and Lord Anson, First Lord of the Admiralty, 1751–6. These and others were supported in their work by increasingly long-serving permanent officials. In the case of the Treasury, for example, 27 of the 60 men who worked in the principal office between 1714 and 1760 did so for more than 25 years.[57] In addition, service in particular offices began to run in families – forty-seven contributing three or more members of the Navy Office staff between 1660 and 1800.[58] Although lengthy periods of service and even inherited knowledge may have lent weight to the advice they were called upon to give, it also had its negative effects. Charges of nepotism was one but much more serious from the point of view of efficiency was the demoralising aspect of slow progress up the ladder of promotion, each step leading to fixed and repetitive duties. According to the historian of the Treasury, this led, by 1760, to low morale and apathy.[59]

On the whole, however, the positive aspects of bureaucratisation seem to have outweighed the negative. The Excise Office became a model of efficiency and others coped remarkably well when set a challenge. In the case of the Board of Ordnance, for example, a new and more centrally controlled system of acquiring armaments was devised between 1710 and 1730 that met the needs of the forces during the wars of 1739–48.[60] A convincing argument has been made that both the army and navy boards provided, after a sluggish start, all the necessary logistical and manpower support for the much criticised expedition to the West Indies in 1739–41.[61] Moreover, several studies of naval administration during the testing period from *c.*1740–75 have come to the conclusion that although far from perfect, it was usually effective, particularly during Lord Anson's spells at the helm, 1751–62.[62] Broadly speaking, the evidence suggests the evolution of a bureaucracy that although it began to show signs of inertia in certain areas, was flexible enough to respond successfully to emergencies.

The other significant development was the growth of Treasury influence over the activities of other departments. The underlying reason for this was the escalation in government expenditure and the necessity of keeping closer control of the sources and means of payment, not least to satisfy sceptical backbenchers. The credit systems of the armed forces, which had hitherto operated with a measure of independence, were therefore gradually brought under the control of the Treasury.[63] In the 1720s and 1730s, Walpole increased the department's influence over Customs and Excise, both of which had also operated hitherto on a 'quasi-independent' basis.[64] In addition, it was the Treasury that gradually assumed the dominant voice in the affairs of the American colonies. Its original functions had been largely supervisory, consisting of the authorisation of payments from the Civil List and public funds, auditing the accounts, and overseeing the revenues raised in the colonies. It was therefore expected that the Board of Trade and Plantations, founded in 1696, would become the lead department. By 1714, however, the Treasury had outflanked the Board and was to remain the dominant department until the 1760s.[65]

Yet, although the growth of Treasury influence gave a greater coherence to the activities of some departments, it was insufficient to undermine the spirit of independence that characterised the departments as a whole. There were three reasons for this. One was the fact that the administrative reforms of the post-Revolution had been incomplete. The practices of some offices had been untouched by reform while those of others had been improved and new offices had been established. The new had been grafted onto the old with the result that tradition was as influential as innovation.[66] Another, was the persistence of the view that ministers were first and foremost ministers of the Crown and were entrusted to look after their departments as they, and not other departmental heads, saw fit. This is reflected in the roles of the two Secretaries of State for the northern and southern departments. These were regarded, and regarded themselves, as the monarch's representatives. Thus, in addition to their extraordinary miscellany of overseas, colonial and domestic responsibilities, they had a nominal authority over the Treasury, the Admiralty, the Ordnance, and the victualling departments. And the third, paradoxically, was a resistance to giving too much power to the monarch or any one minister. The prime example of this was the diffusion of military authority. Thus, although the monarch was the supreme commander of the forces, authority within the naval and military departments was shared in each case between three different offices. Further, the Secretary at War, the monarch's representative, was usually a rising, rather than a front-rank, politician who did not sit in the outer or inner cabinets.[67]

What impact, then, did these developments have upon the ways that executive decisions were made? To what extent, for example, did the remarkable growth in the size of the bureaucracy enable officials to make a greater contribution?

In order to answer to these questions, we need to look more closely at the structure and size of the key offices within the executive. Of the two Secretaries of State, for example, the head of the Northern Department was responsible for diplomatic correspondence with France, Switzerland, Italy, Iberia, the Channel Islands and the colonies; while the Head of the Southern Department dealt with the Habsburg Empire, the United Provinces, Scandinavia, Poland and Russia. As for their domestic responsibilities, the

Northern Secretary looked after Scotland when there was no separate
Scottish Secretary while the Southern equivalent was responsible for Ireland.
Taken together, these miscellaneous duties were carried out by the two
Secretaries, four or more Under Secretaries who were usually politicians, a
few officials with specialist duties, and a larger number of clerks. In 1692, it
has been estimated that the total number of officials was about 15; in 1755,
it was 66, 23 of whom were clerks. Another example is the London headquarters of the Treasury and the Exchequer. These housed a dozen or so different offices but the overall structure was the same: a top echelon of offices
held by politicians headed by the First Lord and the Chancellor of the
Exchequer, and a supporting hierarchy of clerks. In 1690 there was a total
of 124 and in 1755, 220, the number of clerks then being in excess of 100.
This was a structure and rate of growth replicated in the other key executive
departments. Thus, although the growth of the bureaucracy as a whole was
spectacular, the growth in the London headquarters of the offices represented in the cabinet still left them remarkably small, given their various
responsibilities.[68] Further, although there was some increase in the number
of offices held primarily by politicians, the largest addition came in the ranks
of the clerks.

This conclusion corresponds with what we know of the functions of the
departments and the input they had into decision making. The chief function
of the clerks, of course, was the execution and overseeing of the decisions
made by departmental heads – for example, by drafting outgoing correspondence and monitoring the incoming. In this period, however, another
function that became increasingly important in some departments was the
accumulation and presentation of information. This was partly due to a
remarkable flowering of interest in the late seventeenth century in 'political
arithmetic' – the measuring of population, national wealth and religious
practice by statistical means. Apart from inspiring the great studies of
population, trade and war by Gregory King and Charles Davenant, this had
its impact on government with the establishment in 1696 of the Inspector-
General of Imports and Customs and the Board of Trade, for whom and for
which the collection of statistics became essential.[69] But it was also due to the
existence of annual parliaments and the need to supply MPs with information. As the bureaucracy grew, particularly in those departments that reached
deep into the localities, such as Customs and Excise, MPs found it necessary
to have information at their disposal on their activities and matters related to
them. The clerks therefore found themselves providing such information at
a steadily increasing rate.

The combination of the relatively small size of the key departmental
headquarters and the growing burden of routine duties that occupied the
clerks meant that key decisions remained where they had always been – with
the heads of department and their political juniors. In the case of the
heads of department, their real input depended on their capacity and
interest as well as political circumstances. Some were clearly incompetent.

Joseph Addison, briefly Secretary of State for the Southern Department, 1717–18, found it difficult, apparently, to compose a despatch. The Duke of Bedford, also of the Southern Department, 1748–51, spent most of his time at Woburn while Lord Holderness who held both Secretaryships between 1751–61, was appointed by the Duke of Newcastle largely because he would do as he was told.[70] The initiative in such circumstances could easily pass to a political junior and there are a number of examples of such men having a very important influence on decisions taken by both weak as well as strong departmental heads. William Lowndes, Secretary at the Treasury, 1695–1724 and John Scrope, his successor in the post until 1752, both had an important influence upon, in Lowndes' case Godolphin's, and subsequently, Walpole's financial policies, particularly on the planning and execution of the Excise Bill of 1733. On the other side of the coin, Andrew Stone, Under-Secretary of State from 1734, is said to have had an undue influence on the much less decisive Duke of Newcastle when he was Secretary of State.[71]

All these men were MPs and belonged to the political strata of the bureaucracy. Evidence of a significant input from lower down the bureaucratic ladder is much more difficult to find. There certainly was some: Brewer has pointed to the importance of ex-officials (as well as aspiring ones) making use of their knowledge to suggest schemes; and D. M. Clark has suggested that the civilian personnel in the Treasury had a considerable impact on policy formation during Pelham's spell as First Lord.[72] On balance, however, it seems that the key input came from the political bosses. To that extent, the expansion of the bureaucracy and the development of 'a fiscal-military state' did not make a significant impact on the workings of the executive.

Summary and conclusion

As mentioned in the preface, John Brewer's charting of the development of 'a fiscal-military state' has had a considerable impact on current perceptions of government and politics in the post-Revolution period. In the hands of the unwary, however, it can be misleading. Thus, although it undoubtedly highlights the state's extraordinary capacity to raise sufficient money to engage in major wars with minimal hostility from the tax-paying public, it can all too easily suggest that this was due, in part at least, to a more coherent, directional, and efficient form of executive government.

The argument developed in this chapter, however, is that a growing expertise in raising funds to engage in war was not matched by a complete overhaul of the executive. Thus, as far as the processes by which the executive came to decisions and the individuals involved are concerned, it is important not to overestimate the degree of change. There certainly were substantial changes to the framework of executive government. The powers of the restored monarchy were reduced. A first minister and a small inner cabinet gradually replaced the Privy Council, hitherto the principal instrument of royal policy. In addition, the executive quickly recognised that policy had to be approved by annual parliaments and receive, in most cases, statutory authority.[73] The bureaucracy, hitherto dispersed pretty evenly between six departments of state, not only grew exponentially in size but became dominated by the Treasury and the revenue and military departments. However, the effects on what Julian Hoppit has referred to as 'the mainspring of government' should not be exaggerated.[74] The power of the Crown still remained substantial and its free exercise was still supported by the vast majority of the parliamentary class. First ministers did sometimes seem to have accumulated sufficient power to challenge the role of the Crown but as we have seen they were vilified as prime ministers when they did so. The development of an inner cabinet certainly distanced the monarch from a forum where key policies were formulated but their execution was in the last analysis dependent on the agreement of the outer cabinet where he could sit, and where his own representatives sat. Further, the growth of the size of the bureaucracy and of Treasury control did not lead to a significant increase in the bureaucratic contribution to executive decision-making or in what is called in today's terms, 'joined-up government'. The 'mainspring of government' therefore ceased to be purely monarchical but it did not become purely ministerial. Rather, it became a mixture of both.

2 The scope, purpose and achievements of the executive

Introduction

As we have observed in the previous chapter, Britain's transformation from a politically unstable second-rank European power in 1688 to a major imperial and commercial power in 1763 was accompanied by the evolution of a system of executive government that contained old and new elements. The key word is 'evolution'. In other European states, autocratic monarchs such as Peter the Great of Russia or Frederick William I of Prussia implemented extensive bureaucratic reforms in order to fulfil their plans for territorial expansion and world-power status. In Britain, on the other hand, no such overhaul was ever contemplated. Instead, there was a reconfiguration of the roles of the existing office holders and institutions coupled with a considerable expansion of some, but not all, departments. Thus, all the composite departments of state – the royal, naval, military, legal, revenue and ecclesiastical – remained in place, the significant development being the growth of the influence of the revenue and the naval and military departments over the others. The influence of the monarch and their senior Court officials on the day-to-day business of government declined but remained decisive on crucial issues of diplomacy, war and peace, and, ultimately, on who governed and, in broad terms, how. Gradually, the space vacated by this withdrawal was filled by the emergence of a first minister and inner cabinet of 4–6 senior office holders who assumed responsibility for advising the monarch on policy. Their authority, however, was by no means clear-cut. The power of the first minister depended on his relationship with the monarch and the latter's personal representatives – the two Secretaries of State and to a lesser extent, the Lord Chancellor. Taking the lead in shaping policy therefore oscillated between a first minister and duumvirates or triumvirates. In addition, the continuing existence of the larger cabinet council containing the senior members of the Royal Household as well as the members of the inner cabinet acted as a break on the latter's assumption of untrammelled authority. As for the critical departments of state – the revenue and the military – the growth of Treasury supervision of the whole and the exponential increase in the size of the Customs and Excise offices should not obscure the fact that change was modest in other parts of what was disparagingly referred to as a 'leviathan', the biblical sea monster that devoured all in its path. The number of officials in the central office of the Treasury and those of the Secretaries of State hardly rose at all during this period and were remarkably small, given the range of their responsibilities. The numbers recruited by the naval and military departments during wartime were impressive but equally noticeable is the fact that they fell back sharply in times of peace. Further, both of these departments shared a characteristic that was common within the bureaucracy as a whole – namely, a diffusion of responsibilities between different departments and, as a consequence, considerable departmental autonomy. Thus, although some developments such as the emergence of the head of the Treasury as a first minister in an inner cabinet encouraged the development of more coherent government, others, such as the persistence of 'departmentalism', hindered its progress. The key issue, then, bearing in mind Britain's extraordinary growth as a world power, is how far this was due to the operations of the executive.

The scope and quantity of government business

Throughout this period the fundamental purpose of the executive was to assist the monarch in the execution of the 'King's business', that is those matters that he or she swore to maintain at their Coronation – the defence of the realm and the supremacy of the Established Church. In practice this meant the following: the shaping and implementation of foreign policy; the maintenance and recruitment with parliamentary consent of sufficient armed forces for the purposes of defence and attack; the raising with similar consent of sufficient revenues to pay for the ordinary and extraordinary expenses of government; the protection of the Established Church and the 'Protestant Constitution'; and, otherwise, the taking of such measures as were necessary to protect the rights of property, to administer justice and to preserve peace and good order. By today's standards, the scope of executive action was therefore limited. It was almost wholly concerned with diplomacy, defence, the raising of revenue and the Protestant Constitution. Neither the welfare of the population nor the day-to-day administration of the inner and outer branches of the empire was its concern. These were left to voluntary organisations and to local authorities in the case of welfare; and to a combination of local authorities and the Crown's representatives in the case of routine internal and external administration. Thus, following the Union with Scotland in 1707, it was only emergencies that brought the routine affairs of England, Wales, Scotland, Ireland and the colonies under the regular consideration of the executive. The only exception to this was the legislation of the biennial sessions of the Irish Parliament, which, under the terms of Poynings' Law (1495), required the consent of the British Privy Council or, in practice, the executive. This was due to the close proximity between the two countries and the potential for, and sometimes the emergence of, disagreement, particularly on financial and commercial matters.

With regard to the quantity of business that these responsibilities generated, the main instruments of action were treaties with foreign powers and acts of Parliament. In the case of treaties, these were negotiated in private, considered by the cabinet, ratified by the monarch and laid before Parliament for approval, there usually being at least one major debate on foreign policy in every session during the Hanoverian period. Although they were negotiated by a small group consisting of the monarch, the senior ministers and their envoys abroad, the shape of treaties had to take some account of parliamentary opinion, especially if they had financial implications; as well as that of the press and those with particular strategic and commercial interests in the subject.[1] On the other hand, it is worth noting that no treaty was rejected by Parliament during this period. This was partly due to the strength of governments in Parliament, particularly after 1715, and it also reflected the view that foreign policy was a special preserve of the monarch.

In the case of acts of Parliament, enumerating the number and type of failed and successful bills which ministers were wholly or largely responsible for is, at the present moment, very problematic. As recent historians of the subject have emphasised, there are difficulties in categorising types of legislation and in identifying who the principal sponsors of bills were. Even in the case of supply bills (one of the major categories of financial legislation) it appears that not all of those presented between 1690 and 1714 were sponsored by ministers.[2] That said, the work of a number of scholars, most particularly Julian Hoppit and Joanna Innes in a monumental study of failed legislation 1660–1800, enable us to draw some general conclusions. Bills at that time fell into two broad categories: the 'general', that is those that applied nationally – to England and Wales, Scotland or Great Britain as a whole; and the 'local' and 'personal', those that applied to localities or to individuals. The bills on subjects that were most likely to have interested ministers fell almost wholly into the general category and consisted of those dealing with the machinery of government, finance, law and order, religion and the armed forces. In this regard, research by others and some of my own on sample sessions in the 1720s and the 1750s leads to the following conclusions. The first confirms the well-established view that general legislation of all kinds was always a minority of the total number of general, local and personal acts: 33.2% 1690–1713, and 28.8%, 1714–60.[3] Further, if only those general acts of the government interest type are considered, the proportions are lower. However, these overall figures disguise the significant variations from one session to another and from one period to another. Thus, a calculation of the average number of general acts passed in each parliamentary session reveals the following: *c.*20, 1688–1705; *c.*26, 1706–16, *c.*18, 1717–44; *c.*24, 1745–54 and *c.*30, 1755–60. Taken together, these statistics lead to the following conclusions. First, that although general (and therefore ministerial) legislation may have taken up a disproportionate amount of parliamentary time in terms of committee work and debate, it only accounts for, on an average, about a third of all legislation. And second, that such legislation rose *c*.1688–1714, declined a little, *c*.1714–40, and then rose steadily *c*.1740–60 to reach an average of thirty successful bills or acts per session.

Further conclusions follow from a closer examination of government interest bills. As we have seen, the ratio of such bills to bills of all types fell, 1689–1760, but Hoppit and others have also shown that their success rate rose from an average of 44% in the period before 1714 to about 68% thereafter. How, then, does this compare with what we know of bills that were not merely of government interest but were definitely sponsored either wholly or partially by ministers? The data available on this point is limited but what there is conforms to the general trends identified by Hoppit. In the period before 1714, for example, David Hayton has shown a success rate for supply bills – those largely (but not always) sponsored solely by ministers of 68%. To this we might add the results of my own research on two sessions, 1724–5 and 1753. In the earlier session, ministers were wholly or partly responsible for 13 of 16 successful general bills (81.25%) and for 5 of 7 unsuccessful ones, although it is noticeable that in each of the last cases the initiative was shared with independent members.[4] Their 'success rate' was therefore 13/18 (72%) and the successful category consisted of a core of bills dealing with finance, government, the military, religion and the law but included two bills providing assistance with trade. In 1753, they were wholly or partly responsible for 24 of 32 successful general bills (75%) and 3 of 10 unsuccessful ones. Their success rate was therefore 24/27 (88.8%) and in this case, the successful ones were much broader in type. Thus, in addition to a core dealing with finance, local government and the military, there were also bills to encourage trade and manufacture, to naturalise Jews, to found the British Museum and prevent clandestine marriages.

This evidence tallies with Hoppit's conclusions on general bill and government interest legislation – that its ratio to all legislation falls but that its success rate rises – but prompts others with regard to ministerial legislation. If the data from these two sample sessions is a reliable guide, the ratio of ministerial legislation to general legislation rises to reach a plateau of about 75–80%. Given that the total quantity of such legislation dipped slightly to about 18–20 acts per annum, 1714–40, and then rose to about 30 by 1760, this meant that ministerial legislation followed a similar trajectory. It also seems that the success rate was comparatively high by 1714 and tended to rise over time. Ministerial legislation therefore consisted of a core of bills dealing with finance, military matters, government, law and order and trade, the size of which grew over time to include bills dealing more with trade, manufacture and miscellaneous improvements. Taking the period as whole, it seems that there was a steady rise, particularly after 1714, in the ability of ministers to steer their legislative proposals to a successful conclusion. This was probably due to improved methods of parliamentary management and the drafting of bills; and to the establishment of the Whig dominance of Parliament.[5]

The assumptions and priorities of policy

Executive policy-making rested on some widely held beliefs about the constitution, the exercise of power and the proper limits of central authority. One of these was that the mixed form of government that had developed after 1688 was, in terms of the ratio of advantages to disadvantages, far superior to the unlimited monarchy that had preceded it and which was common in most other European countries.[6] This explains the readiness to defer *in extremis* to the surviving prerogatives of the Crown and the view that ministers were administering the 'King's business'. In this respect it is instructive that 'administration' was always preferred to 'government' as a descriptor of the executive – the verb 'to govern' being regarded as too autocratic for a balanced system of power.[7] It also explains why the routine affairs of England and Wales, of Scotland after 1707, of the colonies and to a lesser extent, Ireland, were not part of the regular brief of executives. These were left to the Crown's representatives: the lords lieutenants of counties in Britain, the viceroy in Ireland and the governors of the colonies.

Another widely held belief was that full participation in the affairs of the state depended on two qualifications: membership of the Established Church and the possession of substantial real estate. It was a view that had a long history – a largely property-based parliamentary franchise had been established in the fifteenth century – but it was reinforced in this period. In the case of religion, the restoration of the Church of England in 1660 had been followed by acts requiring the taking of oaths abjuring Roman Catholic doctrine and subscribing to the Anglican form in order to vote in Parliament and hold civil or military posts – the Corporation Act of 1661 and the Test Acts of 1673 and 1678. Although the strict enforcement of these measures lapsed in the early eighteenth century, they were not repealed until 1828. Further, their lapsing coincided with the strengthening of the view that the purpose of civil government was to protect the rights of landed property and that the possession of specific and verifiable incomes from real estate was a necessary qualification for membership of parliament, for various forms of local office-holding, as well as for the parliamentary vote. Prior to 1714, the impetus for such a qualification for MPs came from back-bench country gentlemen, alarmed by what they regarded as the increasing influence of the 'monied interest', that is, those whose incomes derived more from finance or trade than from land. This led in 1711 to an act requiring English and Welsh county members to have £600 pa from landed property and borough members, £300 pa. After 1714, however, the Whigs became the principal apologists for landed property being an essential qualification for the exercise of political authority – their view being supported, it appears, by carefully selected parts of the writings of John Locke.[8] In due course, it has been argued, public affairs were seen largely 'as an expression of propertied interests'.[9] Taken together, these definitions of full citizenship and the fundamental purpose of government provided a further context for executive action.

It was also widely believed that the central institutions of the state should not intrude on those that operated locally. In today's more centrally run state, it is sometimes easy to forget that in this period the instruments of authority and welfare that most people encountered were not wielded by the executive or Parliament but by local institutions. Summary justice, policing and other services were provided by county Quarter Sessions and town corporations. The poor law system, involving the raising of rates, the making of payments to the sick, old and unemployed, and the building of workhouses, was administered by the parishes.[10] Churches and private foundations provided schools and hospitals. All these institutions guarded their independence fiercely and although they might look to Parliament, on occasion, for improvements to their position, they did not expect interference from the executive. Nor did they normally receive it.

These widely held beliefs about the constitution, the exercise of power, and the proper limits of central authority co-existed over time with some equally widely held views about what the general objectives of policy should be in key areas of executive responsibility. This was the case in one of the two most important areas of policy throughout this period – international relations. Between 1689 and 1712 Britain was part of European coalitions that fought two successful wars against Louis XIV – Britain contributing a combination of naval power, military leadership and substantial subsidies to her allies. The outcome of the first in 1697 – the 'Nine Years War' – was something of a stalemate but the conclusion of the second – the 'War of Spanish Succession', fought in conjunction with the Dutch United Provinces and the Habsburg Empire – led to the Peace of Utrecht in 1713. The victories and the Peace had important results. They showed conclusively that the might of France – the superpower of the day – could be contained by concerted allied action. The Peace treaties themselves established a new balance of power in Europe – one in which the crucial elements from Britain's point of view were the transfer of the Belgic Provinces from Spanish to Habsburg control, a new Barrier Treaty with the Dutch, and substantial accessions of territory: in north America (Hudson Bay, Nova Scotia and Newfoundland); in the West Indies (St Kitts) and in the Mediterranean (Gibraltar and Minorca). Above all, they established Britain as one of the five leading powers in Europe, a position that was enhanced by the succession of the House of Hanover to the throne, the state of Hanover having expanded considerably in north Germany during the previous fifty years.

As a result of these developments, the principal assumption of those responsible for foreign policy during the next forty years was that Britain's strategic and commercial interests were best served by forging agreements with other European powers designed to maintain an overall 'balance of power'. Admittedly, this raised certain difficulties for contemporaries. Although the five or six individuals involved in foreign policy decision-making constituted a small enough number to make the focusing on specific objectives easier than they otherwise might have been, the division of responsibility for negotiations with the European courts between the two Secretaries of State complicated matters. In addition, while some contemporaries referred to a 'balance of power' as though it was a single system, professionals were well aware that this omnibus term embraced a global balance between the maritime and continental powers as well as a series of subsidiary and regional systems in Europe, each one of which might pose special problems of its own. In Britain's case, the important ones were those in the Baltic, the Low Countries and the Mediterranean. Finally, throughout the reigns of first two Hanoverians, there was a substantial body of opinion opposed to any continental commitments and a preference for what would later be called a 'free hand'. This view, supported strongly by most Tories, rested on the argument that Britain's interests were essentially maritime and overseas, and were best defended by untrammelled naval power.

That said, the search for continental alliances was a persistent theme of this period, albeit with differing levels of intensity and with various partners. Between 1714 and 1731 the importance allocated to the interests of Hanover combined with the readiness of the most influential Secretary of State, Lord Stanhope, to play a forward role in European affairs led initially to a strengthening of the 1713 alliance with France in 1718. This, however, created more friction than harmony with the result that Stanhope's less interventionist successors, Townshend, Newcastle and Walpole looked to alternatives. This led to peace treaties and alliances with Spain and the Habsburg Empire in 1731 that effectively brought the fractious alliance with France to an end. Thereafter, the principal objective of policy became the checking of the growth of French influence overseas (in North America and India), and in Germany where it threatened both the Habsburg empire (the ruler of the Belgic Provinces) and Hanover. This was to lead to war with Spain in 1739; to participation, eventually, on the side of the Habsburgs, in the war of the Austrian succession, 1739–48; and subsequently, to a partially realised search for an alliance system embracing the Dutch, the Habsburg empire and smaller states such as Bavaria and Saxony that was masterminded by the Duke of Newcastle.

The other area of policy that was of continuous importance to the executive was the economic: in particular, financial policy involving the raising of revenue by borrowing and various kinds of taxes; and commercial policy involving the regulation of internal and external trade. In the case of finance, no settled conviction influenced policy at the start of this period. Ministers traditionally relied on borrowing and taxing according to need. Borrowing and assessed or direct taxes on wealth were therefore occasional. Moreover, although indirect taxes on internal and external trade (excise and customs) were constant, they were closely related to existing expenditure. In so far as there were any generally accepted views about taxation, they were, first, that the levying of a general excise on goods would be unacceptable – although such a policy was advocated in the 1690s; and, second, that it would be impossible to devise an income tax that could assess individuals and different localities equitably.[11]

A settled conviction, however, did influence commercial policy. This was based on the view that the total of world trade was 'fixed' and immutable and that in order to survive in a highly competitive international market, each country was bound to maximise and protect its share by any means at its disposal. In Britain's case, the chief means of doing this were by commercial agreements with foreign countries and by maintaining, for its own purposes, a monopoly of trade with its colonies. The first of these was always of an uncertain and short-term kind but the second was made a fixture by the Navigation acts of 1651, 1660 and 1696. These established that the colonies would trade almost exclusively with England/Britain. Raw materials would be imported, thus reducing dependence on foreign sources and providing opportunities for re-export to other countries. Domestic goods would be exported to the colonies, thus providing home producers with secure markets. All of this trade would be conducted in English/British ships manned by English/British seamen, thereby maintaining a merchant marine that could supply the needs of the navy in times of war. Here was the basis of the 'navigation system' that was to be an integral part of official economic thinking until its partial dismantling in the 1820s and its final demise in 1849.

In keeping with their impact on other areas of policy, the great wars of 1689–1713 led to a reshaping of financial policy which although it did not add up to a system as coherent as that applied to colonial trade certainly provided the context for decision-making during the next fifty years. The principal features were as follows. First, approximately one-third of the huge cost of the wars was met by long-term, interest-bearing loans from the public that were largely controlled by the government and guaranteed by parliamentary statute. In 1688 there was no national debt; in 1714 it had risen to just over £36m. This marked the beginning of the funding of a substantial proportion of expenditure by long-term public borrowing – the 'financial revolution' – that amazed contemporaries and has lasted to this day.[12] Second, what became a permanent land tax was established in 1692 and to this were added other, more contingent, taxes assessed on various forms of property that raised, collectively, about 40 per cent of expenditure. This represented a substantial increase in the proportion of taxation that was raised regularly by taxes on property owners. And third, in conjunction with a tightening of the navigation system by the Navigation Act of 1696 and increases in excise duties, there was a near fourfold increase in the level of import duties from 1690–1704. Although excise and customs duties combined contributed only 30% of government expenditure at this time, the increase in import duties established a much more comprehensive system of protection for domestic goods than had existed hitherto.[13]

These developments set the context for economic policy until the 1760s. Financial policy was therefore focused principally on two general objectives: first, the elimination of the National Debt, and when this proved impossible, the reduction of the interest charges on it; and second, the shifting of the burden of taxation from taxes on property to taxes on consumption. In the case of commercial policy, the navigation system remained a fixture but there were repeated adjustments to excise and customs duties in order to tax consumption more highly, to stimulate domestic production by an extension of protection, and to increase overseas trade. Taken as a whole, this was an agenda that was shaped by the demands of the Williamite wars and driven more by practical than theoretical considerations.

In the case of the other principal area of executive action – law and order – the general objective of policy remained much as it had always been: the maintenance of peace by traditional means and with due respect for the existing distribution of authority between central and local government. There were no new settled views comparable to those in other spheres of policy such as the desirability of a balance of power, deficit financing and imperial protection. This was due, in part at least, to the fact that there was no single department such as the Home Office that was responsible. The two Secretaries of State shared responsibility for maintaining 'order' and the Lord Chancellor and the other senior law officers, the Attorney and Solicitor Generals, were more administrative heads and advisers on law than the promoters of legal policy. Thus, the reforms to the fairness and efficiency of the legal system which took place in three phases between 1700 and 1760 were more the result of co-operation between the Law officers and parliamentary activists than the inspiration of the officers themselves.[14] Moreover, with the exception of what were agreed by all classes to be emergencies such as the Jacobite rebellions of 1715 and 1745, the means to impose order were to diffuse and limited. The Bill of Rights stipulated that there should be no standing army in peacetime without parliamentary consent with the result that once a war was over, the army was reduced to skeleton proportions on the mainland with reserves stationed in Ireland. The county militias were nominally under the control of the Secretaries of State but in practice were the preserves of the county elites. As for the JPs and the peace officers (the constables), these operated under the law and not at the bequest of Secretaries of State. As Lord Camden put it famously in 1765, 'except in libels and some few state crimes, as they are called, the secretary of state does not pretend to the authority of a constable'.[15] All in all, the diffusion of responsibility militated against any redefinition of objectives.

Finally, it is worth noting that a similar approach was adopted to the governing of Scotland, the colonies, and to a lesser extent, Ireland. Broadly speaking, the general objective was limited to ensuring that representative institutions (and after 1707, the Scottish MPs at Westminster) did not threaten English interests, particularly in terms of security and commerce. Otherwise, domestic government was left to the Crown's representatives and local institutions. This placed the emphasis on political management rather than any re-evaluation of the responsibilities of central government.

The shaping of policy

So far we have noted the evolution of widely held beliefs and views about the scope of government and the objectives of policy which taken together might said to have constituted the ideological context for policy-making. We now need to look more closely at how *specific* policies were devised and implemented. This is no easy matter. By comparison with the period after *c.*1760, for example, there is much less evidence available that enables us to reconstruct the thinking that lay behind many specific policies. There is less political correspondence to consult; reports of the parliamentary debates are fragmentary; and the materials for estimating the scope and range of public debate on policy, much less numerous. Admittedly, these deficiencies affect our understanding of some areas of policy more than others. It may have had least effect in the major responsibilities of the executive – foreign and financial policy – where departmental records, while not as substantial as they were later to become, have facilitated convincing reconstructions of the shaping of policy. In what were conceived to be the less important areas of policy, however, the deficiencies are more serious. They are particularly notable, for example, in the devising of social policies, in which broad category we might include those dealing with crime and punishment. For example, in the case of the decision taken in 1718 to make transportation to the American colonies the major form of punishment for felony, there is apparently no surviving evidence on the reasoning that lay behind it. All we know is that it required an act of Parliament as well as intervention by the Treasury and the Privy Council to persuade local authorities and the American colonists to bring it into operation.[16] This may be an extreme example, but it may serve as illustration of the difficulties facing the historians of the practice of government in this period by comparison with those of the period after *c.*1760. Taken as a whole, we should be alert to the possibility that the comparative deficiencies in the sources may lead the historian to unwittingly underestimate the ideological input into decision making.

Furthermore, the various beliefs and views that constituted the ideological framework of government were not only widely shared but were also of a kind that were unlikely to attract determined zealots. In the case of their currency, the only significant challenge came from the Tory antipathy to foreign alliances. As for their substance, most, such as the desirability of a mixed system of government or the objective of a balance of power, had emerged from a combination of theory and successful practical application; and were cast in very general terms. By comparison with later doctrines such as free trade, natural rights and utilitarianism, they lacked the intellectual cutting edge likely to persuade believers to insist on putting their ideas into practice at every opportunity.

In fact, although there clearly was an ideological input to policy-making, the evidence also points to a strong element of pragmatism in the framing of specific policies and little desire to co-ordinate policies in the different spheres of government with a view to achieving an overall coherence. The pressure to play a short and often uncoordinated game was certainly considerable. Despite the emergence of a first minister and an inner cabinet providing greater opportunities to co-ordinate policy, departmentalism remained a strong feature of the executive as a whole – a point exemplified by the fact that it was an eighteenth – century convention that ministers did not normally speak in Parliament on matters that were not their departmental responsibility.[17] In addition, there were frequent changes in the political outlook of the executive before 1714 and although this diminished thereafter with the establishment of the Whig hegemony, there were always differences that had to be resolved between the Whigs who supported ministers and those who opposed them. Further, in the wider scale of things, the establishment of annual parliaments meant that policy had to be framed in the light of the highly volatile views of all MPs and the various interest groups that they represented. All of these circumstances encouraged a pragmatic and expedient approach to the framing of specific policies.

Moreover, there is evidence that the propagandists and apologists for the Whigs in office, particularly during the regimes of Walpole and the Pelhams, developed the view that the ideal form of government for the times was one that was both prudential and pragmatic. Reed Browning, for example, has demonstrated that Walpole and other administration Whigs abandoned Cato as a classical model for Whig theory and sponsored Cicero instead on the grounds that he praised government that was flexible, pragmatic, and expedient. 'Cicero', he writes, 'was the single most important theorizing influence on the greatest of the ministerial apologists of the years between 1725 and 1755'.[18] In addition, a number of historians, most notably, Paul Langford, have detected the growth of 'the pursuit of harmony' or 'politeness' in the conduct of politicians in the early Hanoverian period. This, they suggest, was motivated by a wish to soothe the 'rage of party' that had been such a feature of the later-Stuart period in order to establish and maintain political stability.[19] An ideology was therefore developed to justify a particular way of doing things – an indication that the way itself was thought to be prevalent.

The historiography certainly provides evidence that pragmatism and expedience were strong features of executive practice. In the case of foreign policy, for example, the general objective of Whig administrations after the Williamite wars was to form alliances to sustain the balance of power established by the peace of Utrecht and thereby occupy a forward role in European affairs. However, this was sometimes undermined by a reluctance to support the objective by full-scale war for immediate financial and political reasons. One author, for example, has argued that decisions on whether to go to war or not, 1733–56, were largely based on the immediate threats to British interests as opposed to the broader considerations of a continental commitment. In 1733 Walpole kept out of the war of the Polish succession because he could see no threat to such interests whereas he did enter the war of the Austrian succession in 1740 because France threatened the Low Countries. In 1756 Britain engaged in what was to become the Seven Years War not because of a desire to preserve the balance of power – a subject rarely mentioned as an objective in the public debate on the matter – but to counter French aggrandisement in North America.[20] It has also been argued persuasively that Britain was driven to war by the pressure of public opinion rather than long-term strategic or theoretical objectives: in 1739, for example, against Spain in defence of Britain's Caribbean trade and in 1756 against France following the loss of Minorca.[21]

Similarly, despite fulfilling many of the hopes of pre-1688 theorists and therefore seeming to be driven by their ideas, financial and commercial policies were often devised more in the light of immediate circumstances. This was the case with three key props of the overall system that had emerged by the 1730s. The most wide-reaching in its effects was the financial revolution – the system of 'deficit financing' that consisted of funding a substantial proportion of annual expenditure by borrowing capital from the public. This evolved through three phases. The first, 1693–7, has been variously described as one of 'experiment and confusion' or 'trial and error' when a Lottery scheme and the Million Pound Fund (the foundation stone of deficit financing) were devised by a combination of ministers and private 'projectors' to deal with the immediate costs of the Nine Years War. This was followed by a period of 'stricter control' by government, 1697–1713, during which Charles Montagu and his colleagues devised a coherent programme of 'reconstruction', including the floating of new Exchequer bills and a new subscription for the Bank of England. Finally, in the period between 1713 and 1739, ministers modified the existing system by the establishment of a mechanism to pay off the debt (the Sinking Fund), but then used it for more immediate purposes, thereby making its real operation 'capricious'.[22]

The two other props were the 1692 Land Tax and the tariffs established on imported goods, particularly between 1690 and 1704. In the case of the Land Tax, it has been shown that the ministers responsible did not think they were introducing a new and permanent form of direct taxation. Instead, they regarded it as an extension of earlier levies and hit upon it 'more by accident than design'. Further, rather than it becoming permanent as a result of its intrinsic merits, it did so partly because the landed classes agreed that it would be impossible to establish an income tax that would assess individuals equitably and partly because government was able to raise revenue in other ways.[23] As for tariffs on imported goods, their justification changed over time in response to circumstances. Initially, 1690–1714, they were extended unsystematically from one commodity to another to produce an astonishing fourfold increase in their number. This was partly the result of the demands of domestic producers but much more that of the immediate revenue needs of the government. A protective system was therefore established as much by a series of immediate responses to pressing problems as by some overall design. Later, however, the emphasis changed. In the 1720s, Walpole carried out a wholesale consolidation and rationalisation of 'the results of thirty-two years of piecemeal and uncoordinated concessions to protectionism' but the purpose remained divided between protection and the raising of revenue with Walpole himself being prone to make choices on tariffs with a sharp eye on how they might meet the immediate needs of key interests groups in Parliament. It was therefore not until the post-Walpole era that tariffs came to be seen more as a method of protection than as a means of raising revenue.[24]

In other spheres of responsibility some policies were strongly influenced by idealism but in others pragmatism and expediency were prominent. Idealism, for example, was a strong feature of the moral reform movement that was inspired for religious reasons by Queen Mary and then patronised by the Court after 1690.[25] It led to the establishment of metropolitan and provincial 'Reformation of Manners' societies, many of which remained active until the 1740s. In addition, a commitment on the part of many Whigs to the principle of religious toleration was undoubtedly a major reason for the repeal of the Occasional Conformity and Schism Acts in favour of dissenters in 1719 even though the desire to reward them for their political support was another.[26]

The approach to the maintenance of law and order, on the other hand, was more *ad hoc*. Leaving aside the suppressions of the rebellions in Ireland and Scotland, there were three notable developments in this regard. The first took place between the 1690s and the 1720s and consisted of the extension of the death penalty to a large number of crimes and the creation of the so-called 'Bloody Code'. The second worked in a slightly more humane direction and took the form of extending transportation to the American colonies after 1718. Thereafter, the proportion of convicted felons who suffered the death penalty fell and the proportion who were transported rose substantially. And the third took place in the 1720s and 1730s when Walpole used several devices to silence his critics: the raising of the tax on newspapers and a resort to the libel laws to muzzle the press; the deployment of Commons' standing orders to prevent the publication of the debates; and the persuading of the Lord Chamberlain to use his powers to ban politically subversive plays.

Ministerial involvement in these developments, however, was very limited, elusive, or temporary. Ministers did not have a significant input into the development of the 'Bloody Code', the initiative for which came from the localities and from independent MPs.[27] Further, although the executive undoubtedly gave decisive support to the idea of opening the American colonies to transportation in 1718, it is far from clear that this was its own initiative.[28] As for Walpole's campaign to suppress criticism of his regime, it was short lived and proved largely ineffective by the 1740s.[29]

As mentioned earlier, it is notable that there was no single minister or department responsible for law and order, and this was also the case in the other spheres of responsibility we need to consider – Scotland, Ireland and the colonies. In the case of Scotland, the Union itself was largely the result of fears for a future dynastic crisis in the event of Queen Anne's death and the more immediate concern for English security at a critical stage of the War of the Spanish Succession. Subsequently, there was no settled way for administering Scottish affairs and no coherent scheme of administration. Sometimes there was a Scottish Secretary of State (1708/9–1711, 1713–15, 1716–25, 1741/2–1745/6) and sometimes not. This led successive ministries to focus instead on political management.

As for the very small amount of Scottish legislation sponsored by ministers, most was of the 'fiscal-military' kind, the only other initiatives being the occasional bill to 'tame' the Highlands and the piecemeal abolition of inconvenient parts of the Scottish legal system. By 1745 such initiatives were rarer still and it took the rebellion of that year to bring about a more concerted effort – the 'taming of the Highlands'. This undoubtedly involved a substantial measure of coherent forward planning. Indeed, as Bob Harris has recently emphasised, Pelham's administration devised a 'programme of systematic reform' before the rebellion was over – between January and March 1746. This resulted in legislation to disarm the Highlands, to suppress non-juring meeting houses, and to abolish private armies and jurisdictions. Thereafter, the emphasis shifted to providing sufficient military force to ensure that the legislation was effectively implemented and to long-term projects to extend English (or Whig) conceptions of law to Scotland and to encourage industry and commerce. The ministerial input into these developments, however, became more fitful as the immediate threat waned and other issues took precedence. Thus, the initiatives rested more with the military commanders on the ground and a combination of Scottish officials and private individuals, both Scottish and English, who had their own interest in economic improvement. Pelham's administration may have inaugurated a grand scheme of social engineering but it did not have the means or the time to see it through to a conclusion.[30]

The same *ad hoc* approach is visible in Irish and colonial affairs. In the case of Ireland, David Hayton argues that although ministers did deal promptly with security problems, 1690–1714, they were very reluctant to intervene on other matters for fear of offending the sensibilities of the Irish Parliament and undermining the 'Undertaker' system of administration. This was left to backbenchers to achieve: for example, by securing an act of 1699 which prevented the import of Irish wool into English and colonial markets.[31] Later, Walpole pursued various strategies at different times to strengthen the executive's influence over Irish politics – in the mid-1720s, 1731–3, and 1739–41 – but according to the same authority these were not pursued 'consistently or rigorously', and were in any case counter productive.[32] As for the colonies, the diffusion of responsibility between the Secretaries of State and the Board of Trade together with a lack of interest resulted in their being very few legislative initiatives of any significance until the 1750s.[33]

The evidence therefore suggests that although the executive came to be guided by a widely held set of beliefs about the general objectives of policy, the planning of specific policies was often spasmodic and uncoordinated with their final form being strongly influenced by immediate practical considerations. That said, some historians have detected periods when there were signs of a more forward-looking and co-ordinated approach. Prior to the establishment of the Whig hegemony in 1714, the wars, the novelty of annual Parliaments, the intensity of party warfare, and the prevalence of mixed administrations were obstacles to such developments although there are examples of practice edging in their direction. William III's dominance of the executive ensured that his own objectives on the international stage gave strategic policy some coherence and there was an equivalent on the domestic front in the later stages of Godolphin's financial policies. The best example, however, appears to have been Harley's approach when the effective head of administration from 1710. Harley, Hayton argues, tried to act in accordance with a consistent set of policy objectives. This consisted of: 'limited taxation according to accurate estimates; properly audited accounts; altruistic public service; the cultivation of the real wealth of the country, in terms of its land and its trade, as the proper objects of foreign policy; the preservation of the liberties of the subject, and the forms of the constitution'. However, as Hayton makes clear, these had their origin in the 'programme' of the majority of MPs in the early 1690s – the Country party – as opposed to having emerged from the experience of holding high office. They are therefore more aspirational than well-considered in the light of the information that accrues from being in office.[34]

In the period after 1714, however, some historians take the view that the longevity of Walpole's and Pelham's administrations did lead to what amounts to a programme of operations consisting of general objectives that were advanced by specific proposals in different, but what were perceived to be related, areas of policy. In Walpole's case, the first historian in recent times to nail their colours pretty firmly to this view was P. G. M. Dickson. Walpole's general objectives, he argues, were formed in the wake of the political instability of the first years of the Hanoverian succession and the economic crisis created by the collapse of the South Sea 'Bubble' in 1720–1. They were therefore relatively conservative and consisted of 'political unity partly achieved through social and economic progress'. The means used to achieve them, however, were imaginative and extensive. On the social (and political) side of the equation he sought to reconcile to his regime the two mutually antagonistic groups that had made unprecedented contributions to the funding of the two Williamite wars. On the one hand, the landed elite and the farming community that paid the land and other assessed taxes; and on the other, the City and provincial merchants who raised the loans and paid the excise duties. The former were appeased by keeping the land and assessed taxes low and by abandoning schemes to emancipate Protestant dissenters. The latter, by the strengthening of ties between the Treasury and the City of

London. To these we might add the turning away after 1731 from Townshend's relatively 'forward' foreign policy and the adoption of a less interventionist stance – thereby reducing the chance of further expensive and tax-consuming wars.

The economic side of the equation was much more detailed. Progress was to be achieved by a combination of means. First, by reducing the national debt and the interest charges upon it – an objective that Walpole went some way in achieving. Second, by keeping the land and other assessed taxes low – another success story. Third, by stimulating domestic production – in some cases by legislation such as acts of 1721, 1722 and 1731 and 1736 to prohibit the use of imported calicos, removing export duties on English goods and encouraging the domestic manufacture of sailcloth. Fourth, by encouraging foreign trade – as envisaged by the ill-fated Excise Bill of 1733 which would have done away with some of the delays caused by fraud and lengthy customs procedures for the re-exporters of wine and tobacco to Europe. Fifth, by rationalising tariffs in 1722 in order to make them a more effective system of protection for domestic producers. And sixth, by keeping manufacturing costs as low as possible by such means as ensuring that only the most destitute could claim poor relief (and therefore avoid work) and by clamping down on combinations of workers (trades unions).[35]

The argument that Walpole possessed a coherent programme does raise problems of interpretation. The historian is confronted, on the one hand, by Walpole's very general statements of his objectives; and on the other, by a succession of initiatives spread over a decade or so. Two questions arise. To what extent is the historian justified in thinking that there were links between general objectives and specific measures and dignifying them as a programme? And how far were the specific initiatives driven more by the various contingencies of the moment than by the logic of such a programme? These questions are difficult to answer, especially as Walpole often gave the impression that expedience mattered more than long-term planning and sometimes obscured his real intentions in order to maximise support for his measures. The Excise Bill of 1733 is a case in point. The measure was of long gestation and appears to have had one of the objectives ascribed to it by Dickson – the stimulation of English re-exports of colonial goods as well as another – the raising of more Excise revenue and diminishing the burden on the land tax. In Parliament, however, Walpole stressed the more immediately appealing objective of clamping down on the smuggling of wine and tobacco in order to maximise support for the measure.[36] That said, most historians tend to give Walpole the benefit, so to speak, of the doubt. Thus, although some give more emphasis to expediency and others are reluctant to regard so many of his initiatives as part of a programme, the consensus is that there was a much more coherent link between his objectives and his actions than any of his predecessors had managed to achieve.

A similar case has been made for Pelham's policies, particularly after the conclusion of the costly War of the Austrian Succession (1748). Dickson, for example, detects a three-point agenda. First, the continuation of the essence of Walpole's financial policies but rationalising them where possible: for example, by continuing to operate the Sinking Fund as 'a general and flexible reserve' and by simplifying and strengthening the system of public borrowing. Second, by administrative reforms such as the Calendar Act of 1751 which brought British dating into line with that in the rest of Europe and a drastic pruning of the size of the fiscal bureaucracy. And third, social reform which included the Naval Discipline Act of 1749, various criminal statutes such as the Murder Act of 1751, and the Jewish Naturalisation Act of 1753 which in the face of anti-Semitic opposition close to a general election was repealed the following year.[37] Other scholars have also noted that at this time some departments were presided over by particularly dominant personalities such as Lords Anson and Halifax at the boards of Admiralty and Trade respectively. Anson, it is argued, evolved 'a comprehensive naval strategy' during his spell at the Admiralty, 1751–60, to deal with conflict with France.[38] Halifax, for his part, managed to ensure that colonial governors sent their despatches to the Board of Trade as a matter of course, thus enabling him to develop an overview of colonial affairs. This appears to have been part of a concerted effort at this time to strengthen ministerial control over colonial possessions. Richard Connors, for example, points to acts in 1750 restricting iron production in the American colonies and forbidding in some the use of local paper money.[39]

Admittedly, some caution has to be exercised about the extent of the legislative initiatives of the post-war Pelham administration. Thus, as Bob Harris has made clear, in certain areas of policy – trade, manufactures and the relief of poverty – the administration preferred to share the initiative with, or leave it to, independent MPs, parliamentary committees and lobby groups. This, it is suggested, was a strategy designed to prevent the administration being identified with any particular interest and therefore becoming the promoter of disharmony. On the other hand, both he and others recognise a degree of overall coherence and purpose in the principal areas of government concern – national finances, national defence and colonial administration.[40] Broadly speaking, the consensus is that the costs of the war and the social tensions that it created led to a series of related measures designed to restore the kind of stability that Walpole had engineered in his hey day.

A fitful, unco-ordinated, and pragmatic tendency in executive decision-making was therefore superseded from time to time by a more coherent, co-ordinated and long-term approach. To some extent, the contrast can be explained by political circumstances. Insecure administrations facing annual Parliaments were bound to think short-term in order to survive. Secure ones, on the other hand, could afford to think of the longer term and plan accordingly. But it was also a matter of personality and, possibly, changing concepts of statesmanship. Walpole spectacularly, and to a lesser extent, Pelham, were commanding figures who were capable of surveying all areas of government and spotting the wood for the trees. In addition, it was Walpole who accustomed the political world to the spectacle of the first minister explaining and justifying policy on an annual basis to the House of Commons – a practice that was bound to encourage references to past *and* future objectives.

The achievements of the executive

As mentioned at the beginning of this discussion on the executive, there were three outstanding features of British political history in this period. The first was Britain's emergence as one of the five major European powers as a result of a combination of her unrivalled maritime prowess, the depth and extent of her financial and commercial resources, and the real and potential value of her overseas possessions. The second was the establishment of a new method of governing the two weaker members of the multiple kingdoms of the British archipelago – Scotland and Ireland – and the development in England of a mixed system of government that was to prove remarkably stable. And the third was the evolution of a considerable degree of public acceptance of this new system of government. Resistance was greatest in Ireland and Scotland but it was crushed in both cases by force of arms. In England, on the other hand, a mixed form of government became a matter of national self-congratulation rather than condemnation.

In searching for an explanation of these political developments, historians have traditionally pointed to the helpful conditions provided by contemporaneous economic and social factors. The population grew more slowly than it had done before 1688 and was to do after 1760. In fact the most notable social change of a general kind was a rapid urbanisation in parts of England that offered further stimulus to the development of commerce and industry. Foreign trade flourished and so too did agricultural production. Prices were generally stable for the most part and if anything, tended to fall. These factors therefore led to the slack in the economy that was one of the reasons why those with capital were ready to lend and why the government was able to borrow approximately 30% of its ever-growing wartime expenditure.

Yet, although these factors provided conditions that were conducive to the growth of the power and stability of the state, the executive also clearly played a part. Thus, as we have seen, the executive contributed to Britain's rise to great power status in three crucial ways. First, by forming alliances – for example, with the Dutch (1688–1713), with Austria–Hungary (1743, 1753) and with Prussia (1756–63) – that led not only to military victories but also to the substantial additions to overseas territory that enabled Britain to become the dominant imperial and trading power. Dickson, for example, argues that the maintenance and expansion of the North American and West Indian markets as a result of the wars of 1739–63 led to crucial increases in export demand for British producers.[41] Second, by raising sufficient armed forces in wartime despite the considerable diffusion of responsibility for their respective branches and without any significant changes to systems of administration. As Britain was at war for half the period, she therefore became a 'military state' to a degree that had not existed before. In the other half, however, the swift reduction of forces to a constitutionally acceptable peacetime establishment and the continuity in responsibility and administration belied such a description. And third, by raising the unprecedented sums required to engage in war by an ingenious combination of borrowing and direct and indirect taxation. If the degree to which Britain was a 'military state' fluctuated, there is no doubt that she quickly became a 'fiscal state'.

The role that the executive played in the establishment of a new system of government was also considerable. The 1688 Revolution took place to resist arbitrary government and its success meant that henceforth the actions of the executive would be subject to annual scrutiny by the elected representatives of the English/British public. The onus was therefore on the executive to conduct itself in a manner that made the new system both workable and acceptable.

As we have seen, the practical response to this challenge was the evolution of a framework for executive decision-making that allowed for a mixing of royal, ministerial, parliamentary and bureaucratic influences in ways that seemed well suited to the new ideal of mixed government. Monarchs were regarded as having an important role to play throughout this period, and although the practical influence of the first Hanoverians declined, this was due more to their personal characters and interests than opposition to their role. The political world became accustomed during Walpole's time to policy being driven by a first minister and an inner cabinet but neither of these two institutions were regarded as constitutional fixtures. The continuing existence of the outer cabinet containing ministers representing the interests of the Crown and the sometimes equivalent or even superior influence of the Secretaries of State saw to that. As for the government departments and their officials, there was a curious mixture of the old and the new. In the case of the departments, there was hardly any attempt to co-ordinate and harmonise their operations on a regular basis, each one being seen as the peculiar preserve of a departmental head responsible ultimately to the monarch. Departmentalism therefore remained strong. In the case of the officials, although there were some who had an important influence on policy and although this period saw the development in the Excise of a modern bureaucratic ethos with careers open to talent, these co-existed with an older tradition of officials as no more than clerks and their appointment dependent on patronage. Finally, the executive had a far less dominant role in parliamentary business than it was later to acquire. Government bills accounted for only a minority of legislation throughout this period, although it is true that ministers did give support to bills promoted by independent MPs. Further, although government measures (including legislation) attracted the most attention in debate, they were not given the precedence in the allocation of business that was to be accorded to them in the early nineteenth century.

The evolution of this mixed form of executive was accompanied by the development of a distinctive form of executive government. Decisions were increasingly framed within the context of a number of widely-held beliefs about both the scope and purpose of government and the general objectives of policy in the different spheres of responsibility. Day-to-day decision-making, however, was also strongly influenced by immediate and practical considerations. The result, in terms of the relationship between overall objectives and means, the frequency of the application of those means and the co-ordination of policy, was a form of government that varied from one set of ministers to another and from one department to another. To present-day enthusiasts for assessing the performance of governments (or any other institution) by measuring the relationship between goals and outcomes and the coherence of the 'chain of command', such variability may well appear to have been a sign of weakness. It certainly may seem surprising that there was no fundamental reappraisal of the objectives of colonial policy before 1760; no debate on methods of governing; and no annual review of national finances.[42] In its own time, however, it may well have been conducive to stability. This, after all, was a period when although the military, fiscal and commercial resources of the state undoubtedly grew, power remained diffused between central and local institutions. A more *dirigiste* form of executive government may well have sparked serious conflict between them.

Finally, there is the question of the public's acquiescence in the new system. To some degree this was the result of the favourable social and economic climate and the fact that the political system as a whole incorporated a degree of public participation even though this was made less frequent by the 1716 Septennial Act. But the executive also made a contribution. Two of its principal activities – war and the accession of overseas territory – encouraged patriotic fervour while the other – the raising of money – bore heavily on the landed and middle classes as well as the rest. None could be said to have had the potential to generate mass protest. It was also the case that the executive's approach to law and order was piecemeal and intermittent in its effects. In the case of the political exclusion of Protestant dissenters, the refusal to repeal the Test and Corporation Acts was accompanied by the passing of Indemnity Acts from 1727 which rendered their operation nominal rather than real. The clamp down on press and media criticism in the early stages of Walpole's regime was subsequently allowed to lapse. Even the 'Bloody Code', which had the greatest potential to stimulate violent opposition, proves to have been a parliamentary initiative rather than that of the executive. Indeed, other than the quelling of rebellions, no coherent law and order policy is visible, although there are signs of one emerging in Scotland in the wake of the 1745 rebellion. In this respect too, the executive contributed to the achievements of the period.

Summary and conclusion

By comparison to the changes in the framework of the executive, the changes to the scope purpose and conduct of government appear to have been modest. In the case of its scope and purpose, for example, the mind of the executive was focused firmly for most of this period on war and diplomacy, public finances to support the military, the sustaining of the Protestant constitution and the maintaining of law and order. Only at the end of the period was there a modest increase in the quantity of government legislation and a broadening of its subject matter to include commercial measures and others related to a more progressive approach to law and order.

In keeping with this relative stasis in thinking on the scope of government, there was littler change in the assumptions that underpinned policy and what were regarded as its practical objectives. In the former case, these consisted of supporting the concept of a mixed form of government; of taking the view that full participation in affairs of state depended on membership of the Church of England and the possession of substantial quantities of real estate; and of resisting the institutions of central government intruding too far on local and voluntary authorities. As for the practical objectives of policy, these amounted to pursuing agreements with other powers to achieve a balance of power; to influence British commerce to meet the needs of mercantilism; and eventually, to maintain the balance of interest between the three groups who had contributed most to the 'financial revolution' – the purchasers of government stock, the direct payers of the land tax and the payers of indirect taxes. As far as we can tell from admittedly deficient sources, no similarly settled views influenced social policy.

In the case of the ways that specific policies were shaped, the evidence suggests that this was influenced strongly, for the most part, by practical considerations. Ministers may have had an ideological objective in view but they were aware that realising it, even in part, would require the details to suit the immediate and practical objectives of colleagues, supporters and independent MPs. There were some first ministers, however, who, either by the ways they justified particular policies or by the links they established between them, were able to persuade others that they had an underlying purpose. This was to some extent true of Harley and Pelham, and more particularly, of Walpole. This suggests that there were those who were ready to welcome a more systematic approach to policy-making than was usual.

3   Parliament and government

Introduction

Throughout this period, the two houses of Parliament met in different parts of the 'Palace of Westminster' – an aggregation of buildings of various dates stretching back to pre-Conquest times which, as the name implies, had once been the royal residence. Its evolution therefore resembled that of the constitution itself. The Lords met in 'a simple apartment' with a largely mediaeval interior that was little changed between the Restoration and the Union with Ireland in 1801. The throne and the woolsack were placed at one end, the benches facing them were painted red, and dormer windows placed in the barrelled ceiling that concealed the mediaeval roof provided light. With a floor space of 70 feet by 24 feet 6 inches, it was capable of easily accommodating the 160 or so peers at the start of King William's reign.[1] The Commons, on the other hand, met in a space that although it was part of a much more distinguished building architecturally, was far less suited to their full number of 513, soon to be augmented to 558 by the union with Scotland. Since 1550 this had been in St Stephen's Chapel, the upper story of a church finished in 1348, the main part of which had been converted by 1700 into a chamber approximately 57 feet long, 33 feet wide and 30 feet high – a significantly smaller space than that occupied by the Lords. The conversions had begun in 1692 under the direction of Sir Christopher Wren, leaving it by about 1710 in a state that was largely unchanged until it burnt down in 1834. The Speaker's chair was placed on the original alter steps at the east end with four rows of benches painted green on each of the side walls and running behind the Speaker – three of these being the original Collegiate stalls. The walls had been panelled in wood, painted brown, and galleries erected on each side.[2] Overall, both chambers were more functional than grand and much less imposing than Westminster Hall, the largest building in the Palace complex, which housed the four principal Courts of Law and was otherwise used for grand state occasions, including state trials.

   The functions of Parliament, like the buildings in which they were exercised, had also evolved over time. Initially, in the thirteenth century, one of the principal functions consisted of hearing and registering consent to the monarch's tax proposals. This was the reason why the Lords consisted of the leading territorial magnates in the kingdom while the members of the Commons were the representatives of the principal administrative units suitable for tax purposes – the counties and the wealthiest cities and towns. Subsequently, they acquired other functions and it will be useful to consider them here as a prelude to a discussion of how they were exercised.

As far as Parliament as a whole is concerned, the most important developments, of course, were the two decisions it took in 1688–9: on the one hand, to offer the Crown to William and Mary; but on the other, to refuse to grant them for their lifetime sufficient revenue to be able to govern the country. Taken together, these two crucial actions confirmed Parliament's role in what was to become known as a mixed system of government and ensured that it met on an annual basis in order to raise the revenues the executive required for the following year. The impact on parliamentary time and parliamentary business was immediate. In the words of David Hayton, 'Parliament not only met more often than before, but generally stayed in session for longer periods'.[3] Thus, the average length of an individual session of the 10 parliaments, 1690–1714, was 116 days in comparison with 57 for the period 1660–89 during which there were ten years when Parliament did not sit. Thereafter, the average length of a session declined modestly to nearer 100 days, although a more notable fall to about 85 days took place during the 1730s, the decade when Walpole's grip on power was beginning to falter. As for the times of the year and the times of the day when Parliament met, there were changes but none of any equivalent significance. Sessions therefore usually started in late Autumn and finished in late Spring, although they started after Christmas in 16 of the 23 sessions between 1717 and 1739. This naturally placed a premium on daylight with the result that the formal time for business at the start of the period was 8 am to 2 pm. Thereafter, the times got marginally later and by 1736 were 11 am to 1 pm and 4 pm to 6 pm. These, however, were the formal times. When business required longer sittings (usually in the Commons), these took place, sometimes long into the night or the following morning – a practice which seems to have grown as this period progressed and one that might have been due to the tendency for Christmas and Easter adjournments to become longer. It was a practice also facilitated by the improved lighting that accompanied Wren's alterations.[4]

This affirmation of Parliament's permanent and central role in the governing of the country provided the justification for the three principal functions that it fulfilled in that respect during this period. The first and most historic of these was to offer 'counsel to the Crown' by scrutinising the measures proposed by the executive. In some cases, such as motions to approve measures of war and peace, legislation was not required with the result that they were only subject to a process of debate and a decision. In most cases, however, such as those relating to finance, legislation was required with the result that the process was more elaborate. Thus, in addition to debate, legislation was also scrutinised by various types of committees, the general features of which as far as the Commons is concerned are conveniently outlined here.[5] One was a committee of the whole House (all members), which allowed for more free-ranging and pertinent discussion than that often possible in normal plenary session. Another was a 'Grand Committee', also of all members, to discuss particular subjects. And a third was a 'select' committee (although this was not a term used at the time) consisting of a specific number or category of members. Such committees had various functions: to draft bills; to scrutinise petitions; to consider the majority of bills on their second reading; and to consider or inquire into specific topics. Government bills were therefore drafted by a small 'select' committee of, usually 3–6 members; and in the course of their three 'readings' in the House concerned were subject to a committee stage involving either a 'committee of the whole' (which always applied to financial measures) or a 'select' committee.

The second function was to act as the 'Grand Inquest of the Nation' by considering specific subjects that were not normally dealt with by the executive and approving any proposals that were related to them. Historically, the Commons established four Grand Committees for this purpose – on religion, grievances, the Courts of justice and trade – and continued to do so in this period. However, although they did meet infrequently before 1714, they fell into complete disuse thereafter as a result of the continuing growth of requests for legislation by an ever- increasing numbers of MPs, institutions and private individuals. The function of being the 'Grand Inquest' therefore expanded greatly but instead of being focused in the work of four Grand Committees became dispersed over an expanding body of requests. On the other hand, the ways these requests were scrutinised were relatively uniform. Those pressing for the consideration of grievances or for a bill to deal with them had to be made by means of a petition. These were either referred to a drafting committee for the preparation of a bill or to a select committee to consider whether a bill was an appropriate way of dealing with the matter. Once a bill had been prepared, it also went through the same stages of discussion and scrutiny visited on government measures, and it is a testimony to the formal rigours of such scrutiny that those that had emerged from the consideration of one select committee were then consigned on second reading to another. In fact select committees quickly became the 'engine room' of Parliament – more than 80 were appointed in the 1753 session in the Commons alone, most to scrutinise petitions for local improvement bills and many of those with memberships of 50 or more. In this respect it is significant that in due course the membership of select committees appointed on important subjects in that House were chosen by ballot rather than randomly and kept to a smaller size, thus giving the party in power some means of exercising control over their proceedings.[6]

A third function that evolved with the proliferation of business was to be a repository not only of opinion but also of an increasing quantity of information. This took the following forms: petitions and addresses from members of the public for bills or for the redress of grievances; bills and acts; the *Journals* of the two houses that recorded daily business, including the reports of some select committees; the separate reports of select committees; and the accounts and papers requested by members from the government departments. Virtually all such materials existed initially only in manuscript form but in due course an increasing proportion found its way into print. It was this development that transformed this particular function: from one that was directed solely to the needs of parliamentarians to one that informed the wider public.

Although these were the central functions of Parliament as a whole, each house had its own particular role to play. In the case of the House of Lords, this was strongly influenced by its largely, but not wholly, hereditary membership. This consisted of male heirs to the throne; the male heads of the English and after 1707, the British peerage families; the 16 elected representatives of the Scottish peerage after the same date; and *ex officio*, the Lord Chancellor and the 26 archbishops and bishops of the Church of England. It is also worth noting that some of the peers also occupied offices in the Royal Household and therefore the executive; and that others were either ministers of departments or heads of the army and the navy. The House therefore contained representatives of all the important branches of the state – the monarchy, the judiciary, the Church, the executive and the armed forces – as well as being representative of the peerage at large. Thus, as the presence of the Lord Chancellor, the senior member of the judiciary, suggests, the House had a significant judicial role, particularly as the final Court of appeal. In addition, the presence of members of the royal family and the royal households as well as the heads of the Church meant that the House was inclined to regard itself as a guardian of their interests against any unwarranted challenge from the Commons. Finally, the fact that the House as a whole consisted of the largest landowners in the state as well as many of the past and present servants of the Crown meant that it could regard itself as a body of sufficient weight and experience to be an effective check on the Commons in all but one aspect of legislation. Bills could be initiated in either House and the assent of both was required before they could become law. Most bills originated in the Commons but even so the Lords had a role to play by amending or, in the last resort, rejecting them. The exception was 'money bills', that is those providing the executive with the revenue necessary for its operations. By a convention established before the Revolution and confirmed in 1678, the Lords deferred to the rights claimed by the Commons to be the place where all bills dealing with public money were started and for their not being amended in 'the other place'.

The reason why the Commons had a special role as the guardian of the nation's purse strings was largely the result of its members being the elected representatives of the principal administrative units capable of being taxed – the counties and the boroughs (cities and towns). It would be wrong, however, to draw too sharp a distinction between the two houses in terms of membership or outlook. Many kinsmen and dependants of peers sat in the Commons, as did representatives of the royal households and members of the executive. On the other hand, the Commons consisted of a broader range of social and economic interest groups than the Lords and was subject to frequent elections by an even more broadly based electorate. Its members were therefore more representative of the population at large and consequently applied themselves more diligently to the business of scrutiny, enquiry and legislation. In addition, the Commons was usually the first port of call for those who sought 'the redress of grievances' – in other words, pressure groups.

Members of Parliament

As a result of extensive research over the last fifty years, principally on the House of Commons under the auspices of the History of Parliament Trust, we now know a great deal about the men who performed these functions and operated these procedures. Broadly speaking, they constituted a long-established governing elite with a number of characteristics that were notable more for their consistency than change. We may begin with their number. The major change came with the Union with Scotland in 1707 that added 16 representative peers to the Lords and 45 members to the Commons. By 1714, the total number of peers (including the bishops) was 219 and it remained at approximately that figure until the 1780s and 1790s when the Younger Pitt inaugurated a period of expansion. In the meantime the number in the Commons (558) remained static.

In the case of their social status, occupations and economic interests, some preliminary remarks are required on the contemporary view of social stratification and its relationship with political power. In general, contemporaries envisaged society as a gently descending pyramid of 'ranks, orders and degrees', one's position on it being dependent, to some extent at least, on the possession or occupation of landed property. Property was the one element in a still largely rural country that linked the highest with the lowest strata (the owners and small tenant farmers). This was the justification for equating the holding of political power with the possession of substantial amounts of real property. With property went rank. The highest rank was a peerage and peers were meant to be the most substantial of landowners. Below them came the ranks of the gentry consisting of baronets, knights and commoners, the last not bearing titles but usually possessing coats of arms that marked them out as 'gentlemen' of substantial property. By the time of the Glorious Revolution, the peerage and the gentry combined, later to be referred to as 'the aristocracy', were the dominant force in Parliament, in local government, and in the principal professions – the Church, the armed forces and the law.

This propertied elite continued to be the dominant force in Parliament throughout this period and research enables us to identify some of its characteristics. In the case of the Lords, we await the results of research equivalent to that devoted to the Commons, but it appears that the English, British and Scottish peers who sat there continued to be distinguished principally by their substantial property as opposed to any other qualification such as civilian or military state service. The fortunes of once wealthy families, could fall, of course, and it was not unknown for commoners with sufficient property to merit a peerage to decline one, but in general it could be said that the Lords represented the most substantial landowners throughout this period.

As for the Commons, a minimum qualification of £600 income *per annum* from landed property for county members and £300 for borough members was stipulated by an Act of 1711. The background to this was the fear of the incursion into the House of members of the 'monied interest', that is those whose primary economic interest lay in finance or commerce rather than the land. However, although the Act is a useful reminder of the store that the Commons placed on the possession of landed property as a qualification for membership, it did not make any real difference to the composition of the House. Throughout this period, both before and after 1711, the House consisted largely of landed proprietors from at least the ranks of the gentry and others who although they held sufficient property for the purposes of qualification were primarily engaged in the professions and in business.[7] Some of these may have hailed from families below gentry status but virtually all aspired to it once their fortunes were made.

There were other characteristics that were consistent throughout this period. Figures for the percentage of English and Welsh MPs who were the sons and grandsons of former members, 1690–1714 (48.5%), together with those for new MPs at successive general elections from 1715 to 1760 (36>22%) suggest that at least half were from parliamentary dynasties – families that sent members to Parliament for two or more generations.[8] The vast majority were members of the Churches of England or Scotland, the relatively high number of about 70 Protestant dissenters in 1690 falling to a mere handful by 1760. About half were educated at University and many members took their seats comparatively young leading to about half being under 41, 1690–1714, although the trend thereafter was for the proportion to fall. Only 42.3% of those with known ages were under 40 in 1754. As for their occupations and interests, the following figures for the numbers of MPs of various types taken from the *History of Parliament* volumes for selected dates are an indication not only of a certain consistency but also of the overall predominance of landed proprietorship (Table 3.1).

Table 3.1 Occupations and interest of MPs, 1690–1754

	1690–1714	*1722–7*	*1754*
Commissioned officers in the armed forces	77–104	67	*c.*65
Practising lawyers	*c.*35–53	73	*c.*42
Businessmen	105–80	58	*c.*60
Totals	192–262	198	*c.*167

Interpreting these figures is, of course, problematic. Those for 1690–1714 are for the highs and lows in different Parliaments and in the case of practising lawyers are estimates. Some of the figures for the 1722 and 1754 Parliaments are approximations. Further, there are reasons for thinking that the definition of 'businessmen' is more rigorous for the pre-1714 parliaments than those for the subsequent period. That said, they do suggest two principal conclusions. First, that in any given Parliament in this period, the proportion who were not in any of these categories was at least 54–69%. A rising majority were therefore principally landed proprietors or professional politicians, and usually a combination of the two. Second, that although there was a broad consistency in the number of commissioned officers and practising lawyers, there appears to be a decline in the number of businessmen. In short, the Commons tended to become more, rather than less, aristocratic.[9]

Analysing institutions by reference simply to the social and economic status of their membership, however, can be misleading. It too often leads to the imposition of a homogeneity of outlook and behaviour that belies the variety of human character and the ability of individuals to influence events. The pages of the *History of Parliament* volumes certainly act as a check to such over-simplification. A privileged position in society encouraged individuality rather than uniformity and the four thousand or so biographies of members of the Commons, 1690–1760, are vivid testimony to their great variety in terms of character, abilities, interest, habits and appearance. Further, a combination of privilege and the lack of any official remuneration (MPs were not paid until 1911) did not automatically lead to a casual and self-interested approach to their duties. In the case of levels of activity in each of the two Houses, there appears to have been some variation between them and certainly considerable variation within them. In the Lords, for example, it appears that between 1714–84 about one-third of the membership never went to London or made arrangements to cast their vote by a proxy.[10] This seems to have been a much higher proportion of perpetual non-attenders than the House of Commons would have tolerated even though there was certainly a sizeable number who made little or no contribution. On the other hand, as in most institutions when they are scrutinised carefully, there was a respectable number who did. In the case of the Lords, the paucity of research on contributions to debate and to the preparation of bills and other committee work makes judgement difficult, but what it suggests is a solid core of perhaps 20 members who were the principal 'men of business' in these respects; and a 100 or more who attended on controversial issues in contentious times.[11] In the Commons, however, detailed research on the 1690–1714 period, suggests a much higher proportion of men of business. Two estimates, based on analysis of speaking records, the presenting and reporting of bills and committee work, indicate that around 20% (100–110 MPs) fell into that category.[12] Moreover, the fact that the number of acts passed each year increased after 1714 also suggests that this proportion did not subsequently fall. In general, there appears to have been in both houses two extremes of inactive and active members with the bulk somewhere in between, a not unusual scenario in assemblies where members are paid.

The other feature of parliamentary life which underlines its variety as opposed to its homogeneity was the daily testing of opinion by debates and votes – a process that reveals a continuous history of differences on critical issues. The questions that have exercised historians ever since is what the substance of those differences were and the extent to which they divided MPs. It is to these matters and from our point of view the crucial question of their impact on government, that we now turn.

Key developments took place in the decade before the Glorious Revolution. Before 1679, there were two distinct types of parliamentarians. One, designated 'Court' politicians, competed for office in the service of Charles II. The other, designated 'Country' politicians, were suspicious of the doings of the Court and were more concerned to support what they regarded as the interests of the country at large. Between 1679 and 1685, however, a combination of Charles II's attempt to rule without Parliament and the Roman Catholicism of his successor, the Duke of York, led to a new line of division between 'Tories' and 'Whigs', both of which were terms of abuse for opponents – the former deriving from an Irish word understood to mean 'bandit' and the latter being a word used in Scotland to describe sour milk. Thus, those labelled Tories opposed the Whig proposal that York be excluded from the throne on the grounds of his religion; and following his succession in 1685 expressed various degrees of sympathy for the idea of the divine right of kings and the complimentary view that the King's opinion should prevail in any conflict between the King, Lords and Commons. They also favoured a uniform obedience to a state church and some may have come to feel that a Roman Catholic one was better suited to exercise such sovereignty than the broadly based Anglican Church of the time. The Whigs, on the other hand, supported York's exclusion and were critical of divine right theory, believing that government should rest on a partnership between the monarchy and Parliament. In addition, they took the view that the interests of the Anglican Church were probably best served by a degree of tolerance towards dissenters rather than an insistence on uniformity. By the time James II made his escape in 1688, most parliamentarians, whether of a Court or Country disposition, were Tories or Whigs, their differences being replicated in the country at large.

From one perspective, the new labels proved remarkably durable and all-embracing throughout this period, especially as they were initially terms of abuse. Thus, the contributors to the relevant *History of Parliament* volumes, using all the known evidence pertaining to the constituency and parliamentary careers of members of the Commons, 1690–1760, have classified the results of general elections in the following ways (Tables 3.2 and 3.3).

Several explanatory points need to be made about these calculations.[13] In the first place, although they refer to the House of Commons, the persistence of a Whig/Tory terminology also applied to the Lords. However, the balance of power there was different. In that House, there was a permanent Whig majority. Second, they record the immediate results of an election as opposed to the state of play at the end of Parliaments as a result of the unseating of members for misdemeanours (and their replacement by their competitors) and by-elections. In the case of the 1690 election, this led to a small Tory majority being replaced by one for the Whigs. Third, although

Table 3.2 General election results, 1690–1705: for England and Wales (total 513)

	Tories	Whigs	Unclassified
1690	**243**	241	28
1695	203	**257**	53
1698	208	**246**	59
1701(Jan./Feb.)	**248**	220	45
1701(Nov./Dec.)	240	**248**	24
1702	**298**	184	31
1705	**260**	233	20

Note
The majority immediately after general elections in bold type.

Table 3.3 General election results, 1708–1754: for Britain (total 558)

	Whigs	Whigs in opposition	Tories	Unclassified/vacant seats
1708	**303**		229	26
1710	193		**346**	17
1713	177		**370**	
1715	**341**		217	
1722	**379**		178	1
1727	**415**	15	128	
1734	**326**	83	149	
1741	**286**	131	136	5
1747	**338**	97	117	6
1754	**368**	42	109	39

Note
The majority immediately after general elections in bold type.

the members returned for Scotland have been classified as Whigs or Tories, it should be noted that for the whole of the period, 1707–60, the division on the Whig side between two rival factions headed by Scottish magnates – the 'Squadrone' and the 'Argathelians' – was more important than their whiggism. Those loosely defined as Scottish Whigs nevertheless held the majority of Scottish seats throughout the period. Finally, the figures for 1754 are very provisional, the editor of the volumes dealing with that year taking the view that although the terms Whig and Tory were still in use, the number that were classed as Whigs could equally be regarded as followers of nine or so different party leaders, and that the terminology itself 'no longer corresponded to political realities'.[14]

As the comments on the results of the 1754 election suggest, these calculations tell us much about the durability of the Tory-Whig terminology but much less about the internal structures of those groups or the substance of their political beliefs – subjects crucial to the question of governing. Further refinement is necessary and once again we can call upon a substantial amount of research conducted by the contributors to the *History of Parliament* as well as by many others. In the case of internal structures, we may begin by taking note of the political colour of successive administrations. During the reigns of William and Anne, there was a succession of mixed and largely or wholly Whig and Tory administrations: mixed, 1690–4; Whig, 1694–1702; mixed, 1702–8; Whig, 1708–10; and Tory, 1710–14. Following the Hanoverian succession, George I attempted to balance a majority of Whigs with some Tories but in the wake of the Jacobite rebellion and the Whig landslide at the 1715 election, administrations were wholly Whig thereafter.

What, then, were the structural characteristics of the body of MPs that either sustained or opposed these administrations? Before 1715, there is now overwhelming evidence that the wholly Whig or Tory administrations were sustained or opposed by well-organised Whig or Tory parties that functioned in both houses. Further, even during the periods of mixed administrations, 1690–4 and 1702–8, there was a remarkably high level of political partisanship. Both parties had recognised leaders in each House and both had a highly developed system of party organisation that operated within the constituencies and amongst the opinion formers in the press as well as in Parliament. Organisationally, they were far more sophisticated and far reaching than anything that had been seen before. On the other hand, they both reflected the traditional lines of division. Each party therefore had politicians with either a Court or a Country disposition: that is, those who sought office and were aware (in many cases) that responsibility might require compromising principles; and those who were innately suspicious of the executive and were chiefly interested in 'frugal and honest government'.[15] In other words, although the two parties developed remarkable organisational homogeneity, traditional tensions between Court and Country elements remained within them. Further, for sustained periods, between 1690–5 and 1705–10, the two parties were very closely matched in numbers of seats in the House of Commons. We might therefore conclude that in terms of policy, party leaders such as the Whig Junto would have to consider the varied opinions of their colleagues as well as those of the Tories, some of the last of which would not have been so very different from those of their own backbenchers. In periods of mixed administrations, for example, Whigs were found on both sides of the Commons.[16]

The pattern of mixed and alternately Whig or Tory administrations ended with the Hanoverian succession. George I was crowned on 20 October 1714 and following a wholesale dismissal of Tory officeholders, dissolved Parliament in January 1715 and exhorted the electorate to return Whigs. This, together with the ruthless deployment of the influence at their disposal, enabled the Whigs to replace the substantial Tory majority in the Commons with one of their own. In addition, the failed Jacobite rebellion of the same year called into question the fitness of all Tories for office and led to an Act of 1716 which prolonged the maximum life of a Parliament, from the existing three, to seven years. The result until 1760 was that Whigs were the dominant party in Lords and Commons and formed all the administrations of the period. In the Commons, even the largest Opposition grouping never had even sufficient nominal strength to mount a serious challenge.

The prolonged Whig ascendancy in Parliament and, by extension, their control of patronage and the local levers of power led inevitably to changes in the structure of the party. The firm grip that Whigs as a whole possessed on patronage, coupled with an increased ability to influence elections as a result of the Septennial Act, resulted in influence falling under the control of a score or so of prominent families, each with a coterie of dependants. In addition, tighter discipline was exercised by the senior ministers on placeholders and others dependent on their patronage where major matters of government policy were concerned.[17] Ascendancy therefore gave way to a more oligarchic and *dirigiste* structure which although it suffered setbacks in 1733, 1738–9 and 1744, survived into the mid-1750s. It was only then that the discipline imposed by Walpole and the Pelhams began to crumble as the differences between the great families took precedence. As mentioned earlier there were as many as nine principal Whig family political groups by that stage.

The most significant change, however, was successive splits within the Whig confederacy leading to Whigs going into opposition and often acting with Tories. There were three principal reasons for this. One on the Whig side was the ambition of leading politicians who for one reason or the other found themselves out of power. Another was the presence among the Whigs of a sizeable number with a Country or as it soon came to be called a 'Patriot' viewpoint – namely, that administration, especially those with seemingly overwhelming majorities, were prone to act in their own self-interest rather than provide sound government. And the third was the presence througout most of this period of a Tory party with well over 100 members in the Commons, most with a Country outlook and therefore disposed to enlarge the ranks of Whig dissidents. The first of these (ambition) was the basis of an opposition in the Commons engineered by Walpole and headed by the Prince of Wales between 1717–20. Later, all three factors were combined in the oppositions led by William Pulteney, 1725–42, the Prince of Wales from 1746 until his death in 1751, and finally, that of William Pitt from 1753 until his entry to office in the Newcastle administration in 1756. Moreover, similar developments took place in the Lords where Earl Cowper headed an opposition based on Country principles between 1720–3 that consisted of Whig dissidents and Tories. This was replicated in the late 1720s and the 1730s by the formation of a 'Patriot Party'.[18]

As for the Tory party, the Hanoverian succession may have transformed its prospects of office but it did not change its essential structure. Before 1714, Court and Country Tories were less prone to central organisation than the Whigs and contained, largely within their Country wing, about forty or so Jacobites. Afterwards, some Court Tories converted to the Whigs while the Jacobite wing, although it probably grew in size in the immediate wake of the Rebellion, subsequently declined when it became clear that the Hanoverian regime was secure. From the 1720s to the early 1750s the bulk of the party therefore consisted of what were called the Hanoverian Tories, their number in the Commons being led by Sir William Wyndham until his death in 1740 and sharing many of the views of the Whig dissidents. It seems likely that even though numerically weaker than the Whigs in Parliament, the Tories possessed an almost equal measure of support in the 'open' constituencies in England and Wales that possessed comparatively large electorates and where elections were not decided by one or two individual proprietors. The Tories were therefore a significant force in parliamentary and national politics for most of this period, their reasons for retaining a separate identity only beginning to falter in the 1740s, more particularly, after the failure of the 1745 rebellion. During the 1750s, Tory as a self-descriptor faded as a result of its association with the concept of resistance. Erstwhile Tories sought accommodation with Whigs or took up the cause of patriotism increasingly associated with the future George III.[19]

These developments in the early Hanoverian period lead to the following conclusions. First, that although the crude figures of Whig strength in Lords and Commons might suggest that ministers could do very much as they liked with regard to policy, this was very far from the case. As we observed in Chapter 1, George I and George II were not afraid to consider bringing Tories into the government as a way of keeping the Whigs in check. This they did in on six separate occasions between 1717 and 1746.[20] In addition, the Whigs were well aware that although Tory strength in the Commons declined after 1715, not only was it sufficient after the 1741 election to have presented a serious challenge to ministers when combined with the votes of dissident Whigs, but it also represented a substantial body of English public opinion. Moreover the Whigs themselves were clearly not a wholly homogenous body. As we have observed, the number of Whigs in opposition climbed up steadily after 1727 before falling back again in the 1750s. This was one of the reasons why Walpole had to resort to much tighter controls over his core support than either Godolphin or Harley had attempted in the days of King William and Queen Anne. Even then it was not entirely reliable as the reverse of 1733 and his resignation in 1742 showed. Walpole's, and indeed Pelham's, supporters consisted of members with varying ties to administration and various reasons for giving it their support. Whig oligarchy did not necessarily lead to a unanimity of purpose.

The second conclusion we might draw, is that a significant development in the framework of parliamentary government was confirmed and strengthened. As we have observed, 'a formed opposition', that is, a parliamentary opposition held together by party ties – had come into existence before 1714 but there were various factors that had hindered its development. One was the Crown's preference for mixed administrations. Another was the view, most often expressed by Tories, that formed and systematic opposition posed a threat to the Crown's ability to choose ministers freely. And a third was the Court and Country composition of both parties. These were therefore the early days of formed parliamentary oppositions – a point symbolised, perhaps, by the fact that there were then no recognised government and opposition benches in either House. As we have also observed, however, such oppositions became a fixture in both the Lords and the Commons after 1715 and became, in effect, more fully institutionalised. In the 1730s, for example, the Commons gave its official blessing to the convention that ministers and their supporters should sit on the right hand of the Speaker and their opponents on the left. Moreover, the mechanics of opposition became increasingly routine. There were recognised leaders such as Cowper, Pulteney, Wyndham and Pitt and all bar Wyndham (who shared the Tories' disapproval of systematic opposition on constitutional grounds) entered enthusiastically into organising meetings, sponsoring propaganda and concocting programmes. On the other hand, none of the opposition groups of this period could make any serious mark on their own. Whig dissidents had to appeal to Tories and to potential dissidents amongst the administration's supporters in order to make any headway. Thus, although the institutionalisation of opposition as a part of parliamentary life is an important constitutional development, it did not lead to any single purpose or single platform.[21]

The development of the structure of parliamentary politics along these lines went hand in hand with changes in the substance of parliamentary debate. Immediately before the Glorious Revolution, the traditional debate between Court and Country politicians on day-to-day administration had been subsumed into a conflict between Whigs and Tories on critical constitutional and religious issues. In the light of the arbitrary actions of a Catholic monarch, Whigs argued the case for a contractual or limited monarchy and religious toleration while Tories supported the doctrine of the 'Divine right' of Kings and the necessity of religious uniformity. Under the pressure of events, however, some modification of these two extreme positions took place. James II fled his kingdom thereby leaving a vacuum. Whigs and some Tories therefore combined in the Convention of 1689 to offer the throne to William and Mary – a decision which required the sacrifice of some aspects at least of contractual and divine right theory. As one historian has put it 'The men of 1688...were...empiricists coping with practical difficulties'.[22]

This well-known episode is an apposite illustration of a general point that can be made about political ideas and parliamentary actions in this period as a whole. Throughout, and at least until the 1750s, the principal political ideologies were either Whig or Tory but there evolved under those umbrella terms distinct varieties of each: Court and Country whiggism and Jacobite and Hanoverian toryism. Further, there was not only some similarity between the practical propositions of Country whiggism and toryism in general but there emerged from the 1730s onwards a blending of these into fresh formulation – patriotism. Leaving definitions of these ideologies aside for the moment, the key point is that they evolved rather than remain static. The same point may be made about parliamentary politics. This is not unexpected given the engagement of most of the key political thinkers of the time in contemporary politics: from Hobbes, Filmer and Locke to Hume, Bolingbroke and Hoadley. But there were practical considerations. For about 100 or so days a year, ministers proposed measures in response to events and sought support but expected opposition. Given the unpredictability of events, the differing perspectives *within* the Whig and Tory confederacies, and the evenly balanced or after 1714, the often disunited state of parties, it was inevitable that there would be changes in ostensibly Whig or Tory policies.

The degree of change, however, should not be exaggerated as there was considerable consistency on some issues. One of these was foreign policy. During the course of the wars leading to the Peace of Utrecht in 1713, the Whigs became strong supporters of a continental commitment by means of troops, subsidies and alliances in order to resist the threat that Louis XIV posed to the Protestant states. That support was maintained by the Whigs in power after 1714 and was given a further justification by the union with Hanover. The Tories, on the other hand, while agreeing that Britain had to defend itself in the wars against France, took the view that they should be fought principally at sea rather than by expensive land operations in conjunction with unpredictable allies. Moreover, this hostility to continental commitments and the preference for a naval (or 'wooden walls' or 'blue water') strategy as a means for maintaining national security was heightened by the constant fear, post-1714, that foreign policy was being driven as much by the interests of Hanover as that of Britain.

There were also consistent differences on religious matters. Virtually all Whigs and certainly all Tories were members of the Church of England but they took different views on how its interests were best served, particularly in the context of a resurgence of Protestant dissent. Most Whigs took the view that the interests of the state should take precedence over those of the Church and that the Church itself should be sensitive to the interests of the Protestant community as a whole. This led them to believe that the state should be tolerant of Dissenters and therefore not invoke the full force of the pre-Revolution Test and Corporation Acts which prevented them from holding political office. This was the thinking that led in 1727 to the first of a series of indemnity acts, each of which indemnified those who had taken office without taking the necessary oaths specified by the Test and Corporation Acts. Tories, on the other hand, believed that the interests of the state and the Church were virtually the same and that those of the Church needed to be defended vigorously. They therefore opposed successive proposals for 'occasional conformity' of the kind legalised by the 1727 Act and were stern critics of the Whig control of major clerical appointments after 1714 which seemed to symbolise the supremacy of the state over the Church.

On the other hand, there were inconsistencies on what was, arguably, the most important issue of all – the relationship between the executive, Parliament and the electorate. Prior to the Revolution, many Whigs had supported a virtual partnership between the monarchy, Parliament and the propertied nation as represented by the electorate whereas most Tories supported the notion of a strong, unfettered, monarchy, albeit with some having strong reservations on the issue of standing armies.[23] In the case of the Whigs, however, they experienced a prolonged period of power in the two decades after the Revolution with the result that they took on the habits of what David Hayton has referred to as 'a natural party of government'. They therefore sought to strengthen the hands of the executive by restricting 'the liberty of the subject' and 'repeatedly opposed' bills designed to reduce the number of office holders and pensioners able to be MPs and shorten the periods between elections-bills 'which would have strengthened the independence of Parliament'.[24] Moreover, after 1714 the Whigs in power took further steps to strengthen the hand of the executive in Parliament, most notably, by means of the Septennial Act of 1716. By the 1750s 'Revolution principles' for most Whigs did not mean support of the contractual theories of the 1680s but rather an endorsement of the settlement that had taken place between 1688 and 1716 – a settlement that had led to the progressive strengthening of the influence of the executive.

The Tories also altered their position. Initially, in 1688–9, most were supporters of a strong monarchy and there was a substantial number dedicated to the Jacobite cause. By 1701, however, support for Jacobitism appears to have declined and most were ready to accept the limitations imposed on the prerogative by the Act of Settlement of that year, seeing them as a realistic check on what was a 'foreign' dynasty. A further shifting of position took place following the Hanoverian succession. A substantial majority accepted the new dynasty, albeit with only a minority ready to proclaim themselves 'Hanoverian' Tories, but the consignment to permanent opposition after the 1715 election put a severe strain on their erstwhile enthusiasm for a strong executive. Tories therefore took up causes associated earlier with the Whigs and consistently supported measures to reduce the number of office holders and pensioners in Parliament and to make elections less susceptible to the influence of the executive by means of bribery and corruption.

It was this reversal of roles that created the conditions for fruitful collaboration between Whig dissidents and the Tories. Thus, the two principal Whig oppositions of the Hanoverian period, Walpole's and the Prince of Wales's (1717–20) and Pulteney's (1725–42) focused on issues that were known to be likely to attract Tory support. In June 1717 and January 1719, for example, Walpole launched attacks on the Commander-in-Chief for fraud in the costing of the transports bringing Dutch troops to England to deal with the 1715 Rebellion and on Sunderland's proposal to relax certain restrictions on dissent, thereby appealing, respectively, to Tory xenophobia and 'High Church' sentiments. In both cases Tories provided well over half of the votes cast against ministers.[25] Similarly, Pulteney combined attacks on Walpole's ministry for exerting excessive influence in Parliament by means of placemen with those on aspects of his foreign policy, most notably in 1739 on the terms of a Convention with Spain that appeared too generous in its compensation to Spanish merchants. Once again, he was well rewarded with Tory votes.[26] In short, while there was some consistency on foreign policy and religion, there was considerable inconsistency on the all-important questions of the working of the constitution and the exercise of power.

The functions of Parliament

It is within this context that we can return to the functions of Parliament and how they were exercised. A primary function, it will be recalled, was offering of 'counsel to the Crown' by scrutinising measures proposed by the executive. In general, the evidence points to the executive increasingly gaining the upper hand in this respect and the searching quality of scrutiny therefore declining over time. Thus, as we observed in the previous chapter, ministers were responsible for about three-quarters of the general bills proposed at each session and taking the period as a whole, enjoyed high rates of success with them that increased from about 70% to nearly 90%.

There were various reasons for this. One can be found in the history of party politics where the even balance between the parties in the Commons immediately after the Revolution gave way to a large Tory majority, 1710–14, and subsequently, to the Whig hegemony after 1715. Although ministers invariably framed measures in order to diminish the potential of opposition, their numerical superiority after 1710 was such that it was only rarely that they were actually defeated. Ministers also gained advantages from various institutional and procedural developments. Prior to 1714, for example, the growing influence of the Treasury as the dominant department of state was checked by the appointment of House of Commons' commissions, 1690–7, 1700–5, and 1711–14, charged with scrutinising departmental expenditure. From 1714 until the 1780s, however, no such commissions were appointed which meant parliamentary supervision on how money was spent became less and less effective. This left scrutiny of other elements of what would later be called the state's budget to the committees of the whole on 'supply' (the allocation of money to the various departments) and 'ways and means' (the raising of revenue). Before 1714, the obligations for these to be effective guardians of the public interest in the budget had been strengthened by the Commons' decision in 1713 not to consider petitions on matters of public expenditure. Afterwards, however, the dominance of the party in power in such committees meant that opposition to anything other than points of detail became increasingly rare in those dealing with supply; and that although it was often more effective on minor issues in those on ways and means, it was almost wholly ineffective on major issues. Thus only one tax proposal was actually rejected before 1760, namely Pelham's sugar tax in February 1744. These examples relate solely to financial matters though they were part of a general and significant increase in ministerial control over their own measures during the course of this period – a state of affairs assisted by the convention that questions could not be put to individual members, and therefore, ministers.[27]

However, legislation promoted wholly or partly by ministers constituted only a small proportion of the total. This leads us to the second function of Parliament – the consideration and resolution of the many and various requests for legislation or other means of redress by independent MPs, by corporate institutions, and by individuals: a function that may be described as Parliament being 'The Grand Inquest of the Nation'.

The scale of this function and the difficulties of interpreting it require some elaboration. Julian Hoppit and his colleagues have established that there were 8,264 legislative initiatives, 1689–1760, that resulted in 5,301 acts of Parliament. But how should such large numbers be categorised? Two problems present themselves. The first relates to the type of bill or act. Contemporaries did not give different labels to what would later be referred to after 1798 as 'public and general' or 'local' acts – that is, acts that applied generally and those that affected a particular locality or a particular body of people – although they did distinguish all such acts from those of a 'personal' nature – that is those that applied to individuals.[28] This raises obvious difficulties of interpretation. The second relates to the subject matter of legislation. Bills obviously dealt with a substantial number of different issues and even when analysed expertly by Hoppit and his colleagues, these still fall into ten different categories. Although they are undoubtedly the correct categories for research purposes, some simplification is necessary here.

With these problems in mind, it is useful for present purposes to adopt the categorisation established in 1798 and distinguish broadly between three types of legislation – 'general', 'local' and 'personal' – each of which contained bills and acts dealing with specific issues. In the general category – that is bills that applied generally – were bills dealing principally with economic matters such as finance, trade and manufacture, social issues and the law. Local legislation – that is bills relevant to a particular locality – consisted largely of bills dealing with communications (roads, harbours and bridges), the erection of buildings (jails, town halls, workhouses and churches) and enclosure. Finally, personal legislation dealt with the needs of individuals such as naturalization, divorce or the ownership of estates.

On this basis, we may now return to the scale of legislation not promoted principally by ministers. My own research suggests that 1,585 of the 5,301 acts (30%) were of a general as opposed to local or personal type and that approximately 75% of these were generated wholly or partly by ministers.[29] It therefore seems reasonable to conclude that individuals and institutions that were independent of ministers were responsible for, on an average, 25% of general legislation and virtually all of the rest – some 80% of the total number of acts of all kinds. Further, if failed initiatives are taken into account, the proportion would be even higher, the propensity for such legislation to fail being greater than that of the ministerial kind, especially at the beginning of this period. As for the proportions of acts in each type of legislation, the smallest (7% of the total number of acts) is to be found in the general category and the largest in the local and personal kinds (70% of the total number). In addition, it has been calculated that there was a notable increase in the success rate of legislative initiatives in these categories over time. Thus, the success rate for legislative initiatives in the social, economic and communication spheres (those least likely to be of concern to ministers) rose from an average of 34%, 1688–1714, to 66%, 1714–60, with that for the personal category, where contention was far less notable to begin with, rising less dramatically from 73% to 80%.[30]

In the last two decades, research has transformed our knowledge and understanding of parliamentary legislation in general in this period and of this kind in particular. Hitherto, the focus of attention was the development of parties and the substance of debate. Although it was accepted that a sizeable proportion of legislation was of the local or personal kind and that governments were only interested in a restricted number of issues, little was known of the full range of legislative initiatives and successes. We now know, however, that although the headlines were created by the battle between the party leaders, the solid core of parliamentary business consisted of legislation, most of which was sponsored by independent MPs and outside bodies and individuals. It is to the characteristics of such legislation that we now turn.

The least contentious of such bills were those dealing with local and personal issues. The former category consisted of bills sought by a mixture of institutions and groups of individuals to effect improvements, it being established in the course of the eighteenth century that whereas individuals could do anything that did not break the law, corporate bodies could do nothing without statutory authority. Bills were therefore sought by magistrates to build or repair roads; by municipal corporations to erect harbours or new civic buildings such as gaols; and by groups of individuals to cut canals or enclose land. As for the personal category, these dealt principally with naturalisation, divorce and the ownership and management of estates. Taken as a whole, private bills of this kind are a remarkable testimony to, on the one hand, the readiness of local elites to effect genuine improvements for their communities; and on the other, to promote schemes for their own financial and personal ends. There were variations, however, in the levels and extent of self-interest and the degrees of scrutiny to which these were subjected. Elite self-interest was highest and the degree of parliamentary scrutiny lowest, for example, in the cases of enclosure and personal bills. Petitions for enclosure, if approved, usually proceeded directly to the bill stage without the intercession of a select committee of enquiry and failure rates were low in both cases: declining from 26.9% to 19.1%, 1688–1760, in the case of personal bills; and being about 24% for those dealing with enclosure. On the other hand, the fact that one-fifth to one-quarter failed is a salutary reminder that not all such measures were plain sailing.[31]

In the case of bills dealing with communications and new buildings, their failure rate was not significantly different but they were sponsored by a broader range of social groups and subjected, at least nominally, to a greater degree of scrutiny. Petitions for communication bills, for example, were usually sponsored by groups such as 'JPs, gentry and other inhabitants', 'The Mayor and Corporation' or by members of existing road, bridge and harbour authorities, like the turnpike trusts. Such petitions, if accepted, were then put to select committees of 50 or more named MPs, their number usually being augmented by all the members for the counties likely to be affected. Fifteen select committees on communication petitions were established in the Commons in the 1724–5 session and some 72 in 1753. Further, in a number of cases in each session, additional and different select committees were established to scrutinise the bills approved by their predecessors. Indeed, the setting up of such committees and the detail of their reports form a substantial proportion of the *Commons Journals* for these years.

The effectiveness of such scrutiny is, of course, debatable. Many petitions for road bills requested an extension of the authority granted under earlier acts and were therefore probably treated to a nominal scrutiny. Further, failure rates for road bills in particular were low: only three failed, 1724–5, and merely two out of a much larger number of such bills in 1753. On the other hand, close scrutiny of the progress of communication bills as a whole suggests that the Commons in particular could, on occasion, exercise an effective check. Hoppit, for example, has noted that there was a greater propensity to reject bills dealing with inland navigation than with roads, and the evidence suggests that this was due to there being more vested and proprietary interests involved and therefore more potential for conflict.[32] In this respect it is notable that a proposal to cut a new canal into London as part of a Water Supply Bill in 1724–5 was strongly contested and eventually defeated; and that the Nene Navigation Bill of the same session only proceeded after a large division of 114 vs 73 in its favour.[33] Further, there are several examples in the same session of amendments being made to road bills at the committee stage and one example of such a bill being rejected following the hearing of counsel for the opposing sides.[34] Overall, the evidence for such legislation leads to the following conclusions. First, that the landed elite successfully exploited Parliament for its own ends in the forms of enclosure and personal legislation. Second, that a broader range of social groups did so for their own ends but in so doing managed to improve communications and the amenities of their areas considerably. And third, that Parliament generally endorsed such initiatives while at the same time preserving and sometimes exercising the power to prevent them when there was sufficient local opposition.

Much more significant, however, was the general legislation that flowed, in part at least and sometimes wholly, from the initiative of independent MPs and outside agencies and individuals. The typical process was as follows. A petition would be received from individuals or corporate bodies representing a particular interest, such as the woollen manufacturers of Norfolk, requesting legislation in their favour. Very often, local MPs were aware of such an initiative and may have even suggested it. The petition was then considered and permission given or refused for a bill to be prepared or a select committee of enquiry to be appointed with a prominent role allocated to sponsoring or local MPs. This might coincide by design with other petitions on the same topic or act as a catalyst for the presentation of petitions with either the same or an opposite purpose. It might also coincide with the publication of pamphlets and other printed material pressing or refuting the case concerned. It was at this stage that the issue could become known to a government department, particularly if it involved matters of trade and manufacture. If it was deemed of sufficient importance, ministers might then collaborate with the independent MPs and the lobbies they represented to produce legislation agreeable to all parties. Or, they might not.

It was this process that lay behind an impressive quantity, and a significant range, of legislation in this period. We may begin with one of the most important areas of manufacture and trade in Britain – the textile industries. These were not only important in economic terms but their statutory regulation was a highly sensitive political issue, particularly because of the strength of the woollen interest in Parliament. In the early 1990s, several historians published the results of their work on their regulation from 1660 to the 1770s. Such regulation was, of course, of considerable concern to both the Treasury and the Board of Trade: partly, in the interest of stimulating the economy; and partly as a source of tariff income. None of the authors, however, found that the government played more than an equal part with others and usually less than that, the initiative being with independent MPs and pressure groups. In the period 1689–1714, for example, 122 bills designed to support the domestic textile industry, increase overseas trade and raise revenue were proposed and 66% of them passed into law. Virtually all of them came from various interest groups within the industry and were helped on their way by a hard core of about 25–30 MPs who played a prominent role in the relevant committee work. Most of these 'cloth MPs' represented constituencies where the textile industries were prominent and their activities were accompanied by a public debate fanned by pamphlets from the various, and often competing, interests within the industry. A similar process has been identified for the longer period, 1696–1774. The particular focus of the historians concerned in this case was legislation designed to protect the domestic woollen and silk industries against the importation of Asian calicoes. This, they argue, emerged from a 'parliamentary process' in which pressure from the domestic woollen, linen and silk industries was crucial. In 1721, for example, Parliament passed an act making the wearing of any article of clothing made from printed or coloured calicoes subject to a fine of £5 – thereby bringing to an end the further penetration of the domestic market by Asian textiles. This was largely due, they argue, to effective lobbying by the linen merchants.[35]

Two further examples from the sample sessions illustrate the variety of ways that pressure of this kind was dealt with. In 1724–5 the JPs, gentlemen, freeholders and clothmakers of the West Riding petitioned the Commons for a bill to put an end to the abuses that were taking place in cloth manufacture. The matter was put to a select committee and a member of the government and the MP for Scarborough, Sir William Strickland, was appointed to the drafting committee of the bill that it recommended. The bill duly passed.[36] In 1753 at least ten petitions were received by the same House from framework knitters in various parts of the country against the plans of the London Company of Framework Knitters to extend their supervision of manufacture throughout Britain. The matter was put to a select committee but on this occasion it was thought best, having reviewed the extensive evidence on either side, to proceed by a declaration of the House that the London Company would be acting in restraint of trade if it made the attempt.[37]

The same combination of lobbying by interest groups, the commitment of small numbers of MPs, and on occasion, the collaboration of ministers, lay behind many other categories of legislation in the economic sphere.

It certainly played a vital part in the securing of key measures such as the Molasses Act of 1733 and the Sugar Act of 1739[38] and Bob Harris has shown how it led to three successful bills to promote the fishing industry, 1749–51. The process in this case began with a petition to Parliament by a fishing company with interests in Scotland making the case for being able to export fish to foreign countries. This led to a parliamentary committee *containing* a number of MPs with a strong interest in the subject and eventually, to three successful bills: one to promote whale fishing; another to establish a new fish market in Westminster; and a third, which led to the establishment of the Free British Fishery Society in London, to encourage the herring industry. Indeed, Harris has identified more than twenty legislative initiatives 'aimed at promoting or protecting British trade and manufactures', 1748–60, which involved significant 'lobbying by interested parties and individuals'.[39]

Similar examples can be found in the case of the regulation of imports and exports. In 1724–5, two failed bills to encourage the import of naval stores and the export of rice from the American plantations arose from collaboration between Bristol and Liverpool merchants and Martin Bladen, a member of the Board of Trade;[40] and in 1753 a successful and potentially explosive bill to allow the import of wool and woollen yarn from Ireland to Britain was initiated by a petition from the Mayor and inhabitants of Exeter for local needs and then extended by ministers to the whole country.[41] One of the most outstanding cases, however, concerned the London Turkey Company's monopoly of the Levant trade. In 1753, approximately forty petitions were sent to the Commons from merchants in a variety of trades in all quarters of the country pressing for its abolition. Following the presentation of extensive accounts of the Levant trade and the enlargement of the drafting committee to an astonishing twenty-two MPs (including ministers), this resulted in a successful bill which appears to have met the petitioners demands half way by curtailing the monopoly.[42]

In fact, as the earlier example shows, both the executive and Parliament often acted as a reconciler or 'balancer' of conflicting economic and social interests. Studies of the coal industry, for example, suggest that the substantial legislation applied to it in the course of the eighteenth century flowed from attempts to reconcile the different pressures emanating from the owners, transporters and merchants.[43] The Gin industry is such another case. Thus, as Lee Davison has shown, successive acts regulating the industry in 1729, 1736 and 1738 were influenced by three contradictory pressures: the government's need to raise money from it; the distiller's desire for maximum profit; and the argument of well-organised 'moralists' that price and availability should be regulated in order to reduce the incidence of drunkenness and the crime associated with excessive gin drinking. In 1751 the government eventually responded to the wave of post-war disorder and the pressure of a London-led moralists' campaign and succumbed to an Act which increased the tax (but by far less than the sponsors demanded) and doubled the license fees for spirit houses.[44]

The same processes – the pressure of external interest groups, the taking up of issues by interested MPs and negotiation with ministers – have been observed in many other categories of legislation for which the executive did not feel an on-going responsibility. John Beattie, surveying 100 or so initiatives on the subject of criminal legislation, 1689–1718, has shown that they led to a dozen significant statutes which collectively established the foundations of the infamous 'Bloody Code'. These, he says, were principally the work of several dozen MPs and that ministerial involvement was minimal.[45] Wilfred Prest, examining the origins of successive waves of law reform, 1705–6, 1727–1, and 1748–53, argues that they were advanced by a combination of carefully timed external campaigns fuelled by petitions and pamphlets and the setting up of broadly-based parliamentary committees.[46] Tim Hitchcock has shown how the Workhouse Test Act of 1723, the measure which led to a massive increase in the number of workhouses established in England and Wales, was 'backed and probably formulated by the SPCK' and received only passive support from Walpole's administration. Given that this was, in his words, 'one of the most consistent, and best organised social policy reforms to be attempted before the nineteenth century', it is remarkable that between 1703 when the Board of Trade lost interest in the matter and 1751 when there was a parliamentary enquiry into the number of workhouses, 'there was, in effect, no government policy on or interest in workhouses'.[47] In addition, it has been argued that public pressure played the critical role in the passing of four statutes against gaming, 1739–45;[48] and that there was core of about 50 MPs who made the running in over 30 select committees dealing with social welfare issues, 1747–54, and that some of these led to successful legislation.[49]

Of course, not all initiatives of this kind were successful. In 1753, for example, 7 legislative initiatives from largely independent sources succeeded, while 7 failed, a higher proportion than usually pertained before 1714 and somewhat lower than that later.[50] Nor did they deal solely with the subjects enumerated so far. Indeed, the evidence suggests that in keeping with the gradual, and then accelerating, growth in general legislation, there was a broadening of the subject matter of such legislation in the late 1740s and 1750s. In 1753, for example, the issues dealt with by successful and failed bills from these sources included alehouses, the militia, a census, select vestries, insolvent debtors and the improvement of highway regulations.

Overall, there is a mounting body of evidence that in terms of legislation Parliament was very responsive to public pressure organised by a variety of economic and social interest groups and sponsored by supportive and largely independent MPs. Most legislation dealing with issues not in the forefront of ministers' minds – that is, a growing proportion of all public and general legislation – seems to have its origin in this process. Further, it is notable that an increasing proportion of initiatives in these areas led to legislation. What conclusions, then, can we draw from this phenomenon? One, which is particularly relevant to the themes of this chapter, is that it enabled

Parliament to fulfil, and in some respects to expand, its function of being
'The Grand Inquest of the Nation' by addressing and redressing the claims
made upon it: the 'grievances' as they were sometimes called. Admittedly,
the grievances that led to legislation were largely those of the financial,
commercial and professional classes but it was these classes which were of
growing importance in economic and political terms in this period. In that
respect it became an increasingly important function. This leads us to a
second, and more general, point which may be introduced in outline form at
this stage. Research suggests that two processes were at work in this period
in terms of the distribution of power. In the case of Parliament, it was at the
beginning the preserve of a well-established landed elite which tended to
become more oligarchic over time. In the community at large, however,
power was distributed much more broadly across what Paul Langford has
referred to as a plutocracy extending from the landed elite through the lower
branches of landed society, the middling classes, and down to the yeoman
farmer and successful retailer.[51] By redressing the grievances of the middle
classes, Parliament was therefore able to minimise the inevitable tensions
between oligarchy and plutocracy.

The final function of Parliament to be considered is the gathering of
information about various topics. An important issue here, however, is how
much of this information was put into the public domain. We might therefore usefully expand the scope of this discussion to include not only the
various forms of information but also the extent to which it was disseminated
beyond the confines of Parliament.

One of the principal sources of information was the record of parliamentary
business. This took the following forms: the 'Votes', a daily list of the
principal proceedings, usually on a single sheet of paper; the *Journals*, which
was a reasonably full account of business kept by the clerks of the respective
Houses, short of a record of what was said in debate; and the debates themselves, no official record of which was kept except for a brief note in the
Journals of motions and outcomes, with unofficial reporting in the press of
what was said by participants being banned on the grounds that members
should not seek to influence public opinion and should not be influenced by
it when discussing the affairs of state. It was only gradually and to a limited
extent, however, that these sources became available to the public. In the
case of the Votes, it would appear that they did become increasingly available.
In the period before 1714, they were distributed to MPs at no cost and
copies were apparently delivered free to 'friends and constituents' but were
sold afterwards in increasing numbers – 1,000 a day by the 1730s according
to one estimate.[52] The *Journals*, on the other hand, only existed in manuscript form until a decision was taken by the Commons in the 1740s to put
their historic corpus into print. It was not until the late 1760s, however, that
the printing of this backlog had been accomplished and the publication of
proceedings shortly after the session ended began. As for printed accounts of
the debates in either House, these were 'rare' before 1714 but appear to

have became more common by the 1720s: either in the least objectionable form of reports in books and periodicals printed some time after the relevant debate had taken place; or in the more threatening form of contemporary reports in newspapers. The fact that there were approximately seventy periodicals and newspapers published in London alone at the time of the Hanoverian succession indicates the scale of the 'problem' as far as diehard supporters of parliamentary privacy were concerned. The result was first, a crackdown on the opposition press and then, in the 1720s, an attempt to prevent the reporting of the debates in the newspaper press. From 1725 newspapers were obliged to pay a Stamp tax, thereby forcing them to raise their prices, and in 1729 the Commons resolved to take legal action against those which printed reports. The Commons, however, was swimming against the tide. The resolution had some effect in the early 1730s with reports being largely restricted to those in magazines published during recesses but as the opposition to Walpole's administration grew in the latter years of the decade, the attempt to suppress the newspaper press slackened and with it, the ability to prevent the reporting of the debates. Thus although the official ban on printed reports was maintained – it was not lifted until the early nineteenth century – a blind eye was turned increasingly to the more frequent, but by no means comprehensive, reporting in the newspaper press. It therefore became a part of a gradual increase in the politically related print culture that took place throughout this period and which accelerated from the 1740s. A number of periodicals were founded between 1711 and 1716 which provided digests of the debates and facts and figures relating to political events and enjoyed long runs: *The Political State of Great Britain* (1711–40); the *Historical Register* (1714–38); and *Magnae Britanniae Notitia* (1716–55). By 1760, parliamentary politicians had either reluctantly or enthusiastically accepted the presence of the newspaper press as an important part of what was becoming known as 'public life'.[53]

An additional source of information arose from other aspects of parliamentary business. Legislation required the drafting of a bill, its circulation amongst interested members in manuscript form, and more importantly in this context, a decision on whether it would be printed for the benefit of both the members as a whole and the wider public. Petitions for bills or for the redress of grievances were usually dealt with by the establishment of select committees that later reported to the relevant House. Once again, this raised the issue of whether the reports should be printed and in what numbers. Finally, the scrutiny of the executive involved members asking for information from government departments and the departments often providing it in the form of 'accounts' and 'papers'. The same issues of whether to leave the information in manuscript or whether to print it and in what numbers applied.

Broadly speaking, the current evidence on these matters suggests that although the amount of information available to members rose sharply after the Glorious Revolution and steadily thereafter, its availability to the public was limited. In the case of legislation, for example, it appears that before

1714, it was rare for general bills to be printed although there is evidence of them circulating in manuscript form. This would have inevitably restricted the number who would have seen them.[54] This remained the case until the 1730 session when 5 bills were ordered to be printed by the Commons. This inaugurated a Commons' practice of ordering the printing of an average of 6 bills per session in the 1730s rising to 9 in the 1750s, in each case about one-fifth of the total number of public bills. The number of copies usually ordered for printing in each case was 600, thereby indicating that the selected bills were thought to be of interest to all members of the House. In some cases, however, many more copies were ordered: 2,000 for a 1752 bill for the relief of the poor and 1,000 for the Bread Bill of 1758.[55] Taken together, the evidence suggests that in the Commons at least, there was an increasing readiness to inform the members of the details of significant bills and when the subject matter warranted it, to extend that information to the wider public.

In the case of select committee reports, a contrasting picture emerges. In tandem with the growth of legislation, there was a substantial increase in the number of Commons' select committees, 1690–1713 (544), followed by a steady increase thereafter.[56] There were well over 40 appointed in the 1724–5 session and more than 80 in 1753 – numbers that were much greater than those for an average year before 1714. Most select committees after 1714, however, dealt with petitions and bills on specific, often local, issues, and issued short reports that are noted in the *Journals* but were not thought worthy of a separate status. The number that issued longer reports on matters of wider interest therefore seems to be approximately the same as they had been before 1714. In the 1720s and 1730s about 6 of such reports, on average, were issued each session; and about 8 in the 1740s and 1750s. Sheila Lambert has referred to these as reports from committees analogous to those of 'select committees of enquiry' but some care has to be exercised when using the term. By the early nineteenth century it was associated with a committee preparing the ground for legislation and although it has been suggested that a shift in favour of select committees of this type can be dated to the early 1750s, most were appointed for other purposes.[57] In the context of this discussion, however, the striking feature of such select committee reports is that only a small minority (47 out of 356) were ordered to be printed by the Commons, 1714–60, the number being spread pretty evenly during that period. Thus, although some reports did undoubtedly gain a wide currency – 2,000 copies of the 1733 report on fraud in the Customs service were ordered – there seems to have been a general reluctance to disseminate the results outside the House.[58] It was therefore not until 1767 that it was decided to publish the committee reports on a session-by-session basis.[59]

The contrast between the volume of material and the proportion of it appearing in printed form is even more marked in the case of accounts and papers. In this case the current evidence relates principally to the Commons after 1714. This shows a steady increase in the number of papers presented: from an average of 60–70 per session in the 1720s and 1730s to 80–100 in the 1740s and 1750s. Taken together, these dealt mainly with the economy (36%), the armed forces (29%), finance (19%), and the institutions of government (9%), with those dealing with all other matters such as law and order, religion, social issues, communications and those of a personal nature accounting for the rest (7%). The Commons was therefore responsible for providing an accumulating body of information, principally on matters for which the government had some responsibility and on which it was ready to make information available. Thus, although there is some evidence to suggest a growth in the proportion of papers arising from non-governmental or external pressure, the time when a substantial proportion arose from such sources was a long way in the future. The dissemination of this material, however, was very limited. Thus of the 3,037 accounts and papers presented in the period, 1714–60, only 44 were printed, the rest remaining in manuscript.[60] The costs of printing such a large and increasing volume of material may have been one reason for this but the more likely explanation is that as the material itself dealt principally with government business, it was thought unnecessary to disseminate it beyond the House.

Overall, the picture that emerges from this review of Parliament's role as an accumulator and disseminator of information is mixed. There is no doubt that the quantity of parliamentary business increased substantially, particularly in the spheres of debate, legislation and enquiry. On the other hand, members were clearly reluctant to disseminate more than a selective amount of information about their activities to the wider public. The daily order of business – the Votes – were eventually sold to the public but the official ban on the reporting of what was said in debate remained in place. A decision to have the *Journals* printed was taken in the 1740s but only a relatively small proportion of bills, reports and accounts and papers were put into print. However, as the turning of a blind eye to the unofficial reporting of debates and the selective printing of bills and reports suggests, members were also aware of the exponential growth of interest in their activities. Thus the least that can be said is that Parliament was responsible for generating the interest that it was reluctant to satisfy.

Summary and conclusion

In sum, we have observed two sets of contrasting developments. The first relates to the membership of Parliament. In the case of the Lords, there was little significant change, the House being representative of a relatively static number of the most substantial landowners in the realm. In the case of the Commons, on the other hand, it has been argued that in terms of social origins, family experience of parliamentary life, and primary sources of income, the membership tended to become more, rather than less, representative of the landed elite. Greater social, economic and religious homogeneity, however, did not necessarily lead to greater homogeneity in terms of political conduct or political opinion. What is striking about the extensive research on individual MPs is the variety of political behaviour and opinion that it has revealed. Thus, when the full range of parliamentary activities has been considered, there were always sufficient 'men of business' in both Houses to make up for shortcomings of their colleagues. Further, and more importantly, although the development of two parties and the institutionalisation of parties of government and opposition tended to narrow the options in terms of opinion, all were essentially confederations of various types of politicians and various types of beliefs, views and interest. Before 1714, both the Whig and Tory parties contained Court and Country wings. Afterwards, the Whig administrations and their supporters were a confederation of interests while their opponents consisted of Whig dissidents and Tories. Thus, while there was certainly some consistency in Whig and Tory opinions on foreign policy and religion, their approach to the workings of the constitution and the exercise of power was flexible, to say the least. All of these were circumstances that encouraged the framing of policy in order to maximise support amongst waverers, independents, and even nominal opponents. A more oligarchic Parliament did not therefore lead to a more *dirigiste* form of policy-making.

Contrasting developments have also been observed in the history of the major functions of Parliament. On the one hand, it has been argued that the scrutiny of the executive becomes less searching and effective over time and that ministerial influence over business increases. The readiness of the House of Lords to act as a check on the Commons declines, particularly from the 1720s, and in the Commons various procedural conventions and innovations such as the choosing of select committees on controversial issues by ballot strengthened the influence of ministers. The 'success rate' of government legislation therefore increases significantly. On the other hand, there was considerable expansion of Parliament's role as a 'redresser of grievances' of a personal, local or general kind on behalf of both the landed elite and the broader strata of the professional, financial and commercial classes. In addition, Parliament was not only responsible for the accumulation of an ever-growing quantity of information relating to virtually all aspects of the state, it also presided, at first unwillingly but ultimately with resignation, over its dissemination. In these ways, Parliament could be said to have helped to harmonise the interests of the landed elite with the middling ranks of society.

What contribution, then, did Parliament make to government? Three points stand out. The first is that the disposition of members encouraged a pragmatic form of government on the part of the executive and on that of the parties that took the lead in government and opposition. The second is that in terms of legislation, enquiry and the dissemination of information, Parliament responded to the needs of both the elite, the wider body of landed and commercial society, and to some degree, the public. And third, it enabled substantial improvements to take place in commerce and manufacture, in communications and urban amenities, and to a limited extent, the welfare of the poor.

4   The executive, Parliament and the public

Introduction

The two principal features of Britain's domestic history in this period – the evolution of a mixed system of government dominated by a propertied elite and a rapid expansion of commerce and consumption – were accompanied by a third – the gradual, if uneven, growth of various forms of largely 'non-elite' or 'popular' political activity. It used to be thought that elite and popular politics were discrete spheres of activity with little contact between them but as Professor Dickinson has made clear in his masterly survey of popular politics in eighteenth-century Britain published in 1994, this was far from the case. In fact, there were many points of intersection and in summary form, the types of popular political activity that had most impact on the executive and Parliament were as follows. First, the opinion of parliamentary electors, particularly at general elections but also as expressed in 'Instructions' to candidates or MPs on how they should act on specific issues in Parliament. Second, various forms of influence exerted by groups with specific economic, social, religious or moral objectives. This was a broad category that included: the (usually discrete) influence of City institutions; the more overt lobbying by groups representing particular professions and sectors of the economy; the widely organised campaigns of the religious sects; and the more spontaneous forms of protest generated by formal county and borough meetings or by direct action. And third, the opinions expressed in the various forms of print – principally, books, periodicals, pamphlets and newspapers – to which we might add those articulated in coffee houses, pubs, reading rooms and the like. It is to the impact of these various forms of politics involving those other than the propertied elite on executive and parliamentary government that we now turn.

Parliamentary elections

The sphere of politics in which parliamentarians and the non-elite were most routinely and regularly involved was parliamentary representation. As this is a subject that is now very well documented, a mere sketch of its general features will suffice for our purposes. As far as England and Wales were concerned, the basic pattern and purpose of parliamentary representation had been set in the thirteenth century and had changed comparatively little over time. Focussing on the Commons, the basic purpose was to enable the monarch to be able consult and gain the consent of elected representatives of the chief administrative units – the counties and boroughs – on matters of taxation. Two members were therefore elected for each of the English counties (one for those in Wales) by voters who held a lease to property estimated as being worth at least 40s a year in terms of the income it could produce – a sum that was substantial in the fifteenth century when this franchise was established but much diminished by 1690. Under the terms of the Union with Scotland, the Scottish counties returned single members on the same franchise, although in Scotland, the terms of property ownership and the definition of a '40s freehold' resulted in a much smaller number of comparatively wealthier voters. As for the boroughs, most in England, but none in Wales (and subsequently, Scotland) were two-member constituencies in which the franchise varied considerably from one type to another. In some it was attached solely to the possession or occupation of property of a certain value. In others it derived from membership of a corporation. There were also some in which it was a combination of both types of qualification. The overall result, however, was an electorate in England and Wales that was drawn overwhelmingly from the non-elite sections of the population: from small farmers upwards in the counties; and principally (although not wholly) from the artisans, masters, shopkeepers, tradesmen and professionals of the boroughs. The electorate was therefore drawn principally from the middling ranks of male society, the gentry at one end of the social spectrum and the labourers at the other being in the minority.

As far as elections are concerned, there are several features that are common to this period. One, to be found before and after the setting of new property qualifications for MPs in 1711, was the fact that the overwhelming majority of candidates and major players in elections were members of the propertied elite – that is the peerage and the gentry. This was largely due to the extent of such families' property and financial resources. Each family usually possessed an estate with sufficient qualified tenant freeholders or other types of voters to create a 'personal interest' – that is a body of voters likely to support the head of the family's wishes at election time. Preparing for an election therefore involved extensive negotiation between elite groups within the constituencies in order to determine the probable strength of their personal interests in relation to those of their opponents and the electorate at large. On this would depend which candidates would stand.

A second feature was considerable variation in England and Wales (but not so much in Scotland) in the numbers of voters in constituencies of the same basic type – either counties or boroughs. The *History of Parliament's* figures

Table 4.1 Voters in English counties and boroughs in 1713

No. of counties	No. of voters	No. of boroughs	No. of voters
1	Under 1,000	85	Under 100
18	1,000–3,500	60	100–350
18	3,500+	37	351–1,000
		21	1,000+

for English constituencies for a mid-point in this period, 1713, where they can be ascertained, are shown in Table 4.1.[1]

Two points arise from these figures. The first is that they underline the importance of treating each constituency as distinct and of avoiding the temptation of discussing parliamentary representation in terms of aggregates of voters, let alone 'electorates'. Individual constituencies did not have electorates as we know them because there was no system for registering voters before 1832. Electors laid claim to a vote if a poll took place and if unchallenged, voted. The second point is that notwithstanding their variety and distinctiveness, historians have found the concepts of 'open' and 'close' constituencies a useful, although by no means a hard and fast, way of distinguishing between them. The former consisted of those constituencies in which there was sufficient competition between groups of landed families, and sufficient electors who were in some degree independent of those particular groups, to make a contested election necessary and its outcome uncertain. The latter consisted of constituencies in which individual families or groups of families had interests so strong amongst the electors that opposition to them was unlikely to succeed. In such circumstances the candidates representing the family or families concerned were returned without a poll or contest. Broadly speaking, there was a tendency for the county and borough constituencies with the largest numbers of voters to be open and for those with the smallest to be close. It has to be stressed, however, that there were many exceptions to this tendency in constituencies with both large and small numbers of electors. In both, the competition between landed proprietors for party or other reasons could override the temptation to come to a gentleman's agreement.

A third feature common to the period as a whole was the existence of a significant degree of mutual reliance and even political agreement between elite candidates and largely non-elite electors. Candidates might expect their tenants and those of their gentry supporters to support them fully with their votes but they went through elaborate procedures to persuade them to do so. This could take the form of canvassing, of addresses in newspapers or from the hustings and, if necessary, the provision of board and lodgings at polling time. 'Nursing' a constituency, even if the proprietor actually owned it and had it in his 'pocket', was regarded as necessary. Electors, for their part, expected to be 'nursed'. They favoured candidates with connections with their constituency, who, if successful, would look after its interests: for example, by sponsoring bills of relevance to its economy and amenities or by siphoning patronage in its direction. However, there was more to the relationship than mere reciprocity of interest. By the 1690s, whiggism and toryism had become deeply rooted amongst the voters of many constituencies, the traditional source of division between dissenters and Anglicans being added to by differences over kingship and the costs and methods of war. Thus, the customary obligations of voter to candidate and candidate to voter were either reinforced by political agreement or undermined by disagreement.

A fourth and final general feature was the uncertainty that surrounded the results of general elections. These took place over weeks rather than a single day and results dribbled into party managers piecemeal. The main points of contention between government and opposition were well known to candidates but the evidence suggests that these were not necessarily the issues dominant in the constituencies. Further, not only were more members returned for constituencies with a small number of voters than those with larger numbers but many were uncontested. It was therefore difficult to tell what the principal issues that had motivated the voters were. Finally, it took some time for contemporaries to establish what the outcome was in terms of the political allegiances of MPs. A combination of the different timing of individual elections and the slow passage of information to party managers meant that it probably was not until the House assembled that a 'result' became clear and even then it might take weeks for an accurate opinion to be formed. 'General Elections' were therefore quite unlike those of today.

Although these features of parliamentary representation were common to the period as a whole, there were some significant changes over time. The most obvious was the decline in the frequency of general elections as a result of the Septennial Act of 1716. There were ten general elections between 1690 and 1713 but only seven, 1715–54. Further, following a long period after 1714 during which the frequency of contested elections was comparable to that before hand, there appears to have been a sudden decline. Thus, between 1690–1714 the proportions of all English county and corporation and freemen borough elections (including by-elections) that went to a poll ranged from 36% to 39.6%. The comparable figure for the four general elections between 1722 and 1741 when Walpole was in power was 39%. At the 1747 and 1754 elections, however, the proportions dropped in both cases to 22.9%. It also appears that there was a stasis throughout the period in the total number eligible to vote.[2] The Whig ascendancy therefore coincided eventually with a lowering of the political temperature engendered by elections.

What impact, then, did elections and constituency politics have on executive and parliamentary government? As far as the general outlook of governments and the ways parliamentary life was conducted are concerned, the impact was considerable. Most MPs had close ties with their constituents and the types of constituencies varied enormously and included populous counties, thriving towns and cities engaged in different economic activities, and small, sleepy, boroughs with a handful of voters. Thus, although most MPs were either Whigs or Tories, they also fell into a number of other categories determined partly by their own political leanings but also by the communities and the interests that they represented. We have already encountered those disposed to be Court or Country Whigs or Tories but there were also those who supported the economic or religious interests of their particular constituencies or who shared a professional interest with other members. Majorities and minorities in the Commons were therefore coalitions of different interest groups, partly *because* of the electoral system. It was therefore inevitable that this played a part in determining the policies they advanced. A clear indication of this is that Commons' select committees chosen to investigate matters of national concern usually contained a cross section of MPs representing different types of communities throughout the kingdom and from both sides of the House.

Apart from these general effects the principal concern of executives in particular, then as now, was general elections. The reasons for that concern, however, were in at least one respect very different from those of today. Between 1690 and 1835, no government 'lost' a general election by having to give way to their opponents as a result of the verdict of the electorate. There were various reasons for this phenomenon but the principal ones in this period were the executive's influence within both the electoral system and the Commons; and the fact that both parties before and after 1714 contained Court and Country wings that were often opposed to each other. In other respects, however, the immediate results of general elections in terms of 'pros' and 'cons' could have a significant impact on the prospects, composition and policies of governments. Their prospects, for example, could be retarded or advanced, sometimes to a spectacular degree. On the negative side of the equation, mixed or virtually single-party administrations failed to secure clear majorities in the Commons in the five elections, 1690–1701, and Walpole's administration was fatally weakened in the 1741 election by a decline in his paper majority to approximately forty votes. As for the positive results, mixed administrations secured enhanced majorities, albeit for only one side of the coalition concerned, in 1702 (for the Court Tories), 1705 and 1708 (for the Court Whigs); while single-party administrations secured landslide victories in 1710, 1713 and 1715. These were followed by majorities of more modest, but nevertheless comfortable, proportions for the Court Whigs, the 1741 election being the exception.

The immediate impact of these results on the composition and policies of governments is difficult to assess. The closeness of Whig and Tory numbers in the Commons, 1690–1710 (1702–5 excepted), the comparatively large proportion of contested elections, and the prevalence of key issues which divided many voters, were all factors that would have disposed the monarch and senior ministers to form mixed administrations. There were also cases of the prospect of an election, or the result of one, having an influence on policy or on the cast of an administration. In 1695, King William and Sunderland dissolved early in order to forestall Commons' enquiries into alleged corruption. In 1708, Godolphin had hoped before the election to maintain a line that was independent of the two parties but significant Whig gains meant that he was obliged to give two Whigs cabinet office soon after. Further, Harley found that Whig fears of being decimated at the 1710 election, due to be held in the wake of the Sacheverell prosecution and amidst growing opposition to the war, enabled him to dish the Whig Junto and establish a Tory administration that went on to win a landslide victory.[3] On the other hand, the establishment of a Whig administration in 1693 had taken place between elections and when the parties were neck and neck. On balance, the evidence suggests that elections before 1710 made mixed administration desirable but not essential and that although they could have some immediate impact on policy, it was not decisive.

The Tory landslides at the 1710 and 1713 elections and the Whig landslide in 1715 were all achieved by the parties in office, the last helping to establish the Whig ascendancy and the consignment of the Tories to indefinite exclusion from high office. These clearly did have an immediate impact on the composition and policies of government but the manner in which the Whigs overturned the Tory majority in 1715 underlines the enormous advantage the party in power possessed at elections. George I exhorted the electorate to return Whig candidates and the Whig administration used all its influence to have their own supporters appointed as returning officers in all types of constituencies and to ensure that favourable voters were created in key boroughs. The result was therefore an extraordinary demonstration of the influence of the executive in elections with 112 of the 141 Whig gains being made in the English close boroughs – those most amenable to influence and least vulnerable to public opinion. Indeed, with 63 of the 92 English and Welsh county seats being held by Tories, it could be plausibly argued that if public opinion had been the sole determinant, the result would have been reversed.[4]

The establishment of the Whig ascendancy had the effect of diminishing but not eliminating the immediate impact that general elections could have on the composition and policies of governments. The three cases where they did matter were 1734, 1741 and 1754. In 1733, Walpole announced his Excise Bill in the confident expectation that it would be well received in the constituencies at the election due in the following year and that as a result he would be able reduce the strength of the Whig and Tory oppositions. The hostility to the measure, however, not only led him to drop it in 1733 but to abandon all idea of resurrecting it after the 1734 election had led to an increase in the number of his opponents.[5] Later, in 1741, Walpole's majority was reduced to about forty as a result of the decision by a number of controllers of seats, particularly in Cornwall and Scotland, not to return his supporters. Once the new Commons had assembled and his opponents had increased the intensity of their attacks, supporters began to melt away and he resigned. Finally, in 1753 the combination of widespread opposition to the Pelham administration's Jewish Naturalisation Act and the prospect of a general election in the following year was a strong factor in persuading the government to repeal the measure and thus forestall serious electoral losses. By the time of repeal, fifteen constituencies had issued instructions to their MPs to oppose the measure.[6]

As the above example of the instructions from constituents to their MPs to follow a particular line in Parliament suggests, general elections were not the only occasion when voters and constituents could attempt to influence events. The right of individuals or groups of individuals to send addresses to the monarch or to Parliament was well established at the beginning of this period and instructions to candidates on how they should behave at Westminster if elected were a normal feature of Scottish elections and had been resorted to by Whigs in England at the second election in 1701.[7] However, there appears to have been a considerable increase in such expressions of public feeling after 1733, particularly in instructions. In that year, members of the public in 59 constituencies (all but one boroughs) sent instructions to their MPs to oppose the Excise Bill, their efforts being supported by groups of businessmen from the major towns travelling to Westminster to see that the instructions were followed.[8] Between 1739 and 1742 there were successive waves of instructions campaigns either in favour of war with Spain over her interference in the West Indies trade or more generally against Walpole's regime: from 32 constituencies, September 1739–October 1740, from 47, 1741–2 and from 54 between February and August 1742.[9] By the 1750s, the drawing up of addresses or instructions within parliamentary constituencies appears to have become the established way of demonstrating both widespread support and opposition for government measures. In the summer and autumn of 1756, for example, some 40 addresses and instructions critical of the administration for the loss of Minorca were drawn up in 36 constituencies.[10] Two years later, approximately fifty congratulatory addresses to the King on the capture of Cape Breton were printed in the *London Gazette*.[11]

Assessing the impact of such memorials on the executive and Parliament is problematic. The vast majority of MPs rejected the view that they were delegates rather than representatives and in the current state of research it is very difficult to establish the extent to which they were influenced by the instructions they received. On the other hand, it seems undeniable that concerted instruction campaigns contributed with other factors to bringing about the desired ends in at least two cases. The first of these was the campaign against the Excise Bill in 1733 and the second, the decision to go to war in 1739.[12]

Lobbies and pressure groups

In addition to the verdict of elections, governments and Parliament also had to take account of the influence and pressure wielded by various types of extra-parliamentary groups. In this context, the terms 'influence', 'pressure' and 'extra-parliamentary' have to be used with great care. Ministers, their officials and MPs could often advance their own causes by helping to foster support 'out of doors' and at the same time claim that they were acting in response to public opinion – a term that came into use as early as 1731.[13] It is therefore sometimes difficult to establish how far parliamentarians were responsible for what appears to be extra-parliamentary pressure. In addition, some ostensibly extra-parliamentary bodies were so closely connected with the operations of government that they were, in effect, part of them. The London financiers are a case in point. These included the contractors and brokers who undertook to sell the government's debt to the public, the governors of the Bank of England and other bankers, and the directors of the principal City brokerages and insurance companies. Given that deficit financing or public borrowing was such a crucial aspect of government policy from the 1690s onwards, it seems highly likely that such men and such institutions exercised more influence on government than any others of a 'non-parliamentary' kind. After all, governments were reliant on financiers to broker the debt and financiers were reliant on stable governments to sell it at a profit.[14] However, in view of the necessary secrecy or otherwise that accompanied the relationship, the evidence for such influence is sketchy. Attention has been drawn to the fact that the hostility of the financial institutions did weaken some administrations – those of Harley, 1710–11, Stanhope-Sunderland, 1717–19, and Devonshire-Pitt, 1756–7; while others were strengthened by their approval – those of Godolphin, Walpole, Pelham and Newcastle. In addition, it has been argued that they could influence executive decisions. In 1720, the Bank of England was able to shield itself from the damage threatened by the South Sea Company's attempt to take charge of the national debt. And in 1750, it was able to extract compensation from the government following a lowering of interest rates.[15] However, one suspects that there would be many more examples, had the evidence survived.

The more recognisable extra-parliamentary influence of this period was exercised in the context of what Peter Clark has shown to be the exponential growth of British clubs and societies devoted to a large range of subjects and involving all but the humblest ranks of the population. At the time of the Glorious Revolution, such associations were to be found largely in London and a few provincial centres but as the urban population grew and flourished, they were established in towns and cities all over Britain and, indeed, Ireland. Devoted to subjects as diverse as politics, music, the visual arts, morality, immorality and science, their proliferation in London may be taken as a rough guide to their overall growth. Thus, it has been calculated that there were 66 different types of association in the London area by 1760 and about 1,000 different clubs and societies. The famous contemporary estimate that 20,000 men met together every night in London clubs of one sort or another was therefore not far from the mark.[16] Similar developments took place in the provinces. Over 60 different clubs, for example, were apparently established in Norwich between 1715 and 1750.[17]

The groups that appear to have had the most routine relations with government departments and with Parliament were those involved in over-seas trade. There were two types of these: the chartered companies which had been granted monopolies of trade in different parts of the world such as the East India, Hudson Bay, Russia, Turkey and Royal African companies; and independent groups representing merchants trading in specific areas such as the West Indies or the North American colonies or those based in specific towns and cities in Britain.[18] In the case of the chartered companies, governments were inclined in their favour once they had been established. In 1730 and 1744, for example, the East India Company's charter was extended following strong lobbying and in 1734, pressure from the Russia Company resulted in the Anglo-Russian Commercial Treaty of that year meeting many of its objectives. It is also notable that Pelham's administration was able to resist a concerted campaign by independent merchants against the monopoly of the Hudson Bay Company in 1749. However, as the Hudson Bay example illustrates, there was growing opposition to chartered monopolies which both the executive and Parliament found it increasingly difficult to resist. In 1750, Parliament abolished the monopoly of the Royal African Company following concerted merchant opposition and established a new one directed by merchants trading with Africa based in London, Bristol and Liverpool. Three years later, the monopoly of the Turkey Company was also modified as a result of similar pressure.[19]

Despite the successes of the non-chartered merchants involved in African and Levant trade, by far the most influential of such groups were those involved in trade in the West Indies and North America. In 1733, one branch of the West Indies trade – the planters – mounted a successful campaign to have prohibitive duties placed on all imports of foreign sugar, molasses and rum into the north American colonies. In 1739, they were also instrumental in obtaining the passing of the Sugar Act that allowed West Indies' producers to ship their products to southern Europe without having to call first at a British port. And in 1744, they were able to mount an extensive and ultimately successful campaign to dissuade the government from increasing the duty on imported sugar.[20] As for the North American colonies, one authority has argued that not some but *most* trade legislation in the first half of the eighteenth century originated in petitions to the Treasury from discontented groups.[21]

Less routine but far more widespread and tenacious lobbying was applied by groups with their focus on the domestic economy and on social and religious issues. Economic lobby groups took various forms but conducted their activities in similar ways. Some consisted of specific associations or societies such as the West Riding Committee of Worsted Manufacturers or the British Marine Society while others were more *ad hoc* such as those engaged in the leather trades in 100 or so different locations in England who acted together in petitioning Parliament, 1697–9.[22] As for their methods, petitioning Parliament, often by pressing the petitions into the hands of willing MPs in the lobbies of the two Houses, was the common factor. Groups of this kind were usually reacting to a sudden change in fortunes and were pressing for immediate relief. A surge of petitions was therefore calculated to be the best way to bring the matter to Parliament's attention and, hopefully, to have a select committee of enquiry established that might lead to favourable legislation.

Economic groups of this kind represented many branches of domestic trade and manufacture and were often successful in their methods. Unsurprisingly, given its importance to the economy, the most persistent of all such groups were those involved in the textile industries – particularly wool but including silk, linen and cotton. Tim Keirn has shown how extensive lobbying by textile manufacturers combined with the helping hand of 'cloth' MPs representing textile constituencies led to about sixty successful bills, 1689–1714; while Michael Jubb has argued that the wool merchants were the most persistent lobbyists in Walpole's era, mounting intense campaigns in 1720, 1731 and 1739 to prevent illegal exports.[23] The campaign by those involved in the leather trades we have already noticed but to these we can add many others extending throughout this period: by tanners in 1717;[24] by the London and provincial traders in wine and tobacco against the Excise Bill of 1733;[25] by distillers continuously to prevent increases in the rate of tax; by those engaged in the fishing industry in the 1750s; and in the same decade, by iron manufacturers to have American bar and pig iron imported free of duty to any port in Britain.[26] In general, lobbying by economic groups was a constant feature of parliamentary life that had a substantial measure of success.

The other principal category of lobbying consisted of that orchestrated by religious denominations with the objects of sustaining and improving their own position or raising moral standards. There were two contexts here. In the case of the well-being of the various denominations, the Church of England was on its guard as a result of the fillip given to Protestant dissent by the Toleration Act of 1689 and the Occasional Conformity Act of 1711. Protestant dissent, for its part, sought further concessions, most notably by the repeal of the Test and Corporation Acts. As for moral reform, the context was provided by the gradual withdrawal of the Privy Council from any regulating role which coincided with a steep increase in criminality during the Augustan period and an unwillingness of either the executive or Parliament to do anything effective about it.

In the case of the defence or advancement of the denominations, the Church of England was potentially the most powerful lobby of all and focused after 1714 on resisting any further encroachment of its position by the repeal of the Test and Corporation Acts. In this it found initially reluctant, but eventually acquiescent, support from the Whigs in power with the result that it was never required to organise itself effectively until much later in the century. However, it was the successful resistance to repeal on the part of Anglicanism that provided the impetus to the organisation of dissent. The most highly organised dissenting lobby at the beginning of the period was the Quakers with their highest body, the London – based 'Meeting for Sufferings', being in permanent existence to secure concessions. Initially, they met with considerable success with the passage of the Affirmation Act of 1696 and its subsequent amendment in 1722 to remove the requirement to affirm 'in the presence of Almighty God'. The repeal of the Test Acts, however, proved a tougher nut to crack. In this they were joined by the Protestant Dissenting Deputies representing the Presbyterians, Independents and Baptists, founded in 1727. The latter achieved some success when a sustained campaign led to the passage of the Indemnity Act of 1727 which indemnified those who took office without taking the hated Test Acts. However, although this was renewed annually for all but seven of the next 100 years, the Test Acts themselves remained in place for that length of time.[27]

Although the Quakers probably constituted the most sophisticated and well-organised lobbyists in the early stages of this period, the most extensive lobbying was conducted by the moral reform societies. These took root following a series of Royal letters and proclamations against vice and immorality, 1689–99, and led in the last year of the years to the foundation of the Society for the Promotion of Christian Knowledge by Anglicans who were in the foreground of the 'Reformation of Manners' movement. According to Peter Clark, just over fifty English and Welsh towns had one or more religious societies devoted to moral reform by 1714 with the SPCK providing both a spiritual and guiding centre. They appear to have been less successful, however, than the economic or dissenter equivalents. Their campaigns focussed on bills to stamp out blasphemy, sexual debauchery, drunkenness and duelling – pastimes whose practitioners were difficult to suppress and easily provoked into opposition. Thus, although there were some successes – in the SPCK's decisive contribution to the highly influential Workhouse Act of 1723 and in the pressure that led to the Acts of 1736 and 1751 designed to reduce gin consumption – the impetus behind the moral reform movement began to fade from the 1730s.[28]

The operations of organised pressure groups constituted only a part of popular political activity. There was, in addition, a much more diverse range of what might be best described as pressure and protest and a consideration of the addresses, petitions and instructions mentioned earlier provide a clue to some of its principal characteristics. Memorials such as these were drawn up by specific groups in either counties or towns but these different locales tended to generate different forms of politics. In both counties and towns, inhabitants had a constitutional right to call for a meeting to discuss a matter of concern and to agree to send an address to the monarch or Parliament, to petition Parliament for 'a redress of grievances', or, indeed, to send instructions to MPs. However, the degree to which and the purpose for which such meetings were held differed. In the counties, the magistrates and grand jury at quarter sessions had traditionally taken the lead in representing local opinion by drawing up addresses to the Crown. In the course of this period, however, this method was superseded by county meetings leading to petitions and instructions as well as addresses.[29] At these, the principal landed proprietors usually took the lead with lesser landowners following their example. County sheriffs, for example, were invariably appointed with the approval of at least one group of major landowners and their permission was required before a county meeting could take place. County meetings were therefore invariably held with the approval of the proprietors, the bulk of those in attendance being other gentlemen and the humbler freeholders, most of whom would have been beholden to the gentry. As a consequence, county memorials were popular only in the sense that either the gentry as a whole (or a partisan section of it) had enlisted popular support or had approved of the causes to which that support was pledged. Either way, the causes were usually of a 'national' kind, that is, causes of concern to parliamentarians.

Town meetings were also subject to the approval of the authorities (the mayor or his equivalent) but the dynamics of politics were often different. In the larger towns and cities, the traditional rivalry was between Whig and Tory or Court and Country interests, each of which consisted of landed proprietors, professionals, merchants, tradesmen and artisans with antagonism between Anglicans and dissenters being an additional source of friction. The 'deference' factor, which was strong in the counties, was comparatively weaker in the larger towns and cities. On the other hand, the strength of the parliamentary division between Whig and Tory in such places ensured that the various kinds of memorials were invariably related to the parliamentary agenda even though the specific inspiration for them varied according to the diverse economic, social and political circumstances of the town or city concerned.

Although it would be foolish to underestimate the degree of popular political activity that was not associated in some measure with the politics of the propertied elite, the evidence points, as we have seen,[30] to a steady stream that seems to have been of a largely popular kind. Demonstrations of sectarian feeling were common before 1715 but seem to have faded in frequency thereafter, although there were widespread attacks on Catholic chapels in 1746. Popular demonstrations against price rises or food scarcity, on the other hand, were, with the exception of 1693–5, less notable between 1690 and 1715, and although the intervals between them seems to have lengthened thereafter, their scale may have become more extensive. There was widespread food rioting in 1740–1 and again in 1756–7 when it co-existed with violent protests against the Militia Act. According to one authority, these riots were 'unmatched in scale and scope by anything in recent history'.[31]

The response of the executive to such protest was often immediate but short-term. A case in point is the Riot Act of 1715 which, as one authority has argued, was rarely resorted to because magistrates preferred to use the existing body of criminal law to deter protesters.[32] In the case of scarcity riots, the usual response was to shore up supplies of grain by withholding bounties on exports, 1697–1700, or by prohibiting exports after poor harvests as in 1709–10, 1740–1 and 1756–7. In the case of popular protest directed at single political issues, however, judgement is more difficult because it often coincided with parliamentary and extra-parliamentary opposition of a more peaceful if no less serious nature. It is therefore difficult to assess whether the executive was responding to popular protest or to opposition of a more conventional kind. That said, it has been argued that this form of popular protest was of some account in the decisions to abandon the Excise Bill in 1733, to abandon the Gin Act, 1736–43, and to repeal the Jewish Naturalisation Act in 1753.[33]

The print media

A further source of extra-parliamentary pressure consisted of the print media: books, periodicals, pamphlets, sermons, newspapers and ephemera such as the handbills and squibs that circulated at elections. As in the case of clubs and societies, and in some ways complementary to it, there was exponential growth in virtually all forms of printed material, the only probable exception being election ephemera as a result of the decline in the number of contests after 1741. There were various reasons for this expansion. One was the cessation of censorship as a result of the Licensing Act being allowed to lapse in 1695. Governments could, and did, seek to control the media by placing duties on paper and advertisements and by taking legal action against blasphemous, obscene or seditious publications but such methods were only successful on an intermittent basis and were less and less resorted to in the early Hanoverian period. Another reason was a growing public demand. Literacy rates for both men and women were comparatively high by European standards at the beginning of this period and rose during the course of it: to about two-thirds of men, according to one estimate, and about one-third of women.[34] The rates were obviously highest for those in the upper and middling ranks of society but it was these elements that benefited most from the growing profitability of agriculture and commerce in this period, thereby encouraging forms of consumption which included reading materials.

The final reason, of course, was the readiness with which publishers took advantage of this situation. In the case of books, periodicals, sermons and pamphlets, for example, sermons continued to be the most popular single form of literature throughout this period but it is difficult to tell how far their number and that of pamphlets rose. On the other hand, it has been shown that the number of books and periodicals published did grow substantially from the 1680s to the 1730s, and after a period of stasis, from the 1750s. Thus, whereas most booksellers and publishers were concentrated in London in the 1680s, there were some 400 outlets in nearly 200 towns in Britain by 1740.[35] Further, there had been a significant increase in the periodical press with at least seven periodicals being published in London in the 1750s.[36] These provided a livelihood for the growing number of professional writers in the capital.

There was an equally striking growth in the newspaper press. In the first decade of the eighteenth century there were about twenty newspapers published in London and a handful in the rest of Britain – the first English provincial newspapers being published in Norwich and Bristol in 1701 and 1702, respectively.[37] By 1760 the number of newspapers published in London had risen to approximately thirty, where, it has been suggested, they were read by 25% of the population. Expansion in the rest of Britain began in the 1720s, faltered in the late 1740s, and was renewed in the mid-1750s. By 1760 there were about 40 provincial newspapers in England and Wales and about 8 or so in both Scotland and Ireland. Overall, between about 8 and 11 million duty-paid copies were sold annually in Britain in the 1750s. The number who read the London press was naturally very much higher than that of the provincial variety but such was the distribution system that there were few areas of Britain – the highlands of Scotland and parts of Wales – where newspapers of one kind or the other were not available.[38]

Assessing the impact of this burgeoning print media on the conduct of executive and parliamentary government is as problematic for this period as it is for any other. As we have seen in earlier chapters, the scope of the executive's responsibilities was narrow by today's standards and extended little beyond foreign policy, national defence and finance, all of which were complex and specialised topics that required daily attention. This made them peculiarly resistant to regular external influence. Further, although independent members promoted legislation dealing with economic, social, and religious or moral issues, these were often as much the result of their own interests as opposed to external pressure. It is therefore sometimes difficult to establish whether a cause was being promoted chiefly by parliamentarians enlisting the support of the public or the other way around.

That said, some propositions may be ventured. The first, and most incontrovertible, is that parliamentarians were well aware of the power of print to mould, shape and influence opinion. Their own views, whether they be Whig, Tory or the Court and Country variants of these ideologies, were moulded by their education and their reading; and shaped thereafter by an increasing volume of polemical or speculative literature. The basic beliefs or prejudices of the members of all governments and of all Parliaments were therefore influenced to a greater or lesser degree by the printed word. This had two results. The first is that all forms of policy making were influenced to some extent by the flow of ideas generated by the various forms of print but most particularly, by the book and the pamphlet. The practical results of this have been discussed in an earlier chapter. The second is that parliamentarians sometimes sought to control or influence the media, particularly the newspapers. The most notable examples are the astonishingly successful muzzling of the Tory press by the Whigs, 1714–16, the attempt by Walpole to crack down on contemporary reports of the debates in the 1720s, and the sponsorship of the influential *Craftsman* by Pulteney's Whig opposition in the late 1720s and 1730s.[39] Thereafter, however, it appears that ministerial interest in muzzling the newspapers and Opposition interest in sponsoring them declined. Indeed, it has been argued that after the ending of the War of the Austrian Succession (1748), opposition newspapers themselves began to shift the focus of their attention away from the daily routine of parliamentary politics and to the need for a post-war 'national revival' based upon Britain's growing commercial power.[40] We might therefore conclude that parliamentarians had learned to live with a relatively 'free' press.

The other proposition is that although it was difficult for the print media, particularly the newspaper press, to influence the agenda for either government policy or parliamentary legislation, the evidence does suggest that it was increasingly seen as vital to the application of pressure to achieve particular ends. The difficulties should not be underestimated. 'High' politics, that is, court, ministerial and opposition politics, were conducted largely in private. Newspapers usually had editors rather than reporters and were dependent on official sources for information about diplomatic manoeuvres, wars and parliamentary affairs. Further, although they devoted a large proportion of copy to foreign news, including war and diplomacy, it was only from the 1740s onwards that the contemporary reporting of the debates escaped censure, and even then it was very fragmentary. Newspapers, like the print media as a whole, were therefore at a disadvantage when it came to influencing policy.

On the other hand, there seems little doubt that the print media was increasingly used as a means of bringing pressure to bear on Parliament and governments. The storm of popular Tory protest in London and the Midlands against the impeachment of Dr Sacherverell for his 'High Church' sermon in St Paul's on 5 November 1709 in which he appeared to criticise the Revolution settlement, was generated in part by news sheets, broadsides and addresses. It helped Harley to dish the Whig Junto and enabled the Tories to win a landslide victory at the 1710 election. Wilfred Prest has drawn attention to the fact that a significant body of supportive pamphlet material was published during three periods when Parliament was concerned to reform the legal system, 1700–60.[41] Further, the newspapers were an important means of publicising the extent of popular support or opposition on specific issues. The raw material in this case consisted of addresses to the Monarch or to Parliament from specific localities; and instructions to MPs by their constituents on how they should vote. Addresses and instructions were certainly resorted to in the William and Anne period but it was the reporting of them in the growing number of newspapers that could create the impression amongst parliamentarians *and the public* of *concerted* pressure. As mentioned earlier, forty addresses and instructions from 36 constituencies were issued critical of Newcastle's administration for the loss of Minorca in 1756, most of which were published in the London and provincial newspapers between August and December of that year. More significant, however, was that many of these were brought together in a single volume and published in London at the same time under the title, *The Voice of the People: A Collection of Addresses to His Majesty and Instructions to Members of Parliament by their Constituents.* It was developments of this kind which convinced Newcastle and his advisers that public opinion was so hostile that it had to be countered in some way: either by the prosecution of printers and publishers for libel; or by propaganda placed in the newspapers, thereby 'following the opposition', as Lord Chancellor Hardwicke put it, 'in their own way'.[42]

Summary and conclusion

Although mapping the morphology of popular politics can convey little of their richness, diversity and intensity, it does at least enable us to draw some conclusions about their impact on central government. The crucial one is that the evidence points clearly to the interconnection of the politics of the propertied elite and the politics of the people. The elite's power in parliamentary terms rested, ultimately, on its readiness to respond to the grievances of other sections of the population – grievances that were articulated with increasing sophistication and force as the this period progressed. Similarly, its power at constituency level, even in some of the closest of pocket boroughs, rested on accommodating the interests of voters and non-voters or at least being sympathetic to them. There was, in effect, a reciprocity of interest.

The impact of various forms of popular political activity on the executive and Parliament was certainly substantial. In the case of general elections, for example, the results in the 35–40% of English and Welsh county and freemen and corporation boroughs that were contested before 1714, played a role in the composition of ministries, and decisively so in 1710.[43] Thereafter, the combination of the Hanoverian succession, the dishing of the Tories in 1715 and the Septennial Act of 1716 gave the Whigs a virtual monopoly of office but as the continuation of a comparable proportion of contests in the county and larger borough constituencies suggests, public opinion as expressed in elections continued to have an impact. The strength of popular constituency opposition to the executive certainly played a role in denying Walpole sufficient support to prolong his regime in 1741 and the prospect of it was sufficient to persuade Walpole and Pelham to abandon the Excise Bill and the Jewish Naturalisation Act in 1733 and 1753, respectively.

It may also be no coincidence that as the influence of the Whig-dominated executive increased and the potential for elections to topple it appeared to decrease, so did the resort by constituents to addresses and instructions to the monarch, Parliament and individual MPs. In the case of instructions, their number and the frequency with which they were issued increased significantly from the 1730s and were of account in the abandonment of the Excise Bill, the decision to go to war with Spain in 1739, the fall of Walpole, and ultimately, the fall of the Newcastle administration in favour of Pitt following the loss of Minorca.

The impact of institutional and sectional pressure groups, however, was more sustained and in terms of results, more successful. Representing the higher echelons of the middling classes, the London financiers, the chartered and independent merchants, the domestic producers and manufacturers, and the various Protestant sects, all achieved considerable legislative objectives by means of sophisticated and well-organised lobbying. Indeed, in matters of trade and manufacture, it would not be an exaggeration to conclude that legislation usually flowed from a process of consultation between the executive, MPs and the lobby groups concerned. Pressure from manual workers, on the other hand, received only short-term and immediate palliatives. Its most frequent form over the period as a whole was violent protest against food scarcity or high food prices, the immediate answer to which was to ban the export of grain until domestic stocks had recovered.

Perhaps the most challenging pressure of all, however, was that which was expressed in print. The print media expanded at a rapid rate in this period, fuelled by rapid urbanisation, growing prosperity and consumption, and a proliferation of clubs and societies. Public knowledge of the progress of war and international diplomacy, of executive policies and manoeuvres, of parliamentary proceedings, and most importantly, of demonstrations for or against government policy in different parts of the country, grew exponentially. Initially, the political elite was ambivalent in its response: ministers tried to suppress the publicising of parliamentary business and criticism of their own actions while their opponents tried to sponsor it. In due course, however, the elite reluctantly recognised the force of print and all sides began to think of the best ways to harness it to their own advantage. 'Popularity' came into vogue.

Overall, executive and parliamentary government increasingly became a matter of negotiation and accommodation between the propertied elite and the financial, commercial, manufacturing and professional classes – those who although they might possess landed property and aspire to more, derived most of their income from other sources. In some areas of government, therefore, policy emerged from a mingling of oligarchic and plutocratic influences.

General conclusions

Of the various developments in the history of government that we have noted in the last four chapters, three stand out. The first is the evolution of a new mixture of powers at the executive level. Royal power was diminished and in due course a first minister emerged at the head of a small inner cabinet of senior colleagues to fill the vacuum. The civil service grew in size and within it, the fiscal and military departments became particularly powerful. The causes and consequences of these developments, however, need careful assessment. In the case of causes, the terms upon which William of Orange succeeded James II led to a significant reduction in royal power but the emergence of this precise form of mixed executive government depended on a range of personal and circumstantial factors. There was nothing inevitable about it.

As for the consequences, royal power, although diminished, still remained considerable and was sufficient to determine not only who governed but also, how they governed. Further, although the fiscal and military departments became the dominant elements in the bureaucracy, they did not eliminate the influence of other departments of state such as those of the Secretaries of State, the Lord Chancellor and the Archbishop of Canterbury. It was also the case that it was comparatively rare for even senior civil servants to have a significant impact on policy making. In essence, what therefore emerged was a mixture of royal and ministerial power with the whip hand held, *in extremis*, by the Crown.

The second development was that executive government became largely exercised through legislation passed by annual Parliaments. As we have observed, Parliaments met more frequently and for longer than before. In addition, there were more general elections until 1715 and the number of contested elections remained high until the 1740s. This had several consequences. One was that the composition and policies of the executive were strongly influenced by the state of parties, particularly in the Commons. As we have noted, the parties of this period had certain distinct policy preferences but were never homogenous in outlook and rarely secure in their tenure of power. Parties and therefore governments tended to be confederations of interest and opinion. A second consequence was that although the quantity of ministerial legislation was largely static until the 1750s, the amount promoted by independent MPs, often in collaboration with a variety of lobby groups, increased steadily.

The third development was closely associated with the establishment of annual Parliaments, the growth of parties, the frequency of contested elections and the increase in legislation. Taken together, they made parliamentary business much more relevant to the politics of the middling and lower orders and encouraged the growth of new forms of political activity. Thus, in addition to the growth of contested elections, we have noted the interest in parliamentary politics promoted by an increasing number of provincial clubs and societies, by a proliferation of pressure groups and lobby interests, and by a growing body of publishers and writers commenting on parliamentary affairs. These developments were assisted, in turn, by the fact that more information became available about the debates and through the digests of parliamentary papers, about state affairs.

What impact, then, did these developments have on the practices and policies of central government? In order to assess this effectively, it is important to distinguish between the executive and parliamentary branches. In the case of the executive, we noted that the scope of its responsibility remained relatively limited and static for most of this period, being focused on diplomacy, war and public finance. It was only in the 1750s that the scope appears to have broadened slightly. We also noted that the success rate of ministerial legislation tended to increase over time, thereby suggesting that Parliament's role in offering 'counsel to the Crown' was in decline.

In practice, however, the shaping of policy was a highly complex affair. Some widely held beliefs underpinned the outlook of government on the general cast of policy throughout this period: the virtues of a mixed system of government; membership of the established Church and possession of real estate being a qualification for full participation in politics; and the central institutions of the state not intruding on the local and voluntary variety. Moreover, these co-existed with what in due course became some equally widely held beliefs about what the general objectives should be in specific areas of policy. These consisted of the view that Britain should co-operate with other states in establishing a European balance of power; that mercantilism should be the goal of colonial and commercial policy; and eventually, that financial policy should balance the interests of public debt holders with those of direct and indirect tax payers.

The crucial point, however, is that when it came to the shaping of specific policies, ministers were equally influenced by short-term, practical, considerations relating to both the circumstances of the case and the state of parliamentary opinion, particularly in the Commons. Further, contrary to what might have been expected from our review of background assumptions and objectives, there was relative indifference to the necessity of co-ordinating policy in different spheres of operations. It is this characteristic that makes the policies of Godolphin and Harley, and more particularly Walpole and Pelham, stand out. Admittedly judgement in all these cases is problematic due to gaps in the evidence but it does seem likely that in all four cases there was a recognition that policies in different spheres of operations should be co-ordinated.

What can be said, then, of the parliamentary dimension of government? In this respect, we have noted a number of developments. One was a tendency for the membership of the Commons to become more, rather than less, aristocratic. A second was for parties to take firm root in parliamentary and constituency politics and for a parliamentary opposition to evolve as an accepted institution in parliamentary life. A third was for the quantity of parliamentary legislation to increase and within that context, the proportion of legislation promoted by independent MPs and a plethora of national, regional and local interest groups. Finally, there were two other associated developments. One was the growth of parliamentary scrutiny of largely non-ministerial legislation, particularly through the means of committees.

This enhanced Parliament's role as 'The Grand Inquest of the Nation'. The other was a growth of printed information about parliamentary business – the debates, parliamentary accounts and papers and some committee reports. This took place, as we have seen, in the context of a growth of various forms of extra-parliamentary political activity. The consequences of all this were twofold. In the first place, the parliamentary dimension was firmly integrated into central government as a whole. In the second, parliamentary processes acted as a link between the interests of the landed elite and those of the rest of society.

Part II
1760–1848

5 The framework of the executive

Introduction

Of the many momentous changes that took place in Britain between 1760 and 1848, some had a particularly significant impact on the framework and practice of government. It may therefore be helpful to introduce them briefly here, starting with Britain's standing in the world order. The period begins with the conclusion of the Seven Years War (1756–63) which led to Britain acquiring French Canada and breaking French power in India. The Treaty of Peace signed between Britain, France and Spain in Paris in 1763 confirmed Britain's status as one of the pentarchy of major European powers and established her as France's most formidable rival overseas. This had two effects. On the one hand, it did not weaken and may have strengthened the priority that governments traditionally gave to European diplomacy over all other matters of state. And on the other, it led to initiatives designed to strengthen the influence government had over its scattered empire – in India, Ireland and the American colonies. This was to lead to the revolt and cession of the colonies (1775–83) and a major reverse to Britain's growth as a world power.

The ultimately successful wars against France (1793–1815), in which Britain was the longest serving of the other major allied European powers (the Habsburg empire, Prussia and Russia), shaped the context of government in three particularly important ways. In the first place, victory, together with colonial expansion and the lead that Britain acquired in industrialisation, established her as the foremost European and world power. This resulted in European policy retaining its primacy in terms of government priorities even though the object of policy changed. Initially, until about 1830, Britain was a reluctant participant in a form of collective security (the Congress system) designed to maintain the balance of power established by the Paris Treaty and the Vienna settlement of 1815. Thereafter, however, she preferred to look for a 'free hand' in Europe in order to support her position as the world's foremost industrial, trading and imperial power.

Second, the period between the loss of the American colonies and the ending of the war in Europe in 1815 saw a dramatic extension of British colonial territories: in Canada; in the Caribbean, with the permanent accession of additional West Indian islands in 1815; in Asia, with the acquisition of Ceylon, Java and a massive extension of territory in India; and in the southern Africa (the Cape of Good Hope) and the Mediterranean (Malta and the Ionian islands). By 1820, Britain controlled in excess of a quarter of the world's total population. Moreover, there was a further territorial extension of empire over the next 30 years – for example, in Asia (Singapore, Assam, Arakan, Tenasserim, 1819–26), Aden (1839) and Hong Kong (1842); and the establishment of more formal methods of government for what had hitherto been settlements – most notably in Australia and New Zealand. How far the growth of the 'second British empire' effected the priorities of government is difficult to assess. On balance, it seems unlikely that it led to imperial matters superseding European policy as the major topic on any government's agenda even though they probably played an increasingly important part in shaping it. On the other hand, the issue of the slave trade and slavery certainly became one of the key issues in British politics between 1787 and 1833, when first the slave trade (1807) and then slavery (1833) were abolished.

Finally, the outbreak of the Irish rebellion in 1798 at a critical stage of the European war led to the union of the Irish and British Parliaments in 1801 and subsequently, to the gradual assumption by Whitehall of many of the functions of the hitherto separate Irish administration. The creation of a new state with a new name – the United Kingdom – resulted in what were essentially Irish issues becoming much prominent on the government agenda. The most important was the campaign in both Ireland and Britain to enable Catholics to sit in Parliament, which was a major issue from 1805 until it was resolved in 1829. This was followed by the campaign to repeal the Union; by efforts to conciliate Irish grievances by extensive reforms, *c.*1830–45; and finally and tragically, by the Great Famine of 1845–7.

Britain's emergence as the major European and imperial power can be explained, in part at least, by economic growth. At the beginning of this period, the economy was underpinned by an increasingly profitable agricultural sector, which together with forestry and fishing, employed by far the largest proportion of the workforce. In addition, there was a buoyant financial market in London, a growing manufacturing and mining industry, and most notable of all, a flourishing commercial economy sustained by international and imperial trade and growing internal consumption. By the end of it, however, the population of Britain had increased from *c.*8 million to nearly 21 million and that of Ireland from *c.*3.5 million to 6.5 million. Further, although agriculture still accounted for the largest single category of employees in Britain, those employed in various forms of manufacture, mining and industry outnumbered them as a whole. For example, the number employed in every branch of the cotton industry in 1851 amounted to 527,000. In short, although the economy as a whole still retained flourishing agricultural, financial and commercial sectors, it was becoming increasingly dominated by factory-based industry.

These unparalleled developments led to major changes in areas where people lived, the conditions they lived in, and how they perceived their situation. In the midlands and the north of England, in the lowlands of Scotland and in the north of Ireland, increasing numbers inhabited large manufacturing towns. In 1801, it has been estimated that 78% of Britons lived in rural surroundings. By 1851, 50% were living in towns and cities. Urbanisation was accompanied by an increasing gulf between rich and poor and by sharper class-consciousness and class-antagonism. The landed classes, hitherto more conscious of the gradations of rank between them and their position at the top of a gently sloping social pyramid, became increasingly aware of their separateness and common interests in terms of their lifestyles and sources of wealth. They became known collectively from the 1820s as 'the aristocracy' or the 'upper ten thousand'. Similarly, those usually described in the eighteenth century as constituting 'the middling orders' or 'the middle classes' of society – professionals, merchants, manufacturers and traders – were increasingly associated in the early nineteenth century with the term 'middle class' and the productive and progressive forces in the economy and society. It was also the case that the language of class and to some extent, the language of class antagonism, penetrated the consciousness of working people. To what extent and to what degree is a matter of historical debate, but there can be no doubt that from the 1790s onwards and for a variety of reasons, the concept of a working class gained ground – particularly in the industrial cities where close proximity and shared conditions of labour encouraged a collective identity.

These developments confronted governments with three particular problems. One was the threat of class conflict. Throughout this period the landed elite dominated political power. As its consciousness of being an elite grew, so did its fear of being confronted by the hostility of other classes. The ways in which the elite could present itself as acceptable custodians of the body politic and the extent to which it could prevent itself being opposed by the collaboration of other classes therefore became one of its central occupations in the first half of the nineteenth century. It was this thinking, for example, that underpinned the details of the first major reform of parliamentary representation by the Whigs in 1832.

The second problem was how to reconcile the conflicting demands of the principal sectors of the economy – agriculture, industry and commerce. Eighteenth-century governments had not been unfamiliar with this problem but it reached a new intensity in the early nineteenth century. The principal reason was what were seen as the unfair regulations of predominately aristocratic governments and Parliaments. Throughout this period agriculture was protected to some degree from foreign competition, particularly between 1815 and 1846 when the Corn Laws were in force. This antagonised manufacturers and industrialists who felt that they had to pay higher wages than they need have done under a free-trade system in order to enable their workers to buy artificially expensive food. Further, until the 1820s, governments operated a strict system of tariffs on imports and exports designed to favour the imperial trading system – a system which had been in place since the seventeenth century. Many manufacturers and industrialists who looked to profit from trade outside the empire in view of Britain's lead in industrialisation opposed this. The result was a growing demand for freer trade from the 1820s. Finally, the tax system came under increasing criticism. In 1799, the Younger Pitt introduced a 10% income tax to help finance the war – a tax that fell most heavily on the landed classes. In 1816, however, Parliament voted to abandon the tax, leaving the burden of tax receipts falling on articles of consumption. This led to the charge that the landed elite was privileging income derived from property at the expense of profits derived from business and industry which had to cope with wages kept higher than necessary by taxes on the necessities of life. This was not resolved until Peel reintroduced the income tax in 1842.

The third problem was the ills associated with a rapidly growing population, particularly in the industrial cities and towns – food scarcity, ill health, poverty, unemployment, crime, disease and the lack of education. All of these, of course, were prevalent in the eighteenth century but with the exception of food scarcities, for which temporary palliatives had traditionally been applied, they were not thought to be matters that central government could do a great deal about. They were therefore left to private initiatives, local authorities, and charitable foundations. In the early nineteenth century, however, the accumulation of evidence, often by parliamentary enquiry, and challenges to traditional views on the functions of government, led them to rise to the forefront of the government agenda.

Governments were also challenged by significant developments in religious and political culture. In the case of religion, the issues arising from the incorporation of a largely Catholic Ireland into the state have already been noted, but in England and Wales the challenge arose principally from the exponential growth of Protestant nonconformity. In 1760, there were probably no more than *c.*50,000 members of Congregational, Baptist, Methodist, Presbyterian and Quaker sects. By 1801, there were about 150,000 and by 1851, some 810,000. It is also worth noting that in 1851 there were some 900,000 Catholics in England and Wales, the number swollen by emigrants from Ireland. Two key problems arose. One was the issue of political and civil rights. Under the terms of the seventeenth-century Test and Corporation Acts, Dissenters were barred from holding political office, although many did so by taking advantage of the normally annual Indemnity Acts first passed in 1727. Dissenters nevertheless pressed for the repeal of the Acts, which was achieved in 1828. That still left many civil rights, such as the right to celebrate marriages in their own places of worship, unrecognised. The second was how to put the Church of England in a position to be able to compete, particularly in the industrial towns and cities where it was initially thin on the ground. This was a problem highlighted by the famous Census of Religious Worship conducted in 1851. This revealed that slightly more nonconformists attended worship on the chosen Sunday than Anglicans, even though the latter were nominally the much larger sect.

A second challenge arose from a series of political pressure groups organised on a steadily larger and more sophisticated scale and focussing principally on the need for parliamentary reform. Starting in Middlesex and London with John Wilkes and the Bill of Rights Society in the 1760s, continuing with the Revd Christopher Wyvill's Yorkshire Association in the 1770s, such pressure groups proliferated in the 1790s and following their suppression during the war, re-surfaced in an increasingly more widespread and organised form. The principal ones were the Irish Catholic Association, founded on a national scale by Daniel O'Connell in 1823; the Political Unions, which following the foundation of the Birmingham Political Union in 1830, spread to other towns and cities in England during that decade; and most famously, the Chartists. These were the largely working-class supporters of the 'People's Charter' which demanded substantial parliamentary reform and who were at their strongest between 1838 and 1848, when they once claimed (1842) some 3 million subscribers.

This development, together with the founding of many additional pressure groups pressing for other types of reform, presented governments with two key challenges. The first was the realisation by the 1820s that a new form of 'public opinion' had become a permanent and independent force in the body politic. In the 1760s public opinion was a narrowly based and largely metropolitan phenomenon: as much the creature of ambitious politicians than their master. By the 1820s, however, the combination of pressure groups, the growth of a powerful metropolitan and provincial press, and the prominent roles that members of the new middle class played in these two developments, had created a public opinion that was much more widespread and far less easily manipulated than hitherto. The second challenge was presented by the fact that from the 1780s onwards 'reform', in the sense of 'improving' or 'recasting' virtually all aspects of both state and corporate activities, became a powerful and widely accepted concept. Moreover, this coincided with, and was closely connected to, the emergence of a series of sophisticated intellectual critiques of many of the principles upon which the Hanoverian state had been built. Notable examples are Adam Smith's *An Inquiry into the Nature and Causes of the Wealth of Nations* (1776) which advocated free trade; Thomas Paine's *Rights of Man* (1791–2) which attacked the idea of property as being the basis of political rights; and Jeremy Bentham's *Introduction to the Principles of Morals and Legislation* (1789) which set out his theory of utility, or the greatest happiness of the greatest number being the principal objective of government.

The executive and, indeed Parliament, were therefore confronted by a series of challenges, some of which were well established and others of which were new. All of them, however, were of an unparalleled scale. It is to the responses of the executive, beginning with its framework, that we now turn.

The monarchy

Although the Revolution settlement effectively destroyed the monarch's ability to rule without Parliament and placed other restrictions on his freedom of manoeuvre, the sources of royal power remained extensive throughout the period to George III's accession in 1760. The monarch remained the acknowledged head of State in all its principal branches: the Church of England, the judiciary, the armed forces and the executive. It was also acknowledged that the monarch's verdict was final on all senior, and even junior, appointments to civil, religious and military posts and that no-one could be granted an honour without his approval.

In the case of the executive, however, the monarch became a partner with his chosen ministers in the shaping of policy. The necessity of the executive having to raise the financial resources for its operations from annual Parliaments required the monarch, as the head of the executive, to choose ministers who were able to command majorities in the Commons. In due course, the influence of the traditional instruments of the royal will – the Court, the Privy Council and the Cabinet Council – gave way to those devised by ministers for their own convenience – a first minister and an inner cabinet. Executive government was therefore conducted by means of a part-nership between the monarch and his ministers – a partnership in which the monarch held some strong cards. One was the Court, which although its influence as the centre for high political discussion and manoeuvre had receded, still remained a large institution of consequence. Its senior officers, for example, occupied places in the Cabinet Council. Another was the fact that it was the monarch's income that paid for many of the salaries and pen-sions of the principal civilian officers of state – a circumstance that gave real substance to the concept of the 'Kings government'. Its strongest cards, however, consisted of the three prerogatives that virtually all politicians agreed the monarch, *in extremis*, could wield independently and without question: the right to appoint and dismiss ministers of their own choosing; the right to veto measures, including legislation proposed by their ministers; and within the terms of the Septennial Act, to dissolve Parliament and bring about a general election. The executive partnership therefore consisted of a delicate balance between the influence of the Crown and the influence of ministers. It is to the role of the Crown in the second half of this period that we now turn.

Although George III was afflicted intermittently by the adverse effects of genetic inheritance – the porphyria that was mistakenly diagnosed as 'madness' by his doctors – royal business was conducted throughout this period by monarchs who were intelligent and with the general but not com-plete exception of George IV, hard-working. George III (1760–1820) set the standard.[1] He was born in 1738, the eldest son of the then Prince of Wales who died in 1751, leaving him the heir to the throne. His tutoring therefore acquired a political significance, especially as it was conducted principally under the supervision of a Scottish peer unknown to political circles in London, Lord Bute. In fact, Bute and his charge soon developed a particular view of what was required in the new reign. The power of the 'Old Corps' or administration Whigs was now such, they felt, that it had diminished the legitimate influence of the Crown and sapped the confidence of the public in the political system. What was required was a 'Patriot' King who would maintain the proper influence of the Crown, root out corruption, and restore public faith in the virtues of the mixed constitution.

Having succeeded to the throne in 1760, George III set about setting standards of personal morality and attention to business that contrasted sharply with those of his immediate predecessors. In September 1761 he married by arrangement the almost obligatory German princess, Charlotte Mecklenburg-Strelitz, and in conformity with his own strict observance of the rites of the established church, remained faithful to her thereafter, each attempting to impose strict discipline upon their fifteen children. He also maintained throughout his working life – that is until 1810 – a regular pattern for the week with the focus on state business, religion and his family. He usually rose early at 6 am to deal with the ministerial papers that had arrived overnight. Following a morning ride, divine service and breakfast, he settled down again to executive business, reserving mid-afternoons for public occasions such as the weekly receptions or 'levees' for the nobility. He then retired to his study for more affairs of state before returning to his family at about 8.30 pm, to play cards, listen to music and take supper with the Queen. Given the rigours of this schedule and the effects of the porphyria and its mistreatment that afflicted him at times of political crisis – in 1763, 1788, 1801 and 1804 – his stamina and attention to business were remarkable. In fact, the only decline that took place before his confinement at Windsor for madness in 1810 was after 1789, when he felt it wise to reduce the pressure of business following his recovery from the most serious effects of his illness;[2] and more particularly after 1805, when deteriorating eyesight obliged him to make use of a secretary for the first time. From November of that year he dictated all his correspondence.

Although not a man of great intelligence or originality, he had a wide range of interests in the arts and the sciences. He collected pictures and books in substantial quantities, founded the Royal Academy, promoted Handel at the regular 'Concerts of Ancient Music', played the flute, harpsichord and piano, and was instrumental in enabling Herschel to make the most important scientific discoveries of the age – the modern concept of the Universe. His chief interest, however, was state business. In keeping with the concept of the 'Patriot King', he believed that the Revolution had bestowed upon the monarchy an equal role along with that of the Lords and the Commons. He therefore took the view that it was his duty to maintain it. Admittedly there were some areas of policy that interested him more than others. His chief preoccupations were the same as those of his predecessors – foreign policy and the military, especially the army – but he was also determined to maintain the Anglican supremacy and was otherwise increasingly opposed to any fundamental change to the constitution. His policy interests, however, are less significant than the knowledge of government that he accumulated over time. None of the other monarchs of the post-Revolution period worked as assiduously or as consistently at state business as he did. By the end of the 1770s he was probably the best-informed statesman of his time on the full range of policy issues and this was a position that could only have strengthened over the next thirty years.

George IV (Regent, 1811–20, and King, 1820–30) was of different mettle.[3] Born in 1762, he was brought up and educated according to a strict code of discipline imposed by his parents, both of whom made little secret of their preference for his younger brother, the Duke of York. When under the instruction of his tutors, for example, he was allowed only one hour's recreation in alternate days. The result, given some encouragement in his early years by his dissolute uncles, the dukes of Cumberland and Gloucester, was a personal life that was almost the reverse of his father's. Thus, although he also married a German princess in 1795, Caroline of Brunswick-Wolfenbüttel, he conducted a series of relationships with other women before, during, and after a marriage that although it endured in name until 1820, ended for all practical effects the day after its consummation. With his continuous search for the ideal female companion went a restless sociability pursued in the London salons, gaming clubs and drinking dens. Whereas his father was famed for his religiosity and frugality, George was equally famous for his indifference to religion and his profligacy. He accumulated debts, for example, that rose to the staggering sum of £630,000 in 1795, the year in which he consented to an arranged marriage in return for Parliament agreeing to pay them off.

In matters of state, his chief preoccupation was to play a role rather than maintain a particular view of the function of the monarchy in a mixed constitution. This is not to say that he lacked intelligence or was devoid of interest in the arts and politics. His tutoring gave him a fair knowledge of the classics and modern languages (if not of spelling) and later in life he was a notable patron of the arts. He gave his father's library to the British Museum, supported the Royal Academy and its most fashionable member, Sir Thomas Lawrence, and most notably of all, was responsible for building new, or re-fashioning existing, royal residences. In the case of politics, how-ever, it is difficult to find any consistency of purpose or application. From his coming of age in 1783 to 1806, he attached himself to the Foxite Whigs, the critics of his father's allegedly unconstitutional assertion of royal influence. He even headed a personal following of as many as 80 MPs, 1802–6, in an attempt to put pressure on the King to give him a significant military role in the contest with Napoleon and to accept Fox in office. Following the devas-tating impact of Fox's death in 1806, however, his enthusiasm for political leadership faded. As Regent, 1811–20, and as King until 1830, he applied himself only intermittently to state business with the result that although he did act shrewdly and to some purpose in 1812 and 1827–8, he was always out-manoeuvred by his ministers on contentious issues.

The earlier career of William IV (1830–7) was somewhat similar to that of his brother.[4] Born in 1765 as the Duke of Clarence, his tutoring gave way in 1779 to his becoming a midshipman in the Royal Navy and as a consequence, soon succumbing to the temptations of alcohol and prostitutes. On his return from Hanover in 1785 (to which his father had in desperation sent him), he too took up with a series of women until he settled down in 1790 with Mrs Dorothy Jordan, one of the most successful actresses of her day. They lived together openly at Clarence Lodge or St James's Palace for the next twenty years, producing ten children in the process. By 1810, however, Mrs Jordan's attractions for him had faded and his debts were mounting. They therefore drifted apart and in 1818 he married yet another German princess, Adelaide Saxe-Meiningen, who apart from being in Philip Ziegler's memorable words 'the sort of woman whom every man maintains would make an excellent wife for somebody else',[5] was also rich. Thereafter, William's private life was settled and serene, he responding positively to her admonitions to cut down on his drinking and coarse language, and she receiving some of the illegitimate children of his liaison with Mrs Jordan – the 'FitzClarences' – into the household.

As far as state business was concerned, William IV was far more assiduous than his brother had been, particularly where foreign affairs were concerned, and appears to have had a much clearer conception of his role. Prior to his succession he had been of a Whiggish disposition, but his reign coincided with a series of serious challenges to the constitutional status quo: the clamour for parliamentary reform; the call for a repeal of the Union with Ireland; a substantial increase in the number of radical MPs in the Commons in the first general election to follow reform; and the notion of allocating surplus resources of the Established Church in Ireland to Catholic education. The King believed in the maintenance of the roles for the monarchy and the House of Lords laid down in the Revolution settlement and in view of the threat that these developments posed to them, he devoted most of his reign to that objective.

Like her grandfather, George III, Queen Victoria (1837–1901) was reared on the assumption that she would succeed to the throne relatively young.[6] Born in 1819, the death of her father, the Duke of Kent, a year later left her next in line after William IV who succeeded at the age of 64. She was therefore brought up a devout Anglican by her German mother and tutored in history, languages, maths and science according to a strict daily routine that allowed little time for socialising. Indeed, she slept in the same room as her mother until she came of age.

There were other similarities with George III. Victoria's equivalent of Lord Bute consisted of her maternal uncle, Prince Leopold, King of the Belgians from 1831, and Baron Stockmar, Leopold's personal physician and private secretary. Prior to her succession in 1837, Leopold and Stockmar instilled in her a sense of the important role of the monarchy in British government and the necessity of her devoting herself to state business. Although their influence declined subsequently, their message was basically reinforced by Prince Albert of Saxe-Coburg, whom she married enthusiastically in 1840. Thus, like George III, Queen Victoria was an exceptionally hard-working monarch who from the start of her reign kept a journal on political matters and soon acquired a formidable knowledge of state affairs, particularly those pertaining to diplomacy.

What, then, is the history of their influence on government? In the case of the *general* resources at their disposal, there were two significant but contrasting developments: a considerable increase in the public's knowledge of, and identification with, the monarchy; and an accelerating decline in its influence. The context for the first of these was the extraordinary growth of British power, some aspects of which had a direct bearing on the growth in public knowledge of the monarchy. The rapid increase in population in the first half of the nineteenth century, for example, particularly the urban population, led to an exponential increase in the print media, particularly newspapers. Between 1760 and 1783, the number of individual newspapers published in London and elsewhere in Britain and Ireland rose moderately to 19 and 61 respectively. By 1830, however, the number had risen to 55 and 259, their readership extending to perhaps 2.6 million people.[7] Newspapers and other forms of print such as caricatures and engravings required copy and the royals, then as now, were a major source.[8]

To some extent this was fortuitous. The period is notable for an accelerating number of major 'events' involving the royals: George III's accession in the year commemorating the centenary of the Stuart restoration and the bitter controversy occasioned by his alleged attempt at 'despotic' rule in the 1760s; his struggle to retain the American colonies and the dismissal of the Fox–North coalition in 1783; his mental collapse and recovery in 1788–9; the scandal over the Duke of York's misuse of army patronage in 1809; the celebrations of the King's Jubilee in 1810; and the centenary celebrations of the Hanoverian succession in 1814. Thereafter the pace quickened. Between 1820 and 1840, there was one spectacular divorce (1820), three royal funerals, three coronations – one (1821) being on a grand scale – and one royal marriage of fairytale proportions. However, it was also due to an increasing readiness to engage with the public, either through the media of images easily reproduced in printed form or by personal appearances that apart from flattering those present, were certain to attract public notice.[9] In the case of royal travels, for example, their range and frequency certainly increased in the second half of this period. Although George III eventually acknowledged the importance of ordinary members of the public being able to watch the perambulations of his family at Windsor or Weymouth, he hated being in London, travelled sparingly in the southern half of England, and never went to the north or to Scotland and Ireland.[10] George IV, on the other hand, was well known in elite circles in London and Brighton and besides touring the north of England in 1806 when Prince of Wales, made two highly successful visits to Ireland and Scotland in 1821–2 to celebrate his coronation. Although he subsequently became something of a recluse as a result of his infirmities, it was generally accepted by the time of his death that contact with the public was an essential part of royal duties. Queen Victoria, for example, made at least five tours of various parts of England and Wales between 1830 and 1835 at the instigation of her advisers, the last of which started with the York Music Festival and continued to Leeds, Wakefield, Barnsley, Doncaster before ending in East Anglia.[11]

The willingness to meet the public was complemented by the public's increasing readiness to identify with the monarchy. The key figure in this respect was George III and the key event, the famous words that he inserted in the draft of his first speech to Parliament: 'Born and educated in this country, I glory in the name of Britain'.[12] A line was thereby drawn in the sand. Whereas his two predecessors had made no secret of their love of Hanover and had therefore never been regarded with affection even by supporters of the dynasty, George III identified himself from the outset as British. Further, although the popularity that accrued from this was undermined by his political actions in the 1760s, the combination of his stern resistance to American rebels and French revolutionaries and his devout and frugal lifestyle endeared him to a broad and diverse cross section of society as a personification of national virtues.[13]

It was from these beginnings that the full integration of the monarchy into the popular conceptions of the state took place. The process was uneven. Integrating factors such as a growing sense of Britishness, the spread of patriotic loyalism during the Napoleonic wars, and the contributions members of the royal family made to the armed services were undermined by the scandals attached to the private lives of the Duke of York and George IV. On the other hand, there appears to have developed a growing readiness to identify the royals with popular political causes and to see them as their protectors in defiance of the parliamentary elite. The appeals of the radical London Corresponding Society to George III in the 1790s, the widespread radical and popular support for Queen Caroline in 1820, and the reliance that the largely middle-class Political Unions of 1830–1 placed on William IV's support for parliamentary reform all have something of this character.[14] It is also notable that in 1834 about 5,000 London merchants and traders made public their support for William IV's dismissal of the Whigs that year on the grounds that the 'free and legitimate exercise of the Royal prerogative' was 'essential to the maintenance of our own liberties'.[15]

These developments were matched eventually by a decline in the general means by which the monarchy could exert influence in the executive and Parliament. In the case of the Court, its role as a nerve-centre of high politics continued the decline that had started soon after the Revolution even though it was the setting for occasional royal initiatives. The most famous of these took place in January 1801 when George III used a levee to let it be known that he was opposed to Catholic Relief. The influence of the Royal Household and their officers followed a similar path. The size of the Household, for example, declined appreciably between 1760 and 1850 from well over 1,000 to about 760.[16] More significantly, not only did the Cabinet Council in which Household members sat cease to have any political significance, but the Household representatives who sat in Parliament also became increasingly expected to support the government rather than act independently either on their own behalf or that of the Crown. Their number was not inconsiderable – there were 23 in both Houses in 1788–9 and 24 in 1828 – but it was reluctantly conceded by both George IV and William IV that Household officials with seats in Parliament should act as members of the government on important issues or face dismissal. It was in this context that Peel declined to take office in 1839 following Queen Victoria's refusal to dismiss those Ladies of the Bedchamber who were married or related to senior members of the Whig Party. By the time that Peel formed his second administration in 1841, however, the Queen not only agreed that all Household officials in Parliament should be appointed by the prime minister, subject to her approval, but also agreed to the dismissal or resignation of three of her Ladies of the Bedchamber.[17]

There was a similar decline in the wider influence of the Crown. There was something of a paradox here. In view of the fact that many of the salaries of the civilian officers of state based in London were paid out of the monarch's income, the term 'the influence of the Crown' was synonymous with the influence of the executive. Indeed this was inevitable in George III's time given that he regarded his ministers as advisers who did not even have the right to discuss a matter without his sanction.[18] In this regard two developments took place. First, although George III, on his accession, had surrendered the income from the hereditary revenues of the Crown in return for a Civil List of £800,000 pa, the income from the two remaining sources unsupervised by Parliament grew substantially in the early nineteenth century. Thus although George IV's Civil List had been set at an generous £1.4 million pa, the total income including that from Crown Lands and other sources was at least £1.8 million and perhaps as much as £2.25 million. Second, there is no doubt that although the influence of the Crown in the sense of 'the influence of the executive' was checked in times of peace,[19] it grew substantially up to 1815, largely because successive wars required more state officials and therefore provided more favours to distribute. In other words, there was considerable substance to the radical and Opposition case heard with increasing stridency between the 1770s and 1830 that the influence of the Crown according to either definition was growing.[20]

In practice, however, the ability of the monarch to deploy these resources for their own purposes declined, albeit slowly. The trend is visible in the history of the royal income. A landmark in this respect was Burke's Civil List Act of 1782 that made a distinction for the first time between the Crown's personal expenditure and those of the state and set limits on the value of pensions that could be made out of the Civil List. In 1786, Pitt included the Civil List in the Consolidated Fund, thereby bringing it under effective parliamentary scrutiny for the first time.[21] Further restrictions were imposed subsequently culminating in the Civil List Act of 1832. This instituted the formal separation of personal and state expenses, set the appropriation for the King's personal use accordingly and denied him one of the sources of the enhanced royal income – the so-called 'casual revenues'. What had once been in a very real sense the King's government, was no longer so.

Similar developments occurred in the monarch's freedom of manoeuvre in the distribution of pensions, honours and patronage, although these did not take significant effect until the early nineteenth century. George III guarded his influence jealously, insisting upon having the final word on claimants to honours and exercising considerable personal discretion in appointments in the Church, the armed forces and the judiciary – departments of state in which he took a particular interest.[22] It was he, for example, who effectively chose the Archbishops of Canterbury in 1783 and 1805, and the Archbishop of Armagh in 1801.[23] His successors, however, were unable to withstand the demands of ministers to deploy honours and patronage for their own political and other purposes. In 1828, for example, Wellington made the recommendations for the filling up of vacancies occasioned by the death of the Archbishop of Canterbury.[24] By the 1830s the Crown's room for manoeuvre in these respects was negligible.

What, then, was the influence of the Crown on the composition of executives and the policies they pursued? In the previous period, we noted that a partnership had evolved between the first two Hanoverians and the Whig majority in Parliament which had two elements: the unquestioning acceptance of the monarch being the head of the executive and the final arbiter on its personnel and policies; and the willingness of George I and II to allow the Whig leaders to monopolise office and to develop policy increasingly amongst themselves. In this period, however, the nature of this partnership changed. Before 1810, George III became a much more active and effective head of the executive than either of his two predecessors had been. His successors, on the other hand, found his example more difficult and ultimately, impossible, to maintain. The history of royal influence on the executive therefore falls into two distinct parts.

The reasons for George III's more prominent role lie partly in his conception of kingship and partly in the political circumstances of his time. In the case of kingship, he believed that the balance between King, Lords and Commons established by the Revolution made it incumbent on him to play an equal part with the other elements of the trinity and that his predecessors had allowed it to be diminished. In particular, it required his being fully engaged with, as well as generally supportive of, the aims and objectives of his first minister and the handful of other senior ministers that constituted the core of the inner cabinet – particularly the Secretaries of State. As Lord Bute told George Grenville on his becoming first minister in 1763, it was imperative he established a 'strict union' with the Secretaries in order to maintain the King's 'independency'.[25] The fact that he held strong opinions on the conduct of foreign and imperial policy and was determined to maintain the *status quo* in constitutional matters and the relationship between Church and State only served to reinforce this objective.

As for parliamentary politics, circumstances worked to his advantage. Prior to his accession, the traditional parliamentary divide between Whigs in office and dissident Whigs in an opposition alliance with the Tory party was already crumbling due to a decline in Tory numbers but his formal ending of Tory proscription in 1760 brought it to a close. Toryism as an organised parliamentary force ceased to exist and in the following decade MPs fell into one of three principal categories: 'the King's friends' – those 'men of business' whose primary interest was office in the service of the Crown; the supporters of a number of parliamentary groups headed by leading Whig statesmen; and those who prized their independence, the majority of whom were usually ready to support any government supported by the Crown. Moreover the political resources that the Crown could call upon as a result of this re-configuration, although diminished for short periods, most notably in 1782–4 and 1806–7, did not subsequently decline to any significant degree. In fact the basic divide in parliamentary politics from 1770 to 1810 lay between two groups. On the one hand, those politicians who accepted the constitutional propriety of the King's active role in government and who either supported or were prepared to give way to his views on crucial matters of policy that he thought touched on his prerogatives. And on the other, the supporters of the Marquis of Rockingham and subsequently, Charles James Fox, who regarded his role as unconstitutional and who appropriated the name Whig for themselves and organised as a party to prosecute their case. For all but four years, however, the majority of the Commons rallied to the King's friends rather than the self-styled 'true' Whigs.

George III's interpretation of his role, his dedication to business and the political resources available to him resulted in his having a crucial impact on the composition of governments. Throughout, he looked for a first minister who apart from commanding a majority in the Commons, would respect his prerogatives and together with his other senior ministers, treat him as an equal partner in the discussion of policy. For nearly thirty of the fifty years of his effective reign, the King's requirements were broadly met by Lord North, 1770–82, and the Younger Pitt, 1783–1801, but his initiatives in the intervals were frequent. At the start of his reign, his elevation of Bute to Secretary of State in 1761 resulted in the latter succeeding as first minister in 1762 following the resignations of Pitt the Elder and the Hanoverians' longest serving minister, the Duke of Newcastle. The last of these provided the opportunity for the wholesale dismissal of Newcastle's supporters and the beginning of the legend that the King was bent on personal rule. In 1765, his refusal to accede to the demands of George Grenville, Bute's successor since 1763, that as first minister he should have command of patronage, led to his resignation in favour of the Marquis of Rockingham. The King then refused to meet Rockingham's demands for the dismissal of office holders who declined to support the ministry in Parliament with the result that Rockingham resigned in July 1766 in favour of the new royal candidate, Pitt the Elder, now Lord Chatham. Four years later, when a remodelled Chatham administration under Lord Grafton also resigned, the King at last found stability in Lord North.

In the two subsequent 'intervals', 1782–4 and 1801–10, the King's interventions had even more dramatic results. The most famous was the first. In February 1782, North's ministry was defeated in the Commons on its conduct of the American war and George III was obliged to call upon the services of the largest group in opposition, the Rockingham Whig Party. To make matters worse from the King's point of view, the Whigs presented him with a programme of measures and a list of dismissals from office as their price, thereby signifying that they did not regard him as a partner in decision-making. Worse was to follow. Rockingham died in July 1782 and following the defeat of the successor ministry of a similar but not identical hue in April 1783, the King was obliged to resort to what in his view was an 'unnatural' coalition of the two largest political groups – those of Lord North and Rockingham's successor as head of the Whig Party, Charles James Fox. Further, in the summer of that year, the Fox–North coalition proposed to remodel the government of India by, *inter alia*, increasing the influence of ministers. It was the combination of being 'in thrall' to a coalition of erstwhile hostile political parties and the threat to his influence presented by the India Bill that inspired the King to act. Assured that those ready to rescue him from his confinement were waiting in the wings, he rallied his supporters to defeat the India Bill and then dismissed the coalition and replaced it with one headed eventually by Pitt the Younger. He then granted Pitt a general election in 1784 at which the King's and Pitt's cause was presented as a struggle against oligarchy. The combined effects of the advantages that all incumbent governments possessed in general elections arising from their control of patronage together with majority public support for their case ensured that the new administration emerged with a substantial majority. The fact that the Whigs only held office for less than two of the next forty-seven years led to their interpretation of these events becoming central to their ideology.

The King's partnership with Pitt only began to break down seriously in the late 1790s. Hitherto, the relationship has been characterised as one in which George III gave Pitt as much 'latitude' as his prerogatives had allowed and Pitt did nothing that would upset him.[26] By the end of 1800, however, the King had not only become increasingly critical of the government's foreign policy since 1798 but was seriously concerned about the secrecy with which Pitt and sympathetic members of the cabinet were apparently planning a measure of Catholic relief to follow the implementation of the Irish Union in January 1801. Not only had the King become implacably opposed to concession but the secrecy also suggested an element of deception.[27] He therefore announced his opposition in no uncertain terms and Pitt, although possessed of an overwhelming paper majority in the Commons, resigned in favour of the King's choice, the anti-Catholic Speaker of the Commons, Henry Addington, whose allowances happened to be paid for out of the Civil List. The other result was a proliferation of political groups reminiscent of the 1760s. In 1804, three of these – the Pittites, the Grenvillites (the supporters of Pitt's ex-foreign secretary, Lord Grenville) and the Foxite Whigs combined to defeat the ministry. George III therefore intervened to restore Pitt as first minister and as a result of his determination to refuse office to Fox (and by extension, Grenville), to persuade Addington to support him. Pitt died, however, in January 1806 and the King was obliged to send for Grenville and the Foxite Whigs, now joined in what must have seemed as unnatural a coalition as that of North and Fox in 1783.

The central role that George III played in the making and ending of ministries continued until his final mental breakdown in 1810. In March 1807, the Grenville government proposed a measure that would enable Catholics to serve in the higher ranks of the army. The King, knowing that 'friends' were standing by to form an alternative administration, responded by refusing his support and demanding that his ministers never raise the Catholic question with him again. Grenville resigned and the remnants of Pitt's former colleagues gathered together to form a government under the leadership of first, the Duke of Portland, and from 1809, Spencer Perceval. In the view of Perceval, it was the determined support of the King and 'his friends' in the Commons which sustained the administration against what was numerically the strongest opposition seen since that of Rockingham in 1782.[28]

George III's role in determining who governed not only reflected his view that he should be a partner in government with his ministers but also his strong opinions on matters of policy. The subjects that interested him most were foreign and colonial policy, military administration and the maintenance of both the mixed system of government and the Anglican constitution. Assessing his influence, however, is problematic. The King did not believe in personal rule but rather a partnership with his ministers. Nor does he appear to have believed that his views should prevail over those of his ministers, save in those cases where his prerogatives were threatened. It is therefore difficult to establish at times when harmony prevailed between the King and his ministers just how significant his own influence was by comparison with that of others. On the other hand, there is no doubting his view and that of the members of all his administrations (with the exception of those composed of Rockingham or Foxite Whigs) that in the final analysis his sanction of policy was absolute. In 1782, for example, he told Lord Shelburne that it was standard procedure for departmental heads to seek his permission to lay a subject before the cabinet. Shelburne agreed, and it was the evasion of this practice that lay behind the enforced resignations of Pitt and Grenville in 1801 and 1807.[29]

George III certainly had a strong influence on specific policy at particular times. In the case of foreign policy, for example, it has been argued persuasively that his was the most consistent influence between 1763 and 1783: partly because of the alternative sources of information available to him from Hanover and the 'German Chancery' in London; and partly because of the frequent changes in the two secretaryships of State responsible for foreign affairs. However, this did not preclude his having to give way on policy from time to time as he did in 1765–6 (in favour of an alliance with Prussia), in 1781 (in favour of offering Minorca to Russia) and most notably, on the peace that ended the American war in 1783.[30] On the other hand, there is no doubt that it was his determination that frequently stiffened North's faltering resolve to prosecute the American war and that he was closely involved in both military administration and tactics. A study of the Secretaryship at War, 1765–78, for example, argues that 'nearly all the points of day-to-day administration in peace or in war were settled by the monarch and the secretary' and it has also been shown that it was the King's refusal to countenance the augmentation of existing regiments or the creation of new ones at the outset of the war that forced the government to recruit from external sources.[31]

Following his decisive intervention against the India Bill in 1783 and the establishment of Pitt as first minister, the King's influence may have become more intermittent due to the relative stability of the regime and his preference after his illness, 1788–9, for less constant involvement in business and what he called a more 'superintending eye'.[32] He played an important role, however, in the formation of the league of German Princes, the Fürstenbund, in 1785, which hastened the controversial alliance with Prussia two years later;[33] and as we have noted, his disapproval of the government's foreign policy after 1798 was almost certainly one of the factors that led to his ultimatum to the ministry on the Catholic question in 1801. Thereafter, his familiarity with day-to-day policy making may have lessened further, particularly after the rapid deterioration in his eyesight in 1805. Yet, as the events of 1804 and 1807 demonstrated, his determination to uphold the Anglican constitution and his refusal to be excluded from policy formation could still have dramatic effect.

George III's confinement at Windsor in 1810 and his death in 1820 inaugurated the period when the influence of the Crown on the executive began to decline. The underlying causes were the changes that took place in the structure of the executive, the strength of parliamentary parties and the basis of parliamentary representation. In the case of the executive, the size and responsibilities of the cabinet grew and the First Lord of the Treasury came to be regarded more as its head than the first minister of the Crown. In Parliament, the fundamental divide began to lie between two parties which gradually absorbed more and more members and whose differences lay not so much on the working of the mixed constitution but on a range of economic, social and other political issues. The number of King's friends therefore declined steeply. As for parliamentary representation, the 1832 Reform Acts, by enfranchising populous towns and increasing the electorate, tipped the balance of influence decisively in favour of the Commons and against that of the Lords and the Crown.

The trend is clearly visible in the monarch's ability to influence the composition of the executive although it is important not to exaggerate the speed or the consistency of its trajectory. George IV, for example, was sometimes disposed to act as though he was the maker or breaker of governments. In 1812 he made the unexpected but important decision to retain the services of the Pittites rather than turn to his former friends, the Whigs, and later imposed a veto on Lord Grey, the Whig leader, ever holding office again during his reign. Further, the resignation of Lord Liverpool as prime minister in February 1827 and the divisions that had emerged within the two parliamentary parties on reform enabled him to play the role of ministry-maker.[34] The short-lived Canning and Goderich coalition ministries of that year were therefore very much fashioned according to his wishes and when Goderich resigned, he hoped that his chosen successor, Wellington, would continue their broad-bottomed character. In this, however, he was soon to be disappointed.

The decisive events took place in 1834 and 1841. Ever since he had succeeded to the throne in June 1830 William IV had acted in support of first his Tory and then his Whig ministers as long as their actions did not threaten the balance of the mixed constitution which, as he said, he had inherited from his predecessors.[35] Having unsuccessfully denied support to the Whigs to force the Reform Bill through the House of Lords in 1832, he dismissed Lord Melbourne's government from office in November 1834 – the first time a direct dismissal of a ministry had taken place since November 1783. His reasoning was complex but at bottom it rested on his fear that the government's plans for a reform of the Irish Church would weaken the Anglican constitution and lead to a damaging clash between Lords and Commons. The outcome of that, he thought, might be a government dependent on radical supporters in the Commons determined to weaken the influence of the Crown and the Lords still further.[36] Although few criticised his constitutional right to act in this way, the intervention was unsuccessful. Having commissioned the Tories to form what he hoped might be a centre-ground coalition, they failed, unlike Pitt in 1784, to achieve a working majority in the Commons at the snap general election that he allowed to take place. As a result, they tendered their resignation and the King was obliged to call once again on the services of the Whigs. Melbourne was therefore the first (and most unlikely) prime minister to be installed by the electorate – a fact which undoubtedly helped him to extract from the King a free hand over men and measures.[37] The Crown's influence in the Commons and amongst the electorate was therefore clearly insufficient to sustain the ministers of its choice.

Notwithstanding the events of 1834–5, it took Queen Victoria some five years to come to terms with its implications. Although her advisers had told her that the monarch now had to be above party, she made no secret of her preference for the Whigs over the Tories. At the general election in 1837 she lent her name and her money to the Whig cause and two years later refused to signify that that she supported Peel's attempt to form an administration. The decisive turning took place in 1841–2. At the general election in 1841, she once again gave her support to the Whigs[38] but found to her dismay that they were defeated – the first time an incumbent government had ever lost an election. On the day before she was due to give Peel and his colleagues the seals of office she wrote privately to the ex-prime minister, Lord Melbourne, that she was so horrified by the prospect of a Tory government that she wished to correspond privately with him on political matters. This she did for nearly a year until Stockmar, Prince Leopold and Prince Albert persuaded her that the monarch had to give her entire confidence to the ministers chosen, in effect, by the electorate; and Melbourne was incapacitated by a stroke.[39] From that moment, the Queen's interventions, which were numerous, were devoid of partisanship.

Nor surprisingly, there was a similar decline in the royal influence on policy. This was not attributable for the most part to any serious reduction in the attention paid to state business. George IV's attention was intermittent at best but that of William IV and Queen Victoria was regular and on some issues, keen. The real reason was the declining influence of the Crown in the Commons and the growth of parliamentary parties. These reduced the alternatives to a government of whose policy the monarch disapproved. In 1829, George IV's opposition to Catholic relief led him to consider alternatives to the Wellington government but none could be found that would have been able to sustain a majority in the Commons. In 1831 and 1832, William IV's preference for a modified Reform Bill that the House of Lords would accept led him to look to the Duke of Wellington to form a government in May 1832. The Duke could not form one, however, in view of the Whig majority in the Commons. Two years later, as we have seen, the King encountered the same problem on the issue of Church reform. In fact, from that point in time, Bagehot's famous definition of royal influence made in 1867 is broadly accurate. The monarch had the right to be informed of policy and to encourage or warn against it. She could not, however, actively seek its rejection.

First and prime ministers

The decline of the influence of the Crown coincided with a transformation in the political role of first ministers. Between 1760 and the first decade of the nineteenth century, the role as defined by the Younger Pitt conformed to tradition. The 'first minister', he is reported to have said in 1803, should have 'the principal place in the confidence of the King' and 'the chief weight in the [cabinet] council', and, in addition, 'be the person at the head of the finances'.[40] No mention was made of party. Thereafter, however, the position was increasingly held by those regarded as one of the heads of whichever of two major parliamentary parties possessed a majority in the House of Commons. The role of the monarch as the head of the executive therefore became more nominal and that of the first minister more substantial. The change was reflected in the way the post was described. In the later part of the eighteenth century the term 'prime minister' was rarely used, first minister being usually preferred, although 'premier' was not unknown.[41] By the late 1820s, however, prime minister and premier were the more common descriptors, and universally so by the middle of the century.[42]

As suggested above, the fundamental reason for this was the gradual re-emergence of a two-party dominance of the House of Commons. Prior to 1810 or thereabouts, and with the exclusion of the period 1782–3, the government and opposition sides of the Commons consisted of different types of groups. The government side was made up principally of the personal followings of individual ministers, the King's friends and on most issues, the majority of 'independent' country gentlemen. The opposition side, on the other hand, was usually led by the self-styled Whig Party, which sometimes acted in conjunction with the personal following of a dissident major politician. After 1810, however, both the government and the opposition side of the House were increasingly led either by those whose loyalty was primarily to the legacy of the Younger Pitt, soon to be designated, and eventually self-described, as Tories, or by Whigs. By 1830, about half the House of Commons can be identified as active and committed members of parties; by 1841 virtually all were.

The impact of this development is clearly visible in the history of appointment to the office. With the exception of the period, 1782–3, all the first ministers between 1760 and 1804 were appointed on a combination of the following grounds: their acceptability to George III; their ability to command the support of other significant politicians as well as the King's friends; and their ability to manage the business of the executive and of Parliament – particularly finance and the Commons. Being the head of a formed political party that could guarantee a substantial number of votes was not a consideration. Indeed, not only did the King regard such a qualification as an unconstitutional threat to his influence, but none possessed it. The Younger Pitt's personal following when first minister in the 1780s, for example, was no more than 50 MPs. This is why the circumstances of 1782–3 were exceptional. As a result of the loss of confidence in Lord North's conduct of the American war, the King was obliged to turn to the leaders of the opposition to the government – the Whig Party under Rockingham. Rockingham was succeeded by Shelburne and following his resignation, the King found himself at the mercy of the combined power of the Whig Party under Fox in alliance with the personal following of Lord North. Pitt the Younger, the son of Lord Chatham and an ex-Chancellor of the Exchequer, was an obvious person to head a ministry of the King's choice.

Circumstances changed, however, following Addington's appointment by the King in 1801. Addington's government was toppled by a combination of parties in 1804 in favour of Pitt, an appointment made with approval by the King but on terms that prevented Pitt from proposing Catholic relief as a government measure and from employing the services of Fox. Pitt died two years later and it is at that point that three critical developments take place. First, in the course of the next six years, Pitt's ex-colleagues and admirers began to cohere into a recognisable party. Second, both George III and George IV chose to regard such a party as their preferred option, a major reason being its willingness to subscribe to the terms laid down by George III to Pitt on the Catholic question. And third, they tended, as a result, to look to the leaders of the party to suggest who the prime minister might be. Thus, on Pitt's death in January 1806, George III asked all his colleagues in turn to carry on but was advised in each case to call upon the leader of the reconstituted Whig Opposition, led by Lord Grenville. A year later, on Grenville's resignation, he turned to the Pittites who advised him to appoint the Duke of Portland. Similarly, in 1810, 1812 and February 1827, George III and George IV turned to the members of the cabinet for the recommendation of successors to Portland, Perceval and then Liverpool.

From this perspective, the events of 1827–8, are exceptional. Liverpool's colleagues failed to be able to agree on a successor with the result that George IV had to make his own choice. This led to the coalition governments of Canning and Goderich and on the latter's resignation in January 1828, the King hoped for its continuation under first, Lord Harrowby, and following the collapse of that idea and on the advice of his Lord Chancellor, the Duke of Wellington. Thereafter, however, the custom of turning to the recognised leader of either of the two parties took firm root – a custom that with the growth of parties became a practical necessity. This was the reason for the appointment of Grey in 1830, Melbourne in 1834 and 1835, and Peel (in default of Wellington's acceptance) in 1834 and in 1841.

The role and influence of the holders of the post also changed over time. Up to 1760, it was argued in Chapter 1, their influence was constrained by various factors: the influence of the Crown; the less than complete control of patronage; the competing influence of the Secretaries of State; the strength of departmental autonomy; and the strains of a substantial number of managerial, parliamentary and departmental duties conducted with little secretarial support. It was also noted that Godolphin, Harley, Walpole and Pelham nevertheless managed to give the policies of their administrations a degree of coherence.

In this period, significant changes took place from the first decade of the nineteenth century. Before that, there was a tendency for the influence of first ministers to grow but little change in their role. In the case of their influence, although there was hardly any reduction in the constraints imposed by the preferences of the King and by the royal oversight of patronage and the departmental ethos of the executive, there was a notable, if uneven, growth in the authority they assumed over their senior colleagues. The Younger Pitt's first administration may mark the change. Studies of the first ministers between 1760 and 1783, suggest that all bar the Elder Pitt (1766–7) regarded themselves as 'first among equals' as far as their senior cabinet colleagues were concerned. This did not mean they thought it inappropriate to occasionally intervene decisively in the policy of a colleague's department or that policies they opposed should be pursued. Bute, George Grenville and North, for example, all had key roles to play on foreign policy issues at specific times; and as one of North's biographers points out, most of the important decisions of his long administration were essentially his. What it did mean, however, was that they all paid lip service to the notion of a fair degree of departmental autonomy amongst their senior colleagues and that they might, on occasion, give way to others on policy without regarding it as a resigning matter. In the case of war policy during the American conflict, for example, North would have preferred a naval to a land strategy and was rarely involved subsequently in the details of military operations.[43]

However, from 1783, a number of developments appear to have encouraged first ministers to exercise greater influence over their colleagues. One involved the responsibilities of ministers and the size of the cabinet. In 1782 the composite duties of the two Secretaries of State were redefined with one becoming responsible for foreign policy and the other for home affairs. Further, there was a gradual increase in the size of cabinets: 8 at the end of 1784, 11 in 1798 and 13 in 1806–7. Taken together, these had the effect of enhancing the status of the first minister in relation to the Secretaries of State and requiring him to manage a larger number of colleagues. Another was the financial and commercial reconstruction that was required after the loss of the American colonies followed by the onset of the war with France in 1793. Both seemed to require the benefit of a central guiding hand. In July 1794, Dundas told Pitt that there needed to be 'some particular person who has and ought to have a leading and even an overruling ascendancy in the conduct of public affairs' and that 'Such you are at present as the Minister of the King'. The fact that Dundas felt obliged to tell Pitt of this, underlines the strength of the alternative view and the fact that the conception of the role was in transition.[44]

The result was that first ministers began to exercise a supervisory and co-ordinating influence over both a broader range of policies and a larger number of cabinet colleagues. The practices of the Younger Pitt demonstrate the transition. Initially, and rather like North on occasion, Pitt regarded his small cabinet as largely ornamental and established his superintendence of foreign, commercial and colonial policies by working with colleagues of non-cabinet rank. This became more difficult, however, after the reconstruction and expansion of the cabinet in the 1790s led to his being surrounded by more heavy-weight colleagues.[45] The result was that Pitt to some degree but more clearly his successors in this early period, Addington, Grenville and Perceval, assumed a supervisory role of all aspects of government that were considered primarily in the context of an expanded cabinet.[46]

By contrast, the specific departmental and parliamentary duties that were normally expected of first ministers did not change. Based on the precedents of Walpole and Pelham, the expectation was that a first minister, in addition to being First Lord of the Treasury, would also be Chancellor of the Exchequer and leader of the Commons. Not all fulfilled this ideal, of course, but George Grenville, North, Pitt and Addington, who together served for 35 years between 1760 and 1806, certainly did. An expanding managerial role in cabinet therefore co-existed with a heavy departmental and parliamentary burden.

The influence and role of what were becoming termed prime ministers changed again between *c.*1810 and the 1840s. In the case of their influence, the means at their disposal rose as a result of the diminishing role of the Crown in policy-making, the decline in the King's friends in Parliament, and the appropriation of patronage for political management. In addition, it soon became the convention that the Crown called upon the acknowledged senior figure of the majority party in the Commons to form an administration, increasingly giving him a free hand in his choice of cabinet colleagues. Although not always the powerful instrument this might seem in view of the rivalries that existed in the confederative parties that developed, this undoubtedly added to the prime minister's influence. Finally, not only did cabinets continue to grow in size, albeit moderately, but the concept of collective responsibility took firm root, thereby strengthening the hand of prime ministers against any external attempt to undermine their authority.

With these developments came changes to the conventional role of a prime minister. To some extent this was fortuitous. Thus, the ostensible leaders of the two parties that began to re-emerge in the period 1812–41 and who filled the office for virtually all of that time – Liverpool, Wellington, Grey and Melbourne – happened to sit in the Lords. This meant that they could not be Chancellors of the Exchequer. Here began the convention that prime ministers would hold no office other than the essentially non-departmental post of First Lord, Perceval being the last to also be Chancellor before Gladstone resurrected the practice for the last time in 1873 and 1880. But it probably also suited the new demands of the role. The greater independence of the Crown, a larger cabinet, the growing responsibilities of the executive and the competing claims of party heavy-weights required more emphasis on management and co-ordination, and provided less time for a permanent departmental responsibility.

To what extent, then, did these developments advance or retard the ability of the incumbents of the office to develop coherent strategies and impose them on their colleagues? It is not an easy question to answer, not least because there are so many variables. Prime ministers varied considerably in terms of their abilities, their personalities, their time in office, and the problems they confronted. The only consistent theme of this period by comparison with its predecessor is that there was a steady stream of crises demanding immediate responses: the American war; financial reconstruction; the French wars; and a succession of crises revolving around post-war unrest and fiscal, commercial and political reform. These were on a scale sufficient in themselves to place serious obstacles in the way of calm and systematic forward planning.

That said, the historiography of prime ministers in this period suggests the following broad conclusions. The first is that although it has been argued that all of them from Bute to Peel had a set of policy priorities, the focus of these changed at around the same time that their influence and role did, that is, in the first decade of the nineteenth century. Before that time, virtually all the first ministers (Rockingham being the most notable exception)[47] put financial policy at the centre of their strategy until such time as unanticipated emergencies blew them off course. Bute's objectives, it has been argued, were to end the Seven Years War on favourable terms and then focus on rigid economy in the public finances and root out alleged corruption in the executive.[48] George Grenville, who began by dealing with problems as they arose, then developed something approaching a systematic programme, the centrepiece of which was financial reconstruction and a tightening of the reins of colonial administration.[49] North's initial policies, until the advent of the American war, were to redeem the national debt, avoid continental commitments and persist with colonial taxation.[50] Shelburne envisaged a peacetime programme of financial reconstruction, a revision of trading agreements and administrative reform.[51] The Younger Pitt's initial objectives were very similar until the onset of war obliged him to turn his mind to striking a balance between the domestic repercussions of funding unprecedented expenditure and the demands of military and diplomatic strategy.[52] Moreover, this was the central objective of Addington, Grenville and Perceval in the context of Bonaparte's continental hegemony. Grenville's priorities, for example, consisted of a national government, a defensive military strategy and at its centre, 'a new plan of finance' designed to redeem the national debt.[53] Although all of these strategies were more reactions to circumstances and the groundwork laid by predecessors than the result of original thinking on the scope and purpose of government, the centrality of financial policy and the faint but steady hints of a systematic approach are striking.

However, after 1812, the focus of prime ministerial attention became more diffuse and less centred on national finance. This was largely the result of five prime ministers being peers, the increasing importance of management and a succession of domestic political pressures. Prime ministers therefore began to see themselves more as resolvers of crises and as co-ordinators of their colleagues' policies and conciliators of their differences, although this did not mean that they had no special area of interest of their own. Liverpool, Canning, Wellington and Grey, for example, all took a supervisory, and in the case of Canning and Wellington, a directing role in foreign policy. Liverpool, it has been argued, was essentially a conciliator and co-ordinator of his colleagues who, having made the Catholic question an 'open' one for his colleagues on account of its divisiveness, identified the reconciliation of the competing claims of agriculture, manufacturing and commerce as the principal objective of policy.[54] Wellington and Grey devoted most of their time to the resolving of the domestic crises of Catholic Relief and parliamentary reform, the repercussions of the Greek-Turkish war and the French Revolution, but both had broader agendas. Wellington's, essentially, was to maintain the influence of property within the political system while Grey's was to achieve the same results by showing that the aristocracy was capable of good government by implementing the old Foxite policies of 'peace, retrenchment and reform'.[55] As for Grey's successors in this period, Melbourne and Peel, their practice reveals the extremes to which prime ministers could be driven by the new pressures. Melbourne may have had an overall objective of maintaining a mixed system of government controlled by men of property but his method of achieving it was essentially reactive.[56] Peel, on the other hand, still confronted by the problems that he had first encountered when a minister under Liverpool and Wellington, devoted himself and his colleagues to resolving the issues of public finance, protective tariffs and Ireland. Further, in the case of finance and tariffs, he devised solutions that reconciled the discordant interests of the agriculturist, the manufacturer, and the indirect and direct taxpayers for at least a generation. However, the coherence that lay behind Peel's 'fiscal constitution' was the exception.[57] Overall, we might conclude that although the agenda of prime ministers broadened in response to the problems they faced, there are few signs until Peel's second administration of what we might call a systematic approach.

The second conclusion relates to the question of how far first or prime ministers were able to impose an agenda on their colleagues. The answer appears to be that the number who tried and were able to do so was very small. North, arguably, and the Younger Pitt more clearly, were able to do so in years of peace but both ran into difficulties with colleagues during wartime. Later, Grenville, Perceval and Wellington certainly attempted to supervise all aspects of policy but the former failed to spell out his agenda with sufficient clarity to his colleagues and the latter's was too negative to have much appeal. In fact the only prime minister who had clear control of his government's agenda was Peel – a point underlined by the fact that it was he who introduced his major budgets of 1842 and 1845 rather than his Chancellor of the Exchequer.[58]

Cabinets

It was during this period that the 'outer' or 'nominal' or 'Grand' cabinet ceased to play any effective role in government, its place being superseded entirely by the 'inner' cabinet. Thus, although some vestiges of the previous overlapping functions were retained before 1783 by the occasional presence of Household members of the outer cabinet in the inner version, the practice ceased thereafter save for the exceptional case of Lord Ellenborough who, although a member of the 'Grand' cabinet by virtue of being the Lord Chief Justice, was appointed to Lord Grenville's inner cabinet in 1806. The 'Grand' cabinet therefore became a body that did no more than hear the King's speech before the opening of Parliament and otherwise consider proposed capital convictions in the City of London.[59] The inner cabinet, on the other hand, quickly became the sole body responsible for advising the monarch on state business and will consequently be referred to subsequently as the cabinet.

With regard to membership of the cabinet, the turning point in its history bears some resemblance to that of the first minister. Prior to 1794, membership fluctuated between 6 and 8 on average, the core members being the First Lord, the two Secretaries of State, the Lord Chancellor, the chancellor of the Exchequer and two 'dignified' posts with no significant departmental responsibility, the Lord President of the [Privy] Council and the Lord Privy Seal. These last were always occupied by peers, most of whom were experienced and ageing politicians. After 1793, however, two developments led to a significant increase in numbers. One of these, associated with the onset of the French wars and subsequently, with the greater importance accorded to commercial development and colonial government, was the creation of new departments and the elevation of certain departmental heads to cabinet rank. The President of the Board of Trade, for example, elevated to the cabinet in 1791, became a permanent fixture thereafter. In addition, the newly established Secretary for War took over responsibility for the colonies in 1801 and in 1802 cabinet status was given to the President of the [Indian] Board of Control – a position it invariably held subsequently. The other, and probably more influential, development was the fragmentation of parties. In 1793–4 the Whig party split and a section was drawn into a coalition with Pitt. In 1801, Pitt's following broke into 3 groups which with 2 others, made 5 in all. Further, although these were dissolved into 2 principal groups between 1807 and 1822 – the Tories and the Whigs – they broke up again into 5 competing elements between 1827 and 1831. Moreover, even after that date, the differences within the Conservative and the Whig parties were as notable as their similarities. Forming a stable administration therefore involved rewarding the heads of a number of different groups or factions and this required more cabinet posts.

The combined effect of these developments was an increase in the size of cabinets: to between 11 and 13 up to 1812 and from 13 to 16 until 1846. Thus, in addition to the Colonial Secretary and the Presidents of the Boards of Trade and Control, two and sometimes three dignified posts were included in the shapes of the Chancellor of the Duchy of Lancaster, the Commissioner of Woods and Forests, and the Master of the Mint.

Seven administrations even included ministers without portfolio. The balance of peers to commoners, however, did not change. Throughout the period after 1760, at least half, and usually a majority, of the cabinet members sat in the Lords – a fact that reflects the preference for age, experience, extensive property and party requirements over administrative ability for many of the posts that they held.

There was remarkably little change in the ways that the cabinet conducted its business until comparatively late in this period. Throughout, meetings were usually held in the 'Great Room' in what became the Foreign Office and which had hitherto been that of the senior of the two Secretaries of State. This underlined the precedence given to foreign affairs in state business. The conventional times were afternoons or early evenings during the parliamentary session so that members could then attend the debates. As for their frequency, imperfect records and patchy research makes judgement difficult until the latter part of the period. It will be remembered that in 1705 and in the year from June 1710 to June 1711, the cabinet met on 64 and 62 occasions, respectively. Current research suggests that if formal cabinet meetings alone are considered, the cabinet may have met rather less frequently than this until the early nineteenth century but did so as frequently from the 1820s onwards. From 1828 to 1830, for example, Wellington's cabinet met, on average, 60 times per year. These figures, however, reveal only part of the story. Formal cabinet meetings, for example were concentrated in the parliamentary sessions and few took place in the long recesses. Further, they do not include the regular cabinet dinners hosted by members in rotation, usually on Wednesday evenings during the session – the day set aside for private members' business. Contrary to the impression of some participants, cabinet dinners were usually business as well as social occasions – certainly from the 1820s and maybe earlier.[60]

Traditionally, meetings took the following form. Members were occasionally assembled by the monarch but in the vast majority of cases it was at the request of the first minister or some other member of the cabinet – usually to discuss a specific issue and much less commonly, more than one. The most staple topic was diplomacy and members would have been able to prepare themselves by consulting the despatches that were sent around in circulation boxes, having first been seen by the monarch. On other matters, the prime minister or the relevant departmental head might have circulated memoranda on a topic in advance or left copies on the table in the cabinet room. Alternatively, they would simply speak to the topic at the meeting. Following discussion, usually of 2–3 hours, a decision might be reached, normally without recourse to a vote. The decision was then conveyed to the monarch. On highly serious matters, this was done in person by the prime minister but on those that were less so, the decision was conveyed in writing by the prime minister or by the minister who had summoned the cabinet. In exceptional cases, however, the decision would be conveyed in the form of a minute that recorded the agreed advice to the Crown and listed the members of the cabinet in strict order of rank.

Several points arise from this format. One is that the conduct of business was much less formal than it might suggest. Attendance was not compulsory, there was usually no agenda announced in advance, and no record was kept of decisions, copies of minutes being restricted to the monarch, the prime minister, or the minister who had drawn them up. The principal reasons for this were the emphasis placed on the cabinet as an advisory body to the Crown, the precedence given to pressing issues, and the desirability of keeping discussion and more particularly, differences of opinion, confidential. On the other hand, practices were adopted at the end of this period that signify a more bureaucratic and more independent approach. By the late 1820s, for example, copies of foreign despatches were circulated or placed immediately on the table in the cabinet room rather than having been sent first to the monarch. In addition, the preparing of memoranda to guide discussion seems to have become much more common: so much so that they began to be printed by 1840. Further, the establishment of cabinet committees on specific topics also became routine. In the second half of the eighteenth century informal gatherings on specific topics, particularly foreign policy, had been normal and this continued until 1830. However, Wellington consigned certain aspects of the package of Irish measures, 1828–9, to designated sub-committees consisting of cabinet and non-cabinet members and Grey and Melbourne both set up cabinet sub-committees to deal with difficult issues.[61] By 1846, once again, the establishment of such committees was routine. There was also a particularly significant change in the way that cabinet decisions were made known to the monarch. As has been mentioned, decisions were sometimes conveyed in the form of a minute which included the names of those present and in some cases, those who approved and dis-approved of the decision reached. At the time of writing some 200 such minutes exist for the period 1760–1832 and a high proportion were penned either by George Grenville and his son, Lord Grenville, or by Lord Grey whose first experience of cabinet office happened to be when Lord Grenville was prime minister. It is therefore possible that a Grenvillite enthusiasm for minutes that was adopted by Grey has exaggerated their significance. The important point, however, is that after 1832 both Grey and Melbourne aban-doned the resort to minutes to convey decisions and relied solely on personal communication with the monarch. The bureaucratisation of cabinet business therefore went hand in hand with a strengthening of the prime minister's position as the sole channel of communication on what had been decided.[62]

What contribution, then, did the cabinet make to government? The first point to stress in this regard is that throughout this period the members of virtually all cabinets supported the concept of a 'mixed constitution' and took the view that government was conducted in the name of the Crown. In May 1841, for example, Melbourne told Queen Victoria that it would be 'a great affront to the Crown' if the government was obliged by its weakness in Parliament to submit itself to a general election. In Melbourne's mind as in George III's and Shelburne's sixty years earlier, the Crown and the executive were synonymous.[63] Most cabinets therefore thought that their primary function was to advise monarchs on the policies that needed to be taken on matters that touched on their prerogatives and, with the exception of Hanover, the principal affairs of their dominions. In practice, the last category meant war and peace, diplomacy, military matters, law and order, patronage and in the case of the overseas dominions, the governing of Ireland and the colonies. These, after all, were the subjects for which the Crown bore ultimate responsibility, its signature being as necessary for a treaty as it was for the granting of a peerage or the award of a pension on the Civil List.

The notion of the cabinet as primarily advisers on the King's business was as deeply rooted in the forms of cabinet business in this period as it was hitherto. Thus although no monarch of this period ever attended a cabinet meeting, the convention until 1830 was that there would be a member who was known to have special ties with the Crown and who would act as its ears and its eyes. This was usually the Lord Chancellor. After 1830, however, the Lord Chancellorship became a political post.[64] It was also customary for all measures that individual members of the cabinet or the cabinet as a whole wished to have discussed and which were likely to touch on matters of special interest to the monarch to be referred to him or her in advance so that permission could be given for them to be taken further. Both George III and IV insisted that their governments should not even discuss Catholic relief without their permission, 1801–28, and in 1831 Grey had to engage in lengthy negotiation with William IV in order to secure his approval of the discussion of a specific Reform Bill. If it had not been to his liking, he would have refused it. Later, Melbourne also found the King determined to see bills in advance of their introduction in Parliament.[65] Moreover, the dominance of the 'King's business' is reflected in the subjects cabinets discussed. Thus, analysis of the Younger Pitt's cabinet, 1784–90, shows that of the 66 meetings or decisions for which records survive, 40 dealt with foreign affairs, 10 with Ireland, 9 with home affairs and 3 each with India and the colonies.[66] Further, analysis of the much better records for the Wellington cabinet forty years later shows that not much had changed. Approximately half of the 180 or so meetings, 1828–30, dealt with foreign affairs with attention being otherwise focussed on the three 'emergency' issues of the Corn Bill of 1828, the Irish crisis and the distress and mounting disorder of 1830.[67]

The concept of the cabinet as an advisory group also militated against its development as a body that could or should devise policy collectively. Ministers were ministers of the Crown. Each one could approach the monarch individually on matters within their own department and each could summon cabinets to discuss them. This encouraged the practice of 'government by departments' – a state of affairs that might suit the Crown but work against either prime ministerial co-ordination and direction or a collective sense of purpose. In 1783 Lord North said that he had inherited a system of government by departments when he had become first minister in 1770 and that although he had tried, he had been unable to change this to his own advantage over the next twelve years.[68] It was also worth noting that the Younger Pitt, recognising the traditional outlook within his first cabinet, attempted to co-ordinate policy by working with non-cabinet colleagues.[69]

In due course, however, the foundations were laid for the cabinet to become solely responsible for government policy. The keystone in this respect is the concept of 'collective responsibility'. Conventionally, this is defined as meaning that all the members of a cabinet regard themselves as collectively responsible for the decisions they reach. Under the full force of this interpretation, individuals who dissent from a majority view would be bound to resign, as would the cabinet if its decisions were rejected either by the Crown or by Parliament. However, the term also carries with it the implication that if cabinet members are collectively responsible for their decisions, they have also all played a role in how they were reached and what their general objectives might be. Collective responsibility therefore has a constitutional definition and an administrative implication – the last being in conflict with the traditional practice of a government of departments.

The advance of the constitutional definition of the term was largely the result of the declining influence of the Crown in ministry making and the growing strength of parties. The advance was nevertheless slow. The first display of the full impact of the concept took place in February 1782 when George III was forced to call upon Lord Rockingham's Whig party to form an administration, thereby bringing about a wholesale change of ministers. The Whigs then formed a cabinet united on a raft of policies to which the King was obliged to consent. Further, when Rockingham died in July of that year, Fox argued that the cabinet and not the King should choose his replacement – an argument that George III countered by appointing Shelburne.[70] The experiment, however, was short-lived and it was not until the early nineteenth century that the concept made further headway. In the case of the joint cabinet responsibility for measures, a succession of events established it as conventional practice. In March 1807, the Grenville cabinet resigned as a result of a disagreement with the King on the Catholic question. In June 1812, the Liverpool cabinet established the Catholic question as an open question, that is one on which they could disagree, thereby indicating that they would be agreed on all others. In November 1830, the Wellington government resigned as a result of its defeat in the Commons, leading to the appointment of a new set of ministers; and in 1839 the Melbourne government resigned as a result of a majority of just five in the Commons on its Jamaica Bill. Taken together, these events (and others too numerous to mention) mark the establishment of the view that the cabinet as a whole was responsible for its measures, first to the Crown as in 1807, and ultimately to the Commons, as in 1839. As for the view that individual ministers should give up their own views or resign if they disagreed with the policies of the rest of their colleagues, this also took firm root over the same period of time. There were at least four occasions during the Younger Pitt's first premiership when a minister signified his dissent but did not resign but the practice fell into almost complete disuse thereafter.[71]

The view that the cabinet should decide collectively on overall strategy and the individual measures upon which it was based has a much more chequered history. Some factors worked to its advantage. One was the incorporation into the cabinet of all of the leading civilian departments of state. This was a process that began after 1760 with the recognition that the Chancellor of the Exchequer (1766) and the Secretary for War (1794) should sit in the cabinet as of right and accelerated after 1801 with the awarding of cabinet status to the Presidents of the India Board and the Board of Trade. This strengthened the view that the cabinet should have a preponderance of men of ability and political weight as opposed to mere dignity. Another was increased press reporting of the times of, and attendance at, cabinet meetings, and even of the items discussed. This helped to give the impression that it had a life of its own. Finally, it would appear that as the cabinet became increasingly representative of both party and the major departments of state, more time was devoted to preparing business and anticipating snares in the House of Commons, usually on Saturdays. This also encouraged an institutional *esprit de corps*.

Others developments, however, worked in an opposite direction. As has been mentioned before, the Crown played a consistently significant role in cabinet making and policy until 1835, at which point it began to fade. Further, the presence of first, multiple parties after 1801, and then, two highly confederative parties after 1832, placed increased emphasis on the need to reconcile differences *within* cabinets and provided less opportunity to develop a coherent strategy to which all were signed up. Thus although some prime ministers such as Grenville, Liverpool, Wellington and to some extent Grey sought to encourage a collective sense of purpose, the old tradition of a government of departments died hard. Grey, for example, was ambivalent on the subject. He detested what he called Wellington's 'Dictatorship' over his colleagues and said he was dedicated to re-establishing a 'veritable' 'Counsel of the Cabinet'.[72] However, some felt that he and Melbourne allowed their colleagues far too much latitude. Palmerston, for example, took an increasingly independent line at the Foreign Office and there are several cases of ministers making important policy statements in Parliament without previous cabinet discussion. Indeed, in 1839, Lord Howick, Grey's son, went so far as to accuse Melbourne's cabinet of being a government of departments and 'merely ceremonial'. According to the historian of the Whig cabinets in the 1830s, there were only two policies that could be said to be shaped by the cabinet collectively – parliamentary reform and Irish tithe reform. The rest flowed from the departmental heads.[73]

Overall, the evidence suggests that the tradition of cabinet ministers regarding themselves as advisers to the Crown and therefore being resistant to having too strong a corporate identity was very slow to wither. Kriegel points very persuasively to 1835 as being the date at which the Crown ceases to be of much account in influencing membership or policy; and to 1839 when the cabinet recognised that its ultimate responsibility was to the Commons rather than to either the Lords or the Crown. On the other hand, although something approaching a bureaucratic system for managing cabinet business had come into existence, the evidence of the Melbourne government suggests that it had yet to result in a coherent system of cabinet government.

Departments of state

By comparison with the gradual and intermittent changes in the roles of the Crown, the prime minister and the cabinet, the increase in the number of officials in the civilian and military departments of state was substantial. Between 1755 and 1815, their number rose from *c.*7,700 to *c.*9,700 in 1782–3, 14,673 in 1797 and 24,598 in 1815, the last figure incorporating *c.*4,000 based in Ireland. It then fell back to 22,367 in 1829 before rising again to *c.*29,000 in 1849.[74] Put another way, there was a threefold increase in the number of officials in Britain from *c.*1760 to 1815 followed by a mere 19% in the next forty-five years. The parallel with what happened, 1688–1760, is clear enough.

The increase, however, needs to put into perspective. If the ratio of civilian and military administrative staff to the population of Britain is considered, for example, the difference between 1760 and 1840 was infinitesimal. Further, there was considerable variation not only in the size of different departments but also in the scale and significance of the increases in their staff. By far the largest at the start and the end of this period were the Customs and Excise departments and in both there were increases and significant change in their respective strengths. In 1763 there were 3,973 Excise officials and 2,290 in Customs – some 80% of all civilian and military administrative staff. In 1829 the corresponding figures were 6,335 in excise and 11,016 in customs – 77.5% of the total. Even allowing for the fact that the 1829 figures include Irish officials, it is clear that much of the overall increase was due to the exponential growth in these two departments, particularly in customs. In fact, what the overall figures obscure is that the staff of the principal civilian departments represented in the executive remained remarkably small despite their expanding responsibilities. The calculations below illustrate the point (Table 5.1). Thus, although differences in the number of departments and the reliability of the figures make comparisons between the beginning and the end of this period hazardous, there is no doubt that the rate of increase for the London-based staff of these key civilian departments was far less than that for the bureaucracy as a whole.

That said, some significant changes did take place to these departments and their military counterparts although it is important not to overestimate their intent or effect. As a number of historians of administrative change in the late seventeenth and eighteenth centuries have argued, such was the veneration for the ancient structures of the bureaucracy that new arrangements or methods were invariably grafted piecemeal onto the old.[75] Moreover, although the pace of change undoubtedly quickened in the first half of the nineteenth century, there are strong grounds for arguing that the veneration

Table 5.1 Staff of the civilian and military department of state, 1755–1849

	1755	1782	1797	1829	1849
Treasury, Commissariat and Exchequer	[200]	[200]	211	189	112
Foreign Office	[33]	[33]	24	47	49
Home Office	[33]	[33]	26	30	36
Colonial Office	—	—	12	33	37
Board of Trade	17		19	26	36
Board of Control for India			30	46	36
Totals			322	371	306[a]

Notes

a The figures in brackets are taken from Brewer, *Sinews of Power*, p. 66, table 3.1. In the case of those for the Foreign and Home offices, I have divided his overall figure of 66 for the two forerunners of these offices by half. The figures for 1849 are taken from PP. *Estimates… [of]…Salaries and Expenses of Public Departments* 1850 (256.II) xxxiv. 313 and the *Royal Kalendar* for 1851 in the case of the Board of Control. The others are referred to in Jupp, *British Politics*, pp. 108–14.

for the edifice and the habit of piecemeal adaptation and extension rather than radical renovation remained in tact.

In the case of either the abolition of any of the 70–80 different departments that constituted the civilian and military bureaucracy or the creation of new ones, change was spasmodic and limited. Few developments took place between 1760 and 1782 apart from the creation of a Third Secretaryship of State for the American colonies between 1768 and 1782. There then followed a succession of changes between 1782 and 1794, albeit for a variety of reasons. At the specific request of George III and in order to save money, the functions of the two Secretaryships of State were redefined in 1782 leading to the establishment of the Foreign and Home Offices, the last also having charge of colonial affairs. In the same year, the Council of Trade and Plantations was abolished and replaced two years later by a Committee of the Privy Council for Trade and Plantations which was given the more focussed task of recommending policy on trade matters. In 1784 a Board of Control was created to oversee the executive's input into Indian administration and ten years later, in July 1794, a Secretaryship for War was established to deal with the conflict with France and to accommodate the Portland Whigs who had just joined Pitt's government.

After 1800, two processes can be identified: the abolition of departments and the absorption of their responsibilities into those of others; and the creation of new responsibilities for existing departments, in some cases by forming subsidiary branches. In the case of the first of these, the process was once again, intermittent. In August 1801, responsibility for colonial affairs was transferred from the Home Office to that of the Secretary of State for War, the last soon becoming known as the Colonial Office. From then

until 1830 the principal changes consisted of the abolition of virtually all
the separate Irish departments responsible for military and revenue matters
and the taking up of their duties by the British equivalents.[76] The process
of change on the mainland then quickened. Between 1830 and 1834,
the semi-independent Revenue Department was absorbed into the Treasury
and the ancient Office of Receipt of Exchequer abolished with some of its
functions transferred to a newly created Paymaster of Civil Services.[77]
Similarly, the separate Navy and Victualling Offices were abolished in 1832
and their duties absorbed by the Admiralty Office.[78] By the 1830s the
number of government departments had been trimmed from 75 to 48. On
the other hand, despite consistent pressure to do so, no such streamlining
took place of the various branches of army administration. This had to wait
until 1856.[79]

In the case of the creation of new responsibilities, the changes were more
significant but need to be placed in perspective. Thus, even before the process
got under way in earnest, the scope of the responsibilities of the leading
departments and the numbers of individuals within their spheres of interest
were much greater than the small size of their London staff might suggest.
The Treasury was the outstanding example, with a head office staff of 200 or
less but responsibility for 9 or 10 subsidiary offices employing at its height
some 20,000 officials spread around all parts of Britain and Ireland. The same
was true of the other principal civilian departments as well as the military
ones. In 1829, the Home Secretary and his effective staff of twenty-two were
responsible for the following: law and order in England and Wales, the civil
administration of Scotland, the Isle of Man, the Channel Islands and Ireland;
the stipendiary magistrates of London; the new London police; certain penal
establishments; and the census. Taken as a whole, this brought about 1,000
other officials and public servants under his sphere of influence. Similar points
could be made about the other offices at any time from 1760 onwards.[80]

The creation of new responsibilities was nevertheless a striking feature of
the early nineteenth century. The foundation of the Board of Control led to
Indian affairs falling increasingly under government control and as we have
seen, the Union with Ireland led to British departments taking on most of the
military and revenue business hitherto dealt with Irish departments. It should
also not be forgotten that the Bank Act of 1819 marked the culmination of
the process by which the Bank of England became a virtual department
of state.[81] The most significant changes, however, occurred in the responsibilities of the Board of Trade and the Home Office. In the case of the first,
its original function as a 'think tank' on trade policy was soon overtaken by
the duty of collecting statistics and regulating commerce and trade. In 1821
it was charged with collecting annual returns of corn production and a fully-
fledged Statistical Department was formed before 1832. It was then made
responsible for regulation: of harbours and industrial design, 1835–7; of the
railways, 1840–6 and after 1851; of joint stock companies from 1844; and
the merchant marine from 1850.[82] As for the Home Office, its multifarious

duties were added to in the 1830s by being made responsible, largely at Parliament's rather than its own request, for the work of the commissioners of the New Poor Law, the newly established mines and factory inspectorates, and finally, the borough and county police forces.[83] It was these developments, together, with the establishment in 1839 of a Department of Education under the auspices of the Lord President of the Council, which marked a significant expansion of state responsibilities.

As one might expect, these developments led to a substantial increase in official business. Measuring it is problematic due to the fact that it affected different departments at different times and at different speeds. However, if account is taken of various estimates of increases in the numbers of letters in and out of particular departments and of similar increases in the preparation of accounts and papers for parliamentary scrutiny and of parliamentary bills, it seems likely that the total volume of business doubled between 1760 and 1793, quadrupled between 1793 and 1830 and doubled again between 1830 and 1848.[84]

Another feature of the history of the bureaucracy in this period was the establishment of more efficient working practices coupled with significant changes to the terms of employment for staff. Beginning with the Treasury in 1776 and sustained for the next 60 years by periodic investigation by commissions of enquiry, by departmental heads and by Parliament, all the major offices were subject to substantial overhaul with regard to the processing of business.[85] Two particular developments in this regard might be noted. One was the establishment of the convention that one of the under-secretaries would be a permanent as opposed to a 'political' appointment, thereby encouraging continuity in the management of business. Senior officials who were, in effect, permanent had been a feature of departments before 1760 and remained so afterwards but they were established as such in the Treasury, the Home, Colonial and Foreign Offices, and the Admiralty between 1805 and 1830. Another consisted of the more effective arrangement of functions and the more efficient processing of business. In the first regard, for example, six divisions of business were established in the Treasury in 1782, later reduced to five in 1834. Similar rationalisation took place in the Foreign and Home Offices in the 1790s and these were followed by a fixed distribution of duties among Navy Office commissioners in 1805. In the Colonial Office, each geographical area was supervised by a senior clerk by 1828 and each colony assigned to a particular junior.[86] As for the processing of business, improvements took place in the context of the huge increase in the work of the departments mentioned earlier, particularly in the first half of the nineteenth century. The registering of incoming and outgoing correspondence, for example, became normal practice as did the making of precis; and in the 1780s the first copying machines were developed for Whitehall use, their cost in 1827 being £30.00.[87] Not all departments, however, were up to the mark. The Home Office, for example, did not keep a register of its correspondence until 1841.[88]

In the case of personnel, the principal change took the form of reducing the tendency of regarding office as a form of private property and strengthening the view that it was a form of public service. Both these attitudes of mind had been prevalent before 1760 but two developments led the one to give way largely, if not wholly, to the other. The first was an assault that was initiated in 1780 by North's Commission of Enquiry into the Public Accounts and continued as part of a parliamentary and extra-parliamentary campaign against 'Old Corruption' that lasted until the 1830s. The net effect was the abolition of a substantial number of redundant posts and perks and the strengthening of the view that the holding of office was for the public good.[89] The second consisted of taking steps in every department to abolish the method of paying clerks by a combination of fees and ex-gratia payments and replacing it with a system in which following a probationary year in some cases, clerks progressed up a salary scale and were promoted according to years of service and could look forward to a pension on retirement. This system undoubtedly made for a less political and 'private interest' service but it did not necessarily make it more efficient and imaginative. The purchase of office and payment by fees gave incumbents a measure of independence from ministers and reasons to expedite business quickly. Under the new system, clerks were usually appointed at the very young age of 16–19 and tended to remain at their desks until retirement. This perpetuated a 'clerical' as opposed to an 'intellectual' ethos in the departments which was not effectively challenged until reforms were initiated following comprehensive enquiries in 1848–9.[90]

The final developments that deserve notice were the evolution of a stronger cohesiveness in the operations of the departments coupled with greater accountability to Parliament. In the case of cohesion, this was advanced on a number of fronts: by Whitehall's post-Union control of the Irish revenue and military departments and the absorption of the Scottish Treasury in 1833; by the strengthening of the control of individual departments over others within its sphere of operations as in the case of the Admiralty over the other navy departments; and by ever-increasing exchanges of information and shared responsibilities between and within the departments.[91] The most notable agent of cohesion, however, was the further strengthening of Treasury control over the spending of the other departments. Even in the 1780s, the Younger Pitt had found that the operations of the biggest spending departments – the army, navy and ordnance – were largely immune to Treasury supervision but this changed during and after the French wars.[92] By the early 1840s a substantial increase in Treasury control over the spending of other departments had been secured as a result of successive government initiatives and parliamentary pressure for intelligible accounts, although as enquiries of 1847–8 made clear, it was far from complete.[93] Moreover, this process was complemented by the bringing of all government spending under parliamentary scrutiny. Such scrutiny had declined between 1714 and 1760 but it began to increase in the wake of parliamentary pressure and the findings of the fourteen reports of North's Commission on Public Accounts, 1780–7. Although progress was intermittent, the accounts of *all* departments were subject to close parliamentary scrutiny by the 1830s and the first step had been taken (by the Admiralty in 1832) of a department formally justifying the spending of the money that had been granted the year before. It was not until 1846, however, that the Ordnance and the War Office followed the Admiralty's lead; and 1856 before the practice became general.[94] Nevertheless, these were developments of very considerable significance. The growth of 'Treasury control' undoubtedly gave cohesion to the operations of the civil service and in so doing threatened the authority of Parliament. The fact that it coincided with the development of much closer parliamentary scrutiny of all aspects of government expenditure helped to maintain a balance of power between these two arms of the state.

What impact, then, did this growing, increasingly professional and more accountable bureaucracy have upon the executive? To what extent did the input of officials into executive decision-making change over time? In answering these questions, it is helpful to distinguish between the principal policies pursued by ministers – those likely to have been discussed in cabinet – and the secondary policies and routine business of the departments – those unlikely to be in the forefront of their minds. In the case of the principal policies, the tradition throughout this period appears to have been that ministers shaped them personally with minimal input from their officials other than the supply of information and secretarial assistance. In some cases, they may have counselled with a senior official but in most they relied either upon the views of colleagues or non-departmental advisers or, increasingly, upon the recommendations of parliamentary select committees and statutory or Royal Commissions. The evidence to substantiate the argument is scattered but points strongly in that direction. This includes studies of Barrington's spell as Secretary at War, 1755–61 and 1765–78;[95] of Bute's policies for the American colonies;[96] of Pitt's policies on all fronts, 1784–90;[97] of the first and second Viscount Melville's initiatives as, respectively, minister for India, 1784–1801 and First Lord of the Admiralty, 1812–27;[98] Perceval's Treasury reforms, 1807–12;[99] and in large measure, Peel's at the Home Office, 1822–30.[100] My own study of the Wellington administration, which focused on this point, came to the same conclusion[101] and it is supported by evidence relating to several ministers in the 1830s, most notably, Lord John Russell.[102]

The reasons for this state of affairs are not hard to diagnose. As we have observed, cabinets tended to concentrate on pressing issues and not to plan ahead in any systematic way. This reduced the opportunities for policies maturing within the departments to make much headway in the cabinet. Ministers, for their part, were much more exposed to searching parliamentary scrutiny than they are now. Speeches of more than an hour or so to justify policy became routine and votes turned more on how much the minister knew about his subject than lobby fodder. This also encouraged personal responsibility for the details as well as the general objectives of policy. In addition, the overwhelming weight of evidence points to officials regarding themselves and being regarded as having administrative and clerical functions rather than policy-forming ones. Thus, although there are examples of senior officials acquiring sufficient weight to influence policy in particular departments for specific periods of time, the general complaint by the 1830s and 1840s was that civil servants as a whole had little time for, and little interest in, anything other than routine administrative tasks. The system of promotion by seniority rather than ability and the lack of an effective entrance examination system were identified as causes with the result that reforms were initiated from 1849 in order to encourage a more intellectual and less mechanical input to policy formation. It is also worth noting that recent research on the nearly 500 inspectors created in the 1830s and 1840s to supervise the legislation affecting twelve new areas of central government responsibility such as the New Poor Law, factories and mines, suggests that these also had little impact on policy making.[103]

However, this is only part of the story. The balance of influence between ministers and their officials, which is our main concern here, may not have changed very much but the influence of officials in the wider concerns of the state certainly did. As the period progressed, but particularly after the onset of the French wars in 1793, there was a huge increase in what we might call the execution of secondary policy and routine business coupled with a significant but much more modest increase in the number of officials. In the particular case of business, for example, there was a significant increase in the amount of information that officials were required to accumulate for statutory or parliamentary reasons; and an equivalent increase in the applications made to departments by lobbies and individuals representing an ever-widening range of special and personal interests. This had three results that deserve special mention. The first, was that senior officials in certain departments did acquire a significant influence over the development of policies that while they did not become cabinet issues, were nevertheless important in their own right. This was the case with the advancing of the anti-slavery cause within the Colonial Office in the 1820s and 1830s and that of freer trade by the Board of Trade in the same period.[104] The second was that there was an increase in the exchange of information between the departments and therefore an increase in what might be called a corporate ethos. To give one example: in the 1820s it was customary for trade legislation such as the annual Customs Duties Act to be the result of extensive discussion between the Treasury, its subsidiary departments of customs and excise, the Board of Trade and the revamped consular department of the Foreign Office.[105] Finally, close inspection of the volume and type of pressure applied by interest groups and individuals suggests that the civil service became fully accepted as an integral and important branch of the state as opposed to a self-interested and incompetent drain on its resources. Thus, the voluminous but under-researched evidence of the applications that poured into the offices on a daily basis for favourable treatment or compensation suggests that most not only accepted that the offices should be their first port of call but also that they would be treated to a considered hearing.[106]

Summary and conclusion

When looked at from an institutional perspective, the pace of change in both the functions of the various branches of the executive and in the relationship between them is remarkably slow. By comparison with the first two Hanoverians, the influence of the Crown on the composition of governments and the policies they pursued probably increased during George III's reign, thereby restoring a real partnership between the monarch and his ministers. Its decline only began with his confinement at Windsor in 1810 but its progress was uneven. Between 1827 and 1841, George IV, William IV, and Queen Victoria all sought to maintain an independent role, bolstered in the last two cases, perhaps, by the growing popularity of the monarchy with the public and the tendency to regard it as bulwark against the exercise of excessive aristocratic power. It was only after 1841 that the monarch ceases to be an effective partner in executive government.

The evolution of the premiership follows a similarly chequered course. For most of his reign, George III's active participation in executive business preserved the concept of a first minister and made any pretensions to be a prime minister seem demeaning of his role and unconstitutional. After 1789 and more particularly, after 1793, however, attitudes and practice changed. The King's gradual withdrawal from the permanently active role he had once played and the strains of prolonged war resulted in an equally gradual acceptance that a directing hand or a prime minister was necessary. On the other hand, circumstances worked against prime ministers acquiring the sort of dominance over their colleagues that was once alleged of Walpole. With the exception of 8 months between 1812 and 1841, all the prime ministers sat in the Lords and were therefore not responsible for the budget – one of the centrepieces of government policy. Further, the growth in the size of the cabinet and the related growth of two parliamentary parties in which various factions competed for office meant that prime ministers had to place as much emphasis on management and conciliation as on the direction of policy. In Walpole's time and to some extent in the Younger Pitt's, the term prime minister smacked of 'government by one man alone', the term used by Lord Grenville to describe the premiership of the Younger Pitt, 1804–6. In the 1820s and 1830s, however, the term was used to describe what most accepted to be necessary: the senior party leader acting as chairman of his colleagues.

Much the same trajectory can be observed in the history of the cabinet. Until the turn of the century, the vast majority of the relatively small number of cabinet ministers saw themselves in three different capacities: as personal servants of the King with whom they could discuss privately the business of their own departments; as heads of department who would normally be solely responsible for the policies of that department; and as a member of a cabinet that with the lead of the first minister would give advice to the King on major issues of policy that effected his particular interests and responsibilities. It was this cast of mind that underpinned the practice of a government of departments. In the early nineteenth century, however, a number of developments encouraged a greater sense of loyalty to the cabinet as the principal instrument of government. One was the declining role of the Crown. Another was the enlargement of the cabinet to include all the major departments. And a third was the growth of party. On the other hand, caution has to be exercised when estimating their practical effects on policy making. They certainly led to the strengthening of the concept of collective responsibility but it is doubtful whether they made significant inroads on the practice of government by departments. The Tories and Whigs probably had different approaches in this respect. The Tories of the 1820s and their predecessors had been in power for a considerable period of time and had therefore become accustomed to having a strong directing hand at their head. This may have predisposed them to the more coherent and collective form of government that Wellington sought. Whigs on the other hand, although the pioneers of collective responsibility in 1782, had little experience of cabinet and seem to have preferred a more departmental approach in the 1830s. Thus, although 'cabinet government' made some headway, the alternative of a government of departments was still practised until 1841.

Finally, there is the case of the one branch of the executive where change was startling – the civilian and military departments of state. In these, there was not only a substantial increase in the number of officials but an even more notable increase in the volume of business and the range of responsibilities. In addition, there was a notable change in the ethos of the bureaucracy with the growth of professionalism and the concept of public service. Yet, even in this case caution needs to be exercised when estimating their effect. In general terms, it should be noted that the increases took place at varying speeds and were at their lowest when the responsibilities of the state were growing at their fastest – in the 1830s and 1840s. It is also worth underlining the point that if the ratio of officials to the population is taken as a more accurate measure of bureaucratic growth, there was little change between 1760 and 1848. More particularly, it does not seem that an expanded and more professional bureaucracy led to officials making any significant intellectual or ideological input into executive decision making. By and large ministers were the principal devisors of the major policies of their departments. Officials were left to accumulate information and to conduct the routine business of their offices. On the other hand, we should not underestimate the cumulative effect of officials dealing with the expanding volume of business of this kind. In some cases, it enabled them to forward important policies under the noses of distracted or disinterested ministers. More generally, by collecting information, by listening to a vast array of lobbies, and by dealing with an ever-increasing body of proposals and claims by individuals, it embedded the bureaucracy in the economic, social and political fabric of the state.

6 The scope, purpose and achievements of the executive

In the last chapter it was argued that by comparison with the unprecedented growth in Britain's economy, population and external power, changes to the influence and working practices of the various branches of the executive were relatively modest. Changes to the quantity, scope and purpose of government, however, were more substantial. It is to these that we now turn.

The quantity of government business

As was suggested in the previous chapter, although the changes to the framework of government were modest, the substantial increases in the number of papers registered in the various departments are testimony to an equally substantial increase in government business. This is a point that is supported to some degree by the following statistics relating first, to all public and general legislation; and second, to the number of such bills sponsored wholly or in part by ministers (Tables 6.1 and 6.2).

As these tables demonstrate, not only did the average number of public and general acts passed annually grow substantially between 1760 and 1840 – by about 170% – but the number of these sponsored by ministers was probably never lower than 74% and was as high as 93%. Further, if the numbers of successful bills involving co-operation between ministers and independent members are included, the proportions would be higher – in the case of 1817, considerably so. We can therefore conclude that the executive was responsible for an increasing quantity of legislation. However, the tables also reveal that although there was growth overall, its rate from decade to decade varied and in the case of government legislation, its proportion of the total actually fell. On these points some additional comment is necessary. Thus, Table 6.1 shows that growth was steady between 1760 and 1790, substantial from 1790 to 1820, at which point a decline sets in before a plateau is reached which extends into the 1840s. The exceptional period of growth therefore takes place between 1790 and 1820 and for this there were two causes: the requirements of the French wars and the need to legislate for Ireland following the Union. Approximately, one quarter of such legislation from 1801–20 applied solely to Ireland and if Irish legislation is deducted

Table 6.1 Public and general Acts passed, 1760–1839[a]

Decade, (sessions), [years]	Average per year
1760–1 to 1769–70, (11), [10]	37
1770–1 to 1779–80, (10), [10]	49
1780–1 to 1788–9, (10), [10]	55
1790–9–1800, (12), [11]	85
1800–9, (11), [10]	123
1810–19, (10), [10]	147
1820–9, (10), [10]	104
1830–9, (10), [10]	100

Notes

a The figures for the period 1760–1800 have been calculated by deducting the number of acts designated 'local', 'personal' and 'private' in the *Chronological Table and Index of All the Statutes* from Lambert's figures for 'Public Acts' listed in *Sessional Papers*, vol. 2. I have given averages per year rather than per session because, as can be seen, the length of sessions and their number per decade varied.

Table 6.2 Ministerial legislation, 1772–1839[a]

Year	Successful ministerial bills	Failed ministerial bills	Proportion (%)	Number involving co-operation
1772	40	4	90.9	3
1792	43	3	93.4	7
1817	99	8	92.5	22
1828–30: average per annum	60	15	80	6
1839	78	27	74.2	1

Notes

a These figures were obtained by: (1) by establishing the promoters of all bills for the years selected from the *Lords and Commons Journals*; (2) by determining whether they were in office or not from the biographies of MPs in the relevant *History of Parliament* volumes or from other sources; and (3) tracking the progress of bills in the records of the debates and the *Journals*.

from the total that was passed between 1830 and 1840, the result is not significantly different from that passed immediately before the Union. On this basis, the real rate of growth is better expressed as being steady until the onset of war in 1793 and if the temporary demands of war and the new requirements in Ireland are omitted, modest thereafter. As for the proportion of government-sponsored legislation, Table 6.2 suggests that it falls. This might be accounted for in two ways. First, as we shall see in Chapter 7, there is little doubt that the quantity of legislation sponsored by private members increases in the first half of the nineteenth century. Second, there is the likelihood that the process of administrative rationalisation in the first third of the nineteenth century, which was particularly notable in the Treasury and the Revenue departments, led to fewer government bills, particularly finance bills, being required.

Although the counting of bills can only provide a very partial indicator of government business, the Tables above do suggest three conclusions. First, governments were responsible for an increasing quantity of legislation. Second, if legislation dealing with the French wars and Ireland are taken out of the account, the growth of all forms of legislation between the 1790s and the 1840s was actually modest. And third, the proportion of government-inspired legislation declined after 1820 while that of private members rose.

The scope of government

These observations on the growth of ministerial legislation are a useful reminder of the need to exercise a similar caution when assessing changes in the scope of executive government. It will be recalled that at the time of George III's succession, ministers focussed their attention principally on diplomacy and war, public finance, the regulation of trade, and when required, the maintenance of law and order. Consideration of other matters that were either formally the 'King's business' such as Scotland, Ireland and the colonies, or had principally interested backbenchers such as welfare and legal reform, were only dealt with when the need arose or when individual ministers took a personal initiative. In the case of the principal items it is important to note that all of them retained their importance throughout this period, albeit with some fluctuation in their individual standing. Foreign policy, for example, retained its pre-eminent position until the 1830s when the records suggest that it gave way to domestic reform. One minister said as much.[1] Further, if the contents of ministerial legislation are a reliable guide to executive priorities, all of the others retained their importance. Thus, in each of the years selected for detailed analysis, 1772, 1792, 1817, 1828–30 and 1839, the bulk of government legislation dealt with national finances, the regulation of trade, law and order and military matters.[2]

It is in this context that the expansion of the scope of government – for which the latter part of this period is so famous – takes place. The first examples occurred in the inner and outer empire – Scotland, Ireland and the colonies. In the case of the inner empire it would appear that Scotland rarely engaged the attention of the executive in this period. With its public finances fully incorporated with those of England and Wales, administration was entrusted for a substantial part of this period – from the 1770s to 1830 – to the Dundas family headed by the Viscounts Melville. It was they and the successive Lords Advocate, the principal minister for Scotland in the Commons, who provided effective government. In general terms this took the form of respecting the distinctive features of Scottish ecclesiastical, legal and municipal institutions and otherwise subduing aristocratic rivalries, appointing effective officials, and filling in by legislation some of the administrative gaps left by the Union Treaty. From a Scottish perspective it has been argued that the 'Dundas Despotism' led to a form of 'semi-independence' from Westminster.[3] From a Westminster perspective, it meant that Scottish affairs rarely troubled ministers and that following the full establishment of the Dundas regime at the end of the 1770s, an increased but nevertheless small and static number of Scottish bills passed through Parliament every year. Some of these were dedicated to assimilating Scottish legal processes with that of England and an increasing proportion were based on extensive consultation with Scottish MPs and interest groups. Although the Dundas hegemony came to an end with the formation of a Whig administration in 1830, it would appear that the system of semi-independence continued thereafter.[4]

Ireland, on the other hand, became a subject of regular executive concern from the 1770s onward. Prior to the Union the focus of this concern was to maintain through the Lord Lieutenant and his Chief Secretary the predominant interest in the Irish Parliament with a view to securing decisions that suited British requirements. These were a ready supply of troops for the wars with the American colonies and subsequently with France, many of whom were Catholic; trade policies which did not conflict with those of Britain; and a kingdom that would be ready to resist a French invasion. Successive British governments therefore sought compliance from a majority of the Protestant propertied elite with policies that they hoped might suit these ends – a hope frustrated by the internal momentum of Irish politics and a series of crises in Anglo-Irish relations. These took place principally in 1780–4 over Irish demands for free trade, legislative independence and in the wake of the latter's concession, an abortive commercial settlement; in 1792–5 over concessions to Catholics; and ultimately in 1798–1800, over the causes of the Rebellion and the British government's preferred consequence – the Union. It was these crises which led to Irish issues playing a much more prominent role in executive deliberations than hitherto.

After the Union, the means of governing Ireland changed. The posts of Lord Lieutenant and Chief Secretary were retained but in due course the fiscal and military responsibilities of the Irish administration were brought under the direct control of the British departments of state. On the fiscal side, the first major step was taken in 1816 when the Irish and British revenue departments were consolidated and the Irish Treasury absorbed into the British, albeit with seats provided for Irish representatives. Thereafter the process quickened. Between 1823 and 1827 the consolidation of the Irish and British customs, excise and stamp departments took place or got under way; and the responsibilities of the Irish departments dealing with Crown lands placed under the care of the Whitehall commissioners of the Royal Woods, Forests and Land Revenues. In 1831–2 the separate Irish Post Office disappeared and the remnants of the accounting offices were placed under the supervision of the British commissioners of Public Accounts. As for the military side of the equation, the unification of the respective command and administrative systems had been decided upon soon after the Union and the process reached its conclusion in the 1820s with the abolition of the five remaining responsible Irish departments.

The development of what was, in retrospect, the most substantial extension of executive authority since the late seventeenth century and the Union with Scotland, coincided with another that although it moved in an opposite direction in terms of where responsibility was placed, impinged with increasing frequency on the ministerial consciousness. It was principally concerned with economic development, welfare, education and policing, and took the form of establishing institutions for their promotion under the authority of the Lord Lieutenant. Ten boards of commissioners answerable to the Lord Lieutenant were constituted between 1801 and 1841 to promote economic development, public health, education and sundry other matters, including the reform of the Church of Ireland; and various new bodies of police were established under his authority in 1814, 1822 and 1836.[5]

How far these developments led to Ireland becoming a more prominent subject of executive concern is difficult to assess. The Union certainly led to a significant increase in legislation, most of which was sponsored by ministers. Between 1801 and 1816, Irish legislation accounted for about a quarter of the total before declining to about 17% in the 1830s as a result of measures pertaining to finance, trade and the military being dealt with in UK acts. However, although its quantity was significantly greater than Scottish legislation, much of it flowed from an equivalent degree of consultation with Irish MPs and other interested parties, and proved to be comparatively uncontroversial. Routine Irish legislation, therefore, rarely became a matter for executive discussion. The Catholic question, on the other hand, which in its broadest sense meant giving Catholics political equality with Protestants and dealing with their social and economic grievances, undoubtedly did. Until 1828 the flagship of the Catholic cause, the right to sit in Parliament, was effectively put on the back burner for all but a few months in 1806–7 as a result of royal disapproval of its consideration and it being officially designated an 'open' question for ministers between 1812 and 1827. O'Connell's election for Co. Clare in July 1828, however, changed all that. Enabling Catholics to sit in Parliament and the terms on which the Protestant interest would be protected at future elections were the chief topics of consideration in the Wellington government between 1828 and 1829. Further, the combination of O'Connell's campaign for a repeal of the Union, 1830–4, the tithe war of the same years, and his pledging of the support of his Irish parliamentary following to the Whig government in 1835 ensured that Irish policy was a prominent executive issue throughout the 1830s; and continued to be so in the 1840s.[6]

The government of the colonies, on the other hand, appeared on the executive agenda far less frequently. At first sight this seems, to say the least, surprising. As has been noted above, this was a period of substantial colonial expansion in the 1760s, dramatic contraction with the loss of the American colonies in 1782, and extraordinary expansion thereafter, leading to the position of Britain being responsible for in excess of one-quarter of the world's population by 1820.[7] It was also a period when the concept of a British empire, only tentatively conceived in the 1760s, became firmly established by the 1790s and was commonplace thereafter.[8]

Admittedly, there was one occasion when the general issue of colonial government appears to have been given serious consideration and others when specific developments and issues either promised or attracted sustained attention. In the case of colonial government as a whole, a number of historians have argued that there was a co-ordinated attempt to tighten the existing means of control in the immediate aftermath of the end of the Seven Years War but as one of its results was the revolt of the American colonies, it does not appear to have been followed through.[9] As for specific developments, the establishment of the India Board in 1784 and the evolution of the Colonial Office after 1802 gave a greater focus for colonial administration and more prominent representation in cabinet but it is doubtful whether these led to colonial issues being a regular subject for discussion. Thus, although there was a modest increase in the quantity of colonial legislation in the 1760s which was sustained at a more or less static level thereafter, the evidence points to colonial policy consisting primarily of reactions to specific problems.[10] It was only then that they received concerted government attention. The only exception would seem to be the campaign against slavery after 1815 – and until 1830 that was more of a departmental than a government initiative.

The most notable expansion of the scope of government, however, was the result of the executive becoming responsible for a variety of services and functions hitherto left to local authorities, private institutions and the legislative initiatives of independent MPs. Most of them were designed to improve the welfare of the poor by overseeing the conditions of emigration and factory work, and the provision of education, poor relief and health, but they also dealt with other matters. One of these – the establishment of police forces – is usually included in accounts of the expansion but two others which are not are worthy of inclusion. One was a much greater involvement in the regulation of religious sects and the other was a greater readiness to adjust the system of parliamentary and municipal representation to suit political ends – a subject not touched by governments since the Septennial Act of 1716.

Although the causes of the extension of government into these areas will be discussed in more detail later, there are two general points that it is useful to make here. The first is that it has been argued persuasively that in England the view that Parliament should enact 'national solutions to national problems' was given a considerable boost in the 1770s by the work of a number of philanthropic reformers on such matters as poverty, prison conditions and infant mortality.[11] At that time it was felt best that such solutions were left to the initiative of independent legislators rather than governments but as statistical evidence of the extent of the problems mounted, it is easy to see why the view that the executive should take the initiative might develop. The second is that Ireland provided an example of central government provision. At the time of the Union, the Irish administration and the Irish Parliament already made annual grants for the Catholic seminary of Maynooth as well as a number of Protestant charter schools. In addition, two Boards sponsored inland navigation and public works. Moreover, as we have seen, further boards were established after the Union to promote public health, education and employment, with police forces being established and then extended under the ultimate authority of the Lord Lieutenant in 1814 and 1822. Ireland therefore not only provided an example of state intervention to English observers – nearly £2.5 million was spent on road building and public works alone between 1823 and 1828;[12] it was also an example familiar to several key figures in British government in the 1820s and 1830s. Most notably, Peel, Lord Lansdowne, Thomas Spring Rice and Lord Melbourne.

With regard to the details of expansion, we might begin with the subjects on the margins of what became formal and continuous 'executive responsibility' – political representation and religion. In the case of politics, the first example of governmental intervention in the system of parliamentary representation since 1716 took place in 1800 when Pitt and his colleagues devised the ways that the Irish peerage and populace would be represented at Westminster. The peers therefore selected 28 of their own number with the voters in the 32 counties, 33 towns and cities and Trinity College, Dublin electing the 100 MPs. In the case of the towns and cities, they were largely selected on the basis of their population and wealth. The next example was also Irish. Thus, in addition to the 1829 act that enabled Catholics of whatever nationality to sit in Parliament, the government also disfranchised the vast majority of the Irish electorate which happened to be poor and Catholic in order to establish more of a balance between Protestant and Catholic interests at elections. By the terms of the Qualification of Freeholders Act (1829), the Irish electorate therefore fell from about 200,000 to 40,000 voters.

These two examples of political engineering preceded the most famous interventions – the English and Welsh, Scottish and Irish Reform Acts of 1832 and the Municipal Reform Acts of 1835 (England and Wales) and 1840 (Ireland). The first, based on the principles of representing constituencies according to their population and wealth and enfranchising middle-class men occupying houses valued as being worth £10 a year, had their biggest impact in Britain. In England and Wales 56 boroughs were disfranchised and another 31 had their number of seats reduced. 41 substantial towns returned members for the first time and 67 additional seats were created for existing constituencies or divisions of such. The total electorate rose by about 50% to 656,000. As for Scotland there were 8 extra seats allocated to a new list of grouped burghs and the electorate rose much more dramatically: from a mere 3,800 to nearly 66,000. The second (Municipal Reform), based on the similar principal of enfranchising the middle classes, created an electorate of £10 ratepayers for reformed town councils. Although none of these measures required any permanent expansion of the scope of government – indeed the first Reform Bills were said to be 'final' – it is hard to resist the conclusion that taken together they represented an acknowledgement that central government should add political reform to its agenda.

A similar case may be made about religion. Governments had traditionally regarded the condition of the Church of England and its protection as one of its responsibilities and throughout the eighteenth century there was a steady trickle of ministerial legislation designed for those purposes. In the late eighteenth and early nineteenth centuries, however, the issue became more urgent as a result of the pressure for equal political rights from Dissenters and Catholics and the failure of the Established Church to adapt to urbanisation and the pressure for internal reform. This had two results. The first was that the issues of 'relief' for Catholics and Dissenters emerged high on the agenda of governments between 1828 and 1836 and led, *inter alia*, to the repeal of the Test and Corporation Acts (1828), the Catholic Relief Act (1829) and at the request of the Dissenters' representatives, the civil registration of births, marriages and deaths (1836). The second was increasing attention by successive governments to the internal reform of the Church of England and the supporting of its efforts in both Britain and Ireland to bring its message to where it was least heard. A series of measures to these ends was promoted after 1800, culminating in attempts in the 1830s to reform the Church of Ireland and in acts relating to England which extended to 1843 and led to the commutation of tithe, the building of new churches and the elimination of abuses. It is also important to note that some of these measures led to the establishment of permanent government offices. This was the case with an 1818 act for the building of new churches; and those providing for Civil Registration and Tithe commutation. By 1850 the last two consisted of 57 and 23 staff, respectively.

Although there were sundry cases of expansion in the formation of a Public Works Loan Office (1817), an Industrial Designs Office (1839) and a Board of Commissioners for the Railways with a staff 19 (1840), the principal areas were in policing and welfare. In the case of policing, we have already noted the establishment of police forces in Ireland under the authority of the Lord Lieutenant in 1814 and 1822 but the equivalent in England took longer to implement. In fact, as far as government was concerned the key issue was the system of 'discretionary justice' that according to one authority was at its height between 1740 and 1820.[13] This had the following features. First, the existence of harsh penalties for crime, the application of which was left to the discretion of local elites, usually following extensive negotiation with other social groups. Second, the tradition that prosecutions could only be brought privately at the prosecutors' expense. And third, a reliance upon unpaid magistrates representative of the elites to try offences, the number that they could try summarily and without an indictment being restricted. The emphasis was therefore placed upon prosecution rather than prevention; and upon responsibility for applying the law resting essentially with local elites rather than the central government.

In due course, however, the state began to acquire a more controlling influence. Parliament increased the range of offences that magistrates could deal with summarily from the mid-eighteenth century and this process accelerated in the 1830s. Further, in response to a decline in the supply and calibre of magistrates, the Pitt government established the principal of paid or stipendiary magistrates for Middlesex in 1792 and after this had been taken up by several other local authorities before 1830, the number who did so increased rapidly thereafter. Finally, following a series of enabling acts passed between 1752 and 1818, Peel's Criminal Justice Act of 1826 compelled the courts to award expenses to prosecutors and their witnesses. Collectively, these led to a steady increase in the number and type of offences that went to trial and a decline in those dealt with in some other, discretionary, way.[14]

The view that responsibility for policing should rest with the responsible citizenry of the localities was also at the heart of the argument for and against the establishment of full-time, uniformed and paid police. The argument against was that they could become an instrument of state oppression. The process by which they were established therefore reflects the enduring force of that argument. Although small numbers of paid police officers had existed in London before and after Pitt's act of 1792, which established them formally, a major step was taken in 1829 with Peel's establishment of the Metropolitan Police under the authority of the Home Office. These replaced the watch and took over some of the duties of the traditional constables. Peel's act, however, was untypical. Thus, three other acts passed or inspired by the Wellington government, 1828–30 – one each for Ireland, England and Wales, and Scotland – left the initiative for establishing more effective policing with what have been called 'ratepayers' democracies' – stated numbers of householders and ratepayers.[15] Further, although some thought was given by Grey's government to the extension of Peel's model throughout England, the idea was dropped in favour of legislation later in the 1830s allowing the reformed town councils and counties to establish their own forces on similar lines if they so wished. It was not until 1856 that an act was passed which obliged local authorities to do so and made a Treasury grant available to help in the process. Thus, although it was the case that successive governments became convinced of the necessity of professional police forces and took steps to establish them, the extension of central authority was limited in Britain to the Metropolitan Police. Otherwise, the initiative was left until 1856 to first, 'ratepayers' democracies' and subsequently, to local authorities.

In the case of the larger and more complex subject of welfare, responsibility was extended by statute and made continuous either by annual grants or inspection, or a combination of the two. The principal examples are well known and can be usefully summarised as follows:

1 Emigration. Between 1803 and 1842 and particularly as a result of a government act of 1828, the Colonial Office began to supervise the conditions on emigrant ships. In 1842 a Passenger Act established agents responsible to the Colonial Office for ensuring that specified types of accommodation and rations were provided. By 1850 there were 3 commissioners, 1 secretary and 16 port agents in a specially created Colonial Land and Emigration Board, 9 being in Ireland.

2 Conditions of work and types of workers allowed in factories and mines. Building on independent member legislation of 1802 and 1818, government acts of 1833, 1842, 1847 and 1850 restricted the employment of women and children and the hours of work, principally in textile factories and mines. Inspectors were appointed to ensure compliance. By 1850 a small central office of six staff and inspectors had been established within the Home Office with 16 sub-inspectors in the field.

3 Education. By a clause of the Factory Act of 1833, education was to be provided for children working in textile factories. In the same year the first government grant of £20,000 for the education of working-class children was made to two educational charities and a committee on Education for England and Wales was established within the Privy Council to oversee its spending. By 1850, the annual grant had risen to £125,000 and the committee had 8 members, an assistant secretary and 23 inspectors.

4 Poverty. The Poor Law Amendment Act of 1834 provided relief only to those who entered a workhouse after passing a stringent 'workhouse test'. Parishes were to be united into Unions and Union workhouses substituted for parish workhouses, to be run by elected boards of guardians. A Poor Law Board was established at Somerset House that in 1850 had 5 commissioners, 13 inspectors and about 50 secretaries, clerks and other staff.

5 Public health. A Public Health Act of 1848 allowed local boards of health to be established with power to appoint medical officers of health. A small General Board was established in Whitehall consisting of a Chief Commissioner, two chairmen and three secretaries.

When assessing the significance of these developments, it is important to remember that many of these functions and services had been provided well before central government took some responsibility for them. Policing, workhouses, poor relief, hospitals and schools for the children of the poor had all existed during part or all of the eighteenth century. Moreover the first steps to control conditions in factories and emigrant ships, in 1802 and 1803, preceded government intervention by twenty-five years or more. What was different was that before the late 1820s in Britain, if not Ireland, provision rested with local authorities and private institutions and was regulated, if at all, by legislation promoted by independent MPs.

That said, there is no denying that the assumption of responsibility by central government, principally from the late 1820s until the 1840s, represented a significant expansion in the scope of government. Taken as a whole, 11 boards and sub-departments were created between 1817 and 1850 by which time they were under the charge of more than 50 commissioners and employed about 175 functionaries and 73 inspectors. On the other hand, the significance should not be exaggerated. The new commissioners and officials constituted only a small fraction of the total number of civil servants, the bulk of whom were still employed in the revenue and military departments. Further, all but one of the new boards and offices were placed under the overall responsibility of the existing principal departments of state, thereby underlining their incorporation into the existing machinery of government rather than heralding a new departure. The exception was the Poor Law Board that had commissioners drawn from several of the existing departments (as well as from none) and which was therefore unique in having a virtually autonomous existence. However, even this is less significant than it might seem. It has therefore been shown that a substantial proportion of Poor Law commissioners (in the region of 33%) were drawn from aristocratic and gentry families, thereby ensuring that in the management of the Board there was some continuity with past practices with regard to relief.[16] Finally, caution should be exercised when assessing the impact of the new inspectors. It has therefore been argued that in the case of factory and mines inspectors in particular, their number was too small and the problems of law enforcement too intractable for them to have much impact either as enforcers of the law or as agents of increasing government control.[17]

How far then did the scope of executive government change and at what pace? To what extent does it merit being called revolutionary? The argument presented so far mirrors that of the previous chapter on the framework of government: change there certainly was but it took the form of additions to traditional functions not their replacement. Foreign policy, national finances, trade regulation, the armed forces and law and order continued to be the staple items on the executive agenda. What happened was a process of accretion which was more drawn out than it is sometimes supposed. It began in the 1760s with the colonies, continued in the 1770s with Ireland and strengthened in the first three decades of the nineteenth century with the full force of direct responsibility for Ireland and the pressures for political and religious reform. This was the long prelude to a more concentrated and extensive phase of expansion, the impact of which, it has been argued, was less significant than was once supposed. There was some continuity and some change, the case for continuity being underlined by the fact that government-inspired legislation for Britain was only marginally greater in quantity in the late 1830s than it had been in the late 1790s. However, as anyone familiar with committee meetings might agree, an analysis based on the topics of executive discussion and the institutional contexts in which they take place may say something about the scope of government but little about the factors that shaped policy. It is to these that we now turn.

The assumptions and priorities of policy

We may begin with the *general* principles and priorities that underpinned the outlook of ministers on the purpose, scope and practice of government. In Chapter 2, it was argued that before 1760 most ministers subscribed to the following list. First, that a mixed or balanced constitution provided the best form of government. Second, that full participation in public affairs should rest in the hands of those who were both Anglican and owners of real property. And third, that central government should not intrude on the authority and responsibilities of local institutions. This rested on the view that the primary purpose of government was to defend the King's dominions, to raise money for that purpose, to protect trade and industry, to secure the rights of property and to maintain law and order. All other matters, such as the provision of education, poor relief, health and policing, should be left to the legislative initiatives of independent members and the care of the local authorities and voluntary agencies.

As is clear from the expansion of the scope of government outlined earlier, there certainly were changes to this list and before assessing them it is important to place them in context. Starting in the 1770s, there was a remarkable growth of interest in reform, that, in so far as it impinged on the business of central government, took three inter-related forms.[18] One was philosophical and theoretical in content and consisted principally of distinguished works by a series of writers from David Hume to John Stuart Mill. To analyse their conclusions in any detail here would take us beyond the boundaries of this study but the following points are relevant. It has been shown, for example, that from the 1780s the terms 'the state' and 'the government' (as opposed to 'the administration') become increasingly referred to by theorists as entities that might, or should, act beneficially for all.[19] Somewhat surprisingly, however, with the exception of Bentham, this did not lead to any significant diagnosis of the institutions and machinery of government. Rather, the majority of theorists were content to accept the virtues of a balanced constitution and that the fundamental purpose of government was the defence of property. Instead, their thinking was dominated by the rise of commerce and industry and the question of how best the existing system could accommodate the new economic and social interests that they spawned. Hume and Adam Smith argued that such interests would be driven by self-interest and that if this went unregulated, it would work in favour of order, good government and the liberty and security of individuals. In the course of the latter eighteenth and early nineteenth centuries, however, this optimistic proposition came to be challenged. Dugald Stewart, the influential political economist at Edinburgh University, argued that the regulation of self-interest was required to secure the ends that Smith envisaged. Jeremy Bentham proposed that the object of good government was the greatest happiness of the greatest number and produced quasi-scientific means for its achievement. Macaulay, on the other hand, scorned scientific method and argued that the renovation of existing institutions was all that was required for the maintenance of good government.[20] It has also been argued with some force that an Evangelical Christian political economy had emerged by the 1830s that supported intervention by government in those areas where the play of unfettered market forces had led to distress. According to some historians, this became the dominant ideology amongst politicians by mid-century.[21]

The other forms were less philosophical and more directly related to the realities of contemporary politics. One of these consisted of a critique of the waste and corruption to be found in the machinery of central government and a demand for its elimination. Implicit in this demand was the view that public office should not be seen as a form of private property but rather as a matter of public trust. Inspired, in all probability, by the example of reputable and efficient standards of administration established through the Court of Equity by private middle-class institutions in the 1750s and 1760s, the political movement took root in the 1770s as a result of Lord North's enthusiasm for more efficient and less costly government and the Whigs' conviction that 'Old Corruption' was sustaining his administration in office.[22] The campaign then grew in strength and fuelled by the growth of bureaucracy that accompanied the French wars, attracted strong support from Whigs, radicals and independent MPs – so much so that the ending of 'Old Corruption' became one of the dominant political issues up to 1830. It has also been shown that most of its objectives had been achieved by that time.[23]

The other, which was more or less contemporary with it, was the demand for parliamentary reform. The basic propositions here were that the existing borough constituencies did not reflect the current distribution of the urban population and that the ancient franchises that created the electorate excluded large numbers who were equally deserving of the vote. A movement for parliamentary reform based initially outside Parliament was founded in the 1760s and grew, albeit with troughs and peaks, until it met with success in 1832. It was then revived in the late 1830s in the form of Chartism.

How far the proliferation of theory and the growing appetite for reform influenced practical politicians is, of course, very difficult to assess. That it had an impact on some of the leading figures seems incontrovertible. Dean Tucker and more particularly, Adam Smith, are said to have had a strong influence on Shelburne, the Younger Pitt and Lords Grenville and Liverpool, with Pitt and Grenville also being keen readers of Locke and Blackstone.[24] Dugald Stewart influenced many of the Whigs in senior positions in the 1830s such as Palmerston, Melbourne, Russell, Baring and Lansdowne;[25]

while Thomas Chalmers, the leading apologist for Christian political economy, had a similar impact not only on some of those but also on senior Tories such as Peel and Sir James Graham as well as a large number of influential backbenchers of differing political viewpoints.[26] Even Bentham, whose ideology was too mechanical and laborious for most, was counselled in his later years by Brougham and Peel.[27] Moreover, it is notable that new and influential political journals were founded in the early nineteenth century such as the *Edinburgh* and *Quarterly Reviews*; that it became commonplace for ambitious politicians to seek advice from their seniors on what to read to prepare themselves for advancement; and that the writing of historical or philosophical works by would-be or senior politicians increased.[28] Although comparisons are difficult to make, it seems likely that theories of government had a greater impact on the thinking and practice of the two generations of politicians who governed Britain from the 1780s to the 1840s than it did on their predecessors.

It was in this context that the general assumptions of senior politicians about the scope and purpose of government evolved. In the case of the virtues of the mixed constitution, one of the central points of the traditional list, there was little change. Virtually all cabinet members of this period endorsed them. This is not surprising. All were participants in the system and beneficiaries of it. Further, there was a significant increase from the later eighteenth century in studies of the constitution that tended to praise its evolutionary history. In so far as there was an argument amongst politicians, it was more about the evenness of the balance between King, Lord and Commons, rather than the advantages of their being one.[29] It is also significant that few theorists of government were hostile to the concept of a balance.

On the other hand, the view that participation in politics depended on the possession of property did undergo amendment. The crucial issue here was parliamentary representation, the terms of which obliged both MPs and most if not all voters to possess various amounts of property. In addition, the concept of the constituencies themselves representing different types of property was firmly rooted – so much so that that those that had decayed or even disappeared over time were still regarded by their proprietors as a personal possession. As we have seen, legislation was enacted in 1800, 1829 and 1832, in the last case by a combination of party commitment and public pressure, which aligned the Irish and British constituencies much more closely with centres of population and by doing so did away with rights of representation possessed by the proprietors of small boroughs. On the other hand, the property qualifications for MPs and electors were maintained, the former only being abolished in 1858 and the latter not being entirely done away with until 1918. Indeed, there is a strong case for arguing that the property qualification for electors was strengthened by its increase to £10 for Irish freeholders in 1829 and the establishment of a £10 householder rate for new borough voters in Britain in 1832.

There were more substantial changes to the other parts of the traditional canon. In the case of support for the Anglican monopoly in Parliament and of the holding of office, this was eroded by a number of factors: a growing liberal sentiment in Parliament; steady pressure from organised Dissent and Catholicism that culminated in the late 1820s; and by their identification with significant social and economic interests that were thought worthy of being incorporated into the political system. Dissenters and Catholics were incorporated as a result of external pressure in 1828 and 1829 and Jews in 1852.

This process coincided with a growing acceptance that the machinery of government should be made more efficient and less liable to charges of corruption; and that its scope should be expanded. In the case of the former, the principal steps taken by successive governments have already been traced but it is important to re-emphasise the point that most had occurred by the 1830s. In the case of the latter, the key word is 'expanded'. As mentioned above, the predominant view before 1760 was that the scope of government should be limited – essentially to foreign policy, national and colonial defence, the raising of money for these purposes, the protection of trade and industry, the protection of property, and the maintenance of law and order. These priorities did not disappear. They remained high on the agenda. What happened was the addition of other responsibilities. Theory undoubtedly played some part in this process but more influential, perhaps, were the changes taking place around ministers and the huge growth in their own and the public's knowledge of them through the press and official and independent enquiries. A particularly significant aspect of this was the apparent congealing of class interests in the early nineteenth century and the threat this posed to a society supposedly held together by vertical ties between innumerable ranks, orders and degrees.

This had different results. One, the assumption of a degree of responsibility for policing and welfare has already been adumbrated but it is worth remembering that this only became a fixture in the executive mentality in the 1830s. Hitherto, most senior politicians shared the view of the Younger Pitt that the best promoters of welfare and improvement were not the functionaries of the state but the voluntary association.[30] However, there was another that needs to be included, namely that government began to take regular account of public opinion. For most of the eighteenth century, governments dealt with public opinion on an exceptional and occasional basis, the nearest they came to dealing with it more regularly being the respect shown for the views of the independent county members on the backbenches in the Commons – the supposed barometers of opinion in the country. Starting, perhaps, in the 1790s when the Younger Pitt took steps to encourage loyalism on a massive scale, it soon became axiomatic that governments had to take regular note of public opinion even if they chose to do nothing about it. A classic illustration of the two different approaches is Wellington's refusal to respond to the growth of support for parliamentary reform in 1830 and Lord Grey's argument to William IV in 1831 that public opinion made an extensive measure of reform essential. Wellington as much as Grey was aware of the force of public opinion but took the view that it should not necessarily dictate what governments did.[31]

These continuities and changes in the general assumptions and priorities that underpinned approaches to government were accompanied by similar developments affecting specific areas of policy. We may begin with foreign policy, which for most of this period was regarded in executive circles as the most important function of government. Until 1815, there was considerable continuity in the fundamentals of policy. As in the earlier period, the principal theme was opposition to France and the principal areas of strategic interest thought to be the Low Countries, Hanover and the Baltic, from which much of the timber for British shipping came until the 1790s and in 1800, 75% of grain imports. In addition, there developed after 1763 a greater readiness to support the old allies of Portugal and the Netherlands (Holland). As for the means of defending these interests, they were once again of a traditional kind. In the case of military force, overwhelming naval power was the objective coupled with the capacity to augment the army to a size sufficient to act as an auxiliary to one or more of the great continental powers in times of conflict. As for diplomacy, this was directed, as before, to a search for alliances: on the one hand to maintain a balance of power and to prevent war breaking out; and on the other, to combine continental armies with British sea power in order to win if that stratagem failed. Between 1763 and the mid-1780s, the search for a suitable alliance was unsuccessful, largely as a result of an inability to realise that the preferred targets, the Habsburg Empire and Russia, had other priorities in eastern Europe. Alliances with Holland and Prussia in 1787–8, however, put diplomacy back on its traditional tracks – a development reinforced by the outbreak of war with France in 1793.[32]

This continuity in diplomatic and strategic thinking was challenged by the conclusion of the war in 1815 and by post-war domestic priorities. The military victory put an end to the French threat in the medium term and the Vienna settlement provided a new basis for a balance of power and new mechanisms to maintain it. In particular, the establishment of the independence of the united Low Countries of Holland and Belgium under allied guarantee provided Britain with greater security in that quarter than she had ever possessed in the eighteenth century. Other changes to Britain's position also took place. Broadly speaking, concern for the future in western and central Europe (including Hanover and the Baltic) declined but grew in the case of eastern Europe and America, particularly south America with which trade had increased substantially. The principal changes, however, affected the economy and domestic politics. After 1815 Britain became dependent on foreign food and materials to feed her growing population and to keep it in work. The logical requirement, therefore, was for freer channels of trade that would generate the expansion that could provide the revenue to pay for imported foodstuffs. In the meantime, the huge costs of the war required severe retrenchment in national expenditure while demobilisation fuelled a rising tide of middle class and plebeian political discontent.

The upshot was that the priorities of foreign policy began to change. Instead of a search for European alliances in order to maintain a balance of power and to defend Britain's western European strategic interests, it made better sense to resist any revision of the Vienna settlement and otherwise, avoid any binding agreements. What was required was 'a free hand': first, because this best suited Britain's worldwide interests; and second, because the state of the economy and the volatile state of domestic politics warned against becoming involved in any further costly European wars. A symbol of these priorities was the establishment of a new naval strategy. In 1817 Lord Castlereagh set a 'two-power' standard for the navy which was to last for the rest of the century: the British fleet would always be equal in size to the next two in the premier league.[33] An immediate result of them was treaties with foreign powers designed to settle specific problems – for example, with France, Spain and Portugal over the Iberian Peninsula (1834); with all the major powers over Belgium (1839); and with the United States over the boundary with Canada (1846).

The changes in the priorities of foreign policy coincided (and were linked) to changes in those affecting national finances. Throughout the period to 1815, the principal objectives of successive chancellors of the Exchequer were substantially the same. At the head of the list was the reduction of the national debt: either by ingenious schemes for its long-term reduction; or by reducing current interest payments; and sometimes by a combination of the two. This provided the 'badge of good faith' that creditors and the financial community required to maintain their confidence and their money in the system – a confidence threatened by the abandoning of the gold standard in 1797. Second was the maintenance of a system of colonial and international customs duties (tariffs) designed to protect British and colonial producers from unwanted competition and, of course, to raise revenue. Indeed, the colonial preference system was reinforced in 1764 and 1783–6. And third, was resort to a system of direct and indirect taxation designed to raise revenue, to regulate internal trade, and to deal reasonably equitably with the different social groups. In the case of direct taxes, the mainstay was the land tax until 1799 when an emergency wartime income tax was added which lasted until 1816. In the case of the indirect variety, there was a substantial number aimed principally at hitting hardest those with the means to pay them.

The changes were concentrated in the immediate post-war years. In the case of the national debt, the huge increase in borrowing brought about by the war led to the abandonment of any hope of paying it off – a step symbolised by the decision to allow Pitt's Sinking Fund to die a quiet death in 1828. Debt redemption as the government's badge of good faith to the financial community therefore disappeared and was replaced in 1821 by a restored gold standard. This, together with an increasing control by government of the Bank of England which culminated in the Bank Charter Act of 1844, brought the money supply to the forefront of policy-makers' minds as regulators of the economy.[34] As for tariffs, the situation was complicated by Lord Liverpool's government being forced by Parliament to impose what were hoped to be permanently high duties on imported corn in 1815. The crucial issue, however, was the need to import food for a growing population as well as materials for an expanding manufacturing economy. The increase in revenue that might accrue from the expansion of trade in manufactured goods would pay for imported food. Instead of maintaining a system of protection, the priority became its progressive dismantling – a process which was completed in 1849. Finally, there is the question of taxation. In the case of indirect taxes, there was not such an immediate shift in priorities, although they eventually became regarded as a way of reducing class conflict. Direct taxation, however, was another matter. In 1816 the government was forced by Parliament to abandon the income tax. From then until 1842, when it was restored, the issue of whether to impose an income tax was prominent in the thinking of successive governments – something that had never been seriously considered as a permanent addition to revenue in the eighteenth century.[35]

There were also changes in the assumptions and priorities that underpinned the approach to empire in both its home and overseas forms. For most of the eighteenth century the essence of empire for the English was not external dominion for its own sake but security in the case of Scotland and Ireland and trade in the case of the overseas empire. Changes took place, however, as a result of the assumption of direct rule in Ireland and the expansion, contraction and further expansion of the overseas empire after 1763, 1783 and 1793. In the case of the domestic empire, the Irish Union and the defeat of Napoleon removed the prospect of invasion by the back door aided and abetted by Irish insurgents. Instead, the priority became the settlement of the historic enmities of Catholic and Protestant on terms that maintained the Union and the maintenance of law and order. This, in turn, raised questions about how far the governing of Ireland in political, economic and social terms could be assimilated with that of Britain.

As for the overseas empire, there seems to have been a shift from the concentration on trade to a focus on forms of government and administration. This was due in part to a decline in the importance of the imperial branch of Britain's overseas trade. Between 1783 and 1812, for example, 83% of the increase in the value of Britain's exports was accounted for by trade with Europe and the Americas, although the West Indies are included in this computation.[36] Another factor was the difficulties thrown up by existing forms of government as in the West Indies over the subject of slavery or, recurrently between 1774 and 1839, in Canada over the competing claims of French and British settlers. Perhaps the most crucial cause, however, was the proliferation within the empire, most notably in India, of a corps of British administrators who took with them a determination to impose the 'institutions and ideologies' that they admired at home and which have been identified with the Younger Pitt. The most notable of these was the drive for honest and efficient administration. This constituted a form of 'constructive authoritarian and ideological imperialism' which, having been exported at one remove from the executive from the 1780s onwards, made its way onto the executive agenda after 1815.[37]

In other areas of policy there was a mixture of continuity and change. Military policy is an example. For most of the eighteenth century, the standard assumption with regard to strategy was that as a maritime power emphasis had to be placed on the capacity of the navy to defeat enemy fleets in sea battles and to capture overseas territories as bargaining chips or permanent acquisitions. This meant that in a continental land war, Britain should only act as an auxiliary to her European allies: providing an army that although enhanced, was smaller than those of the other major powers, and otherwise, troops hired from minor states. Indeed such was the lesser priority given to the army, that it was not the custom to plan its campaigns in advance. The upshot was that the total number of marines and troops rose and fell according to demand, the view being that a peacetime army of more than a modest size was a threat to civil government and individual liberties. On the other hand, there is no doubt that the average size of peacetime forces grew over time although it is important not to exaggerate its extent. In the 1720s the average number of troops, marines and seamen voted by Parliament was 32,000. In the immediate aftermath of the American war, in the mid-1780s, by which time the population had grown by about 25%, it was 51,000. This raises the question of how far the armed forces had become – in defiance of constitutional proprieties – an integral part of the state by the eve of the French wars in 1792. On balance, the consensus amongst military historians is that although peacetime numbers had grown, they had not. It has therefore been argued that with regard to recruitment, the navy still drew heavily on the merchant marine and that the army relied upon the existing structures of authority in the state – principally the gentry and the local authorities. The army in particular has therefore been described as a very decentralised force which existed 'on the margins of society'.[38]

The French wars added a new dimension to military policy. The key was the threat of invasion that lasted from 1797 until shortly after 1807. Thus although the wars as a whole led to unprecedented numbers of regular troops and marines, the threat of invasion also resulted in the creation of an equally unprecedented and massive defence force. By 1814, some three-quarters of a million men and women were recruited into the regular armed forces and the home-defence forces – the militia and the yeomanry. However, the long-term effects of the creation of what was, in effect, a warfare state, should not be exaggerated. In the case of overall strategy, the emphasis remained on naval power with Castlereagh's establishment of the two-power standard in 1817 which was largely achieved by 1830 despite the limitations that Parliament placed on spending. On the other hand, there was a significant change to battle plans. Since 1805 the Navy had developed a formidable capacity to attack enemy coastal fortresses and harbour fleets and it was this, rather than the traditional objective of depriving enemies of overseas territory and trade, that became the focus of naval strategy thereafter.[39]

As for the army, several developments deserve notice. One was that apart from the maintenance of the specially created yeomanry in Ireland, the 'armed nation' that had been created in Britain had all but disappeared by 1831. On the other hand, between Waterloo and the Crimean War, the peacetime army establishment more than doubled over its eighteenth-century counterpart to around 100,000. Moreover, if the size of the Indian army is added to the home establishment, Britain had a greater armed strength during that period than any of the continental powers except France and Russia. Canning's judgement, made in 1813, that a succession of victories had made Britain a military as well as naval power for the first time, therefore seems to have been borne out.[40] However, it is important not to exaggerate the change in the relationship between the state and the army that this development might suggest. As was noted earlier, although some attempt was made to consolidate the various army departments and bring them under Parliamentary control, this was not fully achieved until 1856. Further, there was little change in the traditional strategic role of the army. Thus, the verdict of the chiefs of staff in the 1830s was that the peacetime establishment was insufficient to resist invasion or to mount a quick and substantial intervention on the continent.[41] The advice would have been the same in times of peace in the eighteenth century.

The relationship between the army and society also changed, although once again, the degree should not be exaggerated. In this respect several developments took place. The first, was the standing down of the volunteer home defence force and a reliance, as in the eighteenth century, on the local militia as a reserve force. And a second, most notable after 1815, was the creation of a barracks-based army 'formed around regiments that were veritably self-contained communities' enjoying much improved conditions of service. Soldiering was therefore removed from the margins of society to become a recognised profession. On the other hand, it seems that it took some time before the public shook off its misgivings about a standing army: in the view of one authority, not until after the Crimean War and the Indian mutiny. Finally, it appears that there was a gradual decline in Britain in the use of either regulars or auxiliaries as keepers of the peace, an intermittent but important feature of their role in the eighteenth century. Barracks may have been built close to expected trouble spots after 1815 and the militia prepared on four occasions between 1820 and 1831 to deal with disorder but the trend thereafter was to rely increasingly on the new police forces. The situation in Ireland, however, conformed much more to the old pattern. There, about 20,000 regulars were stationed permanently after 1815 in more than 50 barracks and forts.[42]

In the other areas where government policy was traditionally more intermittent, there are also signs of continuity and change. In the cases of the courts, the costs associated with them and the law, it appears to have been the tradition in the eighteenth century that governments as whole did not keep them under constant review and that reforms were more the personal initiative of individual Lord Chancellors and Lord Chief Justices, such as Hardwicke and Mansfield. It has therefore been argued that the series of steps taken to protect the rights of property were more the result of *ad hoc* responses by Parliament to a series of specific issues that arose in the courts rather than a planned public policy.[43] After 1815, there was certainly greater pressure for reform. The number of laws had proliferated, the number of litigants increased and the case load before the courts became unmanageable. There was therefore a widespread demand for a simplification of the law, an improvement in court procedures and a reduction in legal costs. As a result, Peel consolidated and reformed statute law, reduced drastically the number of capital offences and oversaw the setting up of Royal Commissions of enquiry into criminal and property law, the common-law and the ecclesiastical courts. The last were to lead to a series of reforms in the 1830s and 1840s. However, it is doubtful whether this represented a fundamental change in the approach of the executive to the law. Peel and Lord Brougham, the Whig Lord Chancellor, 1830–4, were unusual in being senior ministers interested in law reform. Further, convincing cases have been made that despite their interest, the real driving forces behind reform consisted, on the one hand, of pressure from a combination of extra-parliamentary lobbies and interested back-bench MPs; and on the other, of the lawyers and the complaints made by their clients. In short, although Peel and Brougham gave more prominence to legal reform on the executive agenda, the impetus was as much bottom-up as top-down.[44]

In the case of law and order, the traditional methods of dealing with crime were to rely on harsh penalties as the deterrent and the discretion of judges and local magistrates as to how firmly they should be applied. In the case of widespread disturbances judged to be endangering the state, the method was to suspend Habeas Corpus, enact special powers, and where absolutely necessary, deploy the military in support of the local forces of authority – the militia and parish constables. By and large these were the methods resorted to in 1777, 1783, 1794–1801 and 1817–20 when the Habeas Corpus Act was suspended. In both cases, considerable reliance was placed on the discretion of local elites.[45]

Change was most notable in the approach to crime. By 1829 the growth of crime and the initiatives taken by local authorities and independent members to control it such as the establishment of more efficient police and the imposition of fixed statutory penalties for specific types of offence had convinced senior politicians that this was the way forward. On the other hand, there was little change in the official approach to the causes of periodic disorder: namely, that they were more the result of a small number of agitators than deep-rooted social and economic problems that needed to be rectified.[46]

Finally, there was continuity followed by a marked change with regard to one of the undoubted causes of disorder – scarcity of food. The traditional method of dealing with this was to embargo the export of grain. Until 1765 this had only been done in wartime but in 1766, when Britain was at peace, it was imposed by royal proclamation rather than by Parliament. This led to a sharp debate about the causes of scarcity and the use of proclamation rather than statute, one of the outcomes of which was support for a less *ad hoc* approach.[47] None took place, however. At subsequent times of scarcity, in 1799–1800 and in 1816–17 in both Ireland and in Britain, the government did not have a coherent response, producing a range of moderate palliatives, including support for the work of private charities although in the case of Ireland, Peel oversaw a novel system of relief which led to the distribution of some £37,000.[48] By then, however, the situation had changed with Britain becoming an importer of grain. The first official recognition of the demise of autarchy – the state of self-sufficiency – came in 1822 when the high levels of protection for domestic corn that had been imposed on government were reduced. It was at that point that the Corn Laws and the issues of the profitability of the agricultural interest and the supply and price of bread to the working classes became a major issue on the executive agenda.

The evidence therefore suggests that in these traditional areas of government policy, some of which were dealt with constantly and others intermittently, there was considerable continuity in approach until the end of the Napoleonic wars. In only one case – the law – is there an example for the continuation of a traditional way of thinking but in all the others significant degrees of change in the assumptions and priorities that underpinned policy occur between 1815 and 1830. From this perspective too, the expansion of the scope of government in the 1830s looks less dramatic than it might be supposed.

The shaping of policy

This review of the conditions, assumptions and priorities that underpinned policy leads us to the question of how far individual governments shaped their policies in the light of a coherent and forward-looking agenda based on agreed principles. In the previous period, it was argued, the traditions of departmental government, the complexities of parliamentary politics and the influence of extra-parliamentary pressure groups led to specific policies being shaped more in the light of immediate circumstances and made it difficult to co-ordinate policy for agreed ends. Thus although there are examples of a more co-ordinated and forward-looking approach, they are not particularly strong ones.

The circumstances encouraging an essentially reactive approach to policy-making certainly did not decline in this period. As we have seen in Chapter 5, the development of the concept of a prime minister who might impose his thinking on his colleagues and the emergence of co-ordinated cabinet government were very slow to take to root and do not seem to have become firmly established by the 1840s. Similarly, parliamentary parties, even when they comprised most MPs (which only happened after 1832), were very much confederations of various interest groups that often differed as much as they agreed over specific policies. Moreover the complexities of negotiating and securing legislation certainly did not diminish. Commercial and ultimately, agricultural, lobbies became more powerful and the role of broadly, rather than narrowly, representative select committees in shaping legislation increased. Finally, this period is notable for a series of critical issues to which governments were bound to make immediate responses. Retrenchment and colonial government following the end of the Seven Years War in 1763; the war of the American colonies and retrenchment after 1783; the French wars and particularly the threat of invasion, 1793–1815; retrenchment and post war distress after 1815; and public pressure for reform, 1828–32. Such crises could, of course, concentrate minds, as to some extent they did; but equally, they militated against coherent long-term planning.

Broadly speaking, the historiography of individual ministers and individual governments suggests that until the 1820s the dominant approach to government was more reactive than doctrinaire and piecemeal rather than systematic. Governments tended to react to individual problems as they arose and to adopt solutions that suited current strategic and political circumstances rather than attempt to apply a specific set of principles. Admittedly, there are two notable exceptions to this proposition and a number of cases where historians have given some credence to the presence of either a comprehensive system and/or the importance of doctrine. One of the exceptions, it has been argued, was a period of 'conscious protectionism' that lasted from 1763 to 1776 and led to a range of increased duties on textiles and paper and prohibitions on the export of textile machinery and tools.[49] Another was Lord Rockingham's Whig administration of February to July 1782 which attempted to implement the essence of its public doctrine, namely that the influence of the Crown and its favoured ministers should be reduced in order to restore the balance between King, Lords and Commons. Underlying this was the conviction that they were better representatives of both property and public opinion than their opponents. It was these beliefs that to some extent moulded their approach to the settlements with the American rebels and the Irish patriots.

The other cases where either system, doctrine, or both, have been considered are principally the administrations of George Grenville, the Younger Pitt, Lord Grenville and Lord Liverpool – in all but one case (Lord Grenville), it should be noted, in the aftermath of war. In the case of George Grenville, Ian Christie, proposes that his colonial policy – strengthening British control in the American colonies and in India – had the hallmarks of 'a logical, inter-locking system' and Philip Lawson, his biographer, draws attention to a seemingly complementary policy – of ending subsidies to European powers. Taken together, these suggest a comprehensive strategy. Lawson's conclusion, however, is that this was unlikely. He therefore stresses that some of these policies were already in the pipeline and that Grenville's method was to deal with problems as they arose.[50] John Ehrman, in his biography of the Younger Pitt, also pays particular attention to the question of how far he merely responded to circumstances and how far he had a systematic purpose based, partly at least, upon doctrine. He notes, for example, that in his King's Speech of December 1782, Lord Shelburne, who was in many respects Pitt's mentor, outlined a series of measures that had more resemblance to a programme than was usual on such occasions. However, when considering Pitt's peacetime policies, he stresses the degree to which they borrowed from ideas and measures already in the pipeline and took advantage of particular opportunities. Overall, Ehrman's peacetime Pitt was a man who shaped policy more in the context of circumstances than in the light of doctrine. Even in the case of trade, he argues, Pitt may have believed in the concept of a balance of trade but he was not committed to free trade as a doctrine or even freedom of trade. Instead, he advocated a greater freedom *to* trade. On the other hand, he sees more than pragmatism in Pitt's policies. Taken together, he solved a financial crisis by restoring a budget surplus, contained the level of debt and improved the system of borrowing and accounting. He also improved the collection of the revenue and reduced smuggling. In addition, he sought a comprehensive commercial settlement with Ireland, repaired the fleet and brought to an end two decades of diplomatic isolation. Each particular strand of policy may have had pragmatic origins but when considered together and more particularly, when explained by Pitt in his speeches, the policies as a whole appears and appeared to have system and purpose.[51]

In the case of Lords Grenville and Liverpool, it was more a matter of a systematic approach to policy than doctrine. The central argument of my own study of Lord Grenville's administration is that his intention was to relate all aspects of policy to what he called a 'defensive and husbanding' system designed to repel any assault by Napoleon until such time as there was a renewed continental alliance against him. This jarred, however, with the priorities of his principal colleagues, the Foxite Whigs and it is doubtful whether his 'system' became theirs.[52] As for Lord Liverpool, Norman Gash makes a case for his government adopting a systematic approach on two occasions. The first, in response to distress, took the form of the government sponsoring acts in 1817 to have wages paid in kind, to encourage savings, to facilitate emigration and to encourage public works. The second came in 1820 when Liverpool made a speech on the economy that Gash regards as a possible blueprint for future government policy. In this he articulated the view that the agricultural, manufacturing and commercial interests were interdependent and that what was required was a national policy dealing with all three. In addition, while agreeing that free trade was theoretically the best policy, he emphasised the substantial support for protection. He therefore advocated a *via media*: the maintenance of protection on corn but its relaxation on textiles. Moreover, he had the speech published as a way of winning over public opinion. However, both these initiatives dealt with only one aspect of government policy and both were more strategic than doctrinal. Indeed Gash points out with regard to the economy, that neither Liverpool nor his colleagues believed in a doctrinaire approach.[53]

There is admittedly, evidence to suggest that some ministers in the 1820s had become accustomed to preparing lists of topics which their colleagues should attend to in the future – a form of systematic forward planning. One notable example is a list prepared by Lord Lansdowne in 1827 in his capacity as Home Secretary of the principal issues he thought the Irish government should deal with in the future. This was then amplified by a supplementary list of 14 'secondary issues' provided by his Under-Secretary, Thomas Spring Rice. Other examples are Wellington's selections of a total of 39 topics that he thought his government should act on in the future and which he presented to his cabinet on three occasions in 1828 and 1829.[54] Analysis of these lists, however, suggests that the presence of many of the items was due to the pressure of parliamentary and departmental business: bills that had been prepared, sometimes by previous administrations; acts that needed amendment in the light of the experience of their operation; and reports of Royal Commissions and select committees that required a response. Indeed, all these lists were prepared on the eve or during the summer recess, suggesting that they were more reminders to colleagues of what they should be thinking about in advance of the next parliamentary session than a comprehensive programme.

Thus, even though the historians concerned have given serious considera-tion in these cases to the prevalence of a systematic and/or doctrinaire approach, there remains considerable doubt as to how far it was achieved. This, together with many other studies of individual governments, individual ministers, particular areas of policy and specific policies, suggests the predominance of the traditional approach. Thus most governments, while operating within the general conditions, priorities and assumptions sketched earlier, shaped specific policies in response to immediate circumstances and opportunities rather than doctrinal considerations and did not seek to bind them together in a system. There was no tradition of comprehensive reviews of current and future responsibilities in specific policy areas followed by forward planning. Policy was essentially reactive and framed in the light of materials lying in the offices and the immediate pressures and requirements. Perhaps the best illustration of this process is Boyd Hilton's analysis of how Lord Liverpool's government adopted the economic policies between 1821 and 1823 that laid the foundations for mid-Victorian prosperity: the gold standard and free trade. Some of the ministers involved were certainly ideologues: as bullionists or free traders. But as Hilton demonstrates, the decisions to return to the gold standard in 1821, to modify the corn law in 1822 and to begin to dismantle the system of protection in 1822–3 were taken in the light of immediate pressures and circumstances. It was only when they were required to justify their actions in Parliament that they resorted to the ideology of free trade, one contemporary definition of which was the free operation of the economy and the establishment of the 'principle of self-correction which the analogy of nature teaches us is the universal law of her [Britain's] constitution'.[55]

The words quoted above are significant in two particular respects. In the first place they link the ideology of free trade with its most famous originator in the 1770s, Adam Smith, while at the same time connecting it with the classic, post-1688 justification of the checks and balances inherent in the mixed constitution. In the second, they are an example of the importance that ideology was assuming in the public doctrine and private thinking of many parliamentary politicians. Contemporaries often referred in the 1820s, usually disparagingly, to the 'march of intellect' or to the 'march of the mind', and there is no doubt that the process of refining existing ideas and developing new ones proliferated in the final stages of the war and its aftermath. In 1807 many of the dominant parliamentary labels were associated with individual politicians: Pittites, Foxite Whigs, Sidmouth's party, the Grenvillites, the Canningites. By 1830, they had been largely de-personalised: ultra Tories, Tories, Whigs, liberals, radicals. This may serve as a symbol of the growing influence of ideology which makes the period from the 1820s to the 1840s essentially different from the past. The question to which we now turn is how far this affected the traditional approach to government.

In recent years, our understanding of the ideologies of the executive class during this period have been transformed. Twenty years ago the prevailing orthodoxy was that most senior politicians were essentially reactive. In the case of the Tories, most were dedicated to the maintenance of what they perceived to be the bastions of aristocratic power: the Church of England; the protection of domestic corn from foreign imports; and in default of their being able to resist the reform of parliamentary representation, the prerogatives of the Crown and the powers of the House of Lords. According to this reading of the newly named Conservative Party, Peel was an exception in that he was prepared to accept the Reform Acts and eventually, to promote free trade and the abandonment of the Corn Laws. Hence the split in the party in 1846. As for the Whigs, they were seen as no less conservative than their opponents. The difference was that they believed that the best way to conserve the aristocracy was to respond to pressure for reform from components of their parliamentary following – the liberals, radicals and O'Connellites – and public opinion. The outcome was legislation designed to protect the essential interests of the aristocracy while at the same time promoting those of other sections of society thought to be sympathetic to whiggism. The ethos of government was therefore seen as predominantly reactive and tactical rather than positive and ideological. This meant that the real promoters of reform were to be found elsewhere: for example, amongst the philosophic radicals; or the utilitarians who managed to worm their way into Royal Commissions and select committees that prepared the ground for legislation; and the free trade ideologues who held minor positions in government departments and were able to promote their ideals by stealth. A very influential argument was also developed by Oliver MacDonagh that in the case of central government taking responsibility for welfare, process was at least as influential as ideology. This consisted of six stages: the identification of the problem by parliamentary enquiry; legislation designed to ameliorate it; the appointment of inspectors to enforce it; fresh legislation and the establishment of a centralised supervisory body to deal with the deficiencies of the original measures; a realisation that executive responsibility and central direction needed to be maintained; and further refinement of the methods of administration, leading it to become 'dynamic' rather than 'static'.[56] In short, if the march of intellect can be associated with the many reforms of this period, this was not the result of the efforts of the governing class.

Current thinking, however, credits post-1830 governments with a far more sophisticated intellectual engagement with the problems and issues that they faced. In the case of the Conservatives, for example, Anna Gambles has shown that the argument for the protection of corn was not solely based on aristocratic and agricultural self-interest, although that undoubtedly motivated some. The intellectual case for protection, she argues, was sharpened by the profound shock that it was perceived the 1832 Reform Acts had delivered to the political influence of the landed classes. Further erosion needed to be prevented. This would prove exceptionally difficult, however, if the Whig enthusiasm for retrenchment and the case for reducing or abolishing the tariff system in favour of free trade gathered strength. The result would be that the state would have insufficient financial or economic means (through retrenchment and the loss of tariff revenue) to regulate and balance the competing claims of agriculture, commerce and industry. This would lead to the eclipse of both agriculture and the landed classes and the triumph of commerce, industry and the middle classes. Severe class conflict might follow. Protectionism therefore had economic, political and social strands. What it stood for was the maintenance of social cohesion under aristocratic leadership using much the same means as had been deployed in very different circumstances in the eighteenth century.[57]

Protectionism, however, was not the only Conservative creed any more than it was solely restricted to Conservatives. Philip Harling has revealed an element of Tory thinking before 1830 that called for moral discipline on the part of the governing class and for governments to encourage such discipline more generally by sponsoring a scheme of national education.[58] James Sack has shown that there was a rich vein of constituency conservatism that revered monarchy, loyalism and the Established Church and Richard Gaunt has demonstrated that ultra toryism was not only more than crude anti – Catholicism but also more influential in party circles than was once thought to be the case.[59] Peel's thinking has also been the subject of reconsideration. Much more stress is now placed on the importance of his political philosophy when explaining his political actions. Peel, it is argued, thought of society as a machine that would run more smoothly if government intervened less and was left to regulate itself by means of a divinely – established set of checks and balances. Hence his growing enthusiasm for free trade which would not only necessitate a minimalist form of government through loss of revenue but also enable the agricultural, commercial and industrial interests to find their own equilibrium. Here too there are echoes of the past: as we have seen, Adam Smith had proposed something of the same in the 1770s, the difference being that Smith left the checks and balances to the market rather than divine intervention.[60]

Our understanding of Whigs and liberals has also been substantially revised. Until the 1980s, the standard interpretation of the Whigs was that they were essentially a caste rather than a group of politicians united by their political principles; and that in so far as they had a political philosophy, it consisted of defending the power of the aristocracy from which they were drawn by making concessions to popular pressure. As for liberals, they were seen as uneasy parliamentary allies of the Whigs but essentially different: not part of the Whig family nexus and driven by conviction on particular issues such as free trade or religious toleration. However, a series of distinguished studies of the Whigs published within the last two decades has established that in many cases ideology played an important part in their politics. This was least notable in the cases of the three Whigs who dominated the earlier historiography: Grey, Melbourne and Palmerston, the last two of whom had been acolytes of Canning. All of them were more practical than theoretical in their thinking and the heavy burden of responsibilities that they shouldered in the 1830s did not encourage a more reflective turn of mind. Grey was probably the most thoughtful of the three but his philosophy did not extend much further than the old Foxite canon of re-establishing good government by reducing the influence of the Crown and restoring the influence of property. Men of property would then be in a position to act beneficially in the public interest: for example, by advancing the cause of religious liberty.[61]

Many of the other senior (and often younger) Whigs, however, were much more committed to specific bodies of ideas. Several categories have been identified. One, described as 'liberal Anglicans' by Richard Brent, consisted of 'constitutional moralists' who believed that a reformed and latitudinarian Church of England could become the flagship for a form of politics that by focussing on 'virtuous and patriotic' reforms would be 'morally elevating' and at the same time secure 'the prosperity of the country'. Subscribers, the most prominent of whom was Lord John Russell, therefore advocated the abolition of church rates, the elimination of the alleged abuses of the Church, the extension of civil rights to Dissenters, and the encouragement of education that would include the teaching of religion on a non-denominational basis. The driving force was a belief in the beneficial effects of the Christian religion not a strategic readiness to succumb to pressure.[62] Two others, labelled 'Liberal' and 'Foxite Whig' by Peter Mandler, were primarily concerned with the economy and the social effects of industrialisation. The Liberals, some of whom were evangelicals and high churchmen, were believers in laissez-faire, that is, the minimal or complete absence of any government interference in trade and conditions of work. Foxite Whigs, for their part, rejected the faith placed in a free-market economy and believed that public support for aristocratic government could be revived by a determined commitment to the centrally-directed improvement of factory conditions, public health and education. Few Whigs, of course, can be fitted solely and continuously into one of these categories: many shifted their ground and there was in any case some overlap between the categories. Further, there is some debate about which particular school was in the ascendant at different points in the 1830s. On the other hand, there is no doubt that contrary to view of the older historiography, this was a period when Whig political philosophy was remarkably progressive and diverse.[63]

The question, however, is how far either Conservative and Whig doctrines or MacDonagh's bureaucratic processes explains government policy. The first point to make in this regard is that it is difficult to find ideology having a significant impact on foreign, colonial, and military policy – three areas which accounted for as substantial a proportion of government business as they had done previously. It certainly had some impact, as the readiness of the Whigs to intervene in the Iberian peninsular after 1830 in favour of the liberal cause demonstrates,[64] but the historiography of these subjects suggests that the predominant factors lay in the strategic and financial considerations outlined earlier. All three areas of policy were therefore conceived within the framework of maintaining the Vienna settlement, protecting and enlarging the empire, and avoiding the expense of major military adventures.

It had a proportionately greater impact on financial and economic policy. In the case of finance, the Whigs, with the exception of a continued commitment to reduce the costs of government, worked within the conventional boundaries of trying to balance the budget and attempted nothing that was new or doctrinaire. Peel, however, certainly did. His re-imposition of the income tax in 1842 was therefore not solely related to the raising of revenue. This was the time of Chartism, the largest working-class political movement in British history. Peel therefore regarded an income tax on those earning more than £150 pa and the lowering of duties on the basic necessities of life for the poor as instruments by which the state could soothe class divisions and produce social harmony. The basic idea was not revolutionary. Taxing the rich directly through the Land Tax and setting indirect taxes at rates that affected the poorest sections of society least was standard policy for most of the eighteenth century. The context in which it was proposed, however, was different. The population was much larger and an apparent congealing of class interests had taken place that seemed to foreshadow serious conflict. Peel's re-worked formula for harmony therefore seemed to be novel and profound.[65]

In the case of trade policy there was a considerable measure of agreement between the responsible Whig and Tory ministers. Most Whigs were committed to the principle of free trade as were the successive chancellors of

the Exchequer, Althorp, Spring Rice and Baring, and the President of the
Board of Trade, Poulett Thomson. So too were their effective successors,
Peel and Gladstone, especially after Joseph Hume's 1840 select committee
on tariffs had shown that the majority of revenue was produced by the duties
on a small minority of the items taxed. Admittedly, there was considerable
disparity between the degree of success to which their respective commitments led. The Whigs made only a modest number of reductions in tariffs
and declined to tackle the Corn Laws because of divisions amongst their own
supporters and the strength of support for protection in the Conservative
opposition. Peel, on the other hand, was able to make substantial cuts,
beginning with his famous 1842 budget, and eventually repealed the Corn
Laws in response to the Irish Famine. On the other hand, it seems clear
that the advancement of free trade was as much the result of the conviction
that it would produce economic and moral benefits as it was of the force
of circumstance. It therefore bears some comparison with the 'conscious
protectionism' of the 1760s and 1770s.

The argument for a new approach to government has been most vigorously advanced in the case in those areas of policy where central government
took special responsibility for the first time: factory conditions; poor relief;
education, policing, and public health. Contrary to the view that this was
largely the result of a reaction to pressure, it has been contended that it was
due either to various ideological commitments or to an administrative
'internal momentum', sometimes described as 'incrementalism'. Either way,
the implication is that the impetus was different to the more pragmatic
approach adopted earlier.

In recent years, there has been an increasing scepticism about internal
momentum as a general explanation. Further research on the factors
that shaped particular legislation and initiatives has therefore stressed the
contribution of particular individuals and the influence of specific political
circumstances. It has therefore been argued that the steps by which the state
assumed responsibility for conditions of emigration, 1828–42, was due
principally to the initiatives of particular individuals outside and within
the Colonial Office and to the impact on emigration of the Canadian revolt
in 1837. On this basis the internal momentum case appeared far too deter-
ministic.[66] A similar argument has been advanced for the processes by which
the state took responsibility for working-class education in 1839 and public
health in 1848. The commitment to state supported education, it has been
argued, was largely due to the initiatives of individual politicians while the
establishment of the Board of Health was the result of the dynamics of
contemporary politics and the specific choices available to its chief promoter,
Edwin Chadwick.[67] In the case of the role of ideology, research has not
removed the influence of parliamentary and public pressure as factors
impelling governments to intervene and in some respects it has underlined
the importance of paying close regard to practical politics as a way of
explaining the specific form that individual initiatives took. In this regard,

attention had been focused principally on the Whigs in the 1830s. Ian Newbould has therefore argued that a key to understanding the Whig approach to government was their perception of parliamentary, and to some extent, national, politics. What was most obvious to them was first, the strength of the extremes: the ultra Tories in Lords and Commons and in rural England; and the radicals in the Commons and in urban England. And second, the fact that after 1835, their majority in the Commons was not only small but rested on the support of liberals, radicals and O'Connellites. From this perspective, the best way to conserve the interests of the aristocracy, property and established institutions while at the same time pressing ahead with reform, was therefore to frame measures in such a way as to attract the support of a majority of their own ranks and to preclude the opposition of moderate Conservatives such as Peel. In other words, it would be wrong to ignore tactical considerations when seeking to explain the details of measures.[68]

There certainly is no doubt that pressure from parliamentary and extra-parliamentary groups as well as tactical considerations did play an important part in leading the Whigs to take up issues and to shape their legislation in particular ways. The decision to frame a new poor law, for example, was clearly due, in part at least, to a combination of circumstances: the escalating costs to the gentry of the existing provision of relief; a series of parliamentary enquiries proposing reform; and the 'Captain Swing' riots in the Home Counties which some ascribed to the failure of the old system.[69] Similarly, it has been shown that the precise terms of the Education Act of 1839 were partially the result of pressure from radicals but also the wish to prevent an unregulated system of grant-aid falling into the hands of the Church of England and its most evangelical members – the natural allies of the ultra Tories. Centralisation was therefore as much a tactic as an end in itself.[70]

On the other hand, the evidence does point to ideology playing a much more significant part than it did in other areas of government, and proportionately, a much more significant part than it had in the past. In the case of the New Poor Law, for example, not only did the Benthamite utilitarians play a major role in the Royal Commission appointed by the Whigs to make recommendations but at least three of the 7-man cabinet sub-committee who accepted them (Althorp, Lansdowne and Graham) were supporters of the political economy of laissez-faire upon which they were partially based.[71] It has also been argued, perhaps more speculatively, that they and other Whigs were enthusiasts for a system which, in effect, would enable the gentry to become agents of a reformed system of local administration and so restore their lost prestige.[72] Similar degrees of commitment and conviction played a role in many other areas of policy. For example, in emigration policy where Stephen, the influential Colonial Office official, was influenced by Benthamism;[73] in education policy which was promoted chiefly by Russell, Lansdowne and Spring Rice, all of whom were committed to various types of the new Whiggism;[74] and more generally in the attempts to reform the Church of England and to extend civil rights to Dissenters where the Liberal

Anglicans were to the fore.[75] In addition, there was a strong current of humanitarianism which affected members of both political parties and which was responsible for the various factory and mines acts. It is notable, however, that this sometimes had to give way to the sterner ideology of laissez faire. Thus throughout the period until 1847 there was successful resistance to proposals to legislate against wage cuts and to limit the hours of work. In the early 1830s, for example, a campaign by over 800,000 weavers to persuade Parliament not to repeal legislation which had offered them protection against wage cuts failed. This, it has been argued, was principally due to the influence of laissez-faire ideologues in the Board of Trade and sympathetic Whigs such as Althorp, Lansdowne and Howick.[76]

Overall, the evidence suggests some continuity and some change in the ways that governments shaped policy. Until the 1820s, decision-making, although set in the context of the general axioms and assumptions outlined earlier, was influenced primarily by practical considerations rather than ideological commitments. Perhaps this was inevitable given the series of unforeseen crises that governments faced: the revolt and loss of the American colonies and the French Revolution and the long war that followed. Admittedly, there is a case for arguing that some first ministers, most notably the Younger Pitt, did develop an overall strategy which linked policies in different departments into a 'system', as it was sometimes referred, to either favourably or critically.[77] Systematic government, however, whether real or imagined, is not necessarily the same as doctrinaire government. In fact, the evidence points to individual strands of policy being developed principally in the light of prevailing circumstances rather than doctrine. In this respect there was continuity with earlier practice.

From the 1820s onwards, however, research suggests that senior members of both parties became, to one degree or another, strongly influenced by what was referred to at the time as 'the march of intellect' – a remarkable proliferation of new or reformulated ideas on the purpose and practice of government. In the light of that research, the view that the expansion of the scope of government was due to bureaucratic processes or the singular influence of utilitarianism has been undermined. Caution has to be exercised, however, when estimating the overall influence of this plethora of ideas on the shaping of policy. In the case of substantial areas of policy, for example – foreign, military, and to some extent colonial – they appear to have made very little impact, practical circumstances and considerations being to the fore. They made a comparatively greater impact on financial and commercial policies but it was not until Peel's second administration that it could be said that a single view of the political, social and economic benefits of a particular line of policy prevailed. On the other hand, there seems little doubt that ideology played a much more significant role in the formulation of what might be loosely described as welfare policies – poverty, factory conditions, working-class education, public health and emigration. However, even in these cases, research suggests that practical as well as party considerations cannot be left out of the account.

The achievements of the executive

The three most notable developments in Britain's history in this period were the enhancement of its position within the ranks of Europe's major powers and its becoming the world's foremost imperial power; its emergence as the major commercial, and the first industrial, power; and the maintenance of political and social stability despite the stresses created by the unprecedented growth in population and urbanisation. The question we need to address next is how far executive policy was responsible.

In the case of the enhancement of its position within the European pentarchy (the Habsburg Empire, Britain, France, Prussia and Russia), government policy was clearly responsible for the favourable terms of the outcome of the Seven Years War and subsequently, the decision to enter the war against France in 1793 and the diplomatic and military strategy that led to victory in 1815. It could also be said that ministers made a substantial contribution to the terms of the Vienna settlement that provided the basis for European diplomacy and the avoidance of serious conflict until the outbreak of the Crimean War in the 1850s. Government responsibility for the main features of imperial history, however, is less clear cut. The decision to enhance the taxing of the American colonies without regard to the likely consequences was certainly largely responsible for their revolt and subsequent loss. Ministerial responsibility for the growth of the second British empire, however, is less easy to pin down. There does not seem to have been any settled policy at Whitehall to expand overseas but rather a readiness to assume a measure of responsibility for territories acquired for strategic reasons in the course of war and by semi-independent merchants and explorers. The massive extension of empire in India, for example, seems to have been largely due to the initiative of the Governor-General, Lord Wellesley, rather than the India Board in London. In this regard, it is surely significant that the decision to incorporate Ireland into a United Kingdom was largely taken for immediate strategic reasons.

The ability to engage in war on this scale and to defend overseas acquisitions depended, of course, on sufficient financial and economic resources. In the case of finance, government was clearly responsible throughout. The key was the system of deficit financing established in the late seventeenth century and continued in this period, albeit with sophisticated fine-tuning by the Younger Pitt in the form, *inter alia*, of his new Sinking Fund. This system was accompanied throughout by the Treasury's increasing regulation and control of fiscal administration. It was this that enabled successive governments to engage in European war in the way that they did: by sea power; by subsidies to allies and mercenaries; and by expeditionary military campaigns.

However, borrowing on this unprecedented scale could not have been achieved without the tax revenue that gave creditors sufficient confidence to invest and be sure that they would receive their interest payments. The standard eighteenth century tax formula was to rely on the Land Tax as the only form of direct taxation and to levy indirect taxes in the form of customs and excise duties for three particular purposes: to raise revenue; to protect colonial markets; and to regulate internal commerce. With regard to the sustaining of the system of borrowing and the annual funding of the costs of civil administration and the military, two points need to be made in the context of Britain's geopolitical power. The first is that government was clearly responsible for what was an extremely efficient Excise department and equally responsible for what was a less efficient customs service. It was also the case that successive steps were taken, most notably by the Younger Pitt, to reduce the black economy that flourished through smuggling and other devices. The second is that government was also responsible for the successful transition from a financial system that rested on the security attached to deficit financing to one that rested on the gold standard, budget surpluses and control of the money supply. Lord Liverpool's administration would have liked to retain Pitt's income tax but was denied by Parliament. The resort to bullion as a badge of good faith (coupled with the reduction of expenditure) proved a successful stopgap until Peel restored the income tax in 1842, at which point it became a fixture on the financial front.

Taxation also had other functions and one of them was to regulate external and internal trade. This raises the question of how far government policy was responsible for the extraordinary growth of commerce and manufacture. In recent years, two books have been published which focus on this issue. One, by Joseph Inikori, deals largely with tariffs and the protected colonial markets and argues that despite the higher incidence of smuggling and fraud associated with the customs service, they 'stimulated import and re-export substitution' and therefore made an important contribution to the early stages of the industrial revolution. The other, by William Ashworth, examines both customs and excise duties over the long time span of 1640 and 1845 and comes to even more positive conclusions. He therefore argues that 'the extension and refinement of the excise tax, 'created an effective framework for the rise of industrial capitalism, while supplying … revenues necessary to protect and guide this development'. In the words of a reviewer of his work 'tariffs and the excise permitted lightly taxed new industries (e.g., cotton, iron, and pottery) to grow to the point where Britain enjoyed a dominant international position in the manufacture and trade of these items. The cost was borne by consumables, such as beer and tea, which were subjected to heavy rates of duty'. The case has therefore been made that government policy contributed significantly to the growth of the economy both before and after its deregulation began in the early 1820s. Admittedly, reservations have been expressed about parts of Ashworth's thesis – in particular on the current paucity of evidence pinning down the precise relationship between the impact of particular taxes on particular traders and manufacturers. On the other hand, the evidence seems sufficient to credit a significant element of growth to indirect tax policy.[78]

Tax policy also had a political purpose – the maintaining of social cohesion. In the eighteenth century, this consisted of taxing the gentry directly (and increasingly lightly) by means of a static Land Tax; but otherwise setting taxes on consumption that would have their heaviest impact on those most able to pay them. Between 1799 and 1815/16, this shadowy form of 'compact' with the various social classes was maintained by the introduction of the income tax, albeit, one collected by officials supervised by the gentry and based to some degree on the principal of self-assessment. It broke down, however, with the establishment of the Corn Laws and the abandonment of the income tax at the end of the war. Yet neither of these measures was government policy: they were decided by Parliament. It was therefore left to Peel to re-fashion the compact by re-introducing the income tax, abolishing the Corn Laws, and reducing taxes on consumption.

Social cohesion was only part of the general equilibrium that Britain enjoyed for a good part of this period. This is a large subject and government on its own could hardly have played a major role. Much more important were a host of general social, economic and cultural factors. Government actions, however, were not insignificant. In the case of law and order, for example, the traditional approach was to use special powers sparingly and to allow local authorities and local magistrates to police their districts and to exercise the harsh penal code with discretion. In addition, the intention throughout was to maintain comparatively small military establishments in peacetime. Government therefore did not try to undermine the power and influence that the gentry had in the localities – one of the principal causes of unrest in eighteenth-century Europe. Moreover, although changes did take place after 1815, they were comparatively modest ones. With the possible exception of Ireland, special powers continued to be used sparingly. The discretionary justice system was allowed to give way to fixed penalties but capital offences were reduced to what, in effect, was the crime of murder. The state took responsibility for police in Ireland and in London but their establishment elsewhere was left, ultimately, to the discretion of the local ratepayers. Further, although the peacetime military establishments grew substantially, the fact that about a quarter of the army was stationed permanently in Ireland and that the remainder only amounted to a maximum of about 70,000 troops before the Crimean War meant that Britain was far from appearing to be a military state. The fact that government sponsored a more liberal and laissez-faire state just at the point when Britain was at the zenith of its international power had the advantage of minimising potential causes of political unrest.

Another factor here was the maintaining of the public's trust in government. To some extent this was done for what were perceived to be reasons of necessity and by arbitrary or propagandistic means. A general influence over the press was maintained by taxation until 1836 and by the subsidising of favourable newspapers, especially in Ireland. In addition, loyalism was encouraged by various means – to some extent during the American war and much more thoroughly during that with France. Perhaps the most significant line of policy, however, was the gradual elimination of the sleaze associated with the machinery of government. Admittedly, this was not a policy promoted continuously or wholly by government. Parliamentary and public pressure played a part as did the continuous support for the ending of Old Corruption by the Whig party, largely because they believed that it was sustaining their opponents in power. On the other hand, a succession of governments – for example, those headed by Bute, North, Rockingham, Pitt, Liverpool and Wellington – did much to trim the establishment of rotten wood in order to increase efficiency and reduce expenditure. This may not have increased trust in government but it did not lead to the widespread contempt for it that such excesses caused in France before the Revolution.

Finally, there are the issues of welfare and political rights. In the former case, government was very slow to identify itself with improvement. In the case of food shortages, for example, the general approach was to make immediate emergency provision but to look to no long-term palliatives. Similarly, government was extremely reluctant to intervene in the wage market, believing for pragmatic or ideological reasons that it was best to leave it to find its own level. Moreover, when government did take responsibility for education, poor relief, factory conditions, and public health, it was done either with a light touch or with modest interference with the local elites and authorities and the voluntary agencies that normally attended to such matters. It is difficult to say whether the approach to food shortages and wages did promote equilibrium or not but it is possible that the concern shown not to override the voluntary and local centres of power did so. On the other hand, it is noticeable that although the establishment of the New Poor Law satisfied the gentry by enabling them to resume responsibility at a much lower personal cost than hitherto, it created widespread and threatening opposition amongst the working classes. Direct government intervention came at a cost. As for the advancing of political rights, the government contribution was minimal until it was almost too late. In the case of the concessions to Dissenters and Catholics in 1828 and 1829, they were more the result of extra-parliamentary pressure than government design. It could also be said that this was a reason for the extent if not the fact of the English and Welsh Reform Act. Further, this also came at a cost. Thus, the Whigs' anxiety to attach the middle classes to the constitution in 1832 and also in 1835 through the medium of the Municipal Corporations Act, served to drive working-class leaders into Chartism.

Summary and conclusion

Although the changes to the scope and purpose of the executive were more substantial than the changes to its institutional framework, caution should be exercised when estimating their extent and their chronology.

In the case of the scope of business, for example, it undoubtedly expanded during the first half of the nineteenth century, particularly from *c.*1829–42. During the longer time span, the government of Ireland became a much more central issue than it had been earlier. In the shorter, governments promoted substantial measures of political and religious reform and established various degrees of responsibility for working-class education, the conditions of work in factories and mines, poor relief, policing and public health.

The degree of change, however, needs to put into perspective. Throughout the period from 1760, the core of government business remained as it had been previously with the dominant topics being foreign policy, public finance, the regulation of commerce, trade and manufacture, military operations and the maintenance of law and order. Foreign policy may have slipped in the 1830s from its traditional place at the top of the agenda, with domestic issues taking precedence, but it did not disappear from that agenda. Further, although the executive took on a degree of responsibility for policing and welfare, the ways that it did this do not suggest that it was intended they should become constant items for discussion at the cabinet table. With the exception of the New Poor Law Board, all the new boards and departments were placed under the authority of existing departments. In addition, the total number of new functionaries constituted only a tiny proportion of the civil service as a whole. It is almost as if those responsible were aware that the time taken up by the staple topics of cabinet discussion left little space for the introduction of new ones. This 'arms-length' approach to these new responsibilities mirrored, perhaps, the 'arms-length' characteristics of the legislation that implemented them: governments established the rules and a system of surveillance but implementation was left to local authorities, voluntary agencies and employers.

It is also unwise to regard these developments as part of continuous process of expansion in the scope of government. As we have noted, the steady increase in the total quantity of legislation came to a halt around 1820 and then decreases. Further, the proportion of government-inspired legislation also falls in that period. Admittedly, these two trends may be due to greater legislative efficiency on the part of both independent MPs and the executive, but they also challenge any assumption that with the acceptance of new responsibilities, the executive becomes more dominant in legislative terms. The chronology of expansion was also more drawn out and disjointed than might be supposed. It began in the 1760s with the colonies, continued in the 1770s with a succession of Irish issues, and strengthened in the first three decades of the nineteenth century with the full force of direct responsibility for Ireland and the pressures for political and religious reform. This was the long prelude to a more concentrated and extensive phase of expansion in the 1830s.

Continuity and change was also a feature of the history of the general assumptions and priorities that underpinned approaches to government.

Starting in earnest in the 1770s, there was a remarkable proliferation of new and powerful propositions in the fields of moral and political philosophy combined with a growing support amongst various social groups for political, religious and humanitarian reform. Caution has also to be exercised, however, when estimating the effects of these developments on the executive mind. On the one hand, the evidence suggests that new ideas on the purpose of government and the practice of politics did have a greater impact on politicians in high office than had previously been the case. On the other, there was comparatively little change in thinking on the traditional canon: the virtues of a balance of power between King, Lord and Commons; the view that political participation depended on the possession of property; and the necessity of maintaining the Established Church. In so far as there was significant change, it was in the recognition that public opinion had become a powerful factor in the constitutional balance; and an acceptance of the necessity of office-holding at whatever level being seen as a matter of public trust rather than private profit.

In the case of the assumptions and priorities that influenced specific areas of policy, there was considerable continuity until the aftermath of the Napoleonic wars – between 1815 and 1830. It was then that the foundations of lasting priorities in key areas of government were laid: the avoidance of enduring continental alliances; the shift from Sinking Funds to the gold standard and the money supply as the badge of sound finance; the dismantling of commercial tariffs; reductions in government expenditure and the recognition that eventually some form of income tax would be required; the realisation that autarchy was unobtainable; and the acceptance of an enlarged peacetime army and a different strategic role for the navy. All these changes pre-date the increases in the scope of government in the 1830s.

With regard to the ways that ministers shaped policy, it has been argued that changes coincide with the period when the assumptions and priorities underpinning policy also changed. From the 1760s until the 1820s policies were framed more in the light of practical considerations than ideological commitments, although there are examples of first ministers who linked different strands of policy together into an overall strategy that had the appearance of constituting a system of government. From the 1820s onwards, however, a significant number of senior politicians of both parties were committed in various degrees to the new ideas that had been developed on the purpose and practice of government. That said, it would be an error to ascribe the changes in either policy or the scope of government simply to ideological imperatives. In substantial and important areas of policy, practical considerations remained paramount. It was only in financial and commercial policy, and more notably in welfare policy, that ideology plays a prominent role and even then, practical and party considerations played their part.

Finally, it has been suggested that executive government made notable contributions to Britain's growth as the major European, imperial and industrial power. These were particularly striking in the case of the ability to wage a prolonged European war and to bring it to a successful conclusion. It has also been argued that the system of customs and excise duties played a role in stimulating the Industrial Revolution. In the case of the growth of empire, the contribution was important initially – in the Seven Years War – but less so following the loss of the American colonies with the initiative resting more in the hands of government officials and British merchants and adventurers on the ground.

There is also the question of how far governments contributed to the comparative political and social stability that developed in Britain at the end of this period, and to some degree, Ireland; and which lasted until the mid-1860s. The factors working in an opposite direction were certainly considerable: the growth of population; the growth of industry and urbanisation; increasing religious pluralism; and growing middle-class and working-class agitation to support political and economic goals. Yet governments certainly made some important contributions to easing the problems that these created. They played a role, substantial at first if modest thereafter, in the gradual reduction of the Old Corruption that had infected all parts of the body politic. This helped to restore trust in the virtues of aristocratic leadership. They also took responsibility for aspects of welfare and policing, while at the same managing to maintain a role for the local authorities and the voluntary agencies that had hitherto been responsible for them. This helped to maintain a partnership between the largely aristocratic governing class and the gentry and progressive middle classes in the localities. Further, there was an increasingly sharper awareness on the part of the governing class from the 1820s onwards that one of the keys to social stability lay in a distribution of public expenditure and a system of taxation that engendered trust in government and a sense of equity on the part of the various interests that sustained the economy: those of agriculture, commerce, industry, trade and labour. This awareness was most effectively translated into action by Peel in the 1840s. In the case of religious and political reform, on the other hand, government actions were either too obviously responses to pressure (as in 1828, 1829 or 1832) or were too socially divisive (as in 1832 once again) to have made much of a contribution to stability.

7 Parliament and government

Introduction

Following nearly a century of sitting in largely unaltered accommodation, a series of changes affecting both houses of Parliament took place in the first half of the nineteenth century. The first coincided with the Act of Union with Ireland and had its greatest affect on the House of Lords. In the latter part of the eighteenth century there had been growing concern about the structural soundness of the Palace of Westminster as a whole and the 'stuffiness' of the Lords' chamber in particular – a problem exacerbated by the notable increase in its membership that was then taking place. The prospect of a further 28 Irish representative peers and 4 Irish bishops therefore led the Lords to move in 1801 to the former Court of Requests, for a larger room measuring approximately 80 feet long, 40 feet wide and 30 feet high and lit by 3 large semi-circular windows on each side.[1] The Commons, on the other hand, although faced with the prospect of an additional 100 Irish members, remained in their much smaller space, the only change being the enlargement of the width of the chamber by 2 feet on either side in order to accommodate an extra row of seats. The disparity in the spaciousness of the two chambers therefore increased in favour of the Lords, there still being insufficient room in the Commons to accommodate more than two-thirds of the 658 members.[2]

The next change was the result of a devastating fire on 16 October 1834 that completely destroyed the House of Commons and left much of the rest of the Palace complex in ruins. Steps were therefore taken for the building of what is the present Houses of Parliament, the Lords being moved in the meantime to the repaired 'Painted Chamber', a smaller room than before, the Commons taking over their previous accommodation in the Court of Requests, which had also been renovated. As a consequence, the Commons emerged from the fire with much more spacious accommodation than hitherto while the Lords fared far worse, the Painted Chamber being described by Charles Greville as 'a wretched dog-hole'.[3] It was not until April 1847 that the Lords were able to move to their new accommodation in Barry's Gothic masterpiece, and May 1850 before the Commons sat there for the first time.

These perambulations were accompanied by a number of developments in the history of Parliament, which had a major impact on the ways that Britain and Ireland were governed. Three aspects may be mentioned here by way of a preface to the assessment that follows. One was the re-emergence of something approaching a two-party system that laid the foundations for the more comprehensive version that lasted until the advent of the Labour Party at the turn of the last century. Another was a substantial increase in the quantity of parliamentary business in the forms of legislation, enquiry and receipt of petitions for the 'redress of grievances'. And the third was an equally substantial increase in public knowledge of parliamentary proceedings and public engagement with them. Taken together, they raise the question to which this chapter is principally directed: how far the influence of Parliament on government was transformed.

SECTION 1: MEMBERS, PARTIES AND THE SUBSTANCE OF DEBATE

Members of Parliament

The number of members of both houses increased significantly in this period. In the case of the Lords, the reasons were the creation of a substantial number of new English, British or UK peerages, particularly between 1783 and 1820, and the addition of the 28 Irish representative peers and 4 Irish bishops in 1801 under the terms of the Irish Union. The rate of the increase, which was at its fastest, 1784–1830, is indicated in Table 7.1:

By contrast, the increase in the membership of the Commons took place at one fell swoop in 1801 with the addition of the 100 Irish MPs. Thereafter, despite radical pressure to increase membership at the time of the Reform debates in 1831–2, the number remained at 658 until 1844 when it fell by two as a result of the disfranchisement of Sudbury. It did not rise above 658 until 1885.

Although the increase in the number of legislators from 782 in 1760 to 1097 in 1850 is of interest, the much more important question is whether a significant change took place in the social composition of the two houses. This is a much-debated issue and there are two aspects that have a particular bearing on the approach to government. The first is how far Lords and Commoners shared a similar social standing. Convergence in this respect would encourage harmony between the two houses and divergence the opposite. The second, and related, aspect is how far the members of either house represented the interests of the landed proprietor as opposed to those of the financier, the merchant, the industrialist and members of the professions. If the overwhelming majority of members of Parliament were primarily

Table 7.1 Membership of the House of Lords, 1760–1850

Year	1760	1784	1798	1820	1830	1840	1850
Total	224	238	302	372	399	448	441

concerned with the management and profitability of their estates, this would clearly have a bearing on their priorities as legislators.

In the case of social standing, all the evidence points to there being considerable similarity between the Lords and a significant number of Commoners throughout this period. One measure of this is the number of sons of peers and peeresses who sat in the Commons along with the number of Irish peers like Lords North and Palmerston who did so as of right. Calculations by the editors of the relevant *History of Parliament* volumes show that in any one Parliament between 1760 and 1820, the proportion gradually increased from an average of 20% before 1790 to 25% thereafter. Further, if this measure is broadened to include relatives of peers, the proportion is considerably greater. Between 1830 and 1851, for example, contemporary calculations show a gentle fall from 253 (38.4%) to 224 (34%) members with peerage family connections, but still more than a third of the House. These figures dovetail with those of another measure: the number of members of the Lords who had served in the Commons. By the 1830s this amounted to nearly 49% of peers, a figure that was probably greater than it had been in the 1760s. Indeed, the evidence strongly suggests that instead of an increasing divergence between the social standing of the members of each house, especially after 1832, the opposite was actually the case.[4] Admittedly, this is a difficult point to substantiate because of the effect of peerage creations on the statistics, but if it is true, it explains why radicals in the 1820s and 1830s were so ready to dub Lords and Commoners collectively as 'the aristocracy'.[5]

With regard to the interests that parliamentarians represented we may begin with the Lords. Prior to this period, peerages or advancement in the ranks of the peerage – from an earldom to a dukedom, for example – were granted on the basis of two principal criteria. The first was the possession of sufficient property to sustain the dignity of the title over a long period of time. As the peerage as a whole contained as many as fifteen ranks between an Irish barony at the bottom to an English or British dukedom at the top, the amount of land required obviously varied but it has been suggested that in the middle of the eighteenth century some 10,000 acres was required for promotion to the English peerage.[6] The second was to have performed some service to the Crown and the executive. Historically, this had normally taken a military form but by the eighteenth century it included political services such as the holding of senior political offices or the wielding of significant electoral influence. The important point, however, is that the two had to go together. Peers were meant to be distinguished by the possession of substantial real estate, as opposed to any other form of property such as a business or stocks and shares; and to be either the descendants of men who had made important military or political contributions to the state or to have made such contributions themselves.

In this period, two developments took place that affected the balance between real estate and state service. The first, attested to by substantial research in recent years on the peerage and the wider aristocracy or landed elite of which they formed a part, was that an increasing number of peers became involved in the transformation that took place in the economy. Some were the beneficiaries of urban expansion; others took advantage of the exploitation of natural resources on their estates such as coal. In addition, many became partners with others in the development of roads, canals and railways and some eventually accepted directorships in the burgeoning number of private and joint-stock companies. The economic interests of the peerage therefore became more diversified. Instead of being focused almost exclusively on the profitability of rural tenancies and farming, more and more peers had connections with other forms of property and other forms of capital.

The second development was that not only did the size of the peerage double but a significant proportion of the new peers were ennobled more on the grounds of their military, political and legal services than the possession of the conventional amounts of landed property. Professor McCahill has therefore shown that about 50% of all peers created between 1801 and 1830 were politicians, lawyers, judges, generals and admirals and that very few possessed the amount of landed property regarded as a necessary qualification in the middle of the eighteenth century. This is a conclusion that seems to be confirmed by detailed information to be found in the *History of Parliament* on the fifty-one members of the Commons who were ennobled between 1790 and 1820.[7]

These developments led to a number of changes in the social and economic interests that the Lords represented. In the case of landed property, for example, the Lords ceased to be an exclusive club of the most substantial proprietors. Instead, it became an institution that represented not only a greater range of property owners but also one in which a significant number had interests in urban property, in commerce and in industrial development. On the other hand, it would be wrong to underestimate the continuing importance of the conventional forms of property to membership of the house. 'Old property' still existed – about a quarter of the House in 1850 had titles that had been granted before 1760; and as McCahill's calculations demonstrate, a significant number of peers created, 1801–30, did possess property that would have been sufficient to qualify them in the eighteenth century. Further, it has also been shown that in the 1830s an attempt was made by the Whigs to ensure that new peers had a minimum of 3,000 acres and £3,000 pa to their name. In this they were not entirely successful but the fact that two-thirds of those ennobled between 1833 and 1885 apparently did possess such a qualification indicates the continuing importance that was attached to landed property as a qualification for membership.[8]

That said, the House clearly became more notably the resting-place for those who had performed significant service to the state and to the principal parties of government and opposition – a 'public service elite' in McCahill's words. One of the probable losers in this respect was the Church of England, whose bishops became a declining proportion of the total, but lawyers, diplomats, colonial governors, generals, admirals and most of all, politicians, became more prominent. In the case of politicians, for example, the Whigs created 86 peers in the 1830s in a failed effort to establish more of a balance between the parties, most of these having performed political service on their behalf. How far this transformed the character of the House – from a club of substantial landed proprietors into an assembly of professionals – is difficult to say. McCahill makes the case for a definite shift in that direction having taken place by 1830 but E. A. Smith is more cautious, pointing to the 'new' men with military and state service behind them as 'mainly drawn from the old governing families or shared their educational experience and social environment'.[9] Perhaps the least that can be said is that the new creations broadened the range of interests represented in the House and kept it in touch with developments taking place in the wider society. One indicator of this is that of the approximately 430 presidents, patrons and trustees of some 130 London voluntary societies dealing with education, literature, science and medicine in 1827, 370 were peers.[10]

But what of the Commons? To what extent did similar or even more dramatic changes take place there? In what always seems to be a matter of surprise to those unfamiliar with the subject, the answer is that they were modest. Admittedly, this is a judgement that is tentative as far as the last decades of this period are concerned. At the time of writing, we have the results of exhaustive research for the period 1760–1820 and the prospect of equally reliable sources for the period to 1832 in the not too distant future. Research on the post-Reform period, however, is patchy. Nevertheless, what does exist suggest that more systematic research on the lines conducted by the *History of Parliament* project would not produce significantly different results. It is on this assumption that the following assessment is based.

In the case of the social standing of Commoners, the characteristics identified in the earlier period continued to be prominent in this. Thus throughout the period the overwhelming majority of members were drawn from the ranks of peerage families and those of the landed gentry. The latter was a capacious group soon to be categorised by the genealogist, Sir J. B. Burke, but for present purposes it can be defined as comprising the baronets, knights and commoners possessing landed property measured in thousands rather than hundreds of acres. In addition, an even greater majority – near 97% from 1790 to 1820 – were Anglican, although this proportion was slightly less than it had been hitherto and was to diminish further following the repeal of the Test and Corporation Acts in 1828, although not to any significant extent. Moreover, the Union with Ireland did not alter this familiar profile. Prior to Catholic relief in 1829, virtually all Irish MPs were of gentry rank or above and there was little change subsequently. Even the number of Catholic MPs did not rise above 30, there being 26 Irish Catholic members out of a total of 28 in 1851. On the other hand, the evidence also points to the size of this majority diminishing over time. It has therefore been argued that the number of members who have been described variously as 'self-made' or of 'non-elite' origins rose from an average of just over 15% of members in any given Parliament between 1715 and 1780 to nearly 23% in those from 1780 to 1820. Further, on the basis of other calculations it seems likely that that this upward trend was continued thereafter, although perhaps not to the same degree. The main conclusion, therefore, is that despite the economic, social and political changes taking place around it, the House retained its predominantly 'aristocratic flavour' throughout this period. The only significant change in terms of the social standing of members was that the proportion of self-made men rose to perhaps 25%.[11]

When turning to the interests that Commoners represented, it is important to note that only a proportion of those who came from peerage or gentry backgrounds relied solely on the income from their estates for a living and that not all self-made men were bankers, merchants and industrialists. Establishing the interests of MPs is therefore a subject fraught with difficulties. That said, the categories of occupation other than that of landed proprietor established by the *History of Parliament* enable us to construct a reasonably clear picture of the profile of the House and the ways that it changed in the period, 1760–1820. This is represented in Table 7.2.

Table 7.2 Occupations and interests of MPs, 1754–1820[a]

Occupations	Maximum, minimum and approximate numbers for individual Parliaments, 1754–90	The same, 1790–1820
Holders of political/ legal offices	40–50	71 (1812)
Court officials/ sinecurists/pensioners	39	38 (1812)
Army officers not on half pay or retired	49–68	69–94
Serving Naval officers	14–22	*c.*25
Bankers/financiers/ merchants/industrialists	60	78 (1802) 75 (1818)
Practising barristers/ attorneys/solicitors	*c.*30	*c.*30
E. India Co. officials/ soldiers. E. India traders	26–45	*c.*55
W. Indian proprietors/ merchants/agents	9–15	20+
Totals	*c.*267/*c.*329	*c.*383/*c.*411
The rest, principally proprietors	*c.*291/*c.*229	Post-1801: *c.*247

Notes

a These figures have been extracted from Namier and Brooke, *The Commons*, i, pp. 99–162 and Thorne, *The Commons*, i, pp. 278–332. In the case of the West India interest in Parliament, it was, as Thorne states (i, p. 325), 'diffuse' and there has been some debate about its extent. In a recent article, A. J. O'Shaughnessy estimates it at between 20 and 50 in 1781 which puts it higher than any of those of Namier and Brooke. Thorne says (i, p. 325) that the interest as a whole was greater than that of the East Indian interest in 1818 but does not suggest a figure for an average Parliament. My estimate is of the number of proprietors, merchants and agents only and is provisional, see O'Shaughnessy, 'The formation of a commercial lobby: The West India interest, British Colonial Policy and the American Revolution', *HJ*, vol. 40 (1997), pp. 71–95.

Several conclusions can be drawn from these, admittedly, proximate figures. If we consider the last category, for example, it seems clear that a gently declining proportion of about 40% of members, when not attending to parliamentary business, were principally engaged in looking after their estates. As indicated in the table, some caution needs to be exercised on this point. In the calculation of the number of 'Bankers-industrialists', for example, members who were exploiting the extraction of coal and minerals on their estates were omitted. Moreover, there is some evidence for the post-1820 period that more Commoners occupied seats on the boards of commercial companies than the table suggests. In 1827 some 97 were directors of 60 City institutions and insurance companies.[12] On the other hand, the figures are close to the 200 'country gentlemen' suggested by Namier and Brooke for the parliaments of 1754–90 – an estimate repeated for the later period by a number of other authorities. However, it also clear that despite the House consisting throughout this period of an overwhelming majority of substantial landowners, a rising majority of all members (over 62% after 1801) were drawing an income from politics, the professions and various forms of business. Some of these were self-made men but the important point is that majority was clearly not. This leads us to the even more important general point, that although the House of Commons retained its predominantly aristocratic character up to *c*.1820, it continued to represent a broad cross-section of the *established* interests in the state: the Church, rural and urban property and therefore agriculture; the armed forces, the legal profession; and commerce in general and colonial trade in particular. On the other hand, it was responding only modestly to the emerging *new* interests. There was certainly a steady number of 'self-made men', a small proportion of which represented the new forms of industrial production but there were hardly any representatives of the fast-growing nonconformist communities.[13]

Although the *History of Parliament* volumes for the period 1820–32 are yet to appear and research on the next twenty years, is patchy, current knowledge suggests that there was little subsequent change to this spread of interests. Professor Aydelotte's now venerable analysis of the 1841 Parliament, for example, reveals roughly the same distribution that existed in the later eighteenth century. Of the 815 men who sat in that Parliament, 25.4% were of peerage stock; 16.6% were baronets and their descendants and 29.4% were landed gentry. In his judgement, the Commons was 'overwhelmingly aristocratic in composition'.[14] In fact the only significant change that can be detected is an increase from about 1830 in the number of new members returned at general elections. Between 1760 and 1820 this had fallen from about 23% to 19% of all members. It then rose to 28% in 1830, and 38% in 1832 (when there was an influx of liberals and radicals), before settling down to around 33% until at least 1852. However, more new members than usual did not alter either the social profile of the House or the range of interests that it represented. In the 1847 Parliament, for example, I have so far been able to identify only eight MPs who were directly associated with industrial manufacture.[15] Given the changes taking place to the economy in the first half of the nineteenth century, it would seem that the trend after 1820 was for the Commons to become *less* representative of the dynamic sectors – industry, the emerging middle-class and nonconformity – than it had been before.

Parties

Although the social composition of Lords and Commons and the economic interests that their members represented clearly have a bearing on Parliament's contribution to government, a more important factor is the way that they aligned themselves politically.[16] In the previous period, a Whig–Tory polarity had dominated parliamentary politics until the 1740s, albeit one that had been complicated by differences within each of the two camps on broadly 'Court' and 'Country' lines. In the course of the 1750s, however, the decline of Jacobitism and overtures from the Pelhams and subsequently Pitt led an increasing number of Tories to support government with the result that that party disintegrated as a cohesive force. The old polarity therefore faded to the point that George III was able to declare in February 1762 that no party divisions existed.[17] The question, then, is what happens subsequently and in this respect there are two related issues to address. The first is the structural characteristics of the supporters or opponents of government and how far they were governed by the discipline of party. And the second is to what extent such discipline was based on allegiance to a coherent ideology. It is to these issues that we now turn.

In the case of the disciplines of party, several general points need to be made by way of introduction to what is a complex subject. As we have already observed, the vast majority of parliamentarians throughout this period consisted of men of substantial property, many of whom had a variety of occupational interests other than the management of their estates. In addition, a considerable number were elected as a result of their own electoral interests or those of kinsmen and allies in their constituencies. These were the kind of characteristics that encouraged an independence of mind rather than a readiness to submit to the dictates of an organised party. It was also the case that a substantial numbers of peers and commoners spent only a modest amount of time in Parliament during sessions and some hardly any at all. This might be due to the press of business in the country or to the tedium and expense of travelling long distances to London and then finding accommodation there. This would account for the fact that barely half of the members of either House were regularly engaged in parliamentary business during the course of a session and probably only one-quarter who were permanently and actively so. These were also factors that militated against the development of a fully fledged party system. The most powerful inhibitor, however, until at least the second decade of the nineteenth century, was a widespread, although far from total, disapproval of party on constitutional grounds – a point underlined by the eighteenth-century Commons' convention that members should make no allusion in their speeches to collective action by parties.[18] Contemporaries therefore drew a distinction between two types of parties: the personal party, that is, the acolytes of a particular individual such as the Younger Pitt; and a party that had been formed to promote a particular set of policies on a systematic basis. The former, although not necessarily welcomed, was regarded as the inevitable outcome of a parliamentary system and one which being attached to an individual was likely to be too small and too short-lived to offer any serious threat either to the monarch's prerogative to choose ministers freely or the collective judgement of Parliament. Parties that were formed to promote specific policies on a systematic basis, on the other hand, could clearly offer such a threat, especially if there were just two of them commanding the allegiance of a majority of members. If that were the case, there would be a return to what were now regarded as the divisive and damaging state of affairs that had existed in the post-Revolution era. Further, the key prerogative of the monarch would be rendered, in effect, impotent. It was only when George III became incapable of wielding his prerogatives that those who had been the stoutest defenders of them began to moderate their opposition to parties of this kind.

With these general points in mind, we may turn to the structural characteristics of the supporters and opponents of government and in this respect it is helpful to divide the period into two parts, the dividing line between them being the Reform crisis of 1830–2. It will also be useful to deal with the supporters and opponents separately.

In the period 1760–1830, by far the most consistent polarity lay between, on the one hand, ministers and their supporters; and on the other, what soon styled itself the Whig Party. In the case of the Commons, each side sat on opposite sides of the chamber but this was not formalised in the Lords until the move to the Court of Requests in 1801 when the seating arrangements physically separated them.[19] This new polarity took root in the 1760s. Initially, the accession of a new King in the midst of the Seven Years War had brought about a high degree of unity in Parliament upon which the Pitt-Newcastle administration could draw but this broke down as a result of series of well-known events: Pitt's resignation in 1761; the King's elevation of Lord Bute from political obscurity to a Secretaryship of State to fill the vacuum; Newcastle's resignation the following year; and Bute's becoming first minister and the subsequent dismissal of many of Newcastle's adherents from office. As a result, the Whigs fractured into several personal parties: principally those of Pitt, Bute, George Grenville (who succeeded Bute as first minister), the Duke of Bedford, and Newcastle, whose adherents soon fell under the headship of the Marquis of Rockingham. In the meantime, the Tories, estimated at 113 in the Commons following the 1761 election, went in four different directions. One group took office; a second became regular supporters of government; another was of a more independent frame of mind but generally supported ministers and a fourth went into consistent opposition.[20]

The crucial factor that established a more or less consistent polarity thereafter was the reaction to these events by the Newcastle–Rockingham

Whigs. They concluded that they had been the victims of a plot by George III to establish a degree of influence over the composition and policies of ministries that was incompatible with the mixed system of government established by their ancestors at the time of the Glorious Revolution. They therefore claimed to be the 'true' Whigs – a claim that was re-enforced in their view by the circumstances surrounding the collapse of Rockingham's brief administration which the King had been obliged to ask him to form in 1765–6. Moreover, they later went a step further and proclaimed themselves to be the Whig *Party*, thereby hoping to deny the designation to any of the other personal groups, all of which were largely composed of politicians who thought of themselves as Whigs. It was these events that established the subsequent line of division in both houses. With the exception of two and a half years when the Whigs were in office (March 1782–November 1783 and January 1806–March 1807) ministers and their supporters were opposed principally by the self-styled Whig Party.

There was also considerable consistency in the structures and internal workings of these two bodies. In the case of ministers and their supporters, research has demonstrated that if their total number in either house is analysed at any point between *c*.1770 and 1830, it consisted of a loose amalgam of several types of members, each one having different ties with those in office. Admittedly, the current state of research makes it impossible to substantiate this point in the case of the House of Lords, but as the evidence points to there being considerable similarity between the two houses, the evidence applicable to the Commons is likely to apply to both. What we might call the government side of the House therefore consisted of the following types of members:

1   ministers, other office holders, and the personal supporters of senior ministers;
2   the 'King's friends' or the 'party of the Crown';
3   members occupying seats controlled by patrons who supported government;
4   the majority of Scottish and after 1801, Irish members;
5   a significant number of independent backbenchers (or country gentlemen) sitting principally for English and Welsh county constituencies.

According to detailed research, their total number (and percentage) in the Commons following successive general elections in all but the case of 1828 as shown in Table 7.3.

The key issue that has exercised historians is to what extent the amalgams represented by these figures constituted a coherent political party and therefore led to the re-establishment of the two-party polarity that had existed hitherto. Some factors clearly militated against such a development. In the case of the various types of members adumbrated above, the reasons and circumstances that led each of them to support ministers varied and were not always harmonious. The King's friends, for example, regarded themselves as first

Table 7.3 Supporters of government, 1774–1828[a]

Year	1774	1780	1784	1790	1796	1802	1807	1812	1818	1828
Number	321	260	315	340	424	467	388	400	411	*c.*410
	(57.5%)	(46.5%)	(56.4%)	(60.9%)	(75.9%)	(70.9%)	(58.9%)	(60.7%)	(62.4%)	(62.3%)

Notes

a The figures for 1774–1818 are based on Gregory and Stevenson, *Britain in the Eighteenth Century*, pp. 107–9 and my own calculations from Namier and Brooke, *The Commons*, i, pp. 57–96 and Thorne, *The Commons*, i, pp. 110–277. That for 1828 (following the resignation of the Canningites) is my own calculation, see *British Politics*, pp. 257–8.

and foremost the supporters of the King's chosen ministers as opposed to the ministers themselves or their policies. Their number was considerable throughout the reign of George III and was crucial to the sustaining of the Younger Pitt as first minister following the dismissal of the Fox-North coalition in November 1783 and to doing the same for the Portland and Perceval ministries from 1807 to 1810. Although a 1788 calculation listing 185 as the party of the 'Crown' may have been inflated to meet with the approval of its commissioner, Lord North, it provides some measure of their importance to ministers.[21]

In the case of other types of members, the substantial patronage available to ministers, especially those of a similar political outlook who were in office for such a long period of time, was of some account. They were chiefly responsible for most of the peerages created after *c.*1770 and also for overseeing the election of the Scottish and Irish representative peers and having a say in the nominations to vacant bishoprics and archbishoprics with seats in the Lords. This is one of the reasons for the increasing majority that successive governments possessed in that House. A similar coincidence of interest helps to explain the support of most occupiers of seats under patronage and the majority of Scottish and Irish members. In the case of patrons who sold their not inconsiderable number of seats, many looked to the government of the day to find suitable purchasers while others thought it wise to sell to purchasers who were likely to support it. This clearly worked to the advantage of ministers with a firm purchase on office. As for the Scottish and Irish MPs, a more direct form of management played a part. In the case of Scotland, the Dundas family established a firm grip on Scottish patronage from the 1770s onwards and used it to cement the attachment of the majority of Scottish MPs to the ministerial side of the Commons from then until 1830. Similarly, in Ireland, the Lord Lieutenant and the Chief Secretary deployed the same means to copper-fasten the support of what turned out to be two-thirds or more of the 100 Irish members.

The support of the independent country gentlemen, on the other hand, came largely without ties. Elected by and large for county constituencies with substantial electorates and using their own electoral interests as a base, country gentlemen prided themselves on being the voice of the provinces or 'Country' and therefore charged with keeping a watchful eye on the Court and its ministers. The inclination of the majority was to give general support to the government of the day, reserving the right to turn against it in the national interest when circumstances warranted. This they did to help bring an end to Lord North's government in 1782 and to force Lord Liverpool's government to abandon the income tax in 1816.

The full complement of the ministerial side of the Commons therefore consisted of a variety of different types of members, each disposed to be where they were for a variety of different motives, expectations and convictions. It was probably for this reason that the means of management deployed by ministers were more suited to a confederation than an organised political party. In this respect it is important to take note of some of the characteristics of those who held office. None of the first ministers from North to Wellington, for example, regarded themselves as the leader of a party consisting of all those who supported them. Each of them had varying numbers of personal acolytes and in the cases of Liverpool and Wellington, a larger number of general supporters, but all saw themselves primarily as the King's first minister and not as a party leader in any modern sense. Further, although the number and size of personal parties declined with the formation of Lord North's administration in 1770, they reappeared after Pitt's resignation in 1801 and Liverpool's in 1827, thereby underlining the continuing importance of personal, as opposed to party, loyalties. In 1801 Pitt's ministerial team dissolved into at least three different personal groups – Pitt's, Lord Grenville's and Canning's – and these were soon joined by that of his replacement, Addington. In 1827, Liverpool's cohort was also shattered into ultra Tories, the followers of George Canning, and somewhere between them, the followers of Wellington and Peel. Indeed, the highly personalised state of ministerial politics resulted in first ministers spending a considerable amount of their time trying to persuade individuals with personal followings to join them – even if they were associated with the Opposition. This resulted in the Younger Pitt persuading the Portland Whigs to join him in 1794 and in Lord Liverpool winning over first Canning and his followers in 1816 and then the Grenvillites in 1822. Even Wellington made some effort to neutralise Whig opposition by some judicious appointments. In short, the continuing importance of personal parties and the manoeuvres they encouraged militated against the development of party loyalty.

The methods that ministers used to ensure that a sufficient number of their 'friends' supported them in the division lobbies hardly changed in the course of this period and were also more suited to the needs of a loose confederation than a coherent party. The key figures were the first minister, and if he was in the Lords, the principal minister in the Commons, together with the parliamentary Secretary at the Treasury who looked after the patronage interests of the English and Welsh members and usually kept lists of 'friends' and 'foes'. In addition, one minister managed the Scottish members (usually a member of the Dundas family) while the Lord Lieutenant and the Chief Secretary did the same with the Irish members.

One of the methods used was to issue circulars alerting friends in either House to important debates and expressing the hope that they would attend. Sometimes these might be limited to those who were certain to support and on other occasions to the much larger number whose allegiance was more doubtful. Another was to hold private meetings of various kinds. The most traditional was a general gathering of supporters at the 'Cockpit', a large room in the middle of Whitehall, to listen to an outline of ministerial policies before their being announced in the King's Speech on the opening day of the session. However, these became increasingly unruly during the latter part of the eighteenth century with the result that they had been discontinued by 1802 in favour of more select gatherings at the house of the first minister and if he was in the Lords, a parallel one at the house of the principal minister in the Commons.[22] In addition, there might be other meetings during the course of the session, sometimes taking the form of dinners and usually for only a hard core of supporters. Between 1828 and 1830, for example, no more than 125 ministers and supporters of the government have been identified as attending a series of dinners hosted by Wellington and Peel – a fraction of the total of their supposed strength in both houses.[23]

Apart from these entirely traditional methods, however, there is no evidence of any other forms and forums of organisation. There was no specific club in London which was exclusive to government supporters and the only one which might have become so, the Pitt Club, founded in 1802, became associated in the 1820s with the anti-Catholic cause – one to which Pitt had not subscribed and many of his acolytes did not subscribe. Moreover, although there were numerous political clubs in the constituencies that supported the policies promoted by government, no attempt was made to establish links with these on a permanent basis. In short, organisation was simply designed to secure as much support as was needed to sustain ministers in office on a session-by-session basis and not to lay the foundations for an organised and enduring political party. This is one of the reasons why a good deal of uncertainty surrounded the real strength of government throughout this period. Between 1773 and 1780, for example, the North government lost four divisions due to members who normally voted for it, voting with the Opposition.[24] A half century later, in the aftermath of the 1830 election, the assiduous Treasury secretary, Joseph Planta, could not be certain of the disposition of 129 Commoners and saw his government defeated by the opposition of more than 19 he had regarded as friends.[25]

On the other hand, the evidence also points to the emergence within this confederation of a group that not only acquired the characteristics of a political party but also the readiness to regard themselves as such. There were several reasons for this. One was a decline in the attractions of being one of the King's friends: partly because of the failing powers of George III after 1807 and the fact that his successor could not command equivalent respect; and partly because of a reduction in the means by which the monarch could influence members. Another was the habit of working together over such a long period of time. Thus, there was considerable continuity between the core membership of successive governments, best exemplified by the careers of the first and second Lords Liverpool who were in office almost continuously from 1761 to 1827. A third, and probably the most important, reason was the support for specific policies. Initially, these were associated with the long ministries of North and the Younger Pitt: the prosecution of the American war and resistance to economic and parliamentary reforms in the case of North; financial and modest economic reform coupled with the war against France in the case of Pitt. After Pitt's death in 1806, however, many supporters of the subsequent administrations found common cause in a resistance to Catholic emancipation, parliamentary reform and any reduction in the level of protection offered to agriculture by the Corn Laws of 1815. Although the senior Pittites were in fact divided on the issues of Catholics and Corn, the bulk of their more committed supporters fell into the camp of resistors with the result that their opponents after 1807 began to label them as Tories – the 'resistors' of the past – a label that they soon proved willing to apply to themselves.

As a result of these developments, closer and closer ties were formed between ministers and their more committed supporters. How far this had developed before 1807 is difficult to calculate but it certainly took place thereafter. Contemporary evidence therefore attests to the re-emergence of a Tory party which research suggests consisted in the 1820s of about 75 members in the Lords and between 120 and 150 in the Commons. It did not comprise all the supporters of government and many of its leaders were reluctant to regard themselves as Tories, preferring to see themselves in the less ideologically committed guise of servants of the Crown and 'men of business'. Moreover, although most ministerially-inspired meetings were focussed on this body, party organisation still remained primitive. On the other hand, there is little doubt that the ministerial side of both houses had a more clearly defined and much stronger nucleus than had existed hitherto.

By contrast with the slow evolution of party as an acknowledged nucleus of government forces, the self-styled Whig Party performed that function for those of opposition for all but the two and a half years when they were in office between 1766 and 1830. Estimates of the total strength (and proportion) of the Opposition in the Commons during that period are as follows (Table 7.4):

Substantial research has therefore demonstrated that Whigs not only consistently took the lead in opposing ministers in both houses but that they did

Table 7.4 Opponents of government, 1780–1828[a]

Year	1780	1784	1790	1796	1802	1807	1812	1818	1828
Number	254 (45.5%)	213 (38.1%)	183 (32.7%)	95 (17%)	124 (18.8%)	224 (34%)	196 (29.7%)	198 (30%)	c.200 (c.30.3%)

Note
a Calculated from the same sources referred to in note 22 above and for Jupp, *British Politics*, see p. 292.

so as an organised political party. There were recognised leaders in Rockingham (1765–82), Fox (1782–1806) and Lord Grey (1807–34). The core membership almost constituted a caste, being distinguished by high aristocratic status, considerable landed wealth, close ties of kinship and in some cases, descent from forebears who had played a prominent role in the Revolution settlement, although not as many as were sometimes claimed. In addition, there were various forms of organisation, although not all of them were operated consistently or together. The core parliamentary membership came to possess an exclusively Whig London club in Brooks's and formed the bedrock of the Whig Club founded in Westminster in May 1784 to support Fox's candidature for that constituency but which soon acquired a national significance.[26] There were regular party meetings to discuss tactics, 'whips' to encourage members to attend important debates, and managers of elections. The Whigs also had newspapers intermittently under their control even though most of their leaders regarded the press with suspicion or downright hostility, believing that dealing with it was 'dirty work'.[27]

In constitutional terms, of course, this was a development of considerable significance. Between 1714 and 1760 ministers had opponents but the question mark against the loyalty of elements of the Tory party had cast a doubt on the legitimacy of an 'Opposition' as a permanent and desirable institution. It could also be said that the existence of such an institution might conflict with the monarch's prerogative to be able to choose his ministers freely. However the decision of the Rockingham Whigs to form themselves into a party and to claim that it was necessary to do in order to preserve a mixed constitution, coupled with the fact that they were in almost permanent opposition after 1766, had the effect of giving the concept of the Opposition a degree of legitimacy. The term 'opposition front bench' was apparently in use by the 1770s[28] and although the Opposition as an institution, like that of 'prime minister' or 'the cabinet', was never formally recognised in this period – as 'His [or Her] Majesty's Opposition' – its existence quickly became an accepted fact.

On the other hand, it would be wrong to conclude that the Whig Party was either an entirely homogenous body or that it was the only element in the Oppositions of this period and had complete control of their operations. A number of studies of the party, for example, have shown there to be considerable variation in the degree of commitment on the part of members throughout this period.[29] This has led to the general conclusion that the party consisted of a solid core of active and committed members and a penumbra of less active and less dependable materials. It was also the case that the Whigs often acted in an alliance with other groups that had their own agendas. In the late 1770s, this consisted of groups led by Lord Shelburne, the Duke of Rutland and Sir James Lowther.[30] Between 1784 and 1794 the Foxite Whigs acted in concert with Lord North's followers who at the height of their strength constituted about 40% of their combined number.[31] Ten years later, by which time their own forces had been severely reduced by the defection of the Portland Whigs to Pitt, they formed a junction with the Grenvillites – a junction which lasted until 1817. Moreover the Whigs, like the government, always relied on the support of members who were independent of party. One such welcome source was the independent country gentlemen, a sizeable proportion of whom habitually voted with the Opposition. More problematic was the support of the radicals, who although they never amounted to more than a dozen or so MPs in the first half of this period, grew in number towards the end. Radicals had strong agendas of their own which were often at odds with those of the Whigs. In short, although the Whig Party provided the Opposition with a consistent and substantial nucleus, the Opposition as a whole for a good part of this period was almost as much of a hybrid as the government forces.

So far we have observed the gradual emergence by 1830 of a two-party conflict as the key dynamic in parliamentary politics. Following the dissolution of the Tories as a cohesive force in the 1750s and 1760s, the standard pattern of conflict for the bulk of George III's reign lay between a ministerially led confederation and an Opposition led by, but not exclusive to, the Whig Party. It was only after 1807 that the Pittite ministerial cohort began to cohere and that the most dedicated of their followers began to regard themselves as Tories, thereby restoring the semblance of a two-party conflict. The crucial point, however, is that this did not result in a two-party 'system' – a term that implies that the vast majority of all MPs fell into one or other of the two camps. It certainly was the case by the late 1820s that a two-party polarity dominated the conduct of the 300 or so most active MPs in the Commons but it could not be said of the bare majority which constituted the rest. As will be discussed later, the point is crucial when estimating the impact of party on government. In a multi-party and multi-interest assembly, ministers and their leading opponents have to shape policy to attract the broadest spectrum of support. In a two-party system, there is a greater prospect of direction and coherence.

What happened, then, after 1830? The consensus amongst historians is that although there was change, there was also a fair measure of continuity. The catalyst to current thinking on the subject was Professor Gash's magisterial intervention published almost forty years ago in which he made the case for the emergence of a two-party system by the end of the 1830s. The essence of his argument is that the crisis over Reform, 1830–2, reversed the historic fortunes of the two parties and produced a new political landscape, shorn of the influence of the Crown and the 'rotten' boroughs that it was thought had previously sustained the King's chosen ministers in office. Both parties therefore had to organise themselves more effectively. In the case of the Tories, who were reduced to about 180 MPs at the 1832 election, this led to the adoption of 'Conservative Party' as their new name and the establishment of new forms of parliamentary and electoral organisation. As for the Whigs, who found themselves with nearly 480 supporters in the first reformed Parliament, there were similar developments, most notably a formal agreement between themselves, the radicals and O'Connellites in 1835 to concert measures to oust Peel from office – the Lichfield House 'compact'. In these circumstances, Gash argued, the new Conservative Party and an embryonic, if nor perfectly formed, Liberal Party, each organised centrally at their newly established Carlton and Reform clubs, absorbed virtually all MPs, thereby eliminating the uncertain disposition of so many MPs that was a feature of the situation before 1830.[32]

Since then there has been considerable modification of Gash's thesis. In the case of the reliance that party leaders could now place on their supporters, it appears that it was considerable on motions of confidence in ministers but much less so when it came to divisions on specific policy issues and on a variety of miscellaneous matters. As Ian Newbould has shown, the vast majority of Commoners (80%+) who voted on confidence motions throughout the period, 1830–41, did so consistently for one front bench or the other. As he points out, this casts some doubt on the contention of Gash and others that party solidarity developed *after* 1832, and more particularly, after 1835. In the many more divisions on specific policy issues, however, he found that consistent support for ministers dropped to anything between 11% and 22% of their supposed followers, the rest opposing them on at least 10% of such occasions and some of them consistently. When divisions on all other issues were added, the results were roughly the same. Moreover, as Newbould has also argued, the case for a two-party system developing after 1834 is rendered problematic by the fact that not only did the Whigs look to Conservative support in the Commons in order to resist the pressure of radical MPs but Peel obliged by delivering it on a number of crucial occasions between 1835 and 1839.[33]

Historians have also expressed reservations about the effectiveness of and commitment to, parliamentary and electoral organisation, particularly on the part of the Whigs. In the case of the Conservatives, the argument for the development of a more effective form of parliamentary organisation built around the Carlton Club and consisting of a regular pattern of party meetings supported by whips and managers for MPs from all parts of the UK remains a strong one. The only caveat that might be entered is that apart from the Carlton Club, most of the devices were in place during the period of the Wellington government and appear to have been traditional rather than novel.[34] On the other hand, Francis Bonham's role as a central election manager does appear to be innovatory, although there is now strong evidence that the demand for improved electoral management, particularly of the now all-important matter of voter registration, came from the constituencies rather than from the centre.[35]

There are strong reservations, however, about the formation of a Liberal Party organisation. The Lichfield House Compact, it has been pointed out, was a temporary arrangement for a specific purpose between three distinct groups who had no intention of submerging their different long-term goals. Further, there is abundant evidence that the Whigs, with one or two exceptions, had very little interest in the organisation of their followers in Parliament, in electoral organisation, or in such matters as influencing the press. Broadly speaking, they regarded such activities as demeaning to the power of rational argument as expressed in parliamentary speeches and as unpleasant in so far as it meant their having to negotiate with radicals. Thus, the equivalents to Bonham and the Carlton Club, the Reform Association of 1834 and the Reform Club of 1835, were not the initiatives of the Whigs but of radicals. The Reform Association, for example, was founded by Lord Durham to encourage the spread of registration societies in the constituencies but quickly fell under the control of two radicals, James Coppock and Joseph Parkes. Although it had more success in this regard than some have alleged, it did not have the close association with the Whig leadership that Bonham possessed with Peel. Similarly, the Reform Club was founded by radicals as an alternative to Brooks's, the Whigs' watering hole, but although some Whigs joined, it never acquired the unique position possessed by the Carlton.[36]

Finally, as the earlier points suggest, historians now stress the importance of the differences within these two parties as opposed to the differences between them. In this respect it is important to bear in mind two cardinal points. The first is that at this time there was no formal way an individual became a member of a parliamentary party and therefore no way that he could be formally expelled from it. Being a member of a party meant no more than it being known that the individual was prepared to consider supporting a specific set of front-bench spokesmen. The tradition that party compromised the independence of judgement which men of property were supposed to possess still lived on and it was not until the late nineteenth century that it finally disappeared. The second is that contemporaries used a variety of terms to describe themselves and their political opponents. 'Conservative' was the official new name for erstwhile 'ultra Tories' and 'Tories' as well as those who had avoided any such appellation, but the older terms continued to be used well into the nineteenth century and beyond. There was even greater variety amongst those on the other side. Contemporaries therefore referred to 'old' Whigs, 'new' Whigs, radicals and in an effort to be more inclusive, 'reformers' and 'liberals'. This suggests that labelling all those on one side as Conservatives and all those on the other as Liberals is in danger of being anachronistic.

Recent historians of the Conservatives have therefore laid stress on the differences within the party between the ultras, dedicated to resisting any further changes to the constitution and to maintaining the privileges of the Church of England and the benefits of the Corn Laws; the Tories, who, resembling the country gentlemen of old, were more pliant supporters of the front bench; and the followers of Peel, who as he proclaimed in his Tamworth Manifesto, was prepared to contemplate the rational reform of existing institutions. As a consequence, Bruce Coleman has persuasively described the Conservatives as more of a 'confederacy' of 'interests' than a homogenous party and regards the increasing tensions between the protectionists and the Peelites which led to the split of 1846 over the Corn Laws as symptomatic of this state of affairs.[37] More recent work on the ultra tories as a distinctive force, particularly in registering the voters, and on the strong appeal of protectionism as an antidote to class conflict has tended to reinforce his point.[38]

The case is much stronger for the liberal side of the equation. Grey's first ministry was a coalition of Whigs, ex-Canningite Tories and one ultra Tory and numerous studies have shown that the more predominantly Whig ministries after 1832 were supported by a heterogeneous body of members of which Whigs themselves were probably only a bare majority. Following the 1832 election, for example, it has been calculated that about 190–200 MPs out of the 480 supporters of Grey's government were either various kinds of radicals or followers of O'Connell. Further, although the number of radicals subsequently declined, there were few signs of greater unity. As Greville put it after Peel's victory at the 1841 election, the opposition consisted of 'three distinct sections of politicians, the great Whig and moderate Radical body, owning John [Russell] for their leader, the ultra Radicals following Roebuck, and the Irish under O'Connell'. In view of the fact that Russell detested Roebuck's 'doctrines' and could not be restrained from attacking O'Connell, Greville concluded that Peel had nothing to fear 'from the compact union of his opponents'. Studies of the individual components of the 'Liberal Tabernacle' have also shown that these too contained discordant elements.[39]

The substance of debate

So far we have observed that although Parliament throughout this period consisted largely of substantial landed gentlemen, it also represented a broad range of professional, financial and commercial interests. It is noticeable, however, that in relation to social and economic change, its membership after 1832 failed to represent three new dynamic forces: industry, nonconformity and the middle-class. In addition, it has been argued that both before and after 1832, the principal dividing line lay between two groups each of which was more of a coalition of different interests than a homogeneous political party. We might therefore conclude that from a structural perspective, Parliament encouraged a tactical, pragmatic and accommodatory approach to government on the part of both the ministerial and opposition front benches. This conclusion, however, raises the question of how far such an approach was reflected in the conduct and political views expressed not only by the leading parliamentarians but also by the rank and file. It is to this subject that we now turn.

As indicated in Chapter 6 this period was notable for a remarkable flowering of political theory and moral philosophy. It was also argued that although many ministers were strongly influenced by some of the speculative propositions that flowed from it, policy until the 1820s tended to be formulated within the framework of a set of assumptions conditioned more by practical than philosophical considerations. It was only from about 1820 that what might be called convictions about ideal policies became more influential, although not to the point where they could be called entirely ideological in either conception or execution. Ministers, however, were usually more circumscribed by circumstances and events than their opponents and it is therefore important to consider next the thinking of the Whigs and some of the other groups who acted in opposition.

The basis of Whig thinking was rooted in their experience and memory of the previous period and adapted to changing circumstances. They therefore believed in the capacity of the mixed constitution to resist despotism or revolution and to enable change to take place gradually and peacefully. This was a point of view that was reinforced in the late eighteenth and early nineteenth centuries by the outcome of the French Revolution and the publication of historical works that began to chart a progressive and evolutionary theme in English history to which the Whigs, it was proposed, had made a distinguished contribution.[40] In addition, they began to believe more strongly than they had done earlier that the enduring virtues of the constitution were due to the fact that it was based, as the qualifications for parliamentarians and voters attested, on the preservation and defence of landed property. Hitherto, few had challenged the view that political participation should depend on the possession of such property but as the sales of the '*Rights of Man*' suggested, increasing numbers did in this period. This, together with other developments that seemed to undermine the influence of the landed interest – of which many Whigs were substantial members – therefore made it necessary to emphasise the beneficial role of property as the foundation of the constitution.[41]

On this basis, Whigs constructed a number of working 'principles' that were grounded in practical politics and held to pretty consistently over time. The principal one flowed from what they regarded as their exclusion from office in the 1760s and the ability of the Crown and its chosen to ministers to construct a majority against them for the best part of the next fifty years. The monarch and his lackeys therefore had too much influence under their control. As a consequence, Whigs believed that it should be reduced by means of economical and parliamentary reform in order to re-establish the balanced constitution and enable the sponsors of the Revolution and the wealthier aristocrats in the land to have a fair chance of office once again. This was linked to a second principle, namely that the preservation of the aristocratic element of the constitutional balance could only be achieved if it showed itself to be capable of acting as a patron of popular pressure that was expressed in constitutional forms and had libertarian, although not egalitarian, objectives. Here, Whigs had in mind legally constituted meetings leading to petitions for the removal of civil and religious disabilities. Such patronage would enable the aristocracy to frame legislation in ways that would suit their own interests as well as those of the pressure groups concerned. Taken together, these two principles led to a third, which was that they justified the Whigs acting in Parliament as a party of systematic opposition.

It was these basic principles that ordered Whig priorities and shaped their policies. National finance, for example, never attracted much serious Whig attention until the 1830s, it being a subject that did not touch directly on the distribution of power or aristocratic competence. War, on the other hand, they certainly saw as doing so. Most Whigs had some sympathy for the initial aims of the American rebels and French revolutionaries but the underlying argument against the wars that ensued were twofold. First, that they provided ministers additional reserves of patronage by which they could sustain themselves in office; and second, that they subjected the country to strains that might threaten the stability on which aristocratic power rested.

However, even if we grant the Whigs some consistency of purpose, it was only intermittently that they were able to pursue it without qualification. As mentioned earlier, Whigs were usually in some form of alliance with other groups, most notably Lord North's followers from 1783–90 and Lord Grenville's from 1803–17. In each case, this led to a good deal of negotiation and trimming on policy. With regard to the war against Napoleon after 1807, for example, protracted wrangling over the merits of Lord Grenville's preference for a defensive war and the hankering of the more radical Whigs for a peace settlement led to an agreement that neither policy would be pursued to the exclusion of the other.[42] Further, such was the degree of parliamentary weakness and wrangling over policy that there were times when the leaders virtually ceased their parliamentary activities, thereby abandoning the principal of systematic opposition. Fox seceded from Parliament in 1797 and Lord Grey also went into a form of semi-retirement after 1823.

Of the dozen or so smaller, but nevertheless numerically significant, groups that sometimes acted in government and in opposition before 1830, hardly any were based on a coherent ideology or fixed principles. Instead, they were bound together in varying degrees by other considerations: admiration for a particular leader; support for his specific policies; ties of patronage and kinship; and resentment at losing office or the hope of gaining or re-gaining it. The followers of the Prince of Wales and Addington, for example, significant groups after 1802 and 1804, respectively, were dedicated to supporting the advancement of their heads and held together principally by ties of patronage, kinship and expectation. Those of George Grenville (1765–70), Lord Shelburne (1774–83), and Lord Grenville (1802–17), on the other hand, were focussed more on the specific policies associated with their head, although past obligations, kinship, and in the case of Lord Grenville's followers, ambition, also played a part. George Grenville's party as characterised by Philip Lawson was typical. Amounting to about 74 members in 1766 but to little more than 30 after the 1768 election, Grenville's supporters were bound together by their common experience of office and were dedicated to attacking the circumstances that led to their dismissal, defending their past policies, and opposing those of their successors that deviated from them. Lawson defines their core policies as follows: the exposure of the secret influence of the King and Bute; the reining in of public expenditure; and opposition to any increase in the national debt. However, this did not preclude seizing on other issues and taking advantage of them in order to embarrass ministers. This was the case with Grenville's opposition to the Royal proclamation against grain exports in 1766, his argument being that dearth was due more to the high levels of government taxation than the ostensible reason for the embargo – the high prices being paid to producers.[43]

In fact the only groups that might appear to have been bound together more by fixed principles than the issues of the moment were the 36 or Whigs who joined Pitt in July 1794; the followers of George Canning who numbered some 46 in Lords and Commons in 1827; and the ultra Tories, whose number grew to possibly 80 or so in both houses in 1829. Given the subsequent role of two of its members, Melbourne and Palmerston, the Canningites was probably the most influential of these groups, but it is also the most difficult to assess. Established in the 1796 Parliament and given sustenance subsequently by Canning's attacks on the Addington ministry, the group remained an essentially personal following until the 1820s when his Foreign Secretaryship and brief premiership in 1827, led to its expansion. Following his death in August 1827, his followers pledged their adherence to what they claimed to be his principles. Defining them in abstract terms, however, proved difficult and the best that one of his strongest admirers could do was to say that he was 'anti-revolutionary' but sought to avoid revolution by ensuring that legislation was 'conformable to the spirit of the times'. The Canningites therefore felt more comfortable defining his principles in terms of specific policies: his support for Greek independence and constitutionalism in Portugal and Spain; a readiness to reduce the level of protection for domestic corn producers; a Commons' review of public income and expenditure; and Catholic relief. It was on how these policies were best defended and how much their detail should be amended in the light of changing circumstances that the party disintegrated and went in different directions. It is the classic illustration, perhaps, of the difficulties of reconciling a party of supposedly fixed principles to the shifting sands of a multi-party and multi-interest parliamentary system.[44]

The case for regarding the Portland Whigs and the ultra Tories as parties of fixed principles is somewhat clearer. In the case of the Portland Whigs, so named after their titular leader, the Duke of Portland, their secession from the main body of the party in the company of an equal number of ex-Northites (about 35) was largely due to their agreement with Burke that the French Revolution posed a serious threat to both domestic stability and the international order. The advance of the Jacobins and the occupation of the Low Countries therefore justified the war that Fox opposed.[45] As for the ultra Tories, their principal cause was opposition to the dismantling of the Protestant constitution by the repeal of the Test and Corporation Acts and Catholic relief. However, they did have a broader prospectus which included resistance to the advance of liberalism in matters touching the Corn Laws, the economy, trade and foreign policy. In short, both were parties of resistance and it is noticeable that when the ultra Tories in particular faced the question of what positive policies should be pursued in order to retrieve the situation, they fell out amongst themselves.[46]

Although smaller parties of this kind were less numerous after 1832, there were some: O'Connell's Irish supporters whose number fluctuated between 38 and 31 in the 1830s; the followers of Lord Stanley, later 14th Earl of Derby, who it was said amounted to 86 in the Commons following the 1835 election; and the Peelites, who were about 100 strong after the split in the Conservative party in 1846. The Peelites, however, was the only one with some coherence and longevity. O'Connell's group, it has been persuasively argued, did not regard themselves as a formed party and once repeal was put to one side following its decisive rejection by the Commons in 1834, held a variety of differing views on the key issues of the day.[47] Stanley's followers had only a brief existence and melted away as soon as he and Graham began to prepare their entry into the Conservative ranks.[48] The Peelites, on the other hand, not only possessed a mentor but also the outline of a coherent ideology in his attempt to soothe class conflict by balancing direct and indirect taxation in the context of cheap government and free trade.

Both the Whigs and most of the other smaller parliamentary groups therefore possessed strong preferences about policy but these were framed as much in the light of specific circumstances as deeply held convictions about ideal political systems. With this point in mind, we might enlarge the focus of our discussion to consider the context in which parliamentary debate was conducted.

Two dramatic changes took place in this respect. The most important was the vast increase in public knowledge of what was said in Parliament. In the early 1760s, newspaper reports of the debates were sporadic, especially those in the Lords. However, as a result of sustained pressure from newspapers, from opposition Whigs and the tacit connivance of ministers, both houses had turned an increasingly blind eye to press reporting by the mid-1770s.[49] From that point, daily accounts of the debates increased exponentially leading by the 1820s to virtually continuous coverage by dozens of reporters, even though the daily orders restricting the entry of strangers into the Commons, which were first read in 1711, continued to be so until 1845.[50] Various publishers and editors collected these together to form an annual record, the most famous of which were William Cobbett and T. C. Hansard, the latter's family publishing the most popular series until Parliament entrusted it with the production of an official version in 1908. This development went hand in hand with an equally dramatic increase in the number of national and provincial newspapers, nearly all of which provided extensive reports of the debates. By the end of the 1820s there were probably in excess of two million readers of newspapers in the UK, a number that probably increased following the severe reduction of newspaper duties in 1836. Moreover, public knowledge of parliamentary business was advanced in other ways. A substantial increase took place in the number of division lists printed annually in the press: from an average of 3 each year for the Commons, 1761–93, to 20, 1794–1819, at which point it continued to rise until official records started to be kept in 1836. This was due in some degree to an increase in the number of divisions in both houses after 1760 but was largely the result of the eagerness of the Oppositions that called for them to give the widest possible publicity to their strength. The majority of such lists until the 1820s were therefore only of minorities.[51] In addition, there was an equally substantial increase in the number of select committee and Royal Commission reports and of accounts and papers, that is individual returns of information on a vast array of subjects requested by ministers and private members and supplied by the government offices. In the case of accounts and papers, for example, the number issued and printed tripled between the 1780s to the 1820s, by which time there were about 380 every year. This had two pertinent consequences. The first is that an increasing amount of detailed information, particularly statistical information, became available to members on virtually every subject of policy. The second is that in order to meet an increasing public demand for such information, Parliament began to print sufficient copies to supply it.[52] This resulted in an increased public knowledge, either through copies of the reports and papers themselves or through digests of them in books, pamphlets, periodicals and the press. Although it is always sensible to keep such developments in proportion, it is not too fanciful to suggest that in terms of public knowledge of parliamentary business there was something akin to an 'information revolution' concentrated in the middle of this period – that is, from *c.*1780–1830.

The impact on the substance of parliamentary debate of the flowering of political and moral philosophy, the increased public knowledge of parliamentary speeches, and the exponential growth of information about all aspects of actual or potential policy has never been the subject of the research that it deserves. This, after all, is the period when it might be said that 'public doctrine' takes root. Some developments have been well charted although it is unclear how far they were the result of the expansion of public knowledge and the increase in factual information. Speeches, for example, tended to get longer. At the beginning of the period, it appears that major speeches in the Lords were longer than those in the Commons and that comparatively short speeches of 10 minutes or so were quite normal for the average intervention. As the period progressed, however, the average length of speeches increased in both houses: to 40 minutes or so in the Commons with many major interventions being much longer than this. We also know that only a proportion of members in either house intervened in debate and that the number who did so frequently was comparatively small. In the case of those who made at least one intervention, the proportion in the Lords was much lower than in the Commons – around 25% according to one estimate. Apart from other considerations, this may have been due to the much smaller number of debates and the smaller number of opportunities for back-bench peers to intervene. In the Commons, on the other hand, calculations of the proportion range from 45% to 67% between 1790 and 1830. As for frequent speakers, the evidence, as one might expect, suggests that the burden fell heaviest on the front benches and a relatively small number of enthusiasts. In the Lords, it has been said that in the period before 1784, 10 or so speakers in a debate was normal and that up to 20 or so might get to their feet on major issues. If so, the increase in the size of the House after that date may have led to a greater number speaking regularly by the 1820s. My own calculations for 1828–30 suggest about 45 frequent speakers. A similar trend can be detected in the Commons. According to one authority, a debate before *c.*1780 was unusual if it attracted more than 20–30 speakers. According to another, 5,100 of *c.*9,000 recorded interventions in the 1790s were made by just 19 leading speakers. This compares with my own calculations for 1828–30 which based on the premise that 50 speeches or more in the 3 sessions analysed constituted a frequent speaker, found just over 90 in that category. Although the bases of these different calculations vary, the conclusion seems to be that Commons' debates were dominated by an increasing, but still relatively small, proportion of members, prominent amongst whom were ministers and their leading critics. Indeed, one point upon which all authorities are agreed is that the burden on the leading ministers, particularly the first minister, was immense.[53]

However, on the more important issue of the content of speeches, research is slim. Several authorities have argued that until 1780 or thereabouts the preference of members was for arguments based on common sense and precedence rather than abstract reason or classical allusions.[54] After that time, it is generally agreed that a more classical form of rhetoric, adorned with Greek and Latin quotations, became fashionable amongst the leading speakers, although it is unclear how far this met with the approval of the country gentlemen on the back benches. However, this style seems to have fallen out of favour following the death of Pitt and Fox in 1806 and it has been suggested that a plainer and more straightforward form of speaking came back into fashion. It is even possible that Peel was a pioneer in this respect, almost as a conscious reaction against the excesses of the previous generation.[55] Although there is an undoubted connection between style and substance, my own research for the 1820s, and for sample sessions in the 1830s and 1840s has focussed largely on substance. This leads to the following conclusions. First, that reference to fixed principles as a justification for a particular point of view was a recurring theme in the speeches of some MPs and probably became more prominent over time. In the 1830s and 1840s, for example, the principles of equal civil rights 'without distinction of religion', of the 'utmost liberty' being given to 'individual exertion', and of not restricting the powers of local authorities, were often invoked to justify a point of view. In the course of a speech made in 1844 which was critical of the way MPs deployed principles to justify an argument, Peel defined the ones that should direct legislation as those founded on the 'moral sense' instilled by religion and those 'concurrent with the dictates of justice and humanity'.

Yet when measured against other ways of justifying a point, reference to principle was less common than that to historical, philosophical or scientific premises. Of these, justification by reference to historical example or precedent was the most popular – a not unexpected phenomenon given the increasing professionalism and popularity of the subject itself. In the case of the debates on the Catholic question in 1829, for example, speakers on both sides dwelt at great length on whether Catholics had been granted political equality by the Treaty of Limerick in 1691 or promised it by Pitt at the time of the Union. Similarly, much of the debates on the increase of the grant to Maynooth College in 1845 turned on what had been envisaged by previous grants with respect to the relationship between the State and the Catholic Church.

However, justification by reference to either principle or historical precedent was far outweighed by that based upon a reading of contemporary circumstances and the available facts and figures. Whatever the subject, be it slavery, Catholic relief, parliamentary reform or economic distress, the debates focussed not so much on abstract principles and moral convictions but more on the facts of the matter and whether proposed legislation would lead to real improvements. In the case of slavery, what effects the policy of ameliorating slave conditions had been and what they actually were; in that of Ireland, whether it could be governed without emancipation and whether emancipation would produce a loyal Catholic Ireland; and in that of parliamentary reform, what degree of reform was necessary to regain the public's confidence in the ability of Parliament to deal with its grievances. Above all, it was this approach that dominated debates on economic distress. Dogma undoubtedly played its part but for the majority of members who intervened, arguments were sustained by facts, figures and personal impressions.[56]

SECTION 2: THE FUNCTIONS OF PARLIAMENT

Introduction

In the previous period, three functions of Parliament were identified that had a particular bearing on government: (1) the scrutiny that both houses gave to legislation, particularly ministerial legislation and the 'check' exercised by the Lords on the Commons (and ministers) on behalf of the Crown; (2) the degree to which Parliament addressed public needs and grievances; and (3) the contribution made to the public's knowledge of parliamentary business. It is the exercise of these functions after 1760 that is the subject of this section. The context, of course, is the great increase in the quantity of business that took place, a general outline of which has been provided above. This will be returned to in greater detail later but it is appropriate at this stage to take note of the length of parliamentary sessions. In the first two decades of this period, this was broadly comparable to the previous two, being about 96 days per year. It then began to rise, reaching 114 sitting days on average for the Commons from 1805 to 1816 (excepting 1807), before falling back to nearer 100 in the 1820s. It then rose again during the 1830s and 1840s to an average of 130. It also seems that there was a parallel increase in the number of hours devoted to debate on a daily basis. Charles Abbot, who, in his capacity as Speaker from 1802 to 1817, believed that parliamentary business had tripled between 1760–1801 and doubled between then and 1813, regularly sat for an average of 6–8 hours per day. This appears to have been more than the average at the beginning of this period but bears comparison with estimates for the Commons from the 1820s onwards – the lack of any significant change in the post–Reform period being compensated for by the rise in the number of days that Parliament sat.[57] It is important to take note of the trajectory of this increase. As in the case of the volume of public and general legislation, a steep increase takes place between *c.*1780 and 1820 at which point stasis sets in. Another increase then takes place in the 1830s and 1840s. The increase was therefore neither steady nor continuous.

Scrutiny: the House of Lords

Throughout the period from 1760 to November 1830, the majority of peers supported the key policies of ministers favoured by the Crown: either because they preferred to support the government of the day so long as it had the Crown's support or because they were actively committed to such ministers and their policies – a factor that probably became more important as the influence of the Crown declined. This meant that the potential for conflict between Lords and Commons was largely restricted to periods when the Whigs were in power, which was not very often. In fact, no such conflict occurred because a change of government was effected before they could materialise, the only serious potential clash occurring in 1829 on the question of Catholic relief following its acceptance by the Commons. George IV was known to be hostile to the bill as was a majority in the Lords. However, Wellington persuaded the King to give his assent, at which point a sufficient number of peers also changed their minds and the measure passed. This could be said to demonstrate the increased influence of government over the Crown; and the continuing influence of the Crown amongst the peerage.

If clashes between the two houses on major issues did not occur, what can be said of the function of scrutinising the executive and legislation on a regular, routine basis? Unfortunately, the current state of research does not suggest a clear answer. There were certainly some factors that inhibited scrutiny. Money bills, which constituted a major proportion of ministerial legislation, were, of course, immune to amendment by the Lords. This would have given the house more time to consider other legislation but several factors worked against this. One was that the Lords spent perhaps half the time of the Commons in debate and preferred to focus on one issue only on debating days.[58] Another was that most public bills originated in the Commons and therefore did not get to the Lords until the second half of the session and sometimes, nearing its close. Given that the volume of legislation increased substantially over time, it therefore appears that there was an increasing tendency for the Lords to nod through legislation as summer took its hold.

On the other hand, there are pointers to a more consequential role. The most important was the presence of the Whig Party as the principal opponents of ministers for virtually the whole of this period. Further, not only were peers the effective heads of the party for most of that time – from 1765 to 1782 and 1806 to 1830 – but they also adopted methods of organisation and publicity to further their cause – albeit at a more leisurely pace than their colleagues in the Commons. During Rockingham's leadership from 1765–82, for example, his followers numbered between one-fifth and one-third of the regular attenders of the debates and resort were made to registering 'Protests' against government measures and to having division lists published to gain publicity.[59] In addition, there is some evidence that Whig peers became more active after 1815 in harassing ministers and in highlighting concern about particular issues. For example, there were two general attacks on ministers inaugurated by 'State of the Nation' motions in 1816 and 1819 and several motions on the 'State of Ireland' and the Catholic question in the 1820s. On the other hand, 12 of the 15 addresses in support of the Prince Regent's or the King's Speeches, 1812–27, were passed without a division, with only three being put to a vote by the Opposition (1814, 1819, 1823). This is probably a more realistic measure of the degree of scrutiny of the executive.

With regard to the effectiveness of the Lords in scrutinising legislation we also have very little information, although what there is does suggests an increase starting in the 1780s when it coincided with the beginnings of the practice of asking questions of ministers. Between 1760 and 1780, the Lords voted on only 79 bills. Between 1784 and 1790, however, 69 were amended or lost of which 20 were either government or government-interest bills; and from 1791 to 1800, 137 were amended or lost, of which 56 were associated with the government. Although the current state of research does not allow us to make any firm judgement on what happened subsequently, it seems likely that that trend of increasing scrutiny was continued into the early nineteenth century, if not to any significant degree.[60]

After November 1830 the potential for conflict between the two Houses was considerable. Instead of the majorities in both being of the same political outlook, Conservatives dominated the Lords while the Whigs and their allies were the majority in the Commons. According to one authority, the Whigs never had more than 130 or so supporters in a House of more than 400 peers between 1830 and 1841.[61] This, together with the passage of the Reform Acts, made the constitutional role of the Lords a highly contentious issue. From the Lords' perspective, the declining influence of the Crown and the unpredictable effects of parliamentary reform on both the composition of the Commons and the influence of public opinion raised the question of whether they would have to play a more assertive role in order to maintain the balance between monarchy, aristocracy and democracy. Reformers, on the other hand, questioned whether the Lords now had the right to frustrate the will of the majority in the Commons on behalf of either the Crown or themselves, given that that majority could be said to be much more representative of the public not only in terms of numbers of voters but also of interests other than landed property.

The potential for conflict came closest to reality between 1832 and 1837, when the Whigs' majority in the Commons was at its greatest. Hitherto, during the crisis over the Reform Bill, the majority in the Lords against the measure had been cowed by William IV's support for his ministers. This had been demonstrated by his agreeing to their request for the general election in 1831 that gave them a substantial majority in the Commons; and more crucially, by his reluctant acquiescence to their wish that, if necessary, he would create sufficient peers to get the measure voted through. As supposed protectors of the interests of monarchy and aristocracy, the anti-reformers had no real alternative to submission – a point symbolised by the hard-line opponents of the measure withdrawing from the Lords on its third reading on 4 June as a result of a circular from the King.

However, from 1832 to 1837, a different situation pertained. The Whigs and their allies won a landslide victory at the 1832 election and following a reduction in their majority at the next election in 1835, the Lichfield House compact between them seemed to presage a willingness to force their measures through Parliament. In addition, as his dismissal of Melbourne's administration in 1834 indicated, William IV was becoming increasingly alarmed by the Whig's supposed susceptibility to radical and O'Connellite pressure and made no secret of his hope for a coalition government consisting of Whigs and Tories. As a result, Conservative-dominated majorities in the Lords rejected or made substantive amendments to a series of key Whig bills between 1833 and 1837: a Jewish Relief Bill, a University Test Bill and measures to reform the Church, tithes and municipal corporations in Ireland. In retrospect, these were the most serious clashes between the two houses in the Hanoverian era.

However, after 1837, tension between the two houses eased and a new understanding of the role of the Lords began to develop. Several factors were responsible. One was the accession of Queen Victoria, who was known to favour the Whigs, at least until after the 1841 election. Supporting the

Crown by opposing Whig measures therefore disappeared as a justified course of conduct. In addition, the Whigs' nominal majority in the Commons following the 1837 election declined to about 16 or so. As a result, Whigs were encouraged to moderate their measures to both forestall opposition in the Lords and to look for Conservative support in the Commons in order to resist radical pressure. Probably the most important factor, however, was the influence of Wellington, the Conservatives' leader in the Lords, on how they should conduct themselves. In the immediate aftermath of the passage of the Reform Acts, Wellington had been extremely pessimistic about the chances of the Lords' powers surviving unscathed by radical pressure. He therefore used his considerable influence to persuade his colleagues in the Lords of two cardinal points. First, that they should choose their ground for opposing measures very carefully and with some regard to public opinion. And second, that they should act in concert with their colleagues in the Commons and in the event of a dispute, defer to their leaders there. Although Wellington constructed these views in the light of the particular circumstances of the 1830s, what they amounted to was the doctrine that the Lords should revise but not reject the measures of the party in power in the Commons – the choice of measures being dictated not by the interests of the Crown or the aristocracy but by what was perceived to be the public interest. This, broadly speaking, was the line followed subsequently by the Lords, the severest test coming in 1845 and 1846 on the Conservative government's proposals to increase the parliamentary grant to the Roman Catholic seminary at Maynooth in Ireland and to repeal the Corn Laws. The majority of Conservative peers opposed both measures but were dissuaded by Wellington and Peel from deploying that opposition in a way that might lead to a clash with the Commons. It could be said that in practice the Lords were doing much the same as they had been doing in different circumstances for most of the eighteenth century. The thinking behind such practice, however, was undoubtedly different.[62]

Scrutiny: the House of Commons

Several developments took place in this period that had the effect of strengthening the ability of ministers to secure the passage of their measures – a trend that did not sit easily with the Commons' historic role as the scrutiniser of the executive on the part of the public. Starting in the 1770s, for example, various steps were taken to restrict delays to money bills and to prevent ministers being embarrassed by the relatively new Opposition tactic of asking unanticipated questions. In the last case, ministers quickly established the convention that advance notice of what are now known as 'parliamentary questions' had to be given before an answer was offered. Perhaps the most important development, however, was the reserving of special days for business that were likely to be dominated by the government. By tradition, all members were equal when it came to raising any issue other than money bills, thereby underlining their independence of the Crown and its chosen ministers. However, the increase in all forms of business after 1780 made a change not only practicable but also generally acceptable. Thus, from 1811 'order days' were established on Mondays and Fridays when precedence was given to public and general bills as opposed to notices of motions. As ministers were their principal sponsors, this had the effect of privileging government business. In 1835, Wednesdays were added and for the first time a formal distinction was established between government and other business.[63] This gave ministers the advantage for at least half of the available parliamentary time. It was not until 1852 that two similar 'order days' were established in the Lords.[64]

On balance, however, factors working in the opposite direction may have become stronger as the period progressed. As has already been mentioned, the practice developed in the 1760s of asking questions of ministers and although the possibility of being 'ambushed' was checked by the convention of requiring prior notice, the asking of questions appears to have increased. By 1814, five such questions per day were normal. Moreover, members were able to ask much more searching questions as a result of the vast increase in information about the body politic that Parliament itself made available. Lord North had been notoriously sparing in his release of information but from the 1780s, there was an exponential increase on all aspects of government business.[65] One statistic might suffice to make the general point. Thus, in the case of requests in 1830 for accounts and papers from government departments – only one type of information made available to members – 22 members of the Lords made requests on 56 different occasions and 104 Commoners on no less than 318. Some of these were ministers, anxious to supply members with the requisite information in a time-honoured way. The vast majority, however, were independent members with radicals being particularly prominent.[66]

There are other signs of ministerial control growing weaker rather than stronger in the second half of this period. Scrutiny was, of course, a special function of the Opposition and the fact that this acquired greater legitimacy after 1760 increased its level when Oppositions were strong as they were at the conclusion of the American war and after 1807. The fact that there were an increasing number of divisions every session is an indication of an increasing degree of scrutiny.[67] Moreover there was one particular development that ministers found it difficult to control and which had a considerable influence on a key area of their responsibility. Starting with an initiative of Pitt in 1797 and coming to an end in 1828, the Commons established four select committees every ten years charged with reviewing national income and expenditure. Although ministers had control of the first and some representation on the others, they were not able to control the agenda of those from 1807 – the Committee of that year being particularly influenced by reformers. As a result, the reports of these committees provided a detailed critique of government expenditure and a strong impetus to the campaign for retrenchment. Some, most notably those of 1817 and 1828, also had an equally strong influence on the government's financial and economic policies.[68] Indeed, in the period after the conclusion of the French wars, ministers' control of the Commons appears distinctly weak. Independent and Opposition members, for example, were responsible for the implementation of the Corn Laws, the abandoning of the income tax and later, some of the contents of the 1830 and 1833 budgets. Further, my own study of the most contentious debates between 1828–30 suggests that the majority were not instigated by ministers but by their opponents. The conclusion was that Wellington's ministers had great difficulty in controlling the Commons' agenda.[69]

Overall, the ability of the Commons to scrutinise ministers has a chequered history after 1760. Throughout the period, ministers secured the passage in the House of the great majority of their measures. It was only in the 1830s that key government measures were defeated or amended beyond recovery and that was largely by the Lords. Further, it also seems to have been the case in the earlier part of the period – until about 1800 – that scrutiny of money bills was at best, modest. On the other hand, it appears that ministers subsequently found it increasingly difficult to control the agenda and that the degree of scrutiny, particularly expert scrutiny, began to steadily increase. Some historians have referred to the period after 1846, when the parties were evenly balanced in Lords and Commons, as a period of 'parliamentary government' – that is, a period when ministers were never sure of a majority for their measures and when Parliament (as opposed to ministers) possessed the whip hand. When considering the questions of ministerial control of the Commons and the scrutiny of ministers, it is a concept that might be equally applied to the early nineteenth century.[70]

'The Grand Inquest of the Nation' and the redress of grievances

In the period before 1760, we observed that Parliament received and dealt with the requests of members of the public in a number of ways. In the case of what we might call widespread public grievances – against high prices or taxation, for example – these were made known by means of petitions from different localities that were signed by members of the public and presented by MPs. These might then be received but apart from sometimes placing the subject high on the parliamentary agenda, did not usually lead to action being taken with any immediacy. Petitions from special interest groups pressing for specific legislation, however, often had a more positive response. These might take the form of commercial or industrial organisations or moral reform societies. In such cases, a petition from a private member for a specific bill might be preceded, accompanied or succeeded by petitions in favour of the measure sponsored by the organisation or institution concerned. If the petition for a bill was successful, a process was set in train.

Typically, this took the form of a select committee enquiry, the production of a bill by private members, sometimes with the co-operation of the relevant ministers, debates on its merits, and often the withdrawal of the bill pending resubmission at a later date. Private-member bills for which at least some public support was claimed represented a significant proportion of the total amount of public and general legislation put before Parliament and virtually all that of a local and personal kind. It was in these ways that Parliament acted routinely as a court of enquiry and adjudication on the grievances of the public and the needs of special interest groups.

In this period, resort to these devices not only grew at a rate commensurate with the general growth in parliamentary business but also became an established and prominent feature of parliamentary life. Petitioning is a case in point. Between 1760 and 1848 there was a huge increase in the number of petitions presented to Parliament. In the case of petitions to the Common, less than 100 or so were presented annually at the beginning of the period but about 175 by 1790 and 200 by 1805. A sudden and sustained increase then took place: to 900 annually by 1815, 2,400 by 1826 and 4,900 by 1831. Moreover, the increase did not stop with the Reform Acts. Various steps were taken from the 1830s to provide more detailed statistics about the extent of petitioning and these reveal further sustained growth that only began to tail off in the 1850s. In 1839, for example, 13,657 public petitions on more than 90 different subjects and with over four and half million signatures were presented. It is sometimes assumed that the famous Chartist petitions were an isolated attempt to use an outmoded device to bring pressure on Parliament. This was very far from the case.[71]

Assessing the impact of this extraordinary and still insufficiently studied phenomenon on Parliament is problematic. In general terms, the increase in petitioning affected both public interest and special interest causes in equal measure. In addition, the organisation of petitioning became increasingly sophisticated as a result of the proliferation of what soon became nationally organised associations. The roles played by the Catholic Association in Ireland and the Established Church in England and Wales in sponsoring and organising the huge number of petitions respectively for and against Catholic relief in 1828–9 are good examples.[72] Moreover MPs who were either strong supporters or opponents of particular causes were not slow to encourage petitioning for and against the measure concerned. As a result, there was increasing scepticism on the part of many MPs about the reliability of petitioning as a guide to public opinion. Were they not more of a guide to the ability of special interest groups and zealous MPs to drum up support or opposition, was the gist of the questions asked about them.

That said, there can be little doubt that petitioning played an increasingly important part in enabling Parliament to acquit itself as The Grand Inquest of the Nation. The huge increase in the volume of petitioning is in itself testimony to an equivalent strengthening of the public's assumption that Parliament should attend to the redressing of grievances. Further, the fact that an increasing proportion of public bills became matters for supportive and hostile petitioning – leading to the situation in the 1830s that most were – is an indication that MPs accepted that petitioning was an important part of the legislative process. As mentioned above, more than 90 different issues were the subject of petitioning in 1839, including nearly all the major legislative initiatives of that year. Moreover some 87 petitions on different subjects were printed and circulated as part of the 'Votes and Proceedings' of the Commons, of which about 250,000 copies were sold or distributed. Of these 87, 32 led to motions being made to the House. Although petitioning was a part of the legislative and debating processes before 1760, the evidence suggests that it occupied a much more prominent role after 1810, leading to the situation when virtually all significant public legislation and a fair proportion of debating time was accompanied or determined by petitioning.[73]

However, the question of the effectiveness of petitioning in terms of achieving the required legislation is much more difficult one to answer because research has focussed primarily on the major issues such as parliamentary reform, the abolition of slavery, Dissenters' and Catholic relief, and Chartism. Although campaigns on these issues attracted substantial numbers of petitions, they constituted only a small fraction of the subjects that attracted petitioning. That said, the current evidence suggests the following broad conclusions. First, although sustained petitioning on key issues such as those mentioned above did place them high on the parliamentary agenda, they did not necessarily determine the timing or the content of policy. The majority of English petitions on the Catholic question in 1828–9, for example, were opposed to the concession. Second, on a small proportion of the much larger number of issues of lesser and more routine concern, petitioning did have an impact. In this respect there was continuity with the pre-1760 period. Petitioning then had helped shape legislation effecting trade, industry and other matters and it seems likely that the scale of this increased thereafter, with petitions against proposed legislation perhaps becoming more successful. During the period of the Wellington government, for example, petitions played a significant role in supporting Peel's 1830 bill reducing capital offences applied to forgery, in persuading the government to repeal the beer, cider and leather duties in 1830, and in the decision to drop measures to build new churches in urban areas.[74] My guess is that further research would reveal that this moderate level of effectiveness applied throughout this period.

Another way that Parliament fulfilled the function of being The Grand Inquest of the Nation was by establishing committees of enquiry into matters of public concern whose reports were increasingly regarded as a necessary preliminary to legislation. Committees of enquiry had existed in various forms before 1760 but in this period there was, from the 1790s, increasing resort to the establishment of *select* committees devoted to this task – that is committees requested by a particular member and consisting of a specific and restricted number of MPs selected by the House concerned. Charting their history is difficult, not least because it was eighteenth-century custom to establish *select* committees on routine matters or those of local or private interest and what were, in effect, *open* committees on matters of more immediate and general interest. Indeed a Commons' division of 1772 on whether an enquiry into the East India Company should be conducted in a committee of the whole house or a committee of 31 chosen by ballot suggests that there was considerable opposition to the idea that matters of such general concern should be put to select committees of that kind.[75] Be that as it may, the evidence points, first, to an increasing number of matters of 'public interest' being put to committees of enquiry. And second, particularly from 1795 to 1796, when they were given a separate index entry in the *Commons Journals*, for these to be committees consisting of a selected number of MPs varying between a dozen to about forty. Before the mid-1790s, the number of such public-interest committees seems to have fluctuated between a few to a dozen or so every year, only a small number of which were 'select'. Thereafter, however, the number of select committees established in the Commons increases, as does the proportion dealing with matters of public interest: 18 in 1801; 36 in 1817; 22 on average, 1828–30, and 23 in 1839. The equivalent number established in the Lords was lower but in the early nineteenth century there appears to have been an increasing readiness to launch enquiries on social and economic issues. By the late 1820s around 4–5 Lords' select committees *per annum* was the norm. Overall, there appears to have been a steady increase in the readiness of Parliament to enquire into matters of public interest and at some point in the 1790s, to entrust this to select committees. After 1815, virtually all such matters ranging from food shortages to policing were dealt with in this way which was probably the reason why governments began to prefer the more easily manipulated alternative of Royal Commissions.[76]

Several other points need to be considered when assessing the significance of this development. A number of historians, most notably Professor Finer in a celebrated study published in 1972, have argued that select committees of this kind had less to do with genuine enquiry into matters of public concern and much more with the promotion of a preconceived solution by the MPs who established them. This they achieved by securing a majority of members who shared their point of view, selecting sympathetic witnesses, and deploying other devices, such as writing reports before investigations began.[77] There can be little doubt that in some cases, the sceptics are correct. Many observers throughout this period drew the same conclusion, especially when select committees dealing with matters of general interest proliferated and the issue became more critical. It would be wrong, however, to conclude that all committees were of this kind and that committee evidence as a whole was worthless. Finer's case is based on the evidence for a small number of select committees but my examination of a much larger number for the years 1828–30 suggests a more nuanced interpretation.

What was noticeable then were repeated attempts to construct select committees on national issues that were broadly representative of the counties and towns of the three kingdoms and if dealing with a Scottish or Irish matter, to have a significant number of members from those countries. Partisan committees certainly existed but they were the exception rather than the rule.[78] Further, it is equally noticeable, particularly in the first half of the nineteenth century, that on major issues such as policing, poverty, education and crime and even some of the less contentious ones such as weights and measures, there was not just one select committee established but several. In other words, even if one select committee was persuaded to produce a report based on biased evidence, the others that followed added additional information, possibly on the other side of the argument. There was therefore an accumulation of evidence and interpretation that may have led to a balanced picture.

The contemporary concern about membership of committees was itself indicative of another significant trend – the increasing ties between enquiry and legislation. In the course of the early nineteenth century, enquiries not only covered an increasing number of major topics, they also became more professional and routinely, longer and more detailed. Between 1760 and 1780, 29 reports were printed with an average length of 20 pages and witnesses who gave evidence to them had to pay their own expenses. Witness expenses were paid after 1815 and between 1828 and 1830 the average length of the 54 reports published was about 240 pages. The result was that reports became increasingly closely connected with the process of legislation: either cumulatively as in the case of a series of reports on policing and the operations of the poor law that preceded major legislation in 1828 and 1834; or more directly, as in the case of at least 23 successful bills and 19 unsuc-cessful ones that were considered, 1828–30. Broadly speaking, it would seem to have been the case by the 1820s, that select committee enquiry was the standard precursor to most legislation other than that dealing with ministers' special areas of responsibility – finance and law and order. It is also worth noting in this respect that there was a contemporaneous trend towards making available more printed copies of reports than were required by MPs. In the first part of this period, 600–1,000 copies was normal. By the late 1820s, this had risen to 1,500–2,500 copies and by 1838 they were available for purchase by the general public. In that year over 110,000 copies of reports were issued *gratis* and nearly 32,000 sold. This heightened the ability of the press to provide details of the reports and to comment upon them and, in turn, demonstrate to the public Parliament's role as a Grand Inquest.[79]

Private-members' and public-bill legislation

A further function of Parliament to be considered in this context is its responsiveness to legislative initiatives promoted by private members.

Beginning with public bills, as opposed to those of a local or personal kind, we have already observed that they constituted a significant proportion of the total of such bills in the period before 1760 and that there was a pattern to their subject matter, origins, promotion and outcome. In the case of subject matter, initiatives of this kind were usually taken in areas not deemed by ministers to be their primary responsibility: social, legal and communication matters, and many aspects of trade and manufacture. They were usually instigated by corporate bodies representing a particular interest or by a zealous MP and often, by a combination of the two. Once a bill had been launched it was often accompanied by a petitioning campaign and sometimes by the publication of supportive literature. The sponsoring MPs might at this point seek advice and support from ministers and officials and, if it was forthcoming, this usually gave the bill a much greater chance of success. However, even if such advice and support was not provided and the bill had failed the first time round, it had become the convention to regard this as 'a trial run' before its re-introduction in a revised form in a subsequent session. Overall, private members sponsored an average of 25% of successful public bills before 1760 and a much higher proportion of those that failed.

The crucial point in any understanding of the subsequent relationship between Parliament and governing is that private-member, public-bill, initiatives continued to play a similar role in legislative activity until well into the 1840s. My own research on sample sessions leads to this conclusion. It distinguishes between the different types of promoters of successful and failed public bills: ministers ('Govt.'); a combination of ministers and private members; ('Govt. + pm.'); and private members alone ('Pm.'). The results are as follows:

Table 7.5 Government and private-member bills, 1772–1839

	1772	*1792*	*1817*	*Average 1828–30*	*1839*
Successful bills					
Govt.	40	43	99	60	78
Govt.+pm.	3	7	22	6	1
Pm.	6	7	11	12	18[a]
Total	49	57	132	78	97
Failed bills					
Govt.	4	3	8	15	27
Govt.+pm.	1	1	2		7
Pm.	22	8	17	26	24
Total	27	12	27	41	58

Note
a The Archbishop of Canterbury and the Bishop of London introduced four successful bills affecting the Church of England.

These figures suggest that private members contributed to between 18% and 25% of successful general bills throughout this period; and if the figures for successful and failed bills are combined, to 28–42%. It is also clear that by comparison with government bills, a much higher proportion of private-member bills failed – at least on their first testing.

Moreover, a substantial quantity of other research not only on the crude figures of success or failure but also on the processes leading to public legislation involving private members has confirmed that the incidence and pattern identified for the earlier period continued into this. Joanna Innes and Julian Hoppit were pioneers in this respect and although reference has already been made to their research on the period before 1760, its results also bear on this. In a celebrated article first published in 1990, and which concentrates on social legislation, Innes charts the continuing success of private individuals and members such as John Howard and Thomas Gilbert in promoting bills to reform prisons (1774) and the poor law (1782). She also suggests that towards the end of the century, some MPs sought 'to extend and systematise' the processes of consultation with interested parties so as to enhance the acceptability of their measures. Gilbert, she argues, developed a system that consisted by the 1780s of the circulating of his proposals to magistrates for comment well in advance of introducing a bill; refining the measure and introducing it late in a session so that it might be printed, withdrawn, amended; and then re-introducing it with more chances of success later. These were methods also practised by campaigning societies such as the Proclamation Society which promoted bills from the 1780s onwards designed to promote the moral well being of the working classes. Overall, Innes not only demonstrates the continuance of substantial private-member legislation throughout the century but also the progressive refinement of the methods by which it was promoted – a point reinforced by other scholarly research.[80]

Hoppit's work on the background to the establishment of a uniform system of weights and measures initiated by an act of 1824 demonstrates the continuance of much of the findings of Innes and others for the eighteenth century. Dealing this time with a subject that one might have expected would fall more under the ken of government, Hoppit shows that much of the inspiration for the measure can be credited to successive private members: Lord Carysfort in 1758–9; Sir John Riggs Miller in the 1780s; and Davies Gilbert, Vice-President of the Royal Society after 1815. All three were enthusiasts for a reformed system and besides collecting information on the subject privately, had a hand in the setting up of at least five select committees of enquiry. Eventually, the successful bill was sponsored by Gilbert and a junior minister, Sir George Clerk, Gilbert supplying much specialised information from the Royal Society. Hoppit argues that it was this combination of private-member initiatives, select committee enquiry, expert knowledge, and as in this case, minor government involvement, that led in mid-century to calendar reform and significant improvements in the measurement of longitude, time, pressure and temperature; and later, to the establishment of mean time (1792), the Ordnance Survey (from 1791) and the census (1801).[81]

My own research on the late 1820s reached conclusions that were similar to those of Innes, Hoppit and many other scholars not only on the period before 1760 but also afterwards. Further, there seems no reason at present to think that they would not apply to the next two decades. In the three parliamentary sessions of 1828–30 that were analysed, private members sponsored 125 public and general bills, some 35% of the total. Of these, 46 were successful, 19.8% of the total that were. In terms of their subject matter, they dealt with all categories except UK finance, but principally with social issues, law, the colonies, elections and religion – social issues far outnumbering the others. Several features of these initiatives will now be very familiar. As in the cases of John Howard and Thomas and Davies Gilbert before them, there were the inevitable enthusiasts for particular causes – Robert Slaney for reform of the poor laws, Robert Gordon for the establishment of lunatic asylums, and Robert Wilmot Horton for improved methods of emigration. Similar methods of promoting a measure were adopted. Sponsors therefore sought select committees to bring a subject to parliamentary attention; drafted bills in consultation with interested parties; encouraged petitioning in order to demonstrate that a measure had public support; and were accustomed to re-introducing failed bills in amended form to secure their passage. Finally, there were many cases of collaboration between private members and ministers, the most extraordinary example of which was the Chancellor of the Exchequer giving assistance to a bill extending the Combination Act to the silk trade that had been sponsored by the radical, Joseph Hume.[82]

Although continuity in the incidence and process of private-member legislation is the most outstanding feature of this period, there do appear to have been some significant changes in its subject matter and, ultimately, its prominence. Admittedly the lack of comprehensive research on the subject makes this more a matter of conjecture than conclusion but with that proviso, they seem to have been of the following order. In the first place, it appears that by comparison with the pre-1760 period, the proportion of private-member initiatives dealing with trade and manufacture began to decline. This, we might conclude, was due to the increasing authority and activity of the Board of Trade in that area, particularly after 1786. Even though trade and manufacturing organisations still continued to resort to private-member initiatives, more emphasis began to be placed on lobbying the Board itself. Similarly, it also seems likely that the prominence of private-member initiatives on social issues noted in the late 1820s also began to decline once the Home Office began to assume increasing responsibility for them in subsequent decades. If these two conjectures prove to be accurate, they would correspond with a third, namely, that if the results of the analysis of 1839 legislation are typical for that decade, there was a decline in the number of bills involving ministerial and private-member co-operation. Indeed, the analysis of the origins of legislation in that year strongly suggest much greater ministerial control of measures with which they were associated than has been noted hitherto. The overall conjecture, therefore, is that the number and significance of private-member initiatives began to decline in the 1830s and 1840s although not, perhaps, to the point of being insignificant.[83] Thus, Sir Charles Wood, writing in 1855 of how he remembered parliamentary life on first entering it in 1826, stated that the function of government then was 'chiefly executive' and that 'Changes in our laws were proposed by independent members, and carried, not as party questions, by their combined action on both sides. Now, when an independent member brings forward a subject it is not to propose a measure himself, but to call to it the attention of the government'.[84] One form of parliamentary government had therefore declined, to be replaced by another characterised by the evenly balanced state of parties.

Private-bill legislation

The other form of legislation to be considered in this context is that of private bills – those dealing with local and personal subjects. Their range was considerable but the principal categories were those dealing with agricultural matters – particularly the enclosure of common land; communications – roads, canals and after 1801, railways; town improvements ranging from the building of jails to the improvement of harbours; the establishment of companies providing services; and purely personal requests such as those for naturalisation. Equally considerable was their number. Parliament had always passed more private than public acts and there was a comparable increase in their number in this period. In the period 1760–9 1,177 were passed but this rose to 2,097 in the comparable period, 1800–9, only 59 of which applied to Ireland, that country being consistently undemanding in its requests for private bills. Thereafter, the number passed each decade hovered around the 2,000 mark, 2,187 being passed, 1840–9, when the number was inflated by an extraordinary number of railway acts.

The significance of private-bill legislation in the context of parliamentary government is, of course, considerable. Individuals, groups of individuals, and corporate bodies of a private or quasi-public nature were seeking parliamentary sanction for initiatives that literally transformed the man-made environment. Approximately 6 million acres of land were enclosed in England and Wales between 1760–1844 and thousands of miles of canals cut, roads built, and railway track laid. In addition, hundreds of established or new civic authorities and private companies were empowered to provide a plethora of new buildings, facilities and services. That said, the key issue for present purposes is the way that Parliament exercised this function. How did it deal with private-bill initiatives? And how far were the interests of all the interested parties considered?

As far as procedure is concerned, a number of improvements were made from the 1790s in the definition of private bills, in their distribution to public bodies and officials in the locality concerned, and in keeping a record of them. The most important was the establishment of a Private Bill Office and a Register in 1810. In addition, Parliament took steps to simplify the drawing of bills on certain topics (and thereby reduce their cost) by passing 'model clauses' acts which could then be cited but not spelled out. In 1801 a General Inclosure Act was passed and in 1845 similar model clauses acts were passed dealing with the formation of companies, with land management and with railways. However, the most contentious procedural issue was the composition of the committees of enquiry in both houses to which they were usually consigned. Although nominally regarded as select committees, they in practice usually consisted of a combination of either nominated members and an unspecified number of representatives of counties and towns adjacent to the *locale* of the bill; or of nominated members and all those who had 'voices', that is, those who chose to attend. By the early nineteenth century there was increasing concern about these conventions. Such committees, it was alleged, could easily be suddenly packed with proponents or opponents of the bill who had little knowledge of it but could affect a decision either way. It was also thought that it enabled those with a personal interest in a bill to have undue influence on its outcome. As a result, there was a series of attempts to reform committee procedure in the interests of ensuring that members were dutiful, knowledgeable and impartial. In the case of the Lords, it was decided in 1837 to restrict committees on private bills that had encountered local opposition (other than estate bills) to five peers chosen by a Committee of Selection. Those peers with an interest in the matter in hand were exempted (and presumably deterred) from being chosen. Changes to Commons' procedure, however, took longer to effect. The critical issue was how best to maintain the authority of the House in determining the outcome of private bills while at the same time ensuring that the decision was based on impartiality and knowledge of the matter in hand. Various steps were taken after 1825 to restrict the number of members who could attend committees but it was not until 1855 that in the interests of impartiality, local representatives were excluded from them.[85]

As this brief history suggests, members of both houses became increasingly concerned about the impartiality of private-bill committees and took steps to improve it. However, this was not the only check on the acceptability or desirability of private-bill initiatives as far as local communities were concerned. Would-be promoters were expected to gather a broad spectrum of local support for the petitions for bills that initiated the parliamentary process. The limited evidence that we currently have suggests that this led, at least in some cases, to extensive consultation and bargaining in the locality concerned. It was certainly the case that petitions invariably claimed to be supported by a judiciously selected cross-section of the community. There were other factors that worked in favour of consultation and careful planning. Standing Orders required promoters to insert appropriate notices in county newspapers on three occasions before a bill being presented to Parliament. In addition, they had to send notices to individuals likely to be affected and to affix the same to the doors of session houses and churches. The fact that this, when combined with the employment of a parliamentary agent, could cost substantial sums of money also worked against speculative and opportunistic ventures.

How effective, then, were these requirements and procedures in enabling Parliament to discharge its function of being a fair and impartial judge of local initiatives that could, cumulatively, assume national importance? Although it is more than a century since Frederick Clifford published his pioneering study of the subject, it is only recently that scholars have attempted to build on his work, albeit on different aspects of such legislation and for different periods of time. That said, my own work on all private-bill legislation, 1828–30, and that of others seems to suggest the following tentative conclusions. First, there continued to be a consistent failure rate of between 20–25% for all private-bill initiatives with the exception of those relating to personal matters, for which it was a great deal lower. The reasons for failure varied considerably. In some cases (8% in 1828–30), petitions for bills were rejected on grounds such as insufficient local support. In a greater number of cases, bills failed at the committee stage or in open debate. Once again, the reasons varied. In 1828–30, some categories of bills had a much greater chance of encountering opposition in open debate than others. Those dealing with commercial companies, municipal regulations, canals, railways and harbours were particularly vulnerable. It was in these categories that bills most clearly encroached upon those existing commercial and political interests with sufficient muscle to mount an opposition: either by counter-petitions or by lobbying friends. Such opposition might lead to the withdrawal of the bill. In other cases, sponsors might persevere but have their bills rejected in a division, although this was comparatively rare.

The other side of this coin, however, is that between 75% and 80% of such bills did become acts. In the majority of cases, there is little surviving evidence of any local or parliamentary opposition although this does not mean that some degree of scrutiny did not take place in committee. In a minority of cases, on the other hand, (33% in 1828–30), bills that were ultimately successful did encounter opposition from a mixture of locally generated counter-petitions and in debate.

Overall, the evidence points to Parliament becoming increasingly concerned to deal with private bills in an informed and impartial way. In a majority of cases, it seems to have been guided by the strength of local support for a measure and to have given approval on that basis, even when there was a degree of opposition expressed at a local level or in debate. In a significant minority of cases, however, bills were rejected because they did not meet these standards. On balance, Parliament exercised this function to moderate effect.[86]

Providing information

The final issue to be considered is the extent to which Parliament provided the public with information on matters of common concern. Much has already been said on this point and all that is needed here is a brief summary and some comments on its significance. It is therefore clear that in tandem with the increases in legislation and committee work, there were equivalent increases in the amount of information about parliamentary business that became available to the public. Starting in the 1770s, reports of the debates in the newspapers became more frequent, reaching the point in the 1820s when two competing versions of a virtually full record of the previous session's debates were available. In addition, not only was there a steady, and then from the 1780s to the 1820s, a rapid, increase in the number of parliamentary papers produced in the form of bills, reports, and accounts and papers, but the proportion that was printed increased exponentially. In the Commons, the practice of routinely printing committee reports and accounts and papers appears to have started in the 1770s, in the last case with the alleged encouragement of Irish members new to the House. The Lords took this course a decade later. After 1780, the Commons ordered the printing of bills in increasing numbers and in 1785 was responsible for the printing of the first set of parliamentary papers in the orderly form that became the standard subsequently. The scale and the trajectory of the increase in printed versions follows that of the material itself. In the case of Commons' accounts and papers, for example, about 120 per year were produced in the 1760s; 145 in the 1770s; 217 in the 1780s; 220 in the 1790s; and 312 in 1828. The number of such documents generated by the Lords was consistently smaller over time but it increases at an equivalent rate. By the 1820s, the printing of all such material was a matter of course.

Several points may be made about this development in the context of parliamentary government. The first is that the most dramatic increase in both the publication of debates and the production and printing of bills, report and papers takes place from the 1780s to the 1820s. Prior to 1780 or thereabouts the rate of increase was steady and after 1830 it flattens out. This corresponds to trends in other aspects of parliamentary business. Second, it is worth emphasising that it was MPs who were responsible not only for allowing the increase in the reporting of debates to take place but also for the increase in the proportion of bills and other materials that was printed. In other words, it was Parliament that was the chief engine of the enormous expansion of printed information about virtually every aspect of political, social and economic life. Finally, and most importantly, it was by these means that Parliament either deliberately or accidentally held its ground as the major influence in the shaping of public opinion. Parliamentary debates were prominent copy for most of the burgeoning number of metropolitan and provincial newspapers in the three kingdoms. Possibly 2 million people read newspapers in the late 1820s and with no sport or other media as competition, the debates and foreign relations provided the staple 'national' news. The other forms of parliamentary business, particularly reports and accounts and papers, also became much more widely known. There was a combination of reasons for this: the increasing number of such papers; the increasing number of newspapers and periodicals hungry for copy; the growing proportion that were printed, thereby making the reading and reproduction of them easier; in the case of important subjects, the printing of many more than the number required by MPs and officials; and the broadening scope of such enquiries. From the 1770s onwards a growing number of versions of key papers appeared as books, pamphlets or newspaper articles leading to the situation in the 1820s when it could be said they had become a staple engine of public opinion. In due course, Parliament took the decision to recoup some of the outlay on the costs of printing a mass of papers that were conventionally provided *gratis*. In 1838, over 1.3 million copies of reports, papers, bills and Votes and Proceedings were issued of which nearly a quarter of a million were sold at a cost of just over £5000.00.[87]

The significance of this was considerable. Ministers were responsible for the production of a considerable proportion of this material, especially of accounts and papers in the eighteenth century. This was the reason why the three principal categories concerned matters for which they had prime responsibility: public finance; trade and manufacture; and foreign affairs. Private members, however, had always been responsible for some and their share increased in the nineteenth century, particularly in regard to select committee reports. By 1828–30, a select number of 'active' private members, particularly reformers and radicals, were responsible for most. This was therefore a genuinely 'parliamentary' activity. In addition, it had a profound effect on public opinion. To give just one example. As Philip Harling has made clear, the reports of the decennial select committees on public expenditure, 1797–1828, was a major source for the campaign against 'Old Corruption' – one of the principal targets of reformers and radicals from the 1780s until the 1830s. In particular, one of the seminal tracts, John Wade's *The Extraordinary Black Book*, made extensive use of both those reports and many of the accounts and papers dealing with the income and expenditure of the state. First published in periodical form from 1820 to 1823, it sold 14,000 copies before being revised and reprinted in 1831, 1832 and 1835. Parliament was therefore largely responsible for providing the information upon which a major and influential critique of the workings of the mixed constitution was based.[88]

Summary and conclusion

We may now return to the question posed at the start of this chapter: how far did the influence of Parliament on government change in the course of this period? From a sociological perspective, the potential for substantial change seemed slight. Thus, as we observed, the tendency was for Parliament to become more aristocratic rather than less and therefore decreasingly representative of the new and dynamic forces in society and the economy. This does not appear to have been a likely trigger of change. Yet greater social homogeneity and exclusivity did not lead to greater political consensus.

Thus, from a structural perspective, the following developments are notable. First, daily conflict between the government and opposition front benches was as constant as before and to judge by the increases in the length of sessions and the number of divisions, probably intensified. Second, the established polarity of Whigs in office and Tories in opposition collapsed in the 1760s and was replaced for most of the period from 1766 until 1830 by a new one of a party of government confronting the Whig party in opposition. Third, the gradual cohering of the party of government into a body which from *c*.1810 to 1830 was increasingly ready to refer to itself as a Tory party. And fourth, the gradual absorption in the 1830s and 1840s of virtually all MPs into what were known as the Conservative and Whig-Liberal parties.

But what impact did these developments have on the practice of government? One key issue in this respect is the structure of these various parties. Prior to 1830, the core members of what was for the most part the party of government and the Whig party did not comprise more than half the Commons at most. Indeed, the party of government was a particularly complex amalgam of King's friends, the personal acolytes of individual politicians, and various other interest groups. Moreover, even after 1832, the Conservative and Whig-Liberal parties, although nominally representing all but the O'Connellites, were essentially loose coalitions of discordant elements. The upshot was a form of government and opposition that placed a premium on tactical, practical and accommodatory considerations. Ministers and leaders of opposition had to frame measures and explain them with an eye to maximising support from a heterogeneous and uncertain number of supporters and independents.

This did not mean that politicians lacked political principles or ideological convictions. As we observed in the previous chapter and in this, leading politicians in government and opposition shared some basic assumptions about the ideal polity and an increasing number were influenced by the new and often conflicting ideas that flourished in the early nineteenth century. It is notable, however, that they were also influenced, to a greater or lesser degree, by the specific political situations in which they found themselves. From the 1760s until 1830, for example, the Whigs were principally concerned about the alleged unbalancing of the constitution: initially by George III and then by the hegemony established by Pitt and his successors. Similarly, the personal or minor parties that were almost a constant feature of parliamentary politics until 1850 but which flourished in the 1760s and the early 1800s, were usually formed more for immediate reasons related to personality, ambition and the specific issues of the moment than clearly set out principles. The only exceptions to this appear to be the Portland Whigs in the 1790s; the ultra Tories; and the Peelites.

A further factor that needs to be taken into account is the content of parliamentary speeches. In this respect, four developments were noted. First, the tendency for the speeches of the leading parliamentarians to become longer, reaching an average of 40 minutes or so in the Commons. Second, the increasing and eventually widespread publicity given to the debates by the burgeoning newspaper press. Third, what amounted to a revolution in the factual material made available to politicians and the public on virtually every aspect of state policy. And fourth, the increasing tendency for politicians to base their arguments on a mixture of historical precedents, contemporary facts and figures, and personal observation rather than theoretical principles. Once again, this does not necessarily mean they were lacking in such principles but it does suggest that those that did possess them were aware of the need to draw a distinction between private and public doctrine.

Overall, the survey of MPs, parties and the debates suggests that Parliament had an important impact on the practice of government. Despite the increasing homogeneity of MPs, the ways they disposed themselves politically encouraged a pragmatic and accommodatory form of government. Indeed, the term 'parliamentary government' does not seem out of place.

The appropriateness of the term is strengthened by consideration of the functions of Parliament. In the case of scrutiny, it was noted that with the exception of the period 1832–7, little changed with respect to the Lords acting as a check on the Commons although the reasons why they generally accepted the wishes of the lower House certainly did. Before 1832 it was due either to the majority sharing the views of the party in power or to deference to the Crown. After 1837, it was due to a readiness to defer to the leaders of the respective parties in the Commons. As for the Commons acting as a check on the executive, there were successive steps taken to shield ministers from sudden attacks and to privilege government business but various factors worked against a growth of ministerial control. One, most notable before 1832, was the unpredictable conduct of many supposed government supporters and the many independents. Another was the strength of the Whig opposition at critical times – most notably during and immediately after the American War and from 1807 until the mid-1820s. And a third was the readiness with which opposition and independent members set up or commandeered committees of enquiry on contentious issues – most notably the Finance Committees from 1807–28. For these and other reasons, ministerial control of the Commons' agenda appears to have been weak by the late 1820s and although steps were taken to strengthen it after 1832, it seems unlikely that these had much of an impact before 1846.

In the case of the other functions of Parliament that were considered, the striking features were the scope that private members had to shape legislation and the increasing role played by the public in influencing the parliamentary agenda – particularly in the period before 1832. Private members were responsible either on their own or in collaboration with ministers for, on average, about one-third of all public and general legislation proposed to Parliament and for about one-fifth that became law. Further, they were almost wholly responsible, as promoters or sponsors, for the much larger quantity of local and personal acts that transformed the man-made landscape. In addition, private members in both Lords and Commons were heavily involved in the growth of the number of select committees of enquiry, as both sponsors and participants. By the 1820s such committees were regarded as an almost essential preliminary to legislation on a wide range of social and economic matters and had even encroached on questions of public income and expenditure.

Parliamentarians in general and private members in particular were also responsible to varying degrees for the huge growth in public knowledge of state and parliamentary business and the concomitant increase in the pressure that the public applied to Parliament by petitioning. It was the MPs who turned a blind eye from the 1770s to the publishing of debates in the ever-growing press and it was they who were wholly responsible for the exponential growth from the 1780s in the publication of parliamentary papers. Moreover, MPs themselves were heavily involved in the phenomenal increase in the quantity and range of petitioning. In this respect a distinction needs to be drawn between spontaneous public petitioning for a redress of grievances and premeditated and selective petitioning for or against a particular piece of legislation. In the case of the former, MPs acted more as spokesman than organisers but in the case of the latter, they were often both. The significant point, however, is that both types of petitioning increased exponentially from the 1780s to 1830, leading to the situation where petitioning was regarded as an inevitable part of the legislative process and the parliamentary agenda.

Most of these developments took place in the period *c.*1780–1830 and there are some indications that the scope for private-member initiatives and public pressure diminished thereafter. Even before 1830, the Board of Trade had supplanted Parliament as the first port of call for commercial pressure groups and afterwards, the Home Office played a more significant role in social policy. The opportunity for private-member initiatives in collaboration with ministers therefore seems to have declined but not to the point of insignificance. In addition, steps were taken to prevent petitioning playing such a prominent role in shaping the parliamentary agenda. It is also possible that Royal Commissions began to be resorted to more frequently by ministers in order to circumvent the difficulties of influencing select committees. However, it seems very unlikely that these steps altered the role the private member or the public to any significant degree. Overall, we might conclude that these developments strengthen the case for this being a period when the parliamentary contribution to government increased significantly.

8 The executive, Parliament and the public

Introduction

As we observed in Chapter 4, there was considerable interaction between the executive, Parliament and the public in the period before 1760. Public pressure was therefore applied through a number of well-established channels: parliamentary elections, particularly in the form of 'instructions' from electors to MPs on how they should vote on key issues; pressure groups of various kinds, some of which organised sophisticated campaigns based on petitions to Parliament for the 'redress of grievances'; and the print media, particularly in the form of a growing number of periodicals and newspapers. In the 1730s the term 'public opinion' was coined to describe what was seen as a new and powerful element in politics and historians have argued that when the various channels of public pressure are grouped together and considered in the context of a growing number of clubs and societies in London and elsewhere, that element had acquired a definite structure by the time of George III's accession. However, it was not an element that offered any significant threat to elite power. Public pressure was applied to elicit concessions from government or from Parliament but not to overturn them. Moreover, public opinion tended to be shaped by metropolitan periodicals and newspapers obsessed with the parliamentary agenda and focussed on a relatively narrow range of topics. Some parliamentary politicians, such as the Elder Pitt, may have concluded that it was now necessary to court public opinion but there is little evidence to suggest that it had much of an impact on decision-making at the ministerial level. Parliamentary affairs were therefore central to the more formal aspects of what we might loosely call non-elite or popular politics but were never seriously threatened by them.

In the course of this period, the structure of public opinion changed enormously. To some extent this was due to exponential growth in the sheer number of pressure groups, petitions, newspapers and various types of clubs and societies, but it was also the result of the emergence from the 1760s of a growing clamour for a radical reform of the parliamentary system itself. The issues we therefore need to consider are how far the structure of public opinion had changed by the 1840s and to what extent public opinion came to have a more decisive impact on conduct of government and parliamentary business.

Parliamentary elections

The Union with Ireland, the 1829 Act disfranchising the Irish 40s freeholders, and most famously, the three Reform Acts of 1832 (one each for Ireland, Scotland, England and Wales) were the most important measures affecting parliamentary representation in this period. Their details are well known but a brief commentary on them is essential before we attempt to assess their impact. We may begin with the constituencies. Historically, these consisted of two types – the counties and the boroughs, or towns and cities – each of which were held to represent different types of taxable constituents. The counties therefore represented the landed classes and agriculture; and the boroughs, various types of commerce and manufacture. By the later eighteenth century, however, there was a widespread view that a pattern of representation that had been established in Britain in the middle ages was seriously out of kilter with the changes that had taken place in the size and distribution of the population and in the economic importance of the boroughs that were represented and those that were not. The key issue in this respect was the representation of a large number of boroughs that had diminished in size or importance to the point where they were 'decayed' or 'rotten' and had fallen into the 'pocket' of a proprietor and become 'close'. Thus, although many sizeable and economically important boroughs such as Bristol or Liverpool were represented in Parliament, others such as Birmingham were not. The solution, it was felt, was either to increase the representation of counties or to disfranchise the decayed boroughs and enfranchise those that were flourishing.

The first step along the path of equating population and wealth with enfranchisement (albeit in the context of maintaining a distinction between county and borough constituencies) took place with the Irish Union. In order to reduce Irish parliamentary representation to manageable proportions, all of the 32 county constituencies retained their representation at Westminster but only 33 of the 116 boroughs did so, that number being selected on the basis of their population and taxable wealth. In 1832, the precedent was taken a dramatic stage further. In all, 56 English rotten boroughs were disfranchised (out of 202) and 31 small ones had their number of seats cut from 2 to 1 or, in the unique case of Weymouth and Melcombe Regis, from 4 to 2. This made 143 seats available for redistribution. Sixty five of these went to 42 new English boroughs selected on the basis of their population, 21 acquiring 2 seats and the rest 1; and another 65 went to English and Welsh counties by either dividing them or by adding to the existing number of seats. This left 13 seats available of which 8 were given to Scottish boroughs and 5 to 4 Irish boroughs and Dublin University.

The general significance of these changes needs to be kept in perspective. In the first place, it is important to note that although there was some concession to the view that the number of MPs per constituency should be related to the size of population, the distinction between county and borough constituencies was maintained. This helped to preserve the traditional view that Parliament should represent specific types of communities and interests as opposed to electoral districts with equal numbers of inhabitants. Second, it is also notable that there was a significant increase in the number of MPs representing county constituencies – the bedrock of the landed and agricultural interest. Sixty-four of the 100 Irish MPs after 1801 represented county constituencies and a further 65 seats were allocated to the English and Welsh counties in 1832. The Reform Act of 1832 in particular therefore did as much to shore up the landed interest as it did to enfranchise centres of industry. Finally, although most of the newly enfranchised boroughs of 1832 were populous centres of industry in the midlands and the north of England, their inclusion did not completely alter the pattern of borough representation. Only 27.7% of English and Welsh boroughs were totally disfranchised in 1832 and as we have seen, about half of all available borough seats went to county constituencies. Borough constituencies therefore continued to represent a variety of different types of places of markedly different sizes and electorates. For example, in 1841, some 120 English and Welsh boroughs had less than 1,000 registered electors and a shade more than half of these had less than 500. Huddersfield with a population of about 25,000 and a registered electorate of over 1,000 and Arundel with about 2,000 and 262, respectively, each returned one MP.

There were also significant changes to the bewildering variety of ancient franchises that entitled adult males to the vote. The first to have a significant impact was the 1829 Act disqualifying all freeholders with a title to property below the value of £10 pa (the '40s freeholders') from voting in Irish counties. This had the drastic effect of immediately reducing the total Irish county electorate from in excess of 200,000 to about 37,000. The measures of 1832 worked, of course, in the opposite direction. In the case of the counties, the existing 40s franchises in Britain remained in place but were supplemented by additional qualifications. In Scotland, the intention was to bring the franchise more in line with that in England and Wales by extending it to leaseholders of property worth at least £10 pa as well as yearly tenants paying at least £50 pa in rent. In England and Wales, the decision was also taken to extend it to £50 tenants-at-will, a class that some felt to be particularly vulnerable (or amenable) to landlord pressure. In Ireland too, an attempt was made to broaden the new £10 freehold franchise by including leaseholders of that value who held their property for a stated number of years rather than for the duration of the lives of named individuals.

In the boroughs, the changes were more far reaching. All the electors under the existing franchises (with the exception of non-resident freemen) retained the vote for their lifetime in constituencies that continued to be represented but a new class of voter was created that would eventually become universal – the £10 householder. This was an adult male who had owned or rented property – essentially a building – that had a yearly rental value of £10 and on which the poor rate (if one existed) and all local taxes had been paid by a certain date. Further, in an attempt to establish with some certainty the number of qualified electors, the practice of registering them, which was well-established in Ireland, was extended to Britain. In both the counties and the boroughs, qualifiable property had to have been held for at least six months before registration, with electors in the boroughs (although not in the counties) also having had to be residents of the constituency for at least the same period of time.

Once again, it is useful to put these changes into perspective. It is notable, for example, that with the exception of the disqualification of the Irish 40s freeholders and the non-resident freemen, all the existing classes of electors retained their votes, albeit only for their lifetime in the case of most borough electors but not, significantly, for certain classes of freemen. This ensured that for some time to come the 'ancient rights' electors would form a significant proportion of the electorate. Second, it is also worth underlining the obvious, but sometimes overlooked, fact that the occupation of property either as owners or tenants remained the basic electoral qualification. Indeed by setting the level in the boroughs at a relatively high £10, the framers of the Reform Acts, were reinforcing the emphasis on the possession of property as the pre-requisite for political participation. On the other hand, the introduction of registration and the insistence on residence and the up-to-date payment of local taxes for borough electors marked a new departure in Britain. Hitherto, the requirement that county electors had to be assessed for the land tax had occasionally been enforced but the checking of the qualifications of borough electors had been something of a lottery. The result was that in the majority of English and Welsh constituencies, there was little certainty about the number of individuals who were actually qualified to vote. The Reform Acts put an end to this and also significantly tightened the regulations regarding the qualifications for borough electors.

What then, were the more specific effects of the reform legislation, 1829–32? We may begin with the following estimates of the size of national electorates (Table 8.1 overleaf).

As these figures demonstrate, the electoral legislation had its greatest impact in Ireland and Scotland. The 1829 Disfranchisement Act reduced the Irish county electorate immediately by over 80% before a modest recovery took place in 1832. The effect of the Reform Act in Scotland was even more dramatic. There the electorate increased by a factor in excess of seventeen, having been virtually static for the previous century. In England and Wales, however, the pattern is rather different. Here, there appears to have been a gradual, if modest, increase in the total electorate from 1760 to 1820 followed by a steeper one until 1831. It then rose by approximately 50% as a result of the immediate effects of the Reform Act which were much less than had been anticipated as a result of a reluctance to register. Thus the more realistic measure of its actual effects is the figure for 1839, by which time electors had been encouraged to register by the local party managers. This shows that the electorate had all but doubled in size.

With regard to the significance of these figures, there is no doubt on one point – namely that there remained considerable disparity between the degree

Table 8.1 Estimates of national electorates, 1774–1839[a]

Years	1774 [i]	1790–1820 [ii]	1831 [iii]	1832 [iii]	1839 [iii]
E&W counties	189,400	208,700+	247,000	369,830	490,038
E&W		118,700>			
boroughs	113,800	130,700	188,000	286,428	335,319
Sc. Counties	2,200	2,460	2,500	33,562	48,000
Sc. Burghs	NA	1,280	1,303	32,251	46,000
I. counties		160,000>			
		212,270	37,000	60,597	78,259[iv]
I. boroughs		12,500	21,394	29,471	43,814[iv]
Total E&W		327,400>			
	303,200	339,400	435,000	656,258	825,357
Total S	2,200	3,740	3,803	65,813	94,000
Total I		172,500>			
		224,770	58,394	89,372	122,073
Total GB/UK		503,640>			
	305,400	567,910	497,197	811,443	1,041,430

Notes
a (i) Calculated from Namier and Brooke, *The Commons*; (ii) calculated from Thorne, *The Commons*; (iii) taken from Salmon, *Electoral Reform*, p. 23; Cook and Keith, *British Historical Facts*, pp. 121–6 (I have left universities out); K. Theodore Hoppen, *Elections, Politics, and Society in Ireland 1832–1885* (Oxford, 1984), pp. 1–2. In the case of the figure for Irish boroughs in 1831, it has been calculated from official reports compiled in 1831.The figures for Scotland are taken from, J. I. Brash (ed.), *Papers on Scottish Electoral Politics 1832–1854* (Edinburgh, 1974), pp. ix–x; (iv) these figures are for 1837 and have been taken from B. M. Walker (ed.), *Parliamentary Election Results in Ireland, 1801–1922* (Dublin, 1978). By 1841 the numbers had shrunk to 55,349 in the counties and 38,716 in the boroughs – an overall reduction of nearly 23%.

to which each of the three kingdoms was represented, particularly with respect to the county constituencies. Thus the ratios of electors to inhabitants in Irish, Scottish and English and Welsh county constituencies was 1:116, 1:45 and 1:24, respectively.[1] On other issues, however, there has been keen debate, and two of these are worth dwelling on here. First, the extent of the change brought about by the legislation in terms of the total number of electors. And second, the proportion that had the opportunity and the readiness to vote. In the last respect, many constituencies were traditionally uncontested, either because the number of candidates in a constituency was equivalent to the number of seats available, or if there was more, because some chose to stand down rather than call for what could be a highly expensive poll. Table 8.2 overleaf provides estimates of the number of contested elections and the number of votes cast at selected general elections.

With regard to the first issue – the extent of the growth of the electorate – debate has focused on the increase in the English and Welsh electorate as a result of the Reform Act. Frank O'Gorman has argued that in terms of the ratio of electors to adult males, it was far less than had usually been thought: from 17.2% before 1790 to only 18.4% in 1832. Derek Beales, on the other

Table 8.2 Estimates of votes cast at general elections, 1774–1841[a]

Year	1774[i]	1818[ii]	1830[iii]	1832[iii]	1841[iv]
No. of contests	102	120 (Ir.14)	103 (Ir.30)	273 (Ir.45)	188 (Ir.20)
[Number who] voted in E&W counties	33,800	51,244	28,551	201,962	108,449
Voted in E&W boroughs	57,974	90,387	59,665	188,738	182,861
Voted in S. counties	428	390	239	20,153	7,027
Voted in S. burghs	50	17	31	23,372	16,071
Voted in I. counties		36,800	16,695	23,461	13,564
Voted in I. boroughs		4,500	8,761	22,610	13,604
Totals of those who voted	GB 94,258	GB 142,038 UK 183,338	GB 88,575 UK 113,942	GB 434,225 UK 480,296	GB 314,408 UK 341,576

Notes

a (i) Calculated from Namier and Brooke, *The Commons*. Estimating the actual numbers who voted from the results when a voter could cast either one or two votes in a contest with three or more candidates for a two-member constituency is problematic. The estimates for all these years are approximate. (ii) Calculated from Thorne, *The Commons*. (iii) Taken from Derek Beales, 'The electorate before and after 1832: the right to vote, and the opportunity', *PH*, vol. 11 (1992), pp.146–8. (iv) Calculated from Henry Stooks Smith, *The Parliaments of England*, vols 1–3 (1844); J. Vincent and M. Stenton (eds), *McCalmont's Parliamentary Poll Book of all Elections 1832–1918* (8th edn Brighton, 1971); Walker, *Election Results*.

hand, has calculated that this obscures a fall to 12.4% in 1831, making the real increase by 1832 much greater and even greater again of course by 1841 when the ratio had risen to 20.3%. My own calculations confirm the gist of Beales' case. Thus, the ratio of electors to adult males fell from 1774 to 1818 (from 13.9% to 11.1%) before rising to 12.2% in 1831. The increases in 1832 and by 1841 were therefore substantial.

In the case of the second issue – the extent to which the Reform Act led to higher proportion of electors in England and Wales being able to cast a vote – Beales has also argued for a substantial increase, thereby further undermining O'Gorman's general case for there being continuity between pre- and post- Reform electoral politics. On this point my calculations suggest some modification of those of Beales which were based on the exceptionally low number of contests in the three general elections immediately preceding the Reform Act. Thus, if the ratio of voters to the male population at the relatively highly contested elections of 1774 and 1818 (4.3% and 4.6%) are set against those for 1830, 1832 and 1841 (2.4%, 11% and 7.1%), the differences before and after 1832 are not quite so striking. Moreover, if the ratio of voters to the electorate as a whole is considered, it is even less so: 30.9% and 41.7% in 1774 and 1818; 20.2%, 59.5% and 35.2% in 1830, 1832 and 1841. The Reform Act therefore certainly led to an increase in the number of English and Welsh electors who were able to vote but the proportion who did so in 1841 was actually lower than that in 1818 and not wildly different from that in 1774.[2]

Debate has also focused on the questions of how far there was continuity or change in the social profile of electorates and the factors that determined voting behaviour. In the case of their social profile, there was considerable disparity between the three kingdoms before the 1829–32 legislation, particularly in the case of the counties. In Scotland the '40s freeholder' was in fact a substantial landowner – hence the small number of electors. In Ireland, on the other hand, a considerable proportion consisted of very small tenant farmers with leases from landlords that were held for the lifetimes of individuals other than themselves. County electors in England and Wales, for their part, consisted principally of a broad cross-section of the rural community, the majority of which was made up of modest to substantial farmers, some of whom were freeholders and many more, it seems, leaseholders for their own lifetimes. However, this was not the whole story. A significant number of urban dwellers, particularly those living in towns that were not represented in Parliament, also qualified as county electors as did those who did not reside in the constituency for which they claimed the vote.

As we have seen, the reform legislation had its greatest comparative effects in Ireland and Scotland, where the intention clearly was to produce county electorates that were similar in type to the English model. There was some success in both cases. In Ireland, nearly three-quarters of county electors in 1840 held land between 10 and 50 acres and some 84% had land assessed for the purposes of the Poor Law valuation at more than £10. Two other points are also worth noting. First, the inclusion of leaseholders for years under the terms of the Irish Reform Act had little effect: by 1840 they constituted no more than 10% of the whole. And second, that although there was a rough correlation between the predominant religion in a county and that of its electorate, Protestants were disproportionately represented in the counties outside Ulster.[3] As for Scotland, the county electorate consisted largely of tenant farmers and a smaller proportion of professionals, merchants, shopkeepers and craftsmen who lived in the towns and villages. It therefore became comparable to that in England. In due course, however, competition for seats led to an increasing number of 'mushroom' or fictitious electors being created from amongst lifetime renters of jointly-held property.[4]

In England and Wales, the Reform Act did not greatly alter the social profile of the county electorate. Thus as Philip Salmon has made admirably clear, the granting of the vote to £50 tenants-at-will (the major provision of the Act with regard to the county franchise) did not provide the abundance of electors subject to the landlords' whim that reformers had feared.

By 1840, they were no more than 23% of the electorate. The 40s freeholders therefore continued to constitute the majority although Salmon also provides for the first time reliable estimates of the proportions of urban dwellers and non-resident electors. In both cases, he argues, the proportions rose after 1832 although they clearly varied from county to county: from as low as 10% to as high as 60% in the case of urban dwellers; and from between 12% and 25% in that of non-residents.[5] Overall, Salmon's work suggests there was considerable similarity between the pre- and post-Reform county electorates but that there was a tendency for the proportion of urban dwellers to grow in industrialising areas after 1832.

If we disregard the close and rotten boroughs with very small electorates which were largely disfranchised in 1832 and focus on the 'open' boroughs with sizeable electorates, there would also seem to be considerable continuity in terms of their social profile. As Frank O'Gorman has demonstrated, in terms of its social stratification, the typical borough electorate in England before 1832 was pear-shaped: with gentlemen and professionals at the top; merchants, shopkeepers, master tradesmen, inn keepers and the like in the bulbous middle; and artisans and labourers at the bottom.[6] Studies of equivalent constituencies in Ireland have drawn similar conclusions.[7] Current research suggests that this continued to be the case after 1832 and that the £10 householder franchise led to no significant change. In the case of Ireland, for example, there were considerable variations but a typical profile of a borough electorate consisted of about 10% gentlemen and professionals, 50% merchants, shopkeepers and publicans, and 20% artisans, the rest falling into a variety of smaller categories across the spectrum. The only significant impact of the £10 franchise, albeit an important one, was that it ensured that the Protestant population in the southern provinces was much more disproportionately represented in the boroughs than in the counties.[8]

In the rest of the United Kingdom, the £10 householder franchise produced many more open constituencies but did not alter the social profile of electorates to any significant extent. One reason for this was the persistence of the 'ancient-right' electors who, Salmon estimates, constituted 40% of the English borough electorate after 1832. Further, he also makes the important point that the claim to vote on the basis of ancient-right rather than a £10 household became the more attractive option for those who could do both on the grounds that the latter was more expensive and tied to the payment of local taxes. Thus, the number of ancient-right and freemen electors actually increased in the course of the 1830s, thereby strengthening the continuity with the past.[9] Thus, the social profile of borough electorates revealed by John Vincent's study of the pollbooks of the 1850s and 1860s bears a remarkable resemblance to that found by O'Gorman a century earlier.[10]

There has also been considerable debate on the second issue – the factors that determined voting behaviour. This is an extremely complex subject, not least because of the variety of different types of constituencies and electors, and of imponderables such as uncontested elections. However, there are two central and related issues that we might concentrate upon here. First, the relationship between the landed proprietors (from which the vast majority of candidates were drawn) and the electors. And second, the partisanship exhibited by the electors for the parliamentary parties and local variants of them.

In the case of the relationship between landed proprietors and electors, it used to be thought that most elections, whether contested or uncontested, were decided primarily in one of two ways: either by a combination of the coercion of a sufficient number of tenant electors and a liberal disposal of inducements; or by such electors preferring to defer to their landlords wishes – a preference supposed to be more common after 1832. Current research, however, proposes a different interpretation. Thus while there is little doubt that proprietorial electoral interests were capable of being decisive in small county and borough constituencies, emphasis is now placed on the contractual relationship between the masters of such interests and the electors that they embraced. Proprietors did not so much coerce or bribe the electors as nurse the constituency and be responsive to its needs. Electors, for their part, expected proprietors to take the lead in elections and were ready to support them according to the degree to which they were attentive to these needs. This is an interpretation that has been convincingly developed by O'Gorman for many English county and open borough constituencies before 1832 and although it could not be sensibly applied to Scotland, it was not wholly inapplicable to Ireland.[11] As I have argued elsewhere, for example, the predominately Catholic electors of Ireland were able to exert a powerful influence on the voting behaviour of their Protestant MPs on the Catholic question between 1807 and 1829.[12] Moreover, the case for the continuation and indeed, the strengthening, of a contractual relationship in the English counties after 1832 has received strong support from Salmon's research. He therefore found evidence for the 1830s that was much the same as O'Gorman's for the previous century and stresses that 'Acres…conferred responsibility first and influence only second'.[13]

On the second issue – partisanship – research, principally by O'Gorman and John Phillips, also provides powerful evidence of a steady increase in partisan voting in many English open borough constituencies in the century before 1832.[14] This means that an increasing number of individual electors were influenced consistently over time by political preferences rather than by landed or any other form of 'influence'. In many cases these preferences were dictated by religion with the advance of nonconformity after 1780 encouraging Dissenters to support candidates supportive of the removal of their civil disabilities and Anglicans, the reverse. The religious divide between Protestant and Catholic electors was equally instrumental in many Irish county and some borough constituencies after 1801. Local partisanship, however, was not entirely separate from the parliamentary variety. Candidates were inevitably associated with one side of the Commons or none: as supporters of government or Opposition; as tories, whigs or radicals; and as independents. Partisanship that may have been driven by local circumstances therefore became attached to the parliamentary battle and as this hardened into a Tory-Whig divide in the early nineteenth century, it acquired what historians refer to as 'a national orientation'.

The argument for increasing nationally-oriented partisanship needs to be kept in perspective. It was not, of course, a new phenomenon. It was clearly evident before and after 1714, although it may have faded with the demise of the Tories as a coherent party in the 1750s and 1760s. Further, much of the evidence for it in this period comes from pollbooks recording the ways that individual voters cast their votes in frequently contested English open boroughs. This means that it cannot apply with equal force to constituencies that were usually uncontested such as the majority of Scottish and Welsh constituencies as well as the English counties and English and Irish close boroughs. On the other hand, the evidence of partisanship is so strong for the 'open' constituencies with large electorates that it seems legitimate to argue that partisanship might well have played a part in those where voters were unable to exercise their vote freely or at all.

Research on the post-1832 period suggests that in terms of partisan voting there was some continuity and some significant change. Phillips's study of voting behaviour in selected English open boroughs before and after the Reform Act makes the case for continuity but argues that the measure sharpened divisions and made them more widespread.[15] Salmon's work, however, which focuses on the effects of the newly-introduced registration system, tips the scales in favour of a greater degree of change. O'Gorman and Phillips made the English open boroughs the centre of their attention, but Salmon considers the English counties as well. In their case, his conclusion from a detailed study of voting behaviour is that proprietorial influence cannot account for more than 10–15% of the votes cast. Much more important, was the control taken by local party activists of the registration system and 'the enhanced importance of party affiliation'. In view of the point made earlier that the Reform Act did not change the social profile of county electors to any significant degree, this suggests that partisanship was much more widespread in the counties before 1832 than we had hitherto suspected and that in that respect there was considerable continuity.[16]

It is Salmon's work on the English boroughs, however, which points to a significant degree of change. Thus, while he accepts O'Gorman's and Phillips's conclusions on the high degree of partisanship, his central argument is that the control over the registration system acquired by party activists increases its extent and transforms the context in which it operated. The two parliamentary parties required local activists to oversee the registration of electors in their interest and as it happened, these tended to be liberals rather than Whigs and ultra Tories rather than Conservatives. The activists, for their part, in order to be able to successfully register their supporters in the registration courts, needed to control the institutions that supervised their operation – the parishes and the municipal corporations, most of the latter being subject to election by ratepayers after 1835. The results were first, the establishment of a much closer relationship between specific elements of the parliamentary parties and their enfranchised supporters – elements, it should be noted, that were not in tune with the leadership. And second, that partisanship quickly spread to the institutions of local government.[17]

How far similar developments took place in Wales is, in the current state of research, difficult to say, although the strength of the Conservatives in both counties and boroughs (they took the majority of seats from 1835–47) would suggest that proprietorial influence remained comparatively stronger there than in England. More is known about Scotland and Ireland, however, where some developments were similar and others different. In Scotland, the massive increase in the burgh electorate led to those with a commitment to reform becoming a majority with the result that the burghs became a stronghold for Liberals until the end of the century. In the counties, on the other hand, although an equivalent increase in the size of electorates initially worked to the Whig-Liberal's advantage, the Conservatives responded by quickly exploiting the possibilities of the new registration system. This led to fierce competition in the registration courts between the local landed proprietors who represented the respective parties and a proliferation of fictitious electors. The historian of the subject therefore concludes that by these means, the proprietors who had controlled the Scottish counties before 1832 were able to re-establish their influence by 1841.[18] As for Ireland, the evidence suggests that the intense pro-/anti-Catholic partisanship that developed in many county and some borough constituencies under the umbrella of a much stronger patronal influence than existed in England was dissipated by the Relief and Disfranchisement Acts of 1829. After 1832, candidates presented themselves as supporters of O'Connell, the Whig-Liberals or the Conservatives but it was only the Conservatives who applied themselves with any diligence to the registration process. Thus, although there was a degree of partisanship, it was not so closely tied to the parliamentary parties as became the case in England, and it coexisted as an explanation of voting behaviour with proprietorial and other forms of essentially non-party influences.[19]

The effects of the legislation of 1829–32 on the electoral politics of the United Kingdom were therefore mixed. In the case of constituencies, it had its greatest effect in England and Wales, the changes in Scotland and Ireland being, by comparison, minor. However, the change should be kept in proportion. All rotten and most close boroughs were wholly or partially disfranchised but their seats were distributed in equal measure to the counties and to London boroughs and hitherto unrepresented populous towns. Only slightly more than a quarter of the existing boroughs was wholly disfranchised. Further, although many English counties were divided into two or more separate constituencies, the basic distinction between counties and boroughs was maintained throughout the United Kingdom.

As for electors, the issues boil down to their number, type and voting behaviour. In the case of numbers, the legislation had its greatest impact, relatively speaking, in Ireland and Scotland. There, the electorates were respectively reduced and increased by factors of 4 and 17 and even in 1839, the Irish electorate was till less than half what it had been in 1828. In England and Wales, on the other hand, the electorate grew initially by about 50% and had doubled by 1839. However, being a registered voter did not necessarily mean that there was always an opportunity to vote. If the numbers of those who had an opportunity to vote, 1774–1841, are taken into consideration, the change over time is far less striking than the increase in the nominal electorate would suggest.

The legislation also had its greatest effect in Scotland and Ireland with regard to the types of electors. In England and Wales, county electorates had long consisted largely of tenant farmers with relatively secure tenures and a rising proportion of professionals, traders and craftsmen who lived in the villages and towns. In the boroughs with sizeable electorates, electors consisted of a broad cross-section of the male community with a preponderance of traders and craftsmen. Broadly speaking, the English and Welsh Reform Act, although designed to increase the proportion from the middling ranks of property owners and occupiers, did not significantly alter the social profile of the electorate. In the case of the Irish and Scottish legislation, on the other hand, it certainly did and had the effect of bringing their electorates more into line with their English and Welsh counterparts.

Finally, in the case of voting behaviour, national variations and a strong element of continuity are also evident. Before 1832, proprietorial influence was virtually absolute in Scotland but had been progressively weakened in Ireland, chiefly by pressure from Catholic electors. In England, on the other hand, it has been argued that such influence had traditionally been much more contractual than coercive and was therefore a weaker factor in explaining how electors cast their votes. After 1832, proprietorial influence made a modest recovery in Ireland and following an initial shock to its system, a much more substantial one in the Scottish counties. In England, however, proprietorial influence continued to be of a contractual and conditional type and may have declined. As for the level of support that a significant number electors gave relatively freely for one or other of the parliamentary parties, this seems to have grown in English counties and boroughs before 1832 and to have become stronger thereafter. There also seems to have been some continuity in this respect in Ireland although in the Scottish burghs, it was a wholly novel phenomenon.

The question before us, then, is what impact these developments had upon government and Parliament. If, as O'Gorman argues, 'the quality of political relationships in the [English] constituencies was public, participatory and partisan', did this make any difference to who governed and how they governed?[20] As a preliminary to an assessment, we should take note of two developments with regard to general elections. Twenty-one of these took place between 1761 and 1847 by comparison with eighteen in the period 1688–1760. Elections therefore became marginally more frequent although it is unwise to read too much into this. As in the earlier period, the death of the monarch or the fall of a government could bring about a swift succession of elections as in 1802–7 when there were three and in 1826–37 when there six. The only significant difference is that by comparison with the period of the Whig ascendancy, what was regarded as the politically acceptable lapse of time between elections was reduced from the statutory seven years to six. This was undoubtedly due to governments believing that with the growing force of public opinion, they required the rather more frequent endorsement of the electorate than the law allowed.

There was also a trend towards a select number of 'national' issues dominating the rhetoric of candidates for many contested, and even uncontested, elections. The general election of 1780, it has been argued, was the first one of this period when differences between the government and the Opposition, principally on the conduct of the American war, were the principal topics of debate in a significant number of constituencies.[21] Thereafter, a small cluster of such issues, with one usually more prominent than others, dominated the rhetoric of general elections. In 1784, the key issue was George III's dismissal of the Fox–North coalition and his support for the Younger Pitt; in 1807, his virtual dismissal of the Grenville administration on the issue of Catholic relief; in 1826, in Ireland and some English constituencies, the Catholic question; and in 1830 but much more strongly in 1831, parliamentary reform.[22] In 1841, the prominent issues were free trade and protection, the privileges of the Church of England, and the secret ballot.

These developments might suggest that the fortunes of governments and the policies that they pursued became increasingly determined by the results of general elections but in fact their effects were far less clear-cut. In the case of their effect on which set of politicians was in office, the electoral influence of the government of the day before 1832 was such that it was virtually impossible for a sitting government to be unseated. Indeed all elections bar one between 1761 and 1826 strengthened the party in power, the exception being that of 1780 when North's government suffered such a substantial defeat in the English open constituencies that its credibility with the independent sector of the Commons was severely damaged. Thereafter, however, the sitting government was fatally weakened by the election of 1830; unable to establish a majority in 1835 and actually defeated for the first time in 1841. In 1847, the Whig-Liberal government secured a general election but did not achieve more than a nominal majority of two – a result that would have been unthinkable before 1832. Elections rather than the influence available to the government of the day therefore became the determining factor in who governed.

Their impact on how they governed, however, is much more problematic. The crucial issue is the distinction that contemporaries drew throughout this period between the results of a general election as a whole and the results in particular types of constituencies. As we have seen, the UK's electoral geography was still extremely complex in the 1840s and consisted of different types of constituencies of different sizes and with differing numbers of electors qualified by a bewildering variety of franchises. Contemporaries were therefore well aware that taken as a whole, election results were determined by so many different factors that it made no sense to regard them as an indicator of a public opinion that they should notice of when devising policy. This was as much the case in 1841 as it was in 1761.

On the other hand, they did take notice of the results in the open constituencies, particularly the county constituencies with large electorates, which, it was thought, were a barometer of respectable public opinion. In general terms, for example, ministers before 1832 were very sensitive to the opinions of the MPs for such constituencies, largely because they constituted an independent section of the Commons who could decide their fate. It is therefore likely that most governments had their outlooks in mind when shaping all aspects of policy. Electoral opinion in such constituencies therefore probably had a permanent influence on the official mind, albeit one that was expressed indirectly through their MPs. On the other hand, after 1832 the erstwhile 'independent country gentlemen' (as the MPs for such constituencies were sometimes called) were absorbed, perhaps, uneasily, into the two parties with the result that the constructing of overall policy appears to have fallen more exclusively into the hands of the front bench spokesmen. In this respect the ultra Tory revolt against Peelite conservatism, 1845–6, may be regarded as the last, if decisive, gasp of old-style 'country' independence.

It also appears to have been the case that the movement of opinion in such constituencies did have an impact on specific policies. The principal examples are as follows: (1) the election of a majority of MPs from the English open constituencies who were critical of Lord North's handling of the American war and who hastened his defeat and the end of the war in 1782; (2) the pressure of Catholic electors in Ireland, particularly in the counties, to persuade a majority of Irish MPs to support relief, thereby helping to produce an almost evenly balanced state of opinion in the Commons; (3) the mobilisation of such support to secure O'Connell's election for Co. Clare in July 1828 and which impelled the Wellington government to consider and implement relief and (4) the results of the 1830 and 1831 elections in open constituencies which helped to bring about a government not only committed to parliamentary reform but also a measure that was far more extensive than most had expected.

Two points arise from these examples. The first is that it would be a mistake to regard election results as the sole reasons for these events and policies. The only clear-cut example that made legislation essential is O'Connell's election for Co. Clare. In the case of 1830, on the other hand, the support for parliamentary reform in many open constituencies certainly weakened the Wellington government but its defeat in the Commons was due largely to his refusal to countenance *any* concessions on that head. Further, the 1831 election took place after the details of the Whig's measure were known. The results were therefore as much an endorsement as a demand that could not be refused. The other point is that the number of examples is small and concentrated in the period 1826–31. In other words, there does not appear to have been a trend towards elections having a stronger and stronger influence on specific policies. Overall, we might conclude that although elections came to have a decisive impact on who governed, and although the views of MPs representing large open constituencies may have been a permanent consideration in policy-making before 1832, their impact on specific policies was, with exception of the years, 1826–31, limited.

Lobbies and pressure groups

In the period before 1760, there were several different types of groups that sought to influence the decisions of governments and Parliament. These were the financial institutions of the City of London; the chartered companies and the American, East Indian and West Indian merchants; various other economic pressure groups representing largely internal trade and manufacture; and pressure groups that had religious and moral objectives. The conclusion reached was that each type had some influence on Westminster decision-making and that the most constant and substantial was probably that of the economic pressure groups.

In the period after 1760, this infrastructure grew substantially and acquired new components that rapidly outstripped the others in scale and significance. The general reason for this was the transforming effects of social, economic and cultural change: the more than doubling of the population of Britain by 1841; the industrial 'revolution'; rapid urbanisation; and as one of many cultural developments that might be noted, the evangelical revival that led to a substantial increase in the number of Dissenters, particularly Methodists. These developments, together with a strong current of thought that regarded voluntary association as a feature of a 'civil society', were responsible for a surge in the number of clubs and societies between 1760 and 1800 that was undoubtedly continued to the 1840s and beyond. Peter Clark has therefore shown that there were about 3,000 such institutions of up to ninety different types in London by the late eighteenth century and that an equivalent increase had taken place in other well-established cities such as Edinburgh, Dublin and Bristol. He also noted that they were taking root in growing industrial cities such as Birmingham and were spreading in the English countryside, a habitat that was rare before 1760.[23]

The new feature of pressure-group politics that was grafted onto the traditional infrastructure was the growth of political societies. Although these had existed before 1760, the campaign to have John Wilkes reinstated in the Commons following his expulsion for being found guilty of seditious libel, led to them proliferating at a rapid rate. Amongst the most famous of such societies that helped to define collectively the popular politics of the period were: Wyvill's Yorkshire Association, the London Corresponding Society, Reeves' Loyalist Association, the Catholic Association, the Anti-Slavery Society, the Political Unions, the Chartist Association and the Anti-Corn Law League. Taken together, political organisations such as these added a new dimension to pressure group politics. In the first place, many were seeking not so much concessions from Parliament in favour of a particular interest, but rather a radical reform of the existing political system based on an increasingly detailed and coherent critique of the ways that it worked. Second, the conventional ways of mobilising public support, such as county meetings and petitioning, were deployed on a scale not seen before. The overall quantity of petitioning, for example, rose by a factor of more than seventy between 1780 and 1840 and on key issues, the number of signatures to a specific campaign rose from hundreds to millions. Finally, political pressure groups were an integral part of a process of politicisation on a national and to some degree, a class-based, scale. Nearly all the pressure groups mentioned above, and many others too numerous to mention, aimed at generating support on a national basis. This is evident in the geography of petitioning campaigns. Further, pressure-group activity undoubtedly helped to generate a sense of common purpose or even common identity amongst similar types of people in different parts of the state. Some historians have shown how loyalism and a consciousness of a British national identity developed in a broad cross-section of society in the late eighteenth and early nineteenth centuries.[24] Several have identified increasingly close co-operation between Dissenters in pursuit of civil rights[25] and between different types of trades unions in scattered localities for better wages and conditions of work.[26] Others have described how the concept of a 'middle-class' embracing those associated with the professions, commerce, and the new forms of industry became established as a social descriptor by the 1820s;[27] and more generally, how the language of class conflict became a staple of political literature. All these developments had the effect of encouraging co-operation across the country between similar occupational or religious groups. Pressure-group activity was both a cause and a result of this.

When considering the question of what impact specific types of pressure had upon the executive and Parliament, the first and probably the most extensive in terms of its results – the City of London and the financial institutions it housed – is also the one we know least about. What evidence there is suggests increasingly close ties between the executive and the City. The political rift between the executive and the governing body of the City, the Common Council, which had been caused by the Excise crisis, came to an end in the 1780s.[28] The American and the French wars proved hugely profitable to the financiers and were therefore another reason for harmony. In addition, the ties between the Bank of England and government grew even closer after 1819, especially after the Bank Charter Act of 1844, which made it, in effect, a central bank. On this basis, it seems reasonable to conclude that the relationship between the executive and the City was increasingly co-operative.

In the case of the colonial, overseas and domestically-oriented economic interests, their influence at Westminster was substantial but that of the colonial type changed over time. At the beginning of the period the three leading colonial interests were those involved in the American, West Indian and East Indian trades. Between 1760 and the outbreak of war in 1775, the various Anglo-American groups, hitherto organised on a 'colony-by-colony coffee house' basis, were combined into one for the purposes of applying pressure to the Board of Trade. However, by comparison with the earlier period, when their influence on policy was considerable, it decreased substantially in this. One of the reasons was the lingering differences between the various groups that now constituted a single lobby. Another was the increasingly obdurate and unresponsive approach of a Board that was much more subject to executive and parliamentary oversight on the subject of American trade.[29] Anglo-American commercial interest groups continued to exist after the loss of the colonies, of course, but their ability to exert pressure on policy had less of a focus than hitherto and probably, less influence.

The West Indian lobby also consisted of a number of different groups at the beginning of this period: the agents for the islands; the London merchants trading with them; the planters living in Britain and those MPs with West Indian interests, the number of whom oscillated between 20 and 50 in the earlier part of this period before stabilising at the lower end of that range until 1832. Further, a similar consolidation of these disparate interests into more organised body appears to have taken place in the 1760s and more particularly, during the period of the American war. A Society of West India Merchants was established in the 1760s that began to hold joint meetings with the planters as early as 1772. Then, in response to the economic and strategic threats presented by the war, the interest as a whole became 'a professional and more structured body' under the leadership of Stephen Fuller, the agent for Jamaica. It was on this basis that it organised resistance to pressure from English refiners for cheaper sugar in 1780 and to government attempts to increase sugar and rum import duties in 1781–2. Thereafter, what became the Committee of West India Planters and Merchants with its own opulent headquarters in London and its own journal, the *West Indian Reporter*, was a constant lobbyist of ministers on trade issues and more generally, on slavery.[30] Between 1828 and 1830, for example, they, together with the domestic sugar refiners, were the most frequent commercial lobbyists of all.[31] However, measuring its influence is difficult, not least because of the coincidence that sometimes existed between ministerial policy and that of the merchants and planters. On balance, the evidence suggests that it was a permanent feature of the making of official policy on commercial matters but that it declined substantially in the face of the growing tide of public feeling in favour of the abolition of the slave trade and of slavery. It has also been argued that the West Indian interest in Parliament was severely depleted by the disfranchisement of close boroughs by the 1832 Reform Act.[32]

In the case of the equally diverse East Indian interest, we need to draw a distinction between two elements: one that was principally concerned with the administration of civil and military affairs in India and another more concerned with trade. In the case of the former, it increasingly fell under the sway of the executive and virtually became a part of it. In the case of the latter, there appears to have been a decline in its influence, particularly with regard to the Company's monopoly of the Indian and China trades and a rise in that of the merchants who sought their abolition. The Company was therefore unable to resist the abolition of these monopolies in 1813 and 1833, respectively.

Indeed, in the early nineteenth century the anti-Company interest became part of the extensive and constant lobbying by an array of financial, commercial and manufacturing groups that was as much a central a feature economic lobbying in this period as it was before 1760. In 1828–30, for example, at least 33 different groups of this kind sent representatives to the government departments seeking concessions on at least 77 occasions, one of them being the East India Association that sought the abolition of the Company's monopoly of the China trade.[33] All the evidence we have points to this being a constant feature of the relationship between government, Parliament and the financial, commercial and manufacturing sectors throughout this period. To what extent the lobbyists were successful, however, is equally difficult to determine. The evidence certainly suggests that their activities became increasingly important as the period progresses, particularly in their dealings with the Secretaries of State's Offices, which appear to have been impervious to their efforts before 1783.[34] On the other hand, it is difficult to argue that on crucial issues, pressure of this kind was decisive. In the cases of the abolition of the Company's monopoly of the India trade in 1813 and the repeal of the Corn Laws in 1846, for example, external pressure was not the critical factor. The Liverpool government had already decided to open up the India trade[35] and Peel had long been convinced of the necessity of reducing protective duties on Corn before the Irish Famine persuaded him to abolish them. It might therefore be realistic to conclude that lobbying of this kind was a constant factor in decision-making on trade and manufacture but rarely a decisive one.

Much more eye-catching than the activities of commercial and manufacturing lobbies was the growth of political pressure groups – by far the most distinctive feature of this period. Some, such as the Loyalist associations formed in 1792 to resists the advance of Jacobin-style radicalism in Britain and Ireland, were designed to protect the status quo but the vast majority had reform as their objective. A major stimulus to this development may have been the example of the extra-parliamentary radicalism generated by

John Wilkes in the 1760s. According to John Brewer, this not only extended demands for parliamentary reform to include a redistribution of seats and a wider franchise but also had a new and distinct form of organisation that was not connected to parliamentary groups.[36] In the 1780s, the word 'reform' in its progressive sense became an established part of political discourse and from that point until the 1840s, reform became the objective of a broad spectrum of groups in the political, professional and cultural worlds – hence the recent designation of the period from 1780 to 1850 as an 'Age of Reform'.[37]

Political pressure was applied in various ways and the first type of groups to consider are those that focused on methods that were regarded as constitutionally legitimate. These were: convening county or civic meetings approved by the authorities to prepare and endorse addresses and petitions to the Monarch and to Parliament; seeking pledges from candidates at parliamentary elections; and reliance on the leadership, guidance or encouragement of MPs who supported the cause. Such groups did not necessarily restrict themselves to this repertoire of constitutional pressure but the fact that they made significant use of it distinguishes them from those that concentrated on 'direct action'. These will be considered later.

Of the groups that made some use of constitutional methods, three broad categories can be discerned. The first consisted of those that sought the removal of specific grievances, usually over a prolonged period of time. These included, most famously: the campaign by non-conformists against various disabilities that was sustained for most of this period and only abated after reforms in their favour between 1828 and 1836; the successive campaigns by groups opposed to the slave trade and to slavery; and the mobilisation of support by the Catholic Association in Ireland for giving Catholics the right to sit in Parliament. Broadly speaking, the objective of such groups was not to topple the political system but to gain access to it – hence the emphasis on the 'constitutional' devices of petitions, electoral pressure and the collaboration of friendly MPs. The organisation of such pressure, however, became increasingly extensive and professional. The key resource for all the groups that organised the campaigns mentioned above was the expanding number of non-conformist and Catholic chapels in Britain and Ireland. These enabled leaders to orchestrate petitioning campaigns without recourse to the conventional preparatory county or civic meeting and on an unprecedented scale. In 1828–9, for example, O'Connell was able to mobilise the 40s freeholders to secure his election for Co. Clare and to follow this with a flood of pro-Relief petitions, most of which had a chapel origin.[38] At the general election of 1830, the Anti-Slavery Society demanded pledges from candidates in a number of constituencies and then organised a massive number of petitions to impress the new Parliament, most emanating from Methodist chapels.[39]

The second category consisted of a succession of groups that advocated various degrees of parliamentary reform. Starting with the Society of the

Supporters of the Bill of Rights, founded in 1769 to restore John Wilkes to the Commons as MP for Middlesex, the most notable were Christopher Wyvill's Yorkshire Association, 1779, the Society for Constitutional Information, 1780, the London Corresponding Society, 1792, the Hampden Club and its affiliates, 1812, the Political Unions from 1830, and the Chartists, 1837–48. This is not the place to deal at any length with the internal history of the movement for parliamentary reform but there are two aspects that have generated considerable scholarly debate and require discussion. The first concerns objectives. Broadly speaking, debate has focused on how far reformers were seeking to restore to the existing parliamentary system ancient rights that they thought had been lost in the course of the eighteenth century; and how far they envisaged the replacement of that system with one that was fundamentally different. A key source of controversy in this respect is the demand for annual Parliaments (or general elections), that the LCS championed in 1792 and later became one of the Chartists' 'six points'. To call for Parliaments that lasted for less than the existing maximum of seven years, usually for three, might seem to be a demand for a return to the Revolution period when the executive was supposedly more accountable to the electorate under the terms of the Triennial Act. Annual Parliaments, on the other hand, seems to envisage a state of affairs in which the Commons would become, in effect, the executive.[40] Although there is no clear consensus on this issue, the general trend of research suggests that although the movement was increasingly influenced by the radical 'natural rights' claims of Thomas Paine and others, it never lost touch with the ancient rights propositions of its founders. In a recent study of the Chartists, for example, Paul Pickering stresses this duality in their objectives and on the basis of a study of petitioning, concludes that 'with few exceptions, the ideological horizons of the Chartists were constitutional'.[41]

The other aspect was the methods such groups used. In each case, they deployed the traditional constitutional repertoire, particularly petitioning, but there was an increasing tendency to resort to mass meetings which would alarm the authorities and attract publicity, particularly in the increasingly influential newspaper press. One of the first reform groups to adopt this strategy was the LCS which sponsored a number of mass meetings in London between 1794 and 1797 before they were effectively suppressed by legal bans. Indeed, the Society evidently debated the merits of taking the constitutional path of petitioning and addresses as opposed to what has been called the extra-parliamentary route of mass meetings, some members arguing that the former required too much 'humility' on their behalf.[42] Following the conclusion of the French wars, the strategy was revived, most famously by Henry Hunt at Peterloo in 1819, and subsequently by the Political Unions and the Chartists. However, none of these groups abandoned constitutional methods for the extra-parliamentary variety. As in the case of the mixing of 'ancient' and 'natural' rights theory, they also combined the two strategies.[43]

The third category of constitutional, or partly constitutional, pressure-group politics consisted of more spontaneous protest against economic grievances. Food shortages were periodic causes as in 1766–7 and 1800–1[44] but in the early nineteenth century there were other targets. In 1811–12, there was a widespread campaign against the Orders in Council which restricted trade with Europe and were widely held to be responsible for the recession in manufacturing that led to the breaking of machines by workers in the English midlands known as Luddites.[45] In 1814–16, there was, on the one hand, a petitioning campaign for and against the protection of domestic corn growers;[46] and on the other, resistance to the government's proposal to continue the war-time income tax.[47] And in 1829–30, there was widespread protest against economic distress.[48] None of these campaigns sought to change the political system and in most respects they were advanced by entirely traditional and constitutional means. They were therefore largely based on addresses and petitions generated by legally convened meetings sponsored by local county and civic elites, in some cases encouraged by prominent MPs.

When estimating the impact of the constitutional brand of pressure on the executive and Parliament, it is important to take note of the history of its most widespread and consistent feature – petitioning. As has been mentioned before, the number of petitions presented to Parliament increased substantially between 1780 and 1830 but what needs to be stressed here is that the number continued to increase over the next ten years (Table 8.3).

By 1832, MPs generally were becoming seriously concerned about the amount of parliamentary time taken up by the presentation of petitions while those of a conservative disposition were dismayed at the opportunities that the presentation afforded radicals for initiating debates on their pet topics. As Colin Leys shows in his pioneering article on the subject, steps were therefore taken between 1832 and 1842 that led to petitions being put to a special committee rather than to the House and prevented MPs initiating debates on their subject matter. Although it was agreed for the first time that

Table 8.3 Petitions presented, 1785–1841

5-year periods	Number of petitions presented
1785–9	880
1801–5	1,026
1811–15	4,498
1827–31	24,492
1837–41	70,369

petitions would be received on taxes and duties under the consideration of the House, this amounted to a 'gagging' of petitioners and the MPs who supported their causes.[49] And yet, petitions continued to flow to the House, a record of 33,898 being established for a single year in 1843, and more than 10,000 pa for the rest of the nineteenth century.

This exponential increase in the *number* of individual petitions corresponded with a significant increase in the number of issues they addressed and a much more striking increase in the number of signatories. In the case of issues, it was rare before 1800 for more than two or three issues at most to attract a sufficient number of petitions to warrant MPs thinking that significant campaigns were in operation. However, in the period of the Wellington government, 1828–30, I noted 29 different issues subject to what might realistically called a widespread petitioning campaign.[50] Leys's research confirms that this trend continued into the post-Reform Act period, although he notes that the subject matter of the petitions attracting the largest number of signatures changed over time. Until the 1840s, those supporting political objectives predominated but this was superseded later by religious and social issues.[51] As for the total number of signatories to all types of petitions, these mushroomed from a few thousand to millions. Overall, the sustained increase in petitioning on all counts until the 1840s and the persistently high-level of support for it thereafter is an extraordinary testimony to the public's support for the process.

But, how far was the public's support for petitioning and the other components of pressure-group politics justified? Once again, this is an extremely difficult question to answer with any precision but a number of general propositions may be advanced. The first is that there seems no doubt that extra-parliamentary pressure was critical to placing a subject on the parliamentary agenda. This came to be the principal function of petitioning in particular, with radical and other types of zealous MPs using the presentation of petitions to initiate debates – at least until the Speaker's ruling of 1836 put a stop to this tactic. The role of MPs in this process alerts us to a second point, namely that the growth of both extra-parliamentary pressure and the force of public opinion made MPs aware of the necessity of attaching a significant volume of petitioning to a cause to which they were personally committed. In other words, it becomes increasingly difficult to tell whether the pressure for a specific type of legislation was coming from a largely extra-parliamentary source or whether it was being orchestrated principally by MPs. That said, the key point is that certainly by the 1820s, MPs were taking it for granted that a case for or against any major piece of legislation would be strengthened by the demonstration of a significant degree of public support on the one side or the other. On 9 April 1802, Sir Robert Peel stated in the Commons that the fact that there were no petitions against the bill to continue restrictions on cash payments by the Bank of England was one of the reasons why he would support it.[52] In June 1830 when the Commons was considering 243 petitions supporting, and only 80 opposing, the government's bill to establish free trade in the sale of beer, Sir Edward Knatchbull stated: 'This, I think, is sufficient to show what the general feeling of the public is upon the question'.[53]

However, this still leaves us with the question of how far public pressure persuaded the government and Parliament to do things that they would not otherwise have done. In the case of parliamentary reform, if we leave aside the suppression of radicalism in the 1790s and the years immediately following the end of the French wars, the only example for consideration is the Reform Acts of 1832. Otherwise, all the intermittent pressure from Wilkes to the Chartists came to nothing. However, as has been mentioned before, the Reform Acts are not a clear-cut case. Public pressure certainly made some sort of concession irresistible but the particular form that it took was the responsibility of the Whigs who had long possessed an agenda of their own on the subject. If public opinion is measured by the subject matter of petitions, for example, it was strongly in favour of a secret ballot, but this was not part of the Reform Acts.

More positive points can be made about the removal of nonconformist and Catholic civil disabilities and the abolition of the slave trade and slavery. In all four cases, there is no doubt that sustained pressure-group campaigns helped to convince a sufficient number of MPs and ministers of the political, moral or humanitarian cases for concession. On the other hand, it would be a mistake to ignore high-political factors. For example, in the case of the abolition of the slave trade in 1807, Lord Grenville took advantage of special political circumstances at Court and in Parliament to produce the desired legislation with Wilberforce and others.[54] Similarly, it is sometimes overlooked that there was a majority for some form of Catholic relief in the Commons in 1812–13, a decade before the Catholic Association was formed. In fact, there may be some justification for saying that government and Parliament were most clearly responsive not to sustained campaigns for reform but to spontaneous demands for economic relief. Extensive petitioning following county meetings preceded the protectionist Corn Laws of 1773 and 1815, and the abolition of the income tax in 1816. Further, in making £3 million tax cuts to reduce the cost of living for working families in his 1830 budget, Goulburn, the Chancellor of the Exchequer, stated that the quality of the petitioning campaign protesting against economic distress during the winter had helped him to make his decision.[55]

The other category of pressure that needs to be considered is that generated either partly or wholly by direct action. This took various forms. The most traditional was a ritualistic form of physical-force protest usually referred to as a riot. This was the traditional *modus operandi* of agricultural labourers protesting against the enclosure of common land or the shortage and high price of food; of workers threatened by new technology and wage cuts; and by working people of all types in response to specific political developments. In the last case, the 'No Popery' riots in London and Bath in opposition to the Catholic Relief Act of 1778 are one example. During the course of this period, the riot was supplemented on a more regular basis by other forms of direct action. At one end of the spectrum was the mass meeting and the strike, the last being complementary to the growth of trade 'combinations' or 'unions' in the late eighteenth and early nineteenth centuries. And at the other, there was a more widespread, co-ordinated, and violent form of rural protest such as the 'Captain Swing' firing of agricultural property in the southern counties of England and the anti-tithe 'war' in Ireland in the early 1830s.

By comparison with the previous period, there was a considerable increase in the quantity and frequency of popular protest in this one, particularly in the 1760s, 1790s and from 1810 to 1820 and 1830 to 1834. In the 1760s, for example, some twenty different cases have been listed by Gregory and Stevenson that attracted 'contemporary notoriety or resulted in serious damage to persons or property'. Some were very localised but others were more widespread. In 1761 there were riots against the Militia Act in Gateshead, Morpeth, Whittingham and Hexham; and in January – November 1766, food riots occurred across England but particularly in 'the West Country, Thames Valley, Midlands and East Anglia'.[56] From then until the early 1830s, the scale of such protest and the variety of its targets increased, particularly in the periods of acute tension mentioned above. After 1834, however, it probably began to decline as a result of improved methods of policing.

The greatest impact of such protest on government and Parliament took the form of the legislation designed to contain or suppress it. Apart from individual measures in response to particular protests such as the 1769 Act bringing attacks on mills under the terms of the Riot Act, [9GIII, st.2, *c*.5] there were two periods when a cluster of measures were enacted: 1792–1800 and 1817–19. In the first, Habeas Corpus was suspended, restrictions were placed on political meetings, the law of treason was extended 'to spoken and written words' and the combination of workers to secure improved wages and conditions by such means as a strike made illegal. In the second, a similar battery of measures were taken, including an act to prevent drilling as a prelude to the use of arms [60GIII and 1GIV, *c*.1]. In addition, the steps taken over longer periods of time to promote loyalism and to establish police forces and to garrison troops in areas prone to disturbances would also have to be included in this litany.

Concessionary responses to direct-action popular pressure are, not unexpectedly, far more difficult to find. In many cases a Westminster response was not solicited as protest was related solely to specific local grievances. In others, on the other hand, such as the 'No Popery' riots in London in 1780 or the Reform riots in Bristol in October 1831, it clearly was. However, the number of cases in the last category where protest produced a positive response appears to be very small. At the time of writing, only four stand out. First, the widespread strike action against the terms of the act of 1824 that repealed the laws banning trades unions but seemed to make strikes illegal was a powerful factor in persuading Parliament to make them lawful by an act of 1825. Second, a series of Reform riots, 1830–2, – in London, Bristol and more generally, in the 'Days of May' in 1832 – undoubtedly had some effect in persuading Parliament to agree a substantial measure. And third and fourth, there would seem to have been a causal link between, one the one hand, the contemporaneous Captain Swing riots and the anti-tithe campaign in Ireland, 1830–4, and on the other, the decisions to introduce a new Poor Law and to reform the tithe system.

Overall, we might draw two conclusions from this review of the substantial expansion of pressure-group activity. The first is that pressure upon Parliament continued to be central to the strategies of most groups. In the case of economic interest groups, this is not surprising, but it is much more so in that of the various reform groups. As one historian has put it, 'The centrality of Parliament' in their calculations 'is an indispensable element in any comprehension of their fundamental nature'.[57] The second, is that this expanded activity had mixed results as far as its impact on government and Parliament is concerned. It was probably greatest for the financial, commercial and manufacturing interests that traditionally exerted a regular influence by lobbying and other means, especially in the run up to budgets. However, it is doubtful whether such pressure was ever solely responsible for the decisions that were taken. The more likely scenario is that it was one of many factors that were considered.

Measuring the impact of political pressure is even more problematic. There can be no doubt that in the case of the great issues such as parliamentary reform, religious discrimination and slavery, it was critical to their rising to the top of the parliamentary agenda. Indeed, one of the distinguishing features of this period is the recognition by the promoters of even minor and transitory causes that it was essential to be able to show they had significant public support in order for them to have any chance of parliamentary consideration. On the other hand, the number of occasions when it can be said that pressure was principally responsible for the timing and the content of legislation is very small. This seems to suggest that although extra-parliamentary pressure exercised an increasing influence on the Westminster agenda, governments and Parliament were able to incorporate it into their decision-making processes.

The print media

The increase in the scale and intensity of extra-parliamentary pressure was complemented by an equivalent increase in all forms of printed material: books, pamphlets, periodicals, prints and newspapers. The following estimates of the growth in newspapers may stand as an indication of the scale of the change overall (Table 8.4). Change of this magnitude had an inevitable effect on what historians have referred to as the 'media infrastructure'[58] and led to a considerable increase in public knowledge of parliamentary and other forms of politics. In the case of the infrastructure, it has been argued that

Table 8.4 Numbers and sales of newspapers, *c.*1750–1840[a]

Pub. in	1750s	1780s	1828–30	1836	1837
London	*c.*28	*c.*26	55	71	85
E&W	*c.*40	50+	158	194	237
Scotland	*c.*6	10(1789)	37	54	65
Ireland	*c.*7	*c.*20	64	78	71
Total	*c.*81	*c.*106	314	397	458
Number of newspapers stamped	10.7 million (1756)	12.8 million (1788)	*c.*25 million	35.5 million	53.4 million

Notes

a These estimates are based on: Brian Inglis, *The Freedom of the Press in Ireland 1784–1841* (1954), pp. 19–22; Harris, *Politics and the Nation*, p. 58 for the number of stamped newspapers in 1756. I am also indebted to Professor Harris for the numbers of Scottish newspapers in the 1750s and 1789, for the latter see his 'Scotland's newspapers, the French Revolution and Domestic Radicalism *c.*1789–1794', *The Scottish Historical Review*, vol. 34 (2005), p. 39. Hannah Barker, *Newspapers, Politics, and Public Opinion in Late Eighteenth Century England* (Oxford, 1998), pp. 23, 111; Jupp, *British Politics*, p. 332; *British Almanac and Companion* (1839), p. 196; A. Aspinall, *Politics and the Press c.1780–1850* (1949), p. 6, fn. 6. The substantial increase in 1837 was due to the reduction of the duty from 4d to 1d. However this is not the whole story. Some newspapers evaded paying the stamp duty and more than 40 came into existence between 1816 and 1834, some with sizeable circulations, see Noel W. Thompson, *The People's Science. The Popular Political Economy of Exploitation and Crisis 1816–34* (Cambridge, 1984). In the debate on the reduction of the stamp duty on newspapers on 20 June 1836, the Chancellor of the Exchequer stated that one unstamped newspaper appeared to have an annual circulation of 2 million, the equivalent of one-eighteenth of that of all the stamped newspapers, *Hansard*, 3rd series, vol. xxxiv, clm. 627.

at the start of this period public opinion on political matters was shaped principally by the pamphlet and the periodical and, as a consequence, was focused on a small number of issues. Newspapers tended to follow their lead.[59] By the early nineteenth century, however, books had become as important as pamphlets, the number of periodicals had increased substantially, and newspapers took their own lines. The number of political issues dealt with therefore rose exponentially, one indication being the establishment of specialist periodicals. For example, five different periodicals dealing with foreign and military affairs were established between 1827 and 1833.[60]

In the case of the increase in public knowledge of political issues, this was due, obviously enough, to the fact that a substantial proportion of the different forms of publication dealt with them to some degree or another. Newspapers are the best example because they not only became the major source of information, but their sales also enable us to estimate their readership. Thus, as has been mentioned in a previous chapter, Parliament turned a blind eye to newspapers reporting its business from the 1770s onwards. As a consequence, the debates and other types of business joined foreign affairs to become the staple copy of the majority of the burgeoning number of newspapers. Further, an increasing proportion became partisan in their comments on parliamentary and local politics either for propaganda reasons or because this was a way to generate sales. Often it was a mixture of both.

As for readership (rather than sales), the key point is that contemporaries agreed that a single copy of a newspaper might actually be 'read' in some form or another by far more than one person or even a single household. Various factors were responsible. The principal one is that government imposed a rising level of stamp duty on newspapers in an attempt to restrict readership to the 'respectable' middling sections of society: 1.5d Britain in 1776, 2d in 1789, 3.5d in 1797 and 4d in 1815. The average cost of a newspaper at the highest rate of duty was therefore 7d, a substantial outlay when the average wage of a weaver in Manchester in 1832 was about 15s per week.[61] It was only in 1836 that the duty was substantially reduced to 1d. It therefore became customary for coffee houses, pubs, and all types of clubs and societies to provide copies for their clientele. In 1807, for example, William Cobbett doubted whether there was a pub in existence that did not make newspapers available to their customers.[62] In addition, newspapers benefited from the tradition of printed material being read out to those who were unable to read it for themselves. Literacy levels in Britain were remarkably high by European standards but there were obviously those who could not read and it was in this way that 'readership' levels were regarded as much higher than those provided by sales figures calculated from the stamp duty returns.

Historians have therefore concluded, on the basis of a very conservative estimate of the number who read a single copy of a newspaper, that readership in parts of Britain was very high by the 1780s and that it grew at a rate in excess of that of the population thereafter. Hannah Barker's estimate for England in the 1780s is that one in three of the *total* population of London read newspapers and anywhere between 15% and 50% of the *total* population of the leading towns and cities in which provincial newspapers were published.[63] My own calculations for the UK in the late 1820s suggest that these proportions increased relative to the population in England, especially if the illegal 'unstamped' press is included. Further; although they were very much lower per head of population in Scotland and Ireland as a whole, they were comparable in the leading cities and towns to the English provincial equivalents.[64] Once the duty was lowered to 1d in 1836, the number of readers across the UK rose even higher.

These figures therefore suggest that the readership of newspapers extended well beyond the confines of their traditional customers – the upper and middle classes – and included substantial numbers of working men and women. According to my calculations there were 650,000 readers of newspapers in London in 1830 and 1.3 million in the rest of England and Wales – a total of approximately 2 million. The population then stood at 13.9 million of whom perhaps half were adults. On this basis, we might assume that although newspapers were read predominately by the middling orders of society, they were also read by significant numbers of those small property owners who hovered on the lower edge of the middle-class as well skilled workers in the upper echelons of labour: the shop keepers, publicans, tradesmen, and the artisans and skilled operatives in such enterprises as textiles, shipbuilding and metals. The significance of this, it should be stressed, lies in the fact that newspapers gave considerable coverage to parliamentary politics. It has long been known that there was a substantial increase after *c.*1789 in the amount of literature directed at the working-class reader, much of it being contemptuous of the parliamentary system. This consisted, *inter alia*, of full or abbreviated versions of books such as Paine's *Rights of Man*, popular almanacs, religious tracts, and illustrated radical pamphlets such as Cruikshank's *The Political House that Jack Built*. Most of the unstamped press that flourished in the twenty years after the end of the Napoleonic wars also conveyed a radical message. Newspapers, on the hand, reported parliamentary business and although many were oppositional or radical in outlook, they were cautious in their criticism because of the threat of prosecution for libel. In other words, they offered working-class readers a different perspective.

What impact, then, did the growth of the media have upon government and Parliament? In order to attempt an answer to this question, we need to consider first the relationship between parliamentarians and the media, concentrating principally on newspapers. In recent years there has been some modification and amplification of the standard interpretation of this relationship, first developed by Professor Aspinall nearly sixty years ago. He argued that politicians exercised increasing influence over the press from the 1760s until the end of the Napoleonic wars: on the government's part by stamp duties, prosecution and various forms of direct and indirect subsidies; and on the Opposition's, by purchasing newspapers and such devices as the planting of material. After 1815, however, newspapers became increasingly profitable and had less need of politicians' favours. They therefore concentrated on pleasing their readers and increasing their number. Thus, although politicians still attempted to control newspapers, they were remarkably unsuccessful in England and only managed to do so to any significant extent in Scotland and Ireland where low sales made some newspapers particularly vulnerable to inducements of one sort or another. As a result, English newspapers in particular became, by 1832, the authentic voice of their readers or, of public opinion – a force that was now increasingly dignified, after the Lords and Commons, as 'the third estate'. After 1832, he argues, politicians still sought to influence key London newspapers but instead of resorting to the law, to bribery, or to purchase, relied upon the arts of management. These consisted of such things as the wining and dining of editors, the giving of advance notice of privileged information, and 'a word here and a word there'.[65]

The principal modification of this interpretation concerns the effectiveness of the politicians' attempts to control the press. Aspinall thought that it was extensive in the 1780s due to comparatively small sales, the high costs of production, and the low advertising revenue of many of the key London papers. Hannah Barker, however, has provided convincing evidence that it was much weaker than Aspinall supposed and that the need to appeal to readers was already a stronger factor in the minds of proprietors than the inducements offered by either the government or the Opposition.

It is this point which led Barker to focus on an issue that Aspinall neglected: what the papers said. If proprietors saw themselves as mouthpieces for the views of their readers, then the content of editorial leader columns and the slant given to the reporting of parliamentary politics would provide a clue as to what these were. On this basis, Barker comes to the following conclusions for the 1780s. First, that no matter what view they took of parliamentary politics, most English newspapers, and therefore most readers, assumed that the 'voice of the people' should be a crucial element in political life and that politicians should be measured by the degree to which they respected that maxim. Second, that in the case of the London press, the general issue of reform increasingly took precedence over that of 'parliamentary politics and party divisions' and that on this there were two broad categories of opinion. One group of London newspapers took the view that 'the protection of property and the rule of law [was] more important than extending individual rights' and was therefore opposed to parliamentary reform. Another group took the opposite view and supported a 'radical ideology of constitutional reform'. In other words, what mattered to the London press (and therefore its readers) was not so much the day-to-day issues upon which politicians might have liked to focus their minds but general propositions about the political system. It therefore seems that a significant change had taken place since *c*.1760 when the newspapers had followed the periodicals and had focused on issues of direct relevance to parliamentary politics. The press and its readers had developed an opinion of their own.[66]

My own research on the press in the late 1820s led to very similar conclusions. Based on a reading of the political periodicals as well as the English press, it found that although very considerable coverage was given to all forms of parliamentary business, the day-to-day manoeuvres of parties and their leaders were treated with a large measure of indifference that sometimes bordered on contempt. Most newspapers and periodicals had political agendas of their own but, generally speaking, these were not inspired by admiration for, or loyalty to, the parliamentary parties. General principles and ideas were much more influential. Thus, in line with Barker's findings for the 1780s, about half were committed to the extremes of the political spectrum – ultra toryism and progressive liberalism and radicalism – with the rest occupying points in between. Similarly, there was considerable continuity in the view the press took of its role. Virtually all newspapers regarded the late 1820s as a critical turning point in the relationship between Parliament and public opinion. The common theme was that events were breaking the mould of the 'old system' and that Parliament had to become more responsive to the predominantly middle-class public opinion that the press felt it reflected. As it happened, the readership of liberal newspapers outnumbered their conservative rivals by a ratio of 10:1. It is therefore not surprising that the vast majority of newspapers were in favour of some degree of parliamentary reform when the Wellington government fell in November 1830.[67]

Recent research has therefore refuted the view that the English (if not the Irish and Scottish) press was the politicians' poodle in the 1780s and provided important additional reasons why the influence they did possess weakened progressively until the Reform Bill crisis. Broadly speaking, all forms of media, but particularly the newspapers, were responsible for two developments. First, by providing extensive reporting of parliamentary affairs, they enhanced the public's knowledge, but also its expectations, of Parliament as an institution. Second, by needing to appeal to its readers, it became in England the mouthpiece of a public opinion that was from at least the 1780s, increasingly critical of parliamentary politicians and strongly supportive of what were ideological positions ranging from the extremes of conservatism to advanced liberalism.

How far the gap that had opened up between the politicians and the press was repaired after 1832 is a matter of conjecture. Politicians certainly adopted the path of influencing key newspapers discretely rather than by subsidies and financial inducements, the onus being on the Conservatives in view of liberal newspapers having by far the largest readership. As for the outlook of newspapers, the lack of detailed research makes an assessment highly speculative. It seems likely that they became more sympathetic to the parliamentary parties and in that respect, more supportive of them. We have already noted that party organisation and electoral partisanship in the constituencies increased after 1832 and were extended to the new institutions of local government. It therefore seems plausible to argue that this made the fortunes of the two parties more relevant to readers and editors alike. This, in turn, would have focused opinion more on the essentially constitutional forms of conservatism and liberalism found in Parliament. In this respect it is interesting to note the fate of the unstamped press that rejected the liberal form of political economy and advocated an anti-capitalist alternative in the form of Owenite socialism. Appealing to a working-class readership and priced accordingly, this element of the unstamped press flourished between 1816 and the mid-1830s but apparently withered thereafter. According to the leading authority on the subject, there were two principal reasons. First, the inherent weaknesses of the theoretical propositions on which this particular anti-capitalist ideology was based. And second, the emergence of issues on the *parliamentary* agenda that diverted attention from it.[68]

So far we have noted a substantial increase in all forms of print media, and in particular, that of the newspaper. The print media therefore became a much more powerful engine of public opinion than it had been before. In addition, it has been argued that the relationship between the parliamentarians and the newspaper press, the most powerful component of this engine, changed over time. Attempts were made to control key sections of it but from *c*.1780 to *c*.1832, the English press established itself as an independent voice that reflected the views of its readers. These tended to be dismissive of parliamentarians but enthusiastic for a broad spectrum of political standpoints, particularly on the liberal side. Thereafter, parliamentarians learned to live with an independent press that may have become less dismissive, and more supportive, of their activities in terms of party politics. The final question we need to address, therefore, is what impact the expansion of the print media as a whole and that of the newspapers in particular had upon the decisions that government and Parliament took.

On one point there is no doubt: namely, that politicians viewed the growth of the print media as a whole during the course of this period extremely seriously and did everything they could to harness it for their own purposes. Every government, every Opposition, every faction, and every politician of consequence sought to publicise their views and influence opinion: by the publication of speeches; by pamphlets and books; and in every other form of print. The extent to which they were influenced by the media, however, is a very different issue. In general terms, the influence of the respectable media such as books, pamphlets and periodicals, was, of course immense. It was this that helped to shape the evolving ideologies of the principal parties. However, in the more specific sense of the print media representing the weight of public opinion on a particular issue, its influence seems to have been far more limited. Assessment is made difficult, of course, because of the coincidental role played by other forms of pressure but the only clear cut cases appear to occur between 1828 and 1833. It was then that the weight of media opinion in favour of Catholic relief, parliamentary reform and the abolition of slavery met with positive and tangible results.

Summary and conclusion

At the start of this chapter, two questions were posed: how far did the structure of public pressure on government and Parliament change in this period; and to what extent did such pressure have a more decisive impact on the decisions that these two bodies took. In answer to the first of these questions, it is clear that the quantity of pressure increased enormously, albeit at different speeds, according to its source. In the case of elections, occasional pressure emanating from the results in English open constituencies gave way to more sustained pressure from the Catholic vote in Irish constituencies until 1828. After 1832, the substantially increased electorate in Britain was the source for what was, potentially, very much greater pressure. The histories of the other major component of public pressure, however, have a different chronology. Thus, the number of single-issue pressure groups grew steadily from the 1760s and rapidly from the 1790s. This was not dissimilar to the growth of the print media which accelerated from the 1780s.

Along with growth went changes to the means and infrastructure of pressure. In the case of the means, petitioning became by far the most prominent form of applying pressure constitutionally and quickly overtook, if not eliminate, the presenting of addresses and instructions.[69] It was also the case that there was increasing resort to mass meetings: in the 1790s; in the immediate post-war years; and more consistently from 1830 as the 'monster' meetings of O'Connell and the Chartist demonstrations exemplify. In addition, there were times when the traditional forms of direct action – the riot and machine breaking – were superseded by the more co-ordinated, widespread, and threatening use of physical force. This was particularly apparent in 1830–4. As for the infrastructure, the most notable changes were the growth of political pressure groups and newspapers. The former eventually eclipsed all such other groups in size and importance and the latter became far more influential than all the other forms of print.

The infrastructure of public pressure therefore changed substantially over time and led to public opinion becoming a fixture in the calculations of the governing class. To some extent such pressure became integral to the governing process therefore making it extremely difficult to disentangle its impact from that of other factors. This was the case with the opinion of the independent country gentlemen and therefore the electorates they represented. It was also true of the various economic interest groups whose lobbying of government departments continued to be a constant factor in the shaping of policy. Front-bench and back-bench MPs, for their part, were not slow to use the instruments of pressure on their own behalf. Before 1830, government and Opposition tried unsuccessfully to control the newspapers but made extensive use of the other print media. Moreover, those seeking legislative change soon became adept at organising petitioning campaigns. Indeed, one of the striking features of the relationship between Westminster and some of the instruments of institutional and public pressure before 1832 is how inter-related it was. As has been mentioned earlier, Parliament remained central to the aims and objectives of most pressure groups. To what extent this changed after 1832 is an interesting question. Some developments suggest there was a degree of disengagement on Westminster's part. The growth of a more comprehensive party system, for example, may have diminished the importance of the independent country gentleman as barometers of opinion. It is also possible that the advance of free trade reduced the opportunities for lobbying by economic interest groups. More positively, the leaderships of the two parties certainly appear to have given up trying to control the press and Parliament effectively gagged petitioners. For the moment, however, this is largely a matter of speculation.

In the case of what we might call genuinely extra-parliamentary pressure, three broad conclusions might be drawn. The first is that such pressure undoubtedly had the effect of pushing the issues concerned high up the parliamentary agenda. Indeed, the executive became so concerned about the amount of parliamentary time devoted to matters over which it had no control, many of which were the result of external pressure, that it took steps in the 1830s to regain the initiative. Second, Parliament appears to have been much more responsive to spontaneous pressure arising from immediate, usually economic, grievances than to long-running campaigns for political, religious and social reforms. And finally, that in the case of such long-running campaigns, there was only one short period when their pressure undoubtedly yielded positive results and that was 1828–34. It was then that there was a coincidence of pressure from the various sources we have considered – elections, pressure groups of various types, and the press.

General conclusions

The first principal conclusion to be drawn from the last four chapters is that although the changes in each aspect of government were substantial, they took place for different reasons, at different times, and with varying results. Two examples will suffice to make the point. The influence of the Crown on government probably increased between 1760 and 1810 and although it declined intermittently between then and the 1830s, it was only in 1841 that this became significant. As for public opinion, this increased significantly in structure, shape, and strength throughout the period but genuinely popular pressure was only influential for the short period of 1828–34. The changes were therefore like the elements of a kaleidoscope, floating almost independently of each other.

The second conclusion is that there was considerable continuity between this period and its predecessor. Thus, in the case of the framework of the executive, the influence of the Crown did not decline significantly until after 1841 and although the role of prime ministers and cabinets became institutionalised, their functions, at least until the 1840s, were not significantly different from their predecessors. Prime ministers were more senior managers than leaders and cabinet government often consisted of 'government by departments'. Similarly, although the civil service became more professional and less self-serving, its senior members continued to make little impact on policy making.

There was also considerable continuity in the scope and purpose of government. The core of business remained much as before with foreign policy, public finance, trade, and law and order prominent. Imperial policy and Ireland were intermittent additions when circumstances required, as were policing and welfare. It should be noted, however, that the ways the administration of the last two items was arranged does not suggest that it was intended they would become constant items on the cabinet agenda. Admittedly, change was more substantial in the assumptions and priorities that influenced the thinking of ministers on politics in general and on specific areas of policy. In the case of politics, most continued to believe in the virtues of a mixed constitution, in the possession of property as a qualification for political rights, and in maintaining the Established Church. To these were added the recognition that public opinion was a legitimate political force and that holding public office was a matter of public trust and accountability. As for policy, change was more marked, although this not take effect until the aftermath of the Napoleonic wars. The ideal of a 'free hand' therefore gained precedence over that of European alliances and the faith in autarchy, mercantilism, and deficit financing gave way to ideas of free trade, the gold standard and the income tax. We should not conclude, however, that these changes were driven solely by ideology. As in the previous period, policies were shaped largely in the light of practical considerations until the 1820s and it was only then that ideology became more influential amongst senior politicians. Even so, its real influence was limited to financial, commercial and welfare policies and not to the full range of government business.

The contribution of Parliament to government continued on lines that had been well established in the pre-1760 period. The critical development was the reconfigurations of parties that took place intermittently between 1760 and 1850 and which eventually absorbed virtually all MPs. However, these resulted in both the government and opposition sides of both Houses consisting of loose coalitions, most members of which based their arguments on historic precedents, facts and figures, and personal observations. Taken together, these features encouraged in ministers a tactical, practical, and accommodatory approach to government that was similar to that practised in similar circumstances earlier. Moreover, private members continued to be responsible for a significant proportion of public-bill legislation and nearly all the much larger number of private bills. The only significant change was that it was private members who were to the fore in promoting a growth in the number and significance of select committees, in the public's knowledge of state and parliamentary business, and in the volume of petitioning. A form of parliamentary government had existed before 1760 but its dimensions increased significantly in this period.

The most dramatic change, however, took place in the infrastructure, scale, and strength of public opinion. However, its effects on the practice of government should not be exaggerated. Before 1760, elections, addresses, instructions, lobbying with or without the support of private members, the print media, and crowd action had all played an intermittent role in influencing the decisions of Parliament and the policies of ministers. What happened afterwards was that much of this kind of 'pressure', although transformed in type and scale, became fully integrated into the governing process with ministers and private members making full use of it for their own purposes. The only exceptions were physical-force disturbances arising from economic grievances and the political pressure groups. In these cases, the actions of ministers and Parliament demonstrated a preference for continuity. They were therefore more responsive to the traditional 'scarcity' demonstration than to the political pressure group – the only exception being during the crisis of 1828–34.

Notes

1 The framework of the executive

1 I have drawn freely in this introduction on Jeremy Gregory and John Stevenson, *Britain in the Eighteenth Century 1688–1820* (2000). I am grateful to them and I hope they will not mind.

2 R. Hatton, *George I* (1978), pp. 144–5.

3 In November 1783, George III let it be known in the House of Lords that he opposed the Fox-North government's India Bill and this led to the government's collapse. In January 1801, he made known his opposition to any measure of Catholic relief and this led to the resignation of Pitt's government. In March 1807, he made his opposition known to the government's bill granting a measure of Catholic relief and stipulated that no government should in future propose any measure on that subject. The government refused to accept such terms and resigned. The stipulation remained in force until George IV gave his permission to the Wellington government to consider a measure of Catholic relief in July–August, 1828.

4 Richard Pares, *Limited Monarchy in Great Britain in the Eighteenth Century* (Historical Association Pamphlet, G35, 6th edn, 1967), p. 8.

5 In conversation with Lord Halifax, 18 Aug. [1689], quoted by E. N. Williams, *The Eighteenth Century Constitution* (1977 edn), p. 63. This section on William's kingship is based largely on S. B. Baxter, *William III* (1966), esp. chap. 20.

6 Her own words in her first speech to Parliament, D. W. Hayton, *The History of Parliament. The Commons 1690–1715* (5 vols. 2002), i, p. 454.

7 Based largely on E. Gregg, *Queen Anne* (1980), esp. chap. 5.

8 Hatton, *George I, passim* but partic. pp. 123, 145, 246, 297–8.

9 Quoted by Stanley Ayling, *George the Third* (1972), p. 19.

10 John Brooke, *King George III* (1974 edn), pp. 37–8.

11 Hatton, *George I*, p. 140.

12 R. O. Bucholz, *The Augustan Court* (Stanford, 1993), *passim*, quotation, p. 247.

13 Ibid., pp. 189, 191 (for the quotation).

14 Quoted by J. C. D. Clark, *The Memoirs and Speeches of James, 2nd Earl Waldegrave, 1742–63* (Cambridge, 1988), p. 10. According to the most recent research, George I and II re-invigorated Court ceremonials and thereby ensured that the Court remained an important 'venue for the brokering and staging of politics', Hannah Smith, 'The Court in England, 1714–1760: A Declining Political Institution? *History*, vol. 90 (Jan. 2005), pp. 23–41 (quotation, p. 40).

15 Bucholz, *Augustan Court*, p. 189; J. M. Beattie, *The English Court in the Reign of George I* (Cambridge, 1967), pp. 249–56.

16 E. Cruikshanks, 'The political management of Sir Robert Walpole' in Jeremy Black (ed.), *Britain in the Age of Walpole* (1984), pp. 26–8.
17 Baxter, *William III*, pp. 269–72.
18 Gregg, *Queen Anne*, pp. 134–5, 139.
19 Geoffrey Holmes, *British Politics in the Age of Anne* (1967), pp. 185–210.
20 Hatton, *George I*, pp. 119–20, 126–8.
21 Beattie, *The English Court*, p. 238.
22 Paul Langford, *Modern British Foreign Policy. The Eighteenth Century, 1688–1815* (1976), pp. 8–10; Jeremy Black, *Parliament and Foreign Policy in the Eighteenth Century* (Cambridge, 2004), pp. 2–5. In Chapter 2, Black reviews the historiography of the shaping of foreign policy, 1689–1714, and concludes that a balance emerged between the influence of the monarch, the executive and that of Parliament.
23 Hayton, *The Commons*, i, p. 382.
24 Gregg, *Queen Anne*, pp. 137, 141, 144–50, 405.
25 Hayton, *The Commons*, i, p. 383.
26 Hatton, *George I, passim*, partic. pp. 124, 128–30, 216–7, 294–6; G. M. Townend, 'Religious radicalism and conservatism in the Whig Party under George I: the repeal of the Occasional Conformity and Schism Acts', *PH*, vol. 7 (1988), pp. 24–6; Geoffrey Holmes and Daniel Szechi, *The Age of Oligarchy. Pre-industrial Britain, 1723–1783* (1993), pp. 30–3. As Townend points out, George I's support for Sunderland's measures was not sufficient to ensure their success.
27 Holmes and Szechi, *Age of Oligarchy*, pp. 32–4; J. H. Plumb, *Sir Robert Walpole. The King's Minister* (1960), p. 158; Black, 'Fresh light on the fall of Townshend', *HJ*, vol. 29 (1986), pp. 50–2 and 'Foreign policy in the age of Walpole' in Black, *Age of Walpole*, pp. 152–6.
28 Richard Connors, ' "The Grand Inquest of the Nation". Parliamentary committees and social policy in mid-eighteenth century England', *PH*, vol. 14 (1995), p. 300.
29 G. W. Jones, 'The office of Prime Minister' in H. Van Thal (ed.), *The Prime Ministers*, vol. 1, (1974), p. 13.
30 Quoted by Sir Lewis Namier, *Crossroads of Power* (1962), p. 112.
31 Paul Langford, *The Excise Crisis* (Oxford, 1975), pp. 85, 98, 132.
32 For Walpole's attempt to control patronage, see Plumb, *The King's Minister*, pp. 92–7.
33 M. A. Thomson, *The Secretaries of State 1681–1782* (Oxford, 1932), pp. 15–16; see also, Black, 'Fresh Light', *HJ*, vol. 29 (1986), pp. 58–64 where the limitations on Walpole's ability to determine the composition of the ministry are discussed.
34 P. G. M. Dickson, *The Financial Revolution in England* (1967), p. 244. Paul Foley and Charles Montagu (1st Earl of Halifax) played more important roles, however, see Hayton, *The Commons*, i, pp. 447–51.
35 H. P. Wyndham, *The Diary of the Late George Bubb Dodington, Baron of Melcombe Regis* (1784), pp. 150–1.
36 Plumb, *The King's Minister, passim* but partic. pp. 92, 255–8.
37 Ibid., partic. pp. 76–7, 92, 202; Holmes and Szechi, *Age of Oligarchy*, pp. 22–5; B. W. Hill, *Sir Robert Walpole. 'Sole and prime Minister'* (1989), pp. 3–5; S. Targett, 'Government and ideology during the age of the Whig supremacy: the political argument of Sir Robert Walpole's newspaper propagandists' *HJ*, vol. 37 (1994), p. 290.
38 Plumb, *The King's Minister*, pp. 76–7.
39 Dickson, *Financial Revolution*, p. 203; Holmes and Szechi, *Age of Oligarchy*, pp. 73–81; 'Robert Walpole' by Stephen Taylor in Robert Eccleshall and Graham Walker (eds), *Biographical Dictionary of British Prime Ministers* (1998), pp. 9–10.

40 Holmes and Szechi, *Age of Oligarchy*, pp. 269–71.
41 C. R. Middleton, *The Bells of Victory* (Cambridge, 1985), p. 20.
42 Baxter, *William III*, p. 272; Williams, *Eighteenth-Century Constitution*, pp. 111–12 [doc.58(2)].
43 Based on: J. Plumb, 'The organisation of the cabinet in the reign of Queen Anne', *TRHS*, 5th series, vol. 7 (1957), pp. 137–57; Williams, *Eighteenth-Century Constitution*, pp. 113–16; Gregg, *Queen Anne*, pp. 141–2.
44 Quoted by Romney Sedgwick in 'The inner cabinet from 1739–1741', *EHR*, vol. 34 (1919), p. 290.
45 For the reference to 1757, see Middleton, *Bells of Victory*, p. 21 and more generally, J. W. Croker (ed.), *Memoirs of the Reign of George II….by Lord Hervey*, (2 vols. 1848) ii, pp. 551–72; Sedgwick, 'The inner cabinet', *EHR*, vol. 34 (1919), pp. 290–302; I. R. Christie, 'The cabinet during the Grenville administration 1763–65', *HER*, vol. 73 (1958), pp. 86–92; Michael Jubb, 'The cabinet in the reign of George I', *BIHR*, vol. 55 (1982), pp. 108–10; Plumb, *The King's Minister*, pp. 197–8; Hill, *Walpole*, pp. 3–4.
46 For colonial affairs, see D. M. Clark, *The Rise of the British Treasury. Colonial administration in the 18th century* (Yale, 1960), p. 42 and more generally, Croker, *Hervey's Memoirs*, ii, pp. 551–72 (which record foreign and military affairs being the principal business of seven cabinets in the course of one month in 1740) and Middleton, *Bells of Victory*, p. 21.
47 Croker, *Hervey's Memoirs*, ii, p. 569.
48 Langford, *A Polite and Commercial People. England 1727–1783* (Oxford, 1989), pp. 170–2. After Lord Halifax became President in 1748, he pressed for his inclusion in the cabinet but the most that was conceded was that he could attend when colonial matters were on the agenda, see Thomson, *Secretaries of State*, pp. 50–3.
49 Charles Townshend, Chancellor of the Exchequer, 1766–67, was the first to sit in the cabinet as of right, Peter D. G. Thomas, *Lord North* (1976), pp. 21–3.
50 Julian Hoppit, *A Land of Liberty? England 1689–1727* (Oxford, 2000), pp. 102, 115, 129.
51 John Brewer, *The Sinews of Power* (1989), p. 66.
52 Ibid., pp. 65–7. These figures omit the administrative staff of the army and officials in Scotland. The total number of government employees was therefore higher. However, it seems unlikely they were as high as Geoffrey Holmes' estimate of 12,000 for the 1720s or Joseph Massie's of 16,000 for the 1760s – both referred to by Brewer.
53 Holmes and Szechi, *Age of Oligarchy*, p. 27.
54 Henry Roseveare, *The Treasury, 1660–1870. The Foundations of Control* (1973), pp. 79 (for the quotation) –82.
55 Brewer, *Sinews of Power*, p. 74.
56 Hoppit, *Land of Liberty?* p. 125 (for the quotation); Dickson, *Financial Revolution*, p. 14; Brewer, *Sinews of Power*, pp. 69–74.
57 Roseveare, *Treasury Control*, pp. 81–2.
58 Brewer, *Sinews of Power*, p. 81.
59 Roseveare, *Treasury Control*, pp. 83–4.
60 De Witt Bailey, 'The board of ordnance and small arms supply: the ordnance system, 1714–83', University of London Ph.D., 1988, pp. 247–50.
61 R. W. Harding, 'Sir Robert Walpole's ministry and the conduct of the war with Spain', *HR*, vol. 60 (1987), pp. 299–320.
62 For example, N. A. M. Rodger, *The Wooden World: An Anatomy of the Georgian Navy* (1986), pp. 29–36, 152; and Middleton, 'Pitt, Anson and the admiralty, 1756–1761', *History*, vol. 55 (1970), pp. 189–98.
63 Dickson, *Financial Revolution*, p. 393.
64 Plumb, *The King's Minister*, pp. 233–4.

65 Clark, *Rise of the Treasury*, pp. 7–11, 37–8, 74–5, 107.
66 A point emphasised by Brewer, *Sinews of Power*, p. 69.
67 Ibid., p. 44; Thomson, *Secretaries of State*, pp. 65–6.
68 Brewer, *Sinews of Power*, p. 61.
69 Hoppit, *Land of Liberty?* pp. 190–4.
70 Thomson, *Secretaries of State*, p. 19.
71 Ibid., pp. 131–4; Plumb, *The King's Minister*, p. 234; Langford, *Excise Crisis*, p. 36.
72 Brewer, *Sinews of Power*, p. 82; Clark, *Rise of the Treasury*, p. 86.
73 Hoppit, *Land of Liberty?* p. 43.
74 Ibid., p. 44.

2 The scope, purpose and achievements of the executive

1 For a recent assessment of Parliament's impact on foreign policy, see Black, *Parliament and Foreign Policy*.
2 Hayton, *The Commons*, i, pp. 393–4.
3 Julian Hoppit (ed.), *Failed Legislation 1660–1800* (1997). My figures are drawn from the *Chronological Table and Index of All the Statutes* (2 vols. 1896), vol. 1. This lists all acts designated originally as 'Public' or 'Public and General' (as opposed to those designated as 'local', 'personal' or 'private') and identifies those that in fact dealt with local, personal or private matters. Sheila Lambert in her *House of Commons Sessional Papers of the Eighteenth Century* (2 vols. Wilmington, Delaware, 1975–6) gives figures that conform to the total number of acts per session as listed in the *Chronological Table* as 'Public Acts'. The method, while not foolproof, does, I believe, give a reasonably accurate guide to the number of genuinely public acts passed each session.
4 I have relied principally on the names of those entrusted with the preparation of a bill to establish those who were responsible for it.
5 This section is based on: Hayton, *The Commons*, i, p. 394; Hoppit, *Failed Legislation*, pp. 6–16, partic. 8–10; Lambert, *Sessional Papers, passim*; and the *Lords and Commons Journals*, 1724–5 and 1753. In the case of the last, the petitioners for, and the introducers of, all 'general' bills were identified and the *History of Parliament* volumes used to discover whether they were connected to government by office or by pension. It was on this basis that the number that was sponsored wholly or partly by ministers was established.
6 H. T. Dickinson, *Liberty and Property. Political Ideology in Eighteenth-Century Britain* (1979 edn), pp. 142–5.
7 *Dodington Diary*, pp. 53–4 where Dodington rebuffs the charge that he was attempting, in 1750, 'to govern' the Prince of Wales.
8 Dickinson, *Liberty and Property*, pp. 126–7.
9 Paul Langford, *Public Life and the Propertied Englishman* (Oxford, 1991), chap. 2 and p. 71 for the quotation.
10 For a recent survey, see J. Broad, 'Parish economies of welfare, 1650–1834', *HJ*, vol. 42 (1999), pp. 985–1006.
11 J. V. Beckett, 'Land tax or excise: the levying of taxation in seventeenth- and eighteenth-century England', *EHR*, vol. 100 (1985), pp. 285–308, partic. p. 301.
12 For the size of the national debt, see Hoppit, *Land of Liberty?*, p. 124; and for a succinct survey of its history, Dickson, *Financial Revolution*, pp. 243–5.
13 Hoppit, *Land of Liberty?* p. 124; Ralph Davis, 'The rise of protection in England, 1689–1786', *EconHR* vol. 19 (1966), pp. 306–7.
14 W. Prest, 'Law reform in Eighteenth-Century England' in P. Birks (ed.), *The Life of the Law* (1993), pp. 113–23.

15 W. C. Costin and J. Steven Watson, *The Law and Working of the Constitution: Documents 1660–1914* (2 vols. 1952), i, p. 299.

16 I am much indebted to Joanna Innes for this example and for other points relating to policy-making in this period.

17 Peter D. G. Thomas, *The House of Commons in the Eighteenth Century* (Oxford, 1971), p. 237.

18 Reed Browning, *Political and Constitutional Ideas of the Court Whigs* (1983), pp. 216, 233, 256; Targett, 'Government and ideology', *HJ*, vol. 37 (1994), pp. 289–317.

19 Langford, *A Polite and Commercial People*, pp. 3–6.

20 M. Sheehan, 'Balance of power intervention: Britain's decisions for or against war, 1733–56', *Diplomacy and Statecraft*, vol. 7 (1996), pp. 271–89.

21 Harding, 'Walpole's ministry', *HR*, vol. 60, pp. 299–320.

22 Dickson, *Financial Revolution, passim* but partic. pp. 243–4; Hayton, *The Commons*, i, pp. 393, 447, 450.

23 Beckett, 'Land tax or excise', *EHR*, vol. 100 (1985), pp. 285–6.

24 Davis, 'The rise of protection in England', *EconHR*, vol. 19 (1966), pp. 306–17 (p. 313 for the quotation); see also, Tim Keirn, 'Parliament, legislation and the regulation of the English textile industries, 1689–1714' in Lee Davison *et al.* (eds.), *Stilling the Grumbling Hive* (Stroud, 1992), pp. 10–11; Langford, *A Polite and Commercial People*, pp. 174–5.

25 On the political as well as the religious dimensions of moral reform see T. Claydon, *William III and the Godly Revolution* (Cambridge, 1996).

26 Townend, 'Religious radicalism and conservatism in the Whig Party under George I', *PH*, vol. 17 (1988), pp. 25–6.

27 Hoppit, *Land of Liberty?* p. 476.

28 See note 16 above. I am also grateful to Joanna Innes for the information about the history of capital convictions and transportation.

29 Hill, *Walpole*, p. 14; Jeremy Black, 'Parliamentary reporting in England in the early eighteenth century. An abortive attempt to influence the magazines in 1744', *Parliaments, Estates and Representation*, vol. 7 (1987), pp. 61–9.

30 Holmes and Szechi, *Age of Oligarchy*, pp. 215–16; Joanna Innes, 'Legislating For three kingdoms; how the Westminster parliament legislated for England, Scotland and Ireland, 1707–1830', in Julian Hoppit (ed.) *Parliaments, Nations and Identities in Britain and Ireland, 1660–1850* (Manchester, 2003), p. 26; Bob Harris, *Politics and the Nation* (Oxford, 2002), pp. 165–86, on which the section on the 'Taming of the Highlands' is based.

31 Hayton, *The Commons*, i, pp. 530–4.

32 D. W. Hayton, 'Walpole and Ireland' in Black, *Age of Walpole*, p. 118; *Ruling Ireland, 1685–1742. Politics, Politicians and Parties* (Woodbridge, 2004), pp. 258–9, 266.

33 Based on Clark, *The Rise of the Treasury*, chaps 1–2. See also, Langford, *A Polite and Commercial People*, pp. 170–1.

34 Hayton, *The Commons*, iv, p. 277.

35 Dickson, *Financial Revolution*, pp. 200–4.

36 Langford, *Excise Crisis*, chap. 3.

37 Dickson, *Financial Revolution*, p. 243.

38 Holmes and Szechi, *Age of Oligarchy*, pp. 256–7.

39 Thomson, *Secretaries of State*, pp. 50–3; Connors, 'The Grand Inquest of the Nation', *PH*, vol. 14 (1995), p. 300; J. Gwyn, 'British government spending and the North American Colonies, 1740–55', *JICH*, vol. 8 (1979–80), pp. 77–8 where he notes the increase in government spending in N. America before the outbreak of the Seven Years War.

40 Harris, *Politics and the Nation*, pp. 64–6, 247–9, 275–6.

41 Dickson, *Financial Revolution*, p. 11.
42 Peter Marshall, 'The eighteenth-century empire', in Black (ed.), *British Politics and Society from Walpole to Pitt, 1742–1789* (1990), p. 196; on the lack of debate on methods of government, this is the conclusion I draw from Dickinson, *Liberty and Property*, Part 2; Brewer, *Party, Ideology and Popular Politics at the Accession of George III* (Cambridge, 1981 edn), *passim*; Thomas, *House of Commons*, pp. 76–8.

3 Parliament and government

1 H. M. Colvin (ed.) *The History of the King's Works* (6 vols. 1963–82), v, p. 391.
2 Hayton, *The Commons*, i, pp. 343–5.
3 Ibid., p. 379.
4 Ibid., 379–81; Thomas, *House of Commons*, pp. 89, 92; Pomney Sedgwick, *The House of Commons 1715–54* (2 vols. 1970), i, pp. 3–4.
5 Although there were similar committees in the Lords, it appears that they consisted of all those who were present when they were formed. They were therefore more *ad hoc*. See Anita J. Rees, 'The practice and procedure of the House of Lords, 1714–1784', University of Wales Ph.D., 1978, pp. 461–81.
6 Hayton, *The Commons*, i, pp. 354–8; Thomas, *House of Commons*, p. 267; Sedgwick, *The Commons*, i, p. 8.
7 Hayton, *The Commons*, i, pp. 262–3; Sir Lewis Namier and John Brooke, *The Commons 1754–90* (3 vols. 1985 edn), i, pp. 99–113.
8 Hayton, *The Commons*, i, p. 263; Sedgwick, *The Commons*, i, p. 155; Namier and Brooke, *The Commons*, i, p. 98.
9 The figures for religion, age, occupations and interests are based on Hayton, *The Commons*, i, 282–4, 291, 294–5, 307, 314; Sedgwick, *The Commons*, i, 155; Namier and Brooke, *The Commons*, i, pp. 97, 126–45.
10 Rees, 'The House of Lords', p. 240.
11 Ibid., pp. 268, 394; Langford, *Public Life*, p. 378.
12 Hayton, *The Commons*, i, pp. 416–21.
13 Ibid., p. 236; Sedgwick, *The Commons*, i, pp. 19, 37, 42, 47, 57; Namier and Brooke, *The Commons*, i, pp. 62–3, 184–5.
14 Namier and Brooke, *The Commons*, i, p. 186.
15 Hayton, *The Commons*, i, p. 494.
16 Ibid., p. 436.
17 Holmes and Szechi, *Age of Oligarchy*, pp. 22–8.
18 Clyve Jones, 'William, First Earl Cowper, Country Whiggery, and the leadership of the Opposition in the House of Lords, 1720–23', in R. W. Davis (ed.), *Lords of Parliament* (Stanford, CA, 1995), pp. 29–43.
19 Linda Colley, *In Defiance of Oligarchy: The Tory Party, 1714–1760* (Cambridge, 1982).
20 See above, p. 15.
21 It is interesting that Bubb Dodington made two unsuccessful attempts to get the members of the Prince of Wales's Opposition and those of its successor after the Prince's death in 1751 to sign up to a set of principles that had been set out on paper, *Diary*, pp. 107–8.
22 Williams, *Eighteenth Century Constitution*, p. 3.
23 I am indebted to David Hayton for pointing out that some Tories were critical of unfettered monarchical power.
24 Hayton, *The Commons*, i, pp. 462–3 (from which the quotations are taken).
25 Sedgwick, *The Commons*, i, pp. 26–8, 81.
26 Ibid., pp. 45, 89 (for the vote on the Spanish Convention).

27 Thomas, *House of Commons*, pp. 30–1, 73–4, 76–83, 87–8; Henry Roseveare, *The Treasury. The Evolution of a British Institution* (1969), pp. 74–6, 80, 88–91; Hayton, *The Commons*, i, pp. 403–4.

28 Contemporaries distinguished between two categories of bills – the 'public' and the 'private' – each of which was subject to a different process of scrutiny, with private bills also paying fees for the privilege. More than half the bills in the private category dealt with the interests of a particular locality or a specific body of individuals and were either actually designated public or treated as such.

29 Although it is not without flaws, I have based my calculations on the *Chronological Table and Index of All the Statutes*, vol. i, which distinguishes between public, local and personal acts. In the case of the figure of 75% for ministerial legislation, this is an average, the proportion being lower at the beginning of the period and higher at the end.

30 Hoppit, 'Patterns of parliamentary legislation, 1660–1800', *HJ*, vol. 39 (1996), p. 121.

31 Hoppit, *Failed Legislation*, p. 9. Enclosure bills originating in the Lords were put to select committees in the Commons.

32 Ibid., p. 10. For an analysis of the interests involved, in this case in the Mersey-Irwell Navigation Bill of 1720–21, see Stuart Handley, 'Local legislative initiatives in Lancashire', *PH*, vol. 9 (1990), pp. 27–30.

33 *CJ*, vol. 20 (1724–5), for the references to the London water issue see the index to the *Journals*, under 'London petition for Bill to supply…' and 'Petition of the adventurers', p. 438.

34 Ibid., pp. 386, 412.

35 Keirn, 'English textile industries', in Davison, *Stilling the Grumbling Hive*, pp. 1–24; P. O'Brien, T. Griffiths and P. Hunt, 'Political components of the industrial revolution: Parliament and the English cotton textile industry, 1660–1774', *EconHR*, vol. 45 (1991), pp. 395–423 (quotation, p. 416); Jubb, 'Economic policy and economic development', in Black, *Age of Walpole*, pp. 124–7.

36 *CJ*, vol. 20 (1724–5), see the index to the *Journal* under 'York, West Riding'. The bill became 11GI *c*.24.

37 Ibid., vol. 26 (1753), see the index to the *Journal* under 'Framework knitters company'.

38 H. T. Dickinson, 'Popular politics in the Age of Walpole', in Black (ed.), *Age of Walpole*, pp. 52–7, partic. p. 53.

39 Harris, *Politics and the Nation*, pp. 248 (for the quotations), 256–7.

40 *CJ*, vol. 20, pp. 429, see in the index to the *Journal* under 'Stores, naval'.

41 Ibid., vol. 26 (1753), see in the index to the *Journal* under 'Exeter–petition for a bill to open that port' and 'Wool and Yarn, bill'. The Exeter bill became 26GII, *c*.8; the general importation bill became 26 GII, *c*.11.

42 Ibid., see in the index to the *Journal* under 'Levant trade'. The bill became 26GII *c*.18. See also, Dickinson, *Politics of the People*, p. 65.

43 Langford, *A Polite and Commercial People*, p. 177.

44 Lee Davison, 'Experiments in the social regulation of industry: gin legislation, 1729–51' in Lee Davison (ed.), *Stilling the Grumbling Hive*, pp. 25–48. See also, Peter Clark, 'The "Mother Gin" controversy in the early eighteenth century', *TRHS* 5th series, vol. 38 (1988), pp. 63–84.

45 John Beattie, 'London crime and the making of the "Bloody Code," 1689–1718', in Davison (ed.), *Stilling the Grumbling Hive*, pp. 49–76.

46 Prest, 'Law reform' in Birks (ed.), *The Life of the Law*, pp. 113–23.

47 Tim Hitchcock, 'Paupers and preachers: the SPCK and the parochial workhouse movement', in Davison (ed.), *Stilling the Grumbling Hive*, pp. 145–66, the quotations from pp. 145–7.

48 Langford, *A Polite and Commercial People*, p. 297.
49 Connors, 'The Grand Inquest of the Nation', *PH*, vol. 14 (1995), pp. 285–313.
50 The successful bills were 26GII, cs. 9, 16, 19, 24, 28, 30 and 31. The unsuccessful ones dealt with the militia in England, conveying offenders to jail, the import of French cambrics, a census, select vestries, highways and insolvent debtors.
51 Langford, *A Polite and Commercial People*, p. 5.
52 Hayton, *The Commons*, i, p. 370–1; Brewer, *Sinews of Power*, p. 227.
53 Hayton, *The Commons*, i, pp. 416–7; Black, 'Parliamentary reporting', *Parliaments, Estates and Representation*, vol. 7 (1987), pp. 61–9; P. B. J. Hyland, 'Liberty and libel: Government and the Press during the succession crisis in Britain, 1712–1716, *EHR*, vol. 101 (1986), pp. 863–88; Harris, *Politics and the Nation*, p. 332.
54 Hayton, *The Commons*, i, pp. 371–2.
55 Lambert, *Sessional Papers*, i, pp. 191–7.
56 Hayton, *The Commons*, i, pp. 397–8.
57 Lambert, *Sessional Papers*, i, p. 43. I am indebted to Joanna Innes for advice on this point and for the opportunity to draw on her unpublished paper on select committees *c.*1688–1844 in which she points to three established in 1751 – on crime and the poor, highways and trade – as marking a shift in favour of the type of select committee of enquiry found by the early nineteenth century.
58 Calculated from Lambert, *Sessional Papers*, i, *passim* but partic. p. 193.
59 Brewer, *Sinews of Power*, p. 227.
60 Calculated from Lambert, *Sessional Papers*, i, *passim*, the subject distribution being taken from Hoppit, 'Political arithmetic in eighteenth-century England', *EconHR*, vol. 49 (1996b), p. 522. In the case of the origins of parliamentary papers, most seem to have been presented by ministers on their own behalf or as a result of statutory requirements. In 1753, however, 24 out of a total of 76 papers dealt with the Levant trade and sugar imports, on which there had been a significant volume of petitioning.

4 The executive, Parliament and the public

1 Hayton, *The Commons*, i, pp. 44, 121–2.
2 Ibid., pp. 64, 77, 88 for the proportions before 1714. For those, 1722–47, see Sedgwick, *The Commons*, i, pp. 115–21; and for 1754, Namier and Brooke, *The Commons*, i, pp. 514–19 (my calculations in both cases). There was a similar pattern after 1714, if counties are combined with boroughs designated as having 'medium' (500–999) or 'large' (1000+) numbers of voters: from 49.2%, 1722–41, to 22.9% in 1747 and 32% in 1754. See also on this point, Dickinson, *Politics of the People*, p. 42; Nicholas Rogers, *Whigs and Cities: Popular Politics in the Age of Walpole and Pitt* (Oxford, 1989), pp. 230–1, 254–5.
3 Hayton, *The Commons*, i, pp. 449, 458–60.
4 Sedgwick, *The Commons*, i, p. 20.
5 Ibid., i, pp. 42–3; Langford, *Excise Crisis*, pp. 39–42.
6 Dickinson, *Politics of the People*, pp. 39, 52–3.
7 Hayton, *The Commons*, i, pp. 187–8. For a wide-ranging discussion of 'instructions' see Paul Kelly, ' "Constituents" instructions to Members of Parliament' in Clyve Jones (ed.), *Party and Management in Parliament, 1660–1784* (Leicester University Press, 1984), pp. 169–89.
8 Langford, *Excise Crisis*, pp. 47–61, 77; Kathleen Wilson, *The Sense of the People. Politics, Culture and Imperialism in England, 1715–1785* (Cambridge, 1998 pb. edn), pp. 125–6.
9 Wilson, *Sense of the People*, pp. 150, 165.

10 Ibid., p. 183.

11 Harris, *Politics and the Nation*, p. 113.

12 Harding, 'Walpole's ministry', *HR*, vol. 60 (1987), p. 307; Dickinson, *Politics of the People*, p. 68.

13 J. A. W. Gunn, 'Eighteenth-century Britain: in search of the state and finding the quarter sessions' in J. Brewer and E. Hellmuth (eds), *Rethinking Leviathan. The Eighteenth-Century State in Britain and Germany* (Oxford, 1999), p. 122.

14 On this point see Martin Daunton, *Trusting Leviathan. The Politics of Taxation in Britain, 1799–1914* (Cambridge, 2001), pp. 5–6.

15 Dickinson, *Politics of the People* pp. 61–2. See also, Dickson, *Financial Revolution*, pp. 244–5; Sedgwick, *The Commons*, i, pp. 436–7 (on Newcastle's relations with financiers).

16 Peter Clark, *British Clubs and Societies 1580–1800. The Origins of an Associational World* (Oxford, pb. edn, 2001), chap. 3.

17 Dickinson, *Politics of the People*, p. 97.

18 For a pioneering general survey of lobbying, see Brewer, *Sinews of Power*, pp. 231–49.

19 Ibid., pp. 62–5.

20 Ibid., pp. 66–7.

21 Clark, *The Rise of the Treasury*, pp. 45–8

22 Brewer, *Sinews of Power*, pp. 232–5.

23 Keirn, 'English textile industries', in Davison (ed.), *Stilling the Grumbling Hive*, pp. 1–24; Jubb, 'Economic Policy', in Black (ed.), *Age of Walpole*, pp. 124–7.

24 Brewer, *Sinews of Power*, p. 233.

25 Langford, *Excise Crisis*, p. 77.

26 Harris, *Politics and the Nation*, pp. 256–61; Dickinson, *Politics of the People*, p. 71.

27 Dickinson, *Politics of the People*, pp. 81–5.

28 Davison., 'Introduction', Davison, 'Gin legislation', Robert B. Shoemaker, 'Reforming the city: the reformation of manners campaign in London, 1690–1738', Hitchcock, 'Paupers and preachers' in Davison (ed.), *Stilling the Grumbling Hive*, pp. xvi–xviii, 45–48, 99–120, 145–66; Connors, 'The Grand Inquest of the Nation', *PH*, vol. 14 (1995), pp. 301–7; Clark, *Clubs and Societies*, pp. 64–6, 465–7.

29 B. Keith-Lucas, 'County Meetings', *The Law Quarterly Review*, vol. 70 (1954), pp. 109–14.

30 See above, p. 6.

31 Dickinson, *Politics of the People*, p. 127; Harris, *Politics and the Nation*, p. 62 (for the quotation).

32 M. G. Collinson, 'Law, the State and the control of labour in eighteenth-century England', University of Sheffield Ph.D., 1982, pp. 191–3.

33 Dickinson, *Politics of the People*, pp. 154, 158.

34 Langford, *A Polite and Commercial People*, p. 91. For higher estimates, particularly for women, see Wilson, *Sense of the People*, pp. 30–1 and n. 7. Brewer, *The Pleasures of the Imagination* (1997), p. 167, suggests literacy rates of 60% for men and 40% for women in 1750.

35 Brewer, *Pleasures of the Imagination*, p. 137. For other points in this survey, see pp. 131–2, 144, 163, 172–3.

36 Ibid., p. 146 where the *Busy Body, Bee, Critical Review, Ladies Magazine, London Magazine, and Public Ledger* are cited, to which I add *The Gentleman's Magazine*.

37 Clark, *Clubs and Societies*, p. 69. There appears to have been an increase to 58 newspapers and periodicals published in London, 1714–16, but this declined to

about 38 following a crack down by the government, see Hyland, 'Liberty and Libel', *EHR*, vol. 101 (1986), pp. 863–88.

38 Harris, *Politics and the Nation*, pp. 58, 106–15.

39 Hyland, 'Liberty and libel', *EHR*, vol. 101 (1986), pp. 863–88; Black, 'Parliamentary reporting', *Parliaments, Estates and Representation*, vol. 7 (1987), pp. 61–9.

40 Harris, *Politics and the Nation*, Introduction, partic. pp. 15–17.

41 Prest, 'Law reform', in Birks (ed.), *Life of the Law*, pp. 113–23, partic. pp. 118–9.

42 Wilson, *Sense of the People*, pp. 183 and fn.120, 185.

43 Hayton, *The Commons*, i, p. 459.

5 The framework of the executive

1 In addition to Brooke, *George III* and Ayling, *George The Third*, the sketch that follows is based on the introductions to the correspondence of George III to be found in A. Aspinall (ed.), *The Later Correspondence of George III* (5 vols. Cambridge, 1962–70).

2 Aspinall, 'The Cabinet Council 1783–1835', *Proceedings of the British Academy*, vol. 38 (1952), p. 202.

3 Based principally on Christopher Hibbert, *George IV* (2 vols. 1972–3); E. A. Smith, *George IV* (Yale, 1999); and the introductions to the correspondence of George IV in Aspinall (ed.), *The Correspondence of George IV* (3 vols. Cambridge, 1938) and *The Correspondence of George, Prince of Wales* (8 vols. Cambridge, 1963–71).

4 Based principally on Philip Ziegler, *William IV* (1971); and Henry, Earl Grey (ed.), *The Reform Act of 1832. The Correspondence of the late Earl Grey with His Majesty King William IV* (2 vols. 1867).

5 Ziegler, *William IV*, p. 124.

6 Based on Elizabeth Longford, *Victoria R.I.* (1964); Cecil Woodham-Smith, *Queen Victoria* (vol.1, 1972); Viscount Esher (ed.), *The Girlhood of Queen Victoria. A Selection from Her Majesty's Diaries.... 1832–1840* (2 vols. 1912); Esher and A. C. Benson (eds), *The Letters of Queen Victoria* (lst series 1837–61, 3 vols. 1907).

7 Jupp, *British Politics on the Eve of Reform. The Duke of Wellington's Administration, 1828–30* (1998), pp. 332–4.

8 In the case of engraved portraits, for example, my calculations suggest that 'royals' were second in popularity after actors and singers, *c.*1770–1850, Jupp, 'Pictorial images of the first Duke of Wellington' in Terence Reeves-Smyth and Richard Oram (eds), *Avenues to the Past. Essays presented to Sir Charles Brett* (Belfast, 2003), pp. 108–9.

9 On this theme in general see the pioneering work of Linda Colley, *Britons* (Yale, 1992), chap. 5.

10 Aspinall, *Corrs. of George III*, i, p. xi; Marilyn Morris, *The British Monarchy and the French Revolution* (Yale, 1998), pp. 142–3.

11 *The Times*, 11 Aug. 1830; Longford, *Victoria*, pp. 41–3, 47–8.

12 Brooke, *George III*, pp. 156, 612, n. 7 where he makes it clear that the King wrote 'Britain' and not 'Briton'.

13 Morris, *British Monarchy, passim* but partic. p. 193.

14 Ibid., pp. 84–95; Nancy D. LoPatin, *Political Unions, Popular Politics and the Great Reform Act of 1832* (London, 1999), pp. 63–4.

15 *The Times*, 29 Dec. 1834.

16 According to the *Royal Kalendar* the number in the Royal Household was approximately 940 in 1795 and 760 in 1851. The number in the households of

other members of the royal family was 360 (for 7 households) in 1795 and 103 (for 5) in 1851.

17 Esher and Benson, *Letters of Queen Victoria*, i, pp. 204–17, 254, 344–5, 384, 391.
18 Aspinall, *Cabinet Council*, p. 175 n. 3.
19 The Younger Pitt achieved reductions, 1783–93, see John Ehrman, *The Younger Pitt* (3 vols. 1969–96), i, pp. 317–26.
20 A. S. Foord's pioneering article 'The waning of the "Influence of the Crown,"' *EHR*, vol. 62 (1947), pp. 483–507 needs to be read in conjunction with J. R. Dinwiddy's 'The "influence of the Crown" in the early nineteenth century: a note on the Opposition case', *PH*, vol. 4 (1985), pp.189–200.
21 Ehrman, *Younger Pitt*, i, pp. 304–7.
22 He was aided in this during the Younger Pitt's time because the prime minister took little interest in the distribution of patronage, unlike Walpole, Newcastle, North and Fox, ibid., i, pp. 233–4.
23 For the King's interventions in the appointment to Armagh see A. P. W. Malcomson, *Archbishop Charles Agar. Churchmanship and Politics in Ireland, 1760–1810* (Dublin, 2002), pp. 441, 470, 591–5. For evidence of George III's continuing command of patronage after 1801 see Aspinall, *Correspondence. of George III*, iv, pp. xxiii–iv.
24 The Duke of Wellington (ed.), *Despatches, Correspondence, and Memoranda of…Arthur Duke of Wellington* (2nd series, 6 vols. 1867–77), iv, p. 300.
25 Philip Lawson, *George Grenville* (Oxford, 1984), p. 155.
26 Ehrman, *Younger Pitt*, i, pp. 635–41.
27 Aspinall, *Corrsespondence of George III*, iii, pp. xiv–xviii; Lord Camden lists the disagreements between the King and his ministers on foreign policy in his memorandum on the collapse of the administration, Camden Mss. U840/1027.
28 Aspinall, *Corrsespondence of George III*, v, pp. xxxvii–viii.
29 Aspinall, *Cabinet Council*, p. 175, n. 3.
30 H. M. Scott, *British Foreign Policy in the Age of the American Revolution* (Oxford, 1990), pp. 15–18.
31 Tony Hayter (ed.), *An Eighteenth-Century Secretary at War. The Papers of William, Viscount Barrington* (1988), p. 13 (for the quotation); Stephen Conway, 'The politics of British military and naval mobilization, 1775–83', *HER*, vol. 112 (1997), pp. 1182–4.
32 Aspinall, *Cabinet Council*, p. 202.
33 T. C. W. Blanning, ' "That horrid electorate" or "Ma Patrie Germanique"? George III, Hanover and the *Fürstenbund* of 1785', *HJ*, vol. 20 (1977), pp. 311–44.
34 Smith, *George IV*, chap. 20.
35 Grey, *Corrsespondence of Earl Grey with William IV*, i, pp. 143–6.
36 Ian D. C. Newbould, 'William IV and the dismissal of the Whigs, 1834', *Canadian Journal of History*, vol. 40 (1976), pp. 311–30.
37 Philip Ziegler, *Melbourne* (1976), pp. 193–9.
38 For the Queen's electoral support for the Whigs in 1837 and 1841 see Norman Gash, *Reaction and Reconstruction in English Politics, 1832–52* (Oxford, 1965), pp. 21–7.
39 Woodham-Smith, *Victoria*, i, pp. 234–6.
40 Lord Melville to Henry Addington, 22 Mar. 1803, printed in Williams, *Eighteenth Century Constitution*, pp. 132–3.
41 In 1841 Lord Melbourne gathered from Lord North's daughter, Lady Lindsay, that her father never allowed himself to be known in the family circle as '*prime minister*', Esher and Benson, *Letters of Queen Victoria*, i, pp. 449–50.
42 For the 1820s, see the references from contemporary correspondence in Charles R. Middleton, 'The formation of Canning's ministry and the evolution of the

British cabinet, February to August 1827', *Canadian Journal of History*, vol. 10 (1975), pp. 17–34.

43 For Bute see J. D. Nicholas, 'Lord Bute's Ministry, 1762–1763', University of Wales Ph.D., 1987, partic. pp. 44–7, 77, 111–15; for George Grenville, Lawson, *George Grenville*, partic. p. 155; for the Elder Pitt, Marie Peters, 'The myth of William Pitt, Earl of Chatham, Great Imperialist Part II: Chatham and Imperial Reorganisation, 1763–78' *JICH*, vol. 22 (1994), pp. 393–431; and her 'William Pitt, lst Earl of Chatham' in Eccleshall and Walker, *British Prime Ministers*, p. 58; for North, Thomas, *Lord North*, pp. 39–40, 67, 107. See also, Scott, *British Foreign Policy*, p. 19 and Conway, 'Politics of Mobilization', *EHR*, vol. 112 (1997), p. 1185.

44 Aspinall, *Cabinet Council*, p. 203.

45 Ehrman, *Younger Pitt*, i, pp. 130–3, 180, 186, 309–11, 457, 510, 628–43.

46 Ibid., ii, p. 532; iii, chap. 1, 451–6, 717; C. J. Fedorak, 'The Addington ministry and the interaction of Foreign Policy and domestic politics, 1800–1804', University of London Ph.D., 1990, makes a strong case for Addington's supervision of key policies; Peter Jupp, *Lord Grenville 1759–1834* (Oxford, 1985), pp. 410–12; Aspinall, *Cabinet Council*, pp. 203–5.

47 Rockingham was unique in presenting George III with a comprehensive 'legislative programme', see Langford, *A Polite and Commercial People*, p. 558.

48 Nicholas, 'Bute's ministry', pp. 95, 236 and chap. 8 *passim*.

49 Lawson, *George Grenville*, pp. 181–2, 187–96, 203, 210.

50 Thomas, *Lord North*, pp. 55–8, 90–7.

51 Ehrman, *Younger Pitt*, i, pp. 89–95.

52 Ibid., pp. 613–5.

53 Jupp, *Grenville*, pp. 410–11.

54 Gash, *Lord Liverpool* (1984), partic. pp. 5–6, 101, 157–8, 196–204, 253–4.

55 Smith, *Lord Grey 1764–1845* (Oxford, 1990), chap. 6, partic. pp. 306–7.

56 L. G. Mitchell, *Lord Melbourne, 1779–1848* (Oxford, 1997), chap. 8, partic. pp. 142, 153, 155–62.

57 Boyd Hilton, 'Peel: a reappraisal', *HJ*, vol. 22 (1979), pp. 585–614; Anna Gambles, 'Rethinking the politics of protection and the corn laws, 1830–52', *EHR*, vol. 113 (1998), pp. 928–52; Daunton, *Trusting Leviathan*, pp. 22–7, 80.

58 Boyd Hilton, 'Robert Peel' in Eccleshall and Walker, *British Prime Ministers*, p. 148.

59 Aspinall, *Cabinet Council*, pp. 145–7; for recent assessments of the Grand Cabinet and the death penalty, see J. M. Beattie, 'The cabinet and the management of death at Tyburn after the Revolution of 1688–1689' in Lois G. Schwoerer (ed.), *Revolutions of 1688–9* (Cambridge, 1992) pp. 218–33; and Simon Devereaux 'Peel, Pardon and Punishment: The Recorder's Report Revisited' in Simon Devereaux and Paul Griffiths, *Penal Practice and Culture 1500–1900*.

60 This assessment is based on: Aspinall, *Cabinet Council*, partic. pp. 174–84; Nicholas, 'Bute's ministry', pp. 37, 44; Lawson, 'Further reflections on the cabinet in the early years of George III's reign', *BIHR*, vol. 57 (1984), pp. 237–40; Lawson, *George Grenville*, p. 186; Scott, *British Foreign Policy*, p. 18 (where he refers to Tuesday cabinet dinners); Thomas, *Lord North*, p. 41; Ehrman, *Younger Pitt*, i, pp. 628–35; ii, pp. 419–20; iii, pp. 451–4; Jupp, *British Politics*, chap. 3 *passim*; Abraham D. Kriegal (ed.), *The Holland House Diaries 1831–1840* (1977), pp. lxv–lxvi.

61 In September 1835, for example, Melbourne asked four cabinet colleagues to consider dissenters' grievances, R. Brent, 'The Whigs and Protestant Dissent in the decade of reform: the case of Church rates, 1833–41', *EHR*, vol. 102 (1987), p. 901.

62 B. L. Lansdowne Mss., 3/X2 and 3; Durham University Grey Mss., 3rd Earl Grey's Diary, 26 Aug. 1846; Aspinall, *Cabinet Council*, pp. 171–5, 181–2, 194–8, 210–11, 213; Jupp, *British Politics*, chap. 3, *passim*; Kriegel, *Holland House Diaries*, pp. xlv–xlviii. Cabinet minutes were rare in North's time although four are to be found in his own papers, B. L. Add. Mss. 61867 fos. 217–28.

63 Aspinall, *Cabinet Council*, p. 246 n. 1.

64 Ibid., pp. 231–5.

65 Ibid., pp. 246–8.

66 Ehrman, *Younger Pitt*, i, pp. 628–31.

67 Jupp, *British Politics*, pp. 95–6.

68 Aspinall, *Cabinet Council*, p. 214.

69 Ehrman, *Younger Pitt*, i, p. 186.

70 Richard Pares, *King George III and the Politicians* (Oxford, 1967, pb. edn), pp. 121–2.

71 Aspinall, *Cabinet Council*, pp. 214–24, partic. p. 217; Kriegel, *Holland House Diaries*, pp. xlix–l.

72 Aspinall, *Cabinet Council*, p. 209.

73 Kriegel, *Holland House Diaries*, pp. xliv–xlv, l–li.

74 The figures for 1755 and 1782–3 are taken from Brewer, *Sinews of Power*, pp. 66–7. His table 3.1 omits army clerical staff who in 1797 amounted to 477 in 12 different offices. I have added an estimate of 200 to his figures for 1755 and 400 to those for 1782–3. The official figure for all government employees in 1797 is 16,267 but these include 2,594 Irish officials but omit the *c*.1000 Port of London customs officials – hence the figure for GB being *c*.14, 673. The official figure for 1829 includes 4,126 Irish officials, including those in customs and excise, see Jupp, *British Politics*, pp. 108–114, n. 3. The estimate for 1849 is based on the annual accounts to Parliament, 1830–47, (with the exception of 1830 for which no estimate was made) of the increases and diminutions of the number of persons employed in all public offices and departments to be found in the Parliamentary Papers. These were then compared with the figures provided in PP. *Estimates…[of]…Salaries and Expenses of Public Departments*, 1850 (256.II) xxxiv. 313. According to my calculations, these reveal a net increase of 6,508. The number is significantly lower than that of 39,147 given in Chris Cook and Brendan Keith, *British Historical Facts 1830–1900* (1975), p. 150.

75 See on this point, Brewer, *Sinews of Power*, p. 69 and Ehrman, *Younger Pitt*, i, pp. 317–26 and iii, pp. 846–54.

76 Peter Jupp, 'Government, Parliament and politics in Ireland, 1801–41' in Hoppit (ed.), *Parliaments, nations and identities*, pp. 148–9.

77 J. C. Sainty, *Treasury Officials, 1660–1870* (1972), p. 14.

78 J. C. Sainty, *Admiralty Officials, 1660–1870* (1975), p. 14.

79 George Raudzens, 'The British Ordnance Department 1815–1855', *Journal of the Society of Army Historical Research*, vol. 57 (1979), pp. 88–107; Hew Strachan, 'The early Victorian army and the nineteenth-century revolution in government', *EHR*, vol. 95 (1980), pp. 782–809.

80 Jupp, *British Politics*, pp. 108–14.

81 Huw V. Bowen, 'The Bank of England during the long eighteenth century, 1694–1820', in R. Roberts and D. Kynaston (ed.), *The Bank of England. Money, Power and Influence 1694–1994* (Oxford, 1995), pp. 1–18.

82 J. C. Sainty, *Official of the Board of Trade, 1660–1870* (1974), pp. 8–10.

83 A. P. Donajgrodski, 'The Home Office, 1822–48', University of Oxford D.Phil., 1974, pp. 1–23.

84 The number of papers lodged annually at the Treasury increased from less than 1,000 in 1767 to 3,683 in 1795, 6,168 in 1804 and 19, 761 in 1815 see, Henry Parris, *Constitutional Bureaucracy. The Development of British Central*

Administration since the Eighteenth Century (1969), p. 47; and Lansdowne Mss., 3/Xl, Treasury Board memorial, 19 Aug. 1805. The official return of *Registered Documents, Papers, and Correspondence*, PP. 1852 (116.) xxviii.571, gives the following figures for selected offices at ten year intervals:

	1830	1840	1850
Treasury	22,288	28,390	25,924
Foreign Office	11,546	21,986	31,630
Home Office	–	–	32,250
Colonial Office	12,737	17,986	18,837
War Office	60,931	61,039	85,845

There was a fivefold increase in the Home Office, 1822–48 (Donajgrodski, 'Home Office', pp. 28–35). There were comparable increases in the preparation of departmental papers requested by Parliament and of bills.

85 Landmarks in this respect were: North's Commission on the Accounts, 1780–87; the Commission on Fees from 1785; Pitt's reforms in the Treasury, Customs, Excise, Mint, Exchequer, Post Office and the Foreign and Home Offices; the Treasury Minutes of 1776, 1783, 1805 and 1821; and James Stephen's overhaul of Colonial Office administration in 1837–9.

86 Parris, *Constitutional Bureaucracy*, pp. 42–5; Sainty, *Treasury Officials*, pp. 11–12,14; J. C. Sainty, *Home Office Officials, 1782–870* (1975), pp. 2–3, 5; Sainty, *Colonial Office Officials* (1976), p. 3; J. M. Collinge, *Foreign Office Officials* (1979), pp. 2–5; Sainty, *Admiralty Officials*, pp. 1–6; D. M. Young, *The Colonial Office in the Early Nineteenth Century* (1961), pp. 54–7.

87 Ehrman, *Younger Pitt*, i, p. 576; Lansdowne Mss., Thomas Spring Rice to Lord Lansdowne, 8 Oct. 1827.

88 Donajgrodski, 'Home Office', pp. 25–6.

89 The leading study of a process which had ramifications well beyond the confines of the Whitehall departments is Philip Harling, *The Waning of 'Old Corruption'. The Politics of Economical Reform in Britain, 1779–1846* (Oxford, 1996). For earlier interpretations of the evolution of the concept of office-holding as a matter of public trust rather than private property see, Roseveare, *Treasury Control*, pp. 61–3 and J. Torrance, 'Social class and bureaucratic innovation: The Commission for Examining the Public Accounts 1780–87', *P&P*, vol. 78 (1978), pp. 56–81.

90 Roseveare, *Treasury Control*, pp. 84–96.

91 Ibid., p. 70; Young, *Colonial Office*, chap. 6 *passim*; Jupp, *British Politics*, pp. 125–6.

92 Ehrman, *Younger Pitt*, i, p. 311. For an interesting example of a department (the Admiralty) defeating an attempt by the Treasury to gain more control of its operations, see C. Wilkinson, 'The Earl of Egmont and the Navy, 1763–66', *The Mariners' Mirror*, vol. 84 (1998), pp. 418–33.

93 Roseveare, *Treasury Control*, pp. 64–8.

94 Ibid., pp. 70–1.

95 Hayter, *Barrington*, partic. pp. 11–13.

96 Nicholas, 'Bute's ministry', pp. 322–4, 334–6.

97 This is the conclusion I have drawn from the first volume of Ehrman's, *Younger Pitt*.

98 Michael Fry, *The Dundas Despotism* (Edinburgh, 1992), pp. 118–23; Douglas M. Peers, 'The Duke of Wellington and British India during the Liverpool Administration', *JICH*, vol. 17 (1988–89), p. 7; Andrew Lambert, 'Preparing

for the long peace: the reconstruction of the Royal Navy 1815–1830', *The Mariners' Mirror*, vol. 82 (1996), pp. 44–5.

99 Denis Gray, *Spencer Perceval 1762–1812. The Evangelical Prime Minister* (Manchester, 1963), chaps 17 and 18 where he identifies Sir George Harrison and J. C. Herries as his principal collaborators.

100 Gash, *Mr Secretary Peel* (1961), chaps 9 and 14; Donadjgrodski, 'Home Office', pp. 64–6, 111, 149,184–6, 522.

101 Jupp, *British Politics*, pp. 117–19.

102 A. Brundage, 'Ministers, magistrates and reformers: the genesis of the Rural Constabulary Act of 1839', *PH*, vol. 5 (1986), pp. 55–64; Jan D. C. Newbould, 'The Whigs, the Church, and education, 1839', *JBS*, vol. 26 (1987), pp. 332–46. For biting criticism of the failure to involve officials in the most important aspects of departmental business, see Sir Henry Taylor, *The Statesman* (1836), chap. 22.

103 P. W. J. Bartrip, 'British Government Inspection, 1832–1875: some observations', *HJ*, vol. 25 (1982), pp. 605–26.

104 Jupp, *British Politics*, pp. 119–22; this a point made in Lucy Brown, *The Board of Trade and the Free-Trade Movement, 1830–42* (Oxford, 1958), see in partic. pp. 51–3, 70–5, 225–30.

105 Jupp, *British Politics*, pp. 125–6.

106 Ibid., pp. 127–8.

6 The scope, purpose and achievements of the executive

1 Durham University Grey Mss., 3rd Earl Grey's Diary, 30 May 1834.

2 The proportions of such British/UK legislation to the total of ministerial legislation (including that in collaboration with private members) were as follows: 1772, 76.7%; 1792, 90%; 1817, 71.9%; 1828–30, 67.3%; 1839, 62%.

3 The argument developed in Fry, *Dundas Despotism*, partic. pp. 129–51, 352–84 on the last of which the quotation can be found.

4 Joanna Innes, 'Legislating for three kingdoms', in Hoppit (ed.), *Parliaments, Nations, and Identities*, pp. 15–47; Jupp, *British politics*, pp. 152–5, 176–8.

5 These developments are reviewed at greater length in my 'Government, parliament, and politics in Ireland' in Hoppit (ed.), *Parliaments, Nations, and Identities*, pp. 146–68.

6 I am indebted to Barbara Henry for demonstrating in her Queen's University MA thesis 'The Monarch's Speeches' (2005) that Ireland was a prominent, and sometimes the most prominent, subject of the Queen's Speeches, 1840–49.

7 C. A. Bayly, *Imperial Meridian. The British Empire and the World, 1780–1830* (1989), p. 3.

8 Marshall, 'The eighteenth-century empire', in Black (ed.), *Walpole to Pitt*, pp. 185, 192–3.

9 See, for example, I. R. Christie, *Crisis of Empire 1754–1783* (1966), pp. 39–45; Alison G. Olson, 'The Board of Trade and London-American Interest Groups in the eighteenth century', *JICH*, vol. 8 (1979–80), pp. 33–50; Huw V. Bowen, ' "The Little Parliament": the General Court of the East India Company, 1750–1784,' *HJ*, vol. 34 (1991), pp. 857–72 traces how government acquired increasing control of the Company, a theme developed further in his *Revenue and Reform: the Indian Problem in British Politics, 1757–1773* (Cambridge, 1991). For a sceptical view of there being a forward policy, see Marshall, 'Eighteenth-century empire', pp. 193–6.

10 C. D. Hall, in *British Strategy in the Napoleonic War, 1803–15* (Manchester, 1992), chap. 4, notes that little emphasis was placed on extending the empire at that time.

11 Langford, *A Polite and Commercial People*, p. 485 (where the quotation can be found)–495.

12 Gash, *Mr Secretary Peel*, p. 512.

13 Peter King, *Crime, Justice and Discretion in England, 1740–1820* (Oxford, 2000).

14 This section and the subsequent one on policing draws on: David Philips, 'A new engine of power and authority: the institutionalization of law enforcement in England, 1780–1830' in V. A. C. Gatrell *et al.* (eds), *Crime and the Law. The Social History of Crime in Western Europe since 1800* (1980), pp. 155–89; David Philips and Robert D. Storch, 'Whigs and Coppers: the Grey Ministry's National Police Scheme, 1832' *BIHR*, vol. 67 (1994), pp. 75–90; and the same authors', *Policing Provincial England 1829–1856* (1999).

15 John Prest, *Liberty and Locality. Parliament, Permissive Legislation, and Ratepayers' Democracies in the Nineteenth Century* (Oxford, 1990), pp. 8–24.

16 Philip Harling, 'The power of persuasion: central authority, local bureaucracy and the New Poor Law', *EHR*, vol. 97 (1992), pp. 30–53.

17 Bartrip, 'British government inspection', *HJ*, vol. 25 (1982), pp. 605–26.

18 The enthusiasm for reform in many spheres is well-charted in Arthur Burns and Joanna Innes (eds) *Rethinking The Age of Reform* (Cambridge, 2003).

19 Gunn, 'In search of the state', in Brewer and Hellmuth, (eds), *Rethinking Leviathan*, pp. 102–19; Joanna Innes, Central government and interference: changing conceptions, practices and concerns 1688–1840' in J. Harris (ed.), *Civil Society in British History* (Oxford, 2003), pp. 39–60.

20 This section draws on Stefan Collini, Donald Winch and John Burrow, *That Noble Science of Politics. A Study in Nineteenth-Century Intellectual History* (Cambridge, 1983), the introduction and chaps 1–3.

21 Boyd Hilton, *The Age of Atonement* (Oxford, 1991 edn), partic. chap. 2. See also, A. M. C. Waterman, *Revolution, Economics and Religion* (Cambridge, 1991).

22 Torrance, 'Social class and bureaucratic innovation', *P&P*, vol. 78 (1978), pp. 56–81; Langford, *Public Life*, pp. 250–63.

23 Harling, '*Old Corruption*' is the best account.

24 For example: Ehrman, *Younger Pitt*, i, pp. 95, 132, 267 and n. 1; Jupp, *Grenville*, pp. 36, 57, 462; Gash, *Liverpool*, p. 118; see also on Pitt and Blackstone, John R. Breihan, 'William Pitt and the Commission on Fees, 1785–1801', *HJ*, vol. 27 (1984), pp. 59–81.

25 Collini, Winch and Burrow, *That Noble Science*, pp. 44–5. For the influence of Professors John Millar and Dugald Stewart at Glasgow on Melbourne's education see his autobiography, pp. 4–32, Herts. R. O. Panshanger Mss. Probably his most devoted admirer amongst MPs was Sir James Mackintosh, see Knud Haakonssen, 'The science of a legislator in James Mackintosh's moral philosophy', *History of Political Thought*, vol. 5 (1984), pp. 245–80.

26 Hilton, *Age of Atonement*, pp. 58–63; Waterman, *Revolution, Economics and Religion*, p. 218.

27 J. R. Dinwiddy, 'Early-nineteenth-century reactions to Benthamism' *TRHS* 5th series vol. 34 (1984), pp. 47–69; S. Conway, 'Bentham and the nineteenth-century revolution in government' in R. Bellamy (ed.) *Victorian Liberalism. Nineteenth-Century Political Thought and Practice* (1990), pp. 71–90.

28 For example, in the case of the former, see Lansdowne Mss., Edward Stanley to Lord Lansdowne, 29 Aug. 1822 where he requests a reading list and says that he wishes 'to fit himself for public life' which he sees as his future 'profession'. In the case of the latter, Lord John Russell's *Essay on the English Constitution* and Brougham's *Political Philosophy* are notable examples.

29 Brougham was of this view as late as 1843, see vol. 1, chaps 1 and 2 and vol. 3, chap. 29 of his *Political Philosophy* (1853 edn).

30 Ehrman, *Younger Pitt*, i, pp. 167–8.

31 I refer to Wellington's famous speech on 2 November 1830 stating that he saw no need for parliamentary reform and in the case of Grey, his letter to Sir Herbert Taylor, 13 Jan. 1831, Grey, *Corrsespondence of Earl Grey and William IV*, i, pp. 51–2.

32 I have drawn here on Scott, *British Foreign Policy* and the same author's review article, 'British foreign policy in the age of the American Revolution', *International History Review*, vol. 6 (1984), pp. 113–25; Ehrman, *Younger Pitt*, i, pp. 516–71, ii, pp. 477–84; and Jeremy Black, *British Foreign Policy in an Age of Revolutions* (Cambridge, 1994). On Hanover, Brendan Simms argues that government gave up responsibility for its security from 1763 to 1806, leaving it entirely to George III and his Hanoverian ministers, ' "An odd question enough": Charles James Fox, the Crown and British policy during the Hanoverian crisis of 1806', *HJ*, vol. 38 (1995), pp. 567–96.

33 Lambert, 'Preparing for the long peace', *The Mariners' Mirror*, vol. 82 (1996), p. 41. It has been argued that trade and commerce played a minor role in shaping foreign policy in the first half of the nineteenth century, see B. Porter, 'British foreign policy in the nineteenth century', *HJ*, vol. 23 (1980), pp. 193–202.

34 Michael Collins, 'Monetary policy and the supply of trade credit, 1830–1844', *Economica* vol. 45 (1978), pp. 379–99.

35 I am especially indebted to the following for this section on public finance: Boyd Hilton, *Corn, Cash, Commerce. The Economic Policies of the Tory Governments 1815–1830* (Oxford, 1977); P. J. Cain and A. G. Hopkins, 'The political economy of British expansion overseas, 1750–1914', *EconHR*, vol. 33 (1980), pp. 463–90; P. K. O'Brien, 'The political economy of British taxation, 1660–1815' *EconHR*, vol. 41 (1998), pp. 1–32; and Daunton, *Trusting Leviathan, passim.*

36 Cain and Hopkins, 'British expansion', (1980), p. 474.

37 The argument of Bayly, *Imperial Meridian*, the quotations from p. 250.

38 John Childs, 'The army and the state in Britain and Germany during the eighteenth century', in Brewer and Hellmuth (eds), *Rethinking Leviathan*, pp. 53–70, partic. pp. 67–8; Conway, 'The politics of mobilization' *EHR*, vol. 112 (1997), pp. 1179–1201; J. E. Cookson, *The British Armed Nation, 1793–1815* (Oxford, 1997), pp. 20–3 where he argues that soldiers had 'an increasing physical presence in British society' by the 1780s and p. 124 for the quotation.

39 Lambert, 'Preparing for the long peace', *The Mariners' Mirror*, vol. 82 (1996), pp. 41–54 and the same author's review of Robert Gardiner, *Frigates of the Napoleonic Wars* (2000), 'reviews-list@ihr.sas.ac.uk, 04/10/00, 20.39'

40 Cobbett's Parliamentary Debates, vol. xxvii, col. 148.

41 Cookson, *Armed Nation*, pp. 246–7.

42 Ibid., pp. 123–5 and chap. 9.

43 See on this point, Chris Evans, 'Tories and Colliers: The fate of the "Act for the security of collieries and mines" of 1800', *PH*, vol. 10 (1991), pp. 63–77.

44 David Eastwood, 'Men, morals and the machinery of social legislation, 1790–1840', *PH*, vol. 13 (1994), pp. 190–205; Michael Lobban, ' "Old wine in new bottles": the concept and practice of law reform, *c.*1780–1830' in Burns and Innes (eds), *Rethinking Reform*, pp. 114–35. On reforms of property law see A. R. Buck, 'Property, aristocracy and the reform of the land law in early nineteenth century England', *Journal of Legal History*, vol. 16 (1995), pp. 63–93. See also, Desmond H. Brown, 'Abortive Attempts to Codify English Criminal Law' *PH*, vol. 11 (1992), pp. 1–39 where he argues that the publication of the statutes between 1811 and 1825 was a stimulus to reform. See also, Phil Handler, 'Forgery and the end of the "Bloody Code" in early nineteenth-century

England', *HJ*, vol. 48 (2005), pp. 683–702, who argues that reformers used scandal surrounding forgery cases to justify reform.

45 Clive Emsley, 'Repression, "terror" and the rule of law in England during the decade of the French Revolution', *EHR*, vol. 100 (1985), pp. 801–25; Philips, 'A new engine of power', in Gattrell (ed.), *Crime and Law*, pp. 157–61.

46 J. E. Cookson, *Lord Liverpool's Administration 1815–1822* (Edinburgh, 1975), pp. 102–16; Hilton, *Corn, Cash, Commerce*, pp. 80–1.

47 Philip Lawson, 'Parliament, the Constitution and Corn: the embargo crisis of 1766', *PH* vol. 5 (1986), pp. 17–37.

48 Ehrman, *Younger Pitt*, iii, pp. 314–6; Hilton, *Corn, Cash, Commerce*, pp. 82–7; Gash, *Peel*, i, p. 224.

49 Davis, 'Rise of protection', *EconHR*, vol. 19 (1966), pp. 313–14.

50 Christie, *Crisis of Empire*, pp. 53–4 (where the quotation can be found); Lawson, *George Grenville*, pp. 135–6 and chap. 6.

51 Ehrman, *Younger Pitt*, i, *passim* but partic. pp. 89, 511–12, 613–15. This is confirmed by Henry's study of the King's speeches in the 1780s, see note 6 above.

52 Jupp, *Grenville*, pp. 345–412, partic. pp. 410–12 which are a summary.

53 Gash, *Liverpool*, pp. 118, 131, 157–8, 220. See also, Cookson, *Liverpool Administration*, pp. 395–401.

54 Lansdowne Mss., Thomas Spring Rice to Lord Lansdowne, 11 Sept. 1827; Jupp, *British Politics*, pp. 99–101.

55 Hilton, *Corn, Cash, Commerce*, p. 79 for the quotation from Edward Copleston in 1819; and pp. 303–14 for a summary of the argument.

56 This was the model proposed in MacDonagh's pioneering article, 'The nineteenth-century revolution in government: a reappraisal', *HJ*, vol. 1 (1958), pp. 52–67 and which led to spirited debate with Henry Parris who argued that Benthamite utilitarianism played a key role.

57 Gambles, 'Rethinking the politics of protection', *EHR*, vol. 113 (1998), pp. 928–52 – a thesis developed in her *Protection and Politics: Conservative Economic Discourse, 1815–1852* (Woodbridge, 1999).

58 Philip Harling 'Robert Southey and the language of social discipline' *Albion*, vol. 30 (1998), pp. 630–55.

59 J. J. Sack, 'The memory of Burke and the memory of Pitt. English conservatism confronts its past, 1806–1829', *HJ*, vol. 30 (1987), pp. 623–40 and more generally on conservative thinking, his *From Jacobite to Conservative. Reaction and Orthodoxy in Britain c.1760–1832* (Cambridge, 1993), chaps 7–9; Richard A. Gaunt, 'The political activities and opinions of the fourth Duke of Newcastle (1785–1851)', University of Nottingham Ph.D., 2000.

60 Hilton, *The Age of Atonement*, pp. 230–1; David Eastwood, ' "Recasting our lot": Peel, the nation, and the politics of interest', in Lawrence Brockliss and David Eastwood (eds), *A Union of Multiple Identities. The British Isles, c.1750–c.1850* (Manchester, 1997), pp. 29–43.

61 The theme of Smith, *Lord Grey*, see pp. 326–7. See also, Mitchell, *Melbourne*, pp. 34–41.

62 Brent, 'The Whigs and protestant dissent', *EHR*, vol. 102 (1987), pp. 887–910; and his *Liberal Anglican Politics. Whiggery, Religion, and Reform 1830–1841* (Oxford, 1987) p. 63 for the quotations. See also Boyd Hilton 'Whiggery, religion and social reform: the case of Lord Morpeth', *HJ*, vol. 37 (1994), pp. 828–59.

63 Peter Mandler, *Aristocratic Government in the Age of Reform: Whigs and Liberals, 1830–1852* (Oxford, 1990); Hilton, 'Whiggery, religion and social reform', *HJ*, vol. 37 (1994), pp. 828–59; Richard Brent, 'New Whigs in old bottles', *PH*, vol. 11 (1992), pp. 151–6; Richard W. Davis, 'Whigs in the age of Fox and Grey', *PH*, vol. 12 (1993), pp. 201–8; Abraham D. Kriegel, 'Liberty and Whiggery in early nineteenth century England', *Journal of Modern History*,

vol. 52 (1980), pp. 253–78; L. G. Mitchell, 'Foxite politics and the Great Reform Bill', *EHR*, vol. 108 (1993), pp. 338–64; Lawrence Goldman, 'The origins of British "social science": political economy, natural science and statistics, 1830–35', *HJ*, vol. 26 (1983), pp. 587–616. Peter Gray, in *Famine, Land and Politics: British Government and Irish Society, 1843–50* (Dublin, 1999) divides the Whigs and Liberals into 'Foxites', 'moderate liberals' and 'moralists' – each having specific ideas on reform and political economy.

64 This led to the Quadruple Alliance with France, Spain and Portugal in 1834, see R. Bullen, 'Party politics and foreign policy: Whigs, Tories and Iberian affairs, 1830–36', *BIHR*, vol. 51 (1978), pp. 37–59.

65 For a recent assessment, see Daunton, *Trusting Leviathan*, partic. pp. 22–7, 80.

66 Peter Dunkley, 'Emigration and the state, 1803–1842: the nineteenth-century revolution in government reconsidered', *HJ*, vol. 23 (1980), pp. 353–80.

67 D. G. Paz, *The Politics of Working–Class Education in Britain, 1830–50* (Manchester, 1980); C. Hamlin, *Public Health and Social Justice in the Age of Chadwick. Britain, 1800–1854* (Cambridge, 1998).

68 Ian Newbould, 'Whiggery and the dilemma of reform: liberals, radicals and the Melbourne administration, 1835–9', *BIHR*, vol. 53 (1980), pp. 229–41. The argument is developed more generally in the same author's *Whiggery and Reform, 1830–41: The Politics of Government* (1990).

69 Peter Dunkley, 'Whigs and paupers: the Reform of the English Poor Law, 1830–1834', *JBS*, vol. 20 (1981), pp. 124–49.

70 J. L. Alexander, 'Lord John Russell and the origins of the Committee of Council of Education', *HJ*, vol. 20 (1977), pp. 395–415; Ian D. C. Newbould, 'The Whigs, the Church, and education, 1839', *JBS*, vol. 26 (1987), pp. 332–46.

71 Dunkley, 'Whigs and paupers', *JBS*, vol. 20 (1981), pp. 36–40; Hilton, 'Whiggery, religion, and social reform', *HJ*, vol. 37 (1994), p. 838 (for Althorp and Graham).

72 For exchanges on this theme see A. Brundage, D. Eastwood and P. Mandler, 'Debate: the making of the New Poor Law', *P&P*, vol. 127 (1990), pp. 183–201.

73 Dunkley, 'Emigration and the state', *HJ*, vol. 23 (1980), pp. 378–9.

74 Hilton, 'Whiggery, religion, and social reform', *HJ*, vol. 37 (1994), pp. 837–8 and I class Lansdowne as an 'economic liberal'.

75 Brent, 'The Whigs and protestant dissent', *EHR*, vol. 102 (1987), p. 888.

76 Paul Richards, 'The state and early industrial capitalism: the case of the handloom weavers', *P&P*, vol. 83 (1979), pp. 93–115.

77 Bentham, writing in the 1770s, stated: 'I write from system: and it is the fashion to hate systems', quoted in Simon Devereaux, 'The making of the Penitentiary Act, 1775–1779', *HJ*, vol. 42 (1999), p. 423.

78 S. D. Smith's review of William J. Ashworth, *Customs and Excise: Trade, Production, and Consumption in England, 1640–1845* (Oxford, 2003) and referring to Joseph E. Inikori, *Africans and the Industrial Revolution in England: A Study in International Trade and Development* (Cambridge, 2003) at www.history.a.uk/reviews/paper/smithSD.html.21/03/04, pp. 1–12.

7 Parliament and government

1 E. A. Smith, *The House of Lords in British Politics and Society 1815–1911* (1992), p. 10.

2 R. G. Thorne, *The House of Commons 1790–1820* (5 vols, 1986), i, p. 333. Thorne says that the extra row made four in all and this is confirmed by the Pugin and Rowlandson print of the House published at Ackermann's on 1 June 1808.

3 Smith, *House of Lords*, p. 14.

4 Namier and Brooke, *The Commons*, i, p. 99; Thorne, *The Commons*, i, pp. 282–6; Smith, *House of Lords*, pp. 63–4. The figures for 1851 have been calculated from *The Royal Kalendar* of that year.

5 [John Wade], *The Extraordinary Black Book* (1831), p. 198.

6 Michael M. McCahill, 'Peerage creations and the changing character of the British nobility, 1750–1830', *EHR*, vol. 96 (1981), pp. 259–84.

7 Ibid.; Thorne, *The Commons*, i, pp. 284–5.

8 Smith, *House of Lords*, pp. 50–4.

9 Ibid., p. 51.

10 Jupp, *British Politics*, p. 357.

11 Namier and Brooke, *The Commons*, pp. 99–105; Thorne, *The Commons*, pp. 282–94; I. R. Christie, *British 'Non-Elite' MPs 1715–1820* (Oxford, 1995), pp. 61–2, 67–8, 206.

12 Jupp, *British Politics*, p. 358.

13 Namier and Brooke, *The Commons* i, p. 146; Thorne, *The Commons*, i, p. 318.

14 W. O. Aydelotte, 'The House of Commons in the 1840s', *BIHR*, vol. 27 (1954), pp. 249–62, p. 255 for the quotation.

15 According to the entries on MPs in the *Royal Kalendar* for 1851, there were eight builders, founders, engineers and manufacturers.

16 The literature on the history of parties after 1760 is substantial and the analysis that follows is my interpretation of it. The following books have been particularly useful: Brewer, *Party, Ideology and Popular Politics*; Frank O'Gorman, *The Emergence of the British Two-Party System, 1760–1832* (1982); and B. W. Hill, *British Parliamentary Parties, 1742–1832* (1985).

17 Namier and Brooke, *The Commons*, i, p. 186.

18 Thomas, *House of Commons*, p. 210.

19 Rees, 'House of Lords', p. 302.

20 There is a substantial literature on these developments but I found the following particularly useful: I. R. Christie, 'Party politics in the age of Lord North's administration', *PH*, vol. 6 (1987), pp. 47–68; Patrick Woodland, 'Political atomization and regional interests in the 1761 Parliament: the impact of the cider debates, 1763–1766', *PH*, vol. 8 (1989), pp. 63–89.

21 Thorne, *The Commons*, i, p. 110.

22 B. L. Add. Mss. 35712 f.134, Charles Abbot to Lord Hardwicke, 21 Nov. 1802; Jupp, *British Politics*, p. 255.

23 Jupp, *British Politics*, p. 256.

24 Namier and Brooke, *The Commons*, i, p. 194

25 Jupp, *British Politics*, p. 257.

26 Donald E. Ginter (ed.), *Whig Organization in the General Election of 1790* (Berkeley, 1967), p. xxi, n. 7. The Whig Club foundered after 1800, however.

27 I. Asquith, 'The Whig Party and the Press in the early nineteenth century', *HR*, vol. 49 (1976), pp. 264–83, p. 277 for the quotation.

28 Thomas, *House of Commons*, p. 132.

29 For example: O'Gorman's *The Whig Party and the French Revolution* (1967) and *The Rise of Party in England. The Rockingham Whigs 1760–82* (1975); Michael Roberts, *The Whig Party 1807–12* (1939); Austin Mitchell, *The Whigs in Opposition, 1815–30*, (Oxford, 1967).

30 Namier and Brooke, *The Commons*, i, pp. 199–200.

31 I. R. Christie, 'The anatomy of the Opposition in the Parliament of 1784', *PH*, vol. 9 (1990), pp. 50–77.

32 Gash, *Reaction and Reconstruction*, chaps v and vi. See also his 'The organization of the Conservative Party, 1832–1846' Pts. I and II, *PH*, vol. 1 (1982), pp. 137–159 and vol. 2 (1983), pp. 131–152.

33 Ian Newbould, 'The emergence of a two-party system in England from 1830 to 1841: roll call and reconsideration', *Parliaments, Estates and Representation*,

vol. 5 (1985), pp. 25–31; 'Whiggery and the dilemma of reform', *BIHR*, vol. 53 (1980), pp. 229–41.

34 Jupp, *British Politics*, pp. 254–7.

35 This is the conclusion of Philip Salmon, *Electoral Reform at Work. Local Politics and National Parties, 1832–1841* (Woodbridge, 2002), see, for example, pp. 46, 51.

36 T. A. Jenkins, *The Liberal Ascendancy, 1830–1886* (1994), p. 40; Ian Newbould, 'Whiggery and the growth of party 1830–1841: organization and the challenge of reform', *PH*, vol. 4 (1985b), pp. 137–156; Peter Brett, 'Constituency organization, and the power of the electoral register: national perspectives and the Bristol battleground 1832–41', *Southern History*, vol. 18 (1996), pp. 88–116. For a convincing rebuttal of Newbould's judgement of the effectiveness of the Whig approach to electoral organisation, see Salmon, *Electoral Reform*, pp. 54–7.

37 Bruce Coleman, *Conservatism and the Conservative Party in Nineteenth-Century Britain* (1988), pp. 73, 118 for specific references but it is the theme of the book as a whole.

38 Salmon, *Electoral Reform*, p. 46; Gaunt, 'The 4th Duke of Newcastle', *passim*; Gambles, 'Rethinking the Politics of Protection', *EHR*, vol. 113 (1998), pp. 928–52.

39 Jenkins, *The Liberal Ascendancy*, chap. 1, partic. pp. 36–7 from which the quotations are taken.

40 See on this point, Clark, *Waldegrave*, pp. 120–1.

41 Of the many studies of Whig principles, the following were particularly helpful in constructing this and the subsequent paragraphs on the subject: Brewer, *Party, Ideology and Popular Politics* chaps 4 and 5; Smith, *Whig Principles and Party Politics. Earl Fitzwilliam and the Whig Party, 1748–1833* (Manchester, 1975); Mitchell, 'Foxite politics and the Great Reform Bill', *EHR*, vol. 108 (1993), pp. 338–64.

42 Jupp, *Grenville*, pp. 424–5.

43 Lawson, *George Grenville*, chaps 7 and 8; and his 'Parliament, the Constitution and Corn', *PH*, vol. 5 (1986), pp. 17–37.

44 Jupp, *British Politics*, pp. 268–9.

45 Frank O'Gorman, *The Whig Party and the French Revolution* (1967), chap. 5 and pp. 238–9.

46 Jupp, *British Politics*, pp. 281–4.

47 Brian D. Crowe, 'The parliamentary experience of the Irish members of the House of Commons 1833–41', Queen's University of Belfast. Ph.D. (1995), chap.1.

48 Angus Hawkins, 'Lord Derby' in Davis (ed.), *Lords of Parliament*, pp. 134–62, partic. pp. 147–8.

49 For the press reporting of the Lords see William C. Lowe, 'Peers and printers: the beginnings of sustained press coverage of the House of Lords in the 1770s', *PH*, vol. 7 (1998), pp. 241–56; Stephen Farrell, 'Division lists and the nature of the Rockingham Whig Party in the House of Lords 1760–1785', *PH*, vol. 13 (1994), p. 174.

50 Thomas, *House of Commons*, p. 138.

51 G. M. Ditchfield, 'Review of Donald E. Ginter's *Voting Records of the British House of Commons, 1761–1820' PH*, vol. 15 (1996), pp. 231–44.

52 Ehrman, *Younger Pitt*, i, p. 605 where he suggests the practice can be dated from 1780.

53 This section on the length and frequency of speeches is based on Rees, 'House of Lords', pp. 394–9; Thomas, *House of Commons*, pp. 203–6; Jupp, *British Politics*, pp. 200–3, 205–6; Thorne, *The Commons*, i, pp. 343–4; Ehrman, *Younger Pitt*, iii, p. 38 n. 4.

54 For example, Thomas, *House of Commons*, p. 7.

55 Thorne, *The Commons*, i, p. 344.
56 This is based on a comprehensive reading of the debates, 1828–30, see my *British Politics*, pp. 207–10; and a representative sample of those in the 1830s and 1840s. The quotations can be found in *Hansard* 3rd series, vol. xlv (1839), col. 278; lxxiv (1844), cols. 631, 650–1 where Peel adds that in his view the only other 'rules' or 'principles' that should direct legislation were those based on the 'observance of facts' and 'the conclusions of wisdom drawn from long experience'. On 8 February 1834 Lord Howick noted in his Diary that the Commons 'for the most part' was 'incapable of appreciating philosophical reasoning, and arguments founded on general principles', Durham University Grey Mss.
57 Parliament was in session for 914 days, 1761–70, and 1,005 days, 1771–80. I owe this information to Professor David Hayton. Thorne, *The Commons*, i, pp. 334–5; see also, Jupp, *British Politics*, pp. 198–9; PP. 1881 (445) lxxiv.109. *Return of Number of Days on which House of Commons sat in each month of Sessions 1831–81.*
58 Rees, 'House of Lords', pp. 212, 232, 268, 394.
59 Farrell, 'Division lists', *PH*, vol. 13 (1994), pp. 174, 186–8.
60 Rees, 'House of Lords', pp. 60, 457–8; Michael W. McCahill, *Order and Equipoise. The Peerage and the House of Lords, 1783–1806* (1978), pp. 41–2 and Appendix A; Smith, *House of Lords*, pp. 44–5, 93–6.
61 Smith, *House of Lords*, p. 96.
62 Ibid., pp. 93–122; R. W. Davis, 'The Duke of Wellington and the resurgence of the House of Lords' in Davis (ed.), *Lords of Parliament*, pp. 97–115.
63 Thomas, *House of Commons*, pp. 11, 30–1, 68, 83–5; Thorne, *The Commons*, i, p. 335; Gary W. Coxe, *The Efficient Secret. The Cabinet and the Development of Political Parties in Victorian England* (Cambridge, 1987), pp. 46–9.
64 Smith, *House of Lords*, p. 34.
65 Thomas, *House of Commons*, pp. 33, 100–3; Thorne, *The Commons*, i, pp. 340–1; Rees, 'House of Lords', p. 54.
66 Jupp, *British Politics*, pp. 266–7.
67 Thomas, *House of Commons*, chap. 13: the average number per session was 50 in the 1760s and 200 by the mid-nineteenth century.
68 Harling, '*Old Corruption*', pp. 72–9, 108–9, 168–72 (on 5 May 1817, 10 bills were proposed as a result of the report of the 1817 Committee); Jupp, *British Politics*, pp. 136–45.
69 Jupp, *British Politics*, pp. 199–200.
70 For an incisive discussion of the concept, see Angus Hawkins, *British Party Politics, 1852–1886* (1998), chap. 1.
71 For petitioning in general, see: Colin Leys, 'Petitioning in the nineteenth and twentieth centuries', *Political Studies*, vol. 3 (1955), pp. 45–63; P. Fraser, 'Public petitioning and Parliament before 1832', *History*, vol. 46 (1961), pp. 195–211; Paul A. Pickering, ' "And Your Petitioners & c": Chartist petitioning in popular politics 1838–48', *EHR*, vol. 116 (2001), pp. 368–88; Joanna Innes, 'Legislation and public participation: aspects of a changing relationship 1760–1830' in David Lemmings (ed.), *The British and their Laws* (Woodbridge, 2005), pp. 102–32. For studies of pressure groups that made particular use of petitioning, see Seymour Drescher, *Capitalism and Antislavery* (1986); his, 'Whose abolition? Pressure and the ending of the British Slave Trade', *P&P*, vol. 143 (1994), pp. 136–66; and J. R. Oldfield, *Popular Politics and British Anti-Slavery* (Manchester, 1995). For reference to 1828–30 and the importance of petitions to the Lords, see my *British Politics*, pp. 216–8. The figures for 1839 are taken from *The British Almanac and Companion* (1840), pp. 219–22.

72 G. I. T. Machin, *The Catholic Question in English Politics 1820 to 1830* (Oxford, 1964), pp. 144–9, 165; Jupp, *British Politics*, pp. 369–75.

73 PP. 1841 (281). xxvii. 33: *Return of the Number of Petitions Printed and Circulated with the Votes in 1839 and 1840*; PP. 1854–55 (531). liv. l: *General Index to Reports of Public Petitions, 1833–1852*, pp. iii–ix.

74 Jupp, *British Politics*, pp. 144, 147, 149, 158.

75 In 1772, 'select' committees were established on several routine matters – on expiring laws, privileges and the reply to the Address as well as on petitions and local bills. Another 12 committees were established on what l construe to be general matters. Eleven of these had two names listed followed by 'and all who come to the committee to have a voice' or '& c.' These therefore seem to be committees open to any member. Only one, to enquire into the operations of the East India Company, was restricted to the 31 MPs balloted on to it, *Commons Journal*, 1772 (Par.13. Sess.5), p. 691.

76 I am grateful to Joanna Innes for letting me see her very helpful unpublished paper, 'The early history of select committees of enquiry, *c*.1688–1844' and for drawing my attention to developments in the Lords. Further research on the last point confirms increasing enquiry there on public-interest matters after 1815. See also, Rees, 'House of Lords', pp. 461–5, 481. The figures for Commons' select committees have been taken from the *Journals* and from my *British Politics*, pp. 210–16. 38 Royal Commissions were appointed, 1807–26, but 53 between 1830 and 1842, see David Eastwood, ' "Amplifying the province of the legislature": the flow of information and the English State in the early nineteenth century', *HR*, vol. 62 (1989), p. 286.

77 S. E. Finer, 'The transmission of Benthamite ideas 1820–50' in G. Sutherland (ed.), *Studies in the Growth of Nineteenth-Century Government* (1972), pp. 11–32. For a discussion of the issue see Lambert, *Sessional Papers*, i, pp. 43–53.

78 Jupp, *British Politics*, pp. 212–13.

79 Based on: Innes, 'Select committees'; Lambert, *Sessional Papers*, ii, pp. 371–81; Jupp, *British Politics*, pp. 215–16; PP. 1840 (130). xv. 250: *Comparative Circulation of Parliamentary Papers Issued 1833–38*, p. 16.

80 Joann Innes, 'Parliament and the shaping of eighteenth-century English Social Policy', *TRHS* 5th series vol. 40 (1990), pp. 63–92 and p. 88 for the quotation. See also, Devereaux, 'The making of the Penitentiary Act', *HJ*, vol. 42 (1999), pp. 405–33.

81 Julian Hoppit, 'Reforming Britain's weights and measures, 1660–1824', *EHR*, vol. 108 (1993), pp. 82–104. The repeal of the 1725 'Bubble' Act in 1825 is another example of co-operation between ministers, private members in the context of vigorous commercial lobbying, see Ron Harris, 'Political economy, interest groups, legal institutions, and the repeal of the Bubble Act in 1825', *EconHR*, vol. 50 (1997), pp. 675–96.

82 Jupp, *British Politics*, pp. 168–78.

83 It appears that private-member initiatives in social policy were still significant in the early twentieth century.

84 Coxe, *Efficient Secret*, pp. 50–1. See also, Eastwood, 'Men, morals and social legislation', *PH*, vol. 13 (1994), pp. 190–205.

85 Frederick Clifford, *A History of Private Bill Legislation* (2 vols. 1885–7), ii, pp. 788–9, 826–43; Prest, *Liberty and Locality*, pp. 6–7, 23–4.

86 Based on: Jupp, *British Politics*, pp. 179–86; Langford, *Public Life*, pp. 156–86; Joanna Innes, 'The local acts of a national parliament: parliament's role in sanctioning local action in eighteenth-century Britain', *PH*, vol. 17 (1998), pp. 23–47; Prest, *Liberty and Locality*, pp. 1–36; Jerome Blum, 'English parlia-mentary enclosure', *Journal of Modern History*, vol. 53 (1981), pp. 477–504; G. E. Mingay,

Parliamentary Enclosure in England. An Introduction to its Causes, Incidence and Impact 1750–1850 (1997), chap. 4.

87 Lambert, *Sessional Papers*, i, pp. 17, 25, 41, 48–9, 60, 62, 69, 71; *Mirror of Parliament* (1828), vol. 3, pp. 2643–63; PP. 1840 (130). xv. 250: *Comparative Circulation of Parliamentary Papers Issued 1833–38*, p. 16.

88 Harling, *'Old Corruption', passim*; Jupp, *British Politics*, pp. 227–8.

8 The executive, Parliament and the public

1 Hoppen, *Elections*, p. 2.
2 Beales, 'The electorate before and after 1832', (1992), pp. 139–150; O'Gorman, 'The electorate before and after 1832', *PH*, vol. 12 (1993), pp. 171–83.
3 Hoppen, *Elections*, pp. 1, 13, 36.
4 Brash, *Scottish Electoral Politics*, pp. xxxix–xl.
5 Salmon, *Electoral Reform*, pp. 132–37.
6 Frank O'Gorman, *Voters, Patrons, and Parties. The Unreformed Electoral System of Hanoverian England 1734–1832* (Oxford, 1989), pp.199–218. O'Gorman uses the metaphor of a 'blunted diamond' to describe the electorate (p. 217) but I prefer the pear.
7 See, for example, P. J. Jupp and Stephen A. Royle, 'The social geography of Cork City elections, 1801–30', *IHS*, vol. 29 (1994), pp. 23–4.
8 Hoppen, *Elections*, pp. 36–7, 40–1.
9 Salmon, *Electoral Reform*, pp. 200–9.
10 J. R. Vincent, *Pollbooks: How Victorians Voted* (Cambridge, 1967), pp. 20–6,165 (for the example of the Rochdale voterate of 1841).
11 O'Gorman, *Voters*, pp. 224–44.
12 P. J. Jupp, 'Irish parliamentary representation and the Catholic vote, 1801–20', *HJ*, vol. 10 (1967), pp. 183–96.
13 Salmon, *Electoral Reform*, chap. 4 and p. 125 for the quotation.
14 O'Gorman, *Voters*, chap. 6, partic. pp. 368–83; J. A. Phillips, *Electoral Behaviour in Unreformed England, 1761–1802* (Princeton, 1982); and his *The Great Reform Bill in the Boroughs. English Electoral Behaviour 1818–1841* (Oxford, 1992).
15 Phillips, *Great Reform Bill*, pp. 295–303.
16 Salmon, *Electoral Reform*, chap. 5 and p. 241 for the quotation.
17 Ibid., Part 3 and for his overall conclusions, pp. 238–48.
18 Brash, *Scottish Electoral Politics*, pp. lix–lxiii.
19 Hoppen, *Elections*, pp. 258–9, 278–85.
20 O'Gorman, 'The electorate before and after 1832', *PH*, vol. 12 (1993), p. 172.
21 Namier and Brooke, *The Commons*, i, pp. 80–6.
22 Thorne states that in the period 1790–1820, 'No election in this period contains as many references to one issue as do the addresses of the candidates in 1807', *The Commons*, i, p. 189.
23 M. Gorsky, 'Mutual aid and civil society: friendly societies in nineteenth-century Bristol', *Urban History*, vol. 25 (1998), p. 302; Clark, *Clubs and Societies*, chap. 3, esp. pp. 131–6. I am indebted to Joanna Innes for pointing out that in the eighteenth century the word 'association' often referred to oath-bound groups formed at times of national crisis and that before 1780 these were invariably loyal in outlook. The word therefore needs to be used with care.
24 Colley, *Britons*.
25 References to this can be found in Burns and Innes, *Rethinking Reform*, pp. 43–4.
26 John Rule, *The Labouring Classes in Early Industrial England 1750–1850* (1986).
27 Dror Wahrman, *Imagining the Middle Class. The Political Representation of Class in Britain, c.1780–1840* (Cambridge, 1995).

28 Langford, *Excise Crisis*, p. 148.
29 Olson, 'The board of trade', *JICH*, vol. 8 (1979–80), pp. 33–50; 'The London Mercantile lobby and the coming of the American Revolution', *Journal of American History*, vol. 69 (1982), pp. 21–41, p. 24 for the quotation.
30 O'Shaughnessy, 'The formation of a commercial lobby', *HJ*, vol. 40 (1997), pp. 71–95, p. 77 for the quotation.
31 Jupp, *British Politics*, p. 366.
32 Miles Taylor, 'Colonial representation at Westminster, *c*.1800–65' in Hoppit (ed.), *Parliaments, Nations and Identities*, pp. 206–19.
33 Jupp, *British Politics*, pp. 366–7.
34 Scott, *British Foreign Policy*, pp. 22–3. Trade played an increasingly important role in foreign policy after 1783, but was rarely a decisive factor, see Ehrman, *The British Government and Commercial Negotiations with Europe, 1783–1793* (Cambridge, 1962); Black, *British Foreign Policy in an Age of Revolutions*, pp. 495–9; D. C. M. Platt, *Finance, Trade, and Politics in British Foreign Policy, 1815–1914* (Oxford, 1968).
35 Anthony Webster, 'The political economy of trade liberalisation: the East India Company Charter Act of 1813', *EconHR*, vol. 43 (1990), pp. 404–19.
36 Brewer, *Party, Ideology and Popular Politics*, pp. 9, 19.
37 Burns and Innes (eds), *Rethinking the Age of Reform* (Cambridge, 2003).
38 Oliver MacDonagh, *O'Connell. The Life of Daniel O'Connell 1775–1847* (1991 edn), pp. 246–7.
39 Jupp, *British Politics*, p. 368.
40 In the case of the Chartists, it has been suggested that this may have been due to their familiarity with the practice of the managing committees of trades unions being elected on a monthly basis, see Clive Behagg, *Politics and Production in the Early Nineteenth Century* (1990), pp. 225–6.
41 Pickering, 'Chartist petitioning', *EHR*, vol. 116 (2001), pp. 368–88, p. 387 for the quotation.
42 John Barrell, http://www.history.ac.uk/04/10/2000 at 20.38pm, p. 2.
43 For the Political Unions, for example, see LoPatin, *Political Unions*, p. 27.
44 Langford, *A Polite and Commercial People*, pp. 446–7 (for 1766–7); Fedorak, 'The Addington Ministry' provides useful information, pp. 23 ff., on petitioning in 1800–1.
45 For a recent assessment, see William Anthony Hay, *The Whig Revival, 1808–1830* (2005), pp. 28–32.
46 Hilton, *Corn, Cash, Commerce*, pp. 5–10.
47 Hay, *Whig Revival*, pp. 55–8.
48 Jupp, *British Politics*, pp. 368–9.
49 Leys, 'Petitioning', *Political Studies* vol. 3 (1955), pp. 45–64.
50 Jupp, *British Politics*, pp. 220–1.
51 Leys, 'Petitioning', pp. 56–61.
52 Cobbett's *Parl. Deb.* vol. xxxvi, clm. 544.
53 Jupp, *British Politics*, p. 220.
54 Jupp, *Grenville*, pp. 388–91.
55 Jupp, *British Politics*, p. 225.
56 Gregory and Stevenson, *Britain in the Eighteenth Century*, pp. 217–25, pp. 218, 225 for the quotations.
57 G. M. Ditchfield, 'Parliament, the Quakers and the Tithe question 1750–1835', *PH*, vol. 4 (1985), pp. 105–6. On [4 Nov.1831], Brougham told Lansdowne, 'I never yet saw the *announcement* of an approaching session [of Parliament] fail to produce a suspension of out-of doors agitation', Lansdowne Mss.
58 Innes, 'Parliament and social policy', *TRHS* 5th series vol. 40 (1990), p. 88.
59 Marie Peters, *Pitt and Popularity* (Oxford, 1980), chap.1, partic. pp. 19–24.

60 *Foreign Quarterly Review* and *United Services Journal*, 1827; *Foreign Review*, 1828; *United Service Gazette* and the *Naval and Military Gazette*, 1833.

61 [John Wade], *History of the Middle & Working Classes* (1833, reprint, New York, 1966), p. 570.

62 Aspinall, *Politics and the Press*, p. 11.

63 Barker, *Newspapers*, pp. 23–4, 115–16.

64 I have revised my calculations for 1828–30 in *British Politics*, p. 333–4, and now suggest the following readerships: London, 650,000; England and Wales, 1.3 million; Scotland, 106,000; Ireland, 169,000. I have estimated that the number of readers of 1 newspaper was 10 for London and 5 for all other parts of the UK. Aspinall suggests that the number of readers per newspaper may have been as high as 25 throughout England, see *Politics and the Press*, p. 25, fn. 1. These figures omit readership of the unstamped press.

65 Aspinall, *Politics and the Press*, pp. 379–84.

66 Barker, *Newspapers*, pp. 72, 81, 93–4 (where the quotations can be found), 177–8.

67 Jupp, *British Politics*, pp. 331–57.

68 Thompson, *The People's Science*, pp. 219–28.

69 In 1810, 82 addresses were sent supporting the parliamentary enquiry into the nepotism of the Duke of York, Peter Spence, *The Birth of Romantic Radicalism: War, Popular Politics and English radical Reformism, 1780–1815* (Aldershot, 1996), pp. 123–4. It also seems to have been the case that more pledges were required of parliamentary candidates at the 1830 and 1831 elections than was normally the case – a version of 'instructions'. On this point see, A. H. Graham, 'The parliamentary candidate society, 1831', in John Bossy and Jupp (eds), *Essays Presented to Michael Roberts* (Belfast, 1976), pp. 104–16.

Bibliography*

Books

Ashworth, William J., *Customs and Excise: Trade, Production, and Consumption in England, 1640–1845* (Oxford, 2003).

Aspinall, A. (ed.), *The Correspondence of George IV* (3 vols, Cambridge, 1938).

Aspinall, A., *Politics and the Press c.1780–1850* (1949).

Aspinall, A. (ed.), *The Later Correspondence of George III* (5 vols, Cambridge, 1962–70).

Aspinall, A. (ed.), *The Correspondence of George, Prince of Wales* (8 vols, Cambridge, 1963–71).

Ayling, Stanley, *George the Third* (1972).

Barker, Hannah, *Newspapers, Politics, and Public Opinion in Late Eighteenth Century England* (Oxford, 1998).

Barrow, J. E. (ed.), *Mirror of Parliament* (1828–41).

Baxter, S. B., *William III* (1966).

Bayly, C. A., *Imperial Meridian. The British Empire and the World, 1780–1830* (1989).

Beattie, J. M., *The English Court in the Reign of George I* (Cambridge, 1967).

Behagg, Clive, *Politics and Production in the Early Nineteenth Century* (1990).

Bellamy, R. (ed.), *Victorian Liberalism. Nineteenth-Century political thought and practice* (1990).

Birks, P. (ed.), *The Life of the Law* (1993).

Black, Jeremy (ed.), *Britain in the Age of Walpole* (1984).

Black, Jeremy (ed.), *British Politics and Society from Walpole to Pitt, 1742–1789* (1990).

Black, Jeremy, *British foreign policy in an Age of Revolutions, 1783–1793* (Cambridge, 1994).

Black, Jeremy, *Parliament and Foreign Policy in the Eighteenth Century* (Cambridge, 2004).

Bossy, John and Jupp, Peter, *Essays presented to Michael Roberts* (Belfast, 1976).

Bowen, Huw V., *Revenue and Reform: the Indian problem in British Politics, 1757–1773* (Cambridge, 1991).

Brash, J. I. (ed.), *Papers on Scottish Electoral Politics 1832–1854* (Edinburgh, 1974).

---

* This lists the sources cited in the endnotes. All were published in London unless otherwise stated.

Brent, Richard, *Liberal Anglican Politics. Whiggery, Religion, and Reform 1830–1841* (Oxford, 1987).

Brewer, John, *Party, Ideology and Popular Politics at the Accession of George III* (Cambridge, 1981 edn).

Brewer, John, *The Sinews of Power* (1989).

Brewer, John, *The Pleasures of the Imagination* (1997).

Brewer, J. and Hellmuth, E. (eds), *Rethinking Leviathan. The Eighteenth-Century State in Britain and Germany* (Oxford, 1999).

The British Almanac and Companion (Society for the Diffusion of useful knowledge, 1828–72).

Brockliss, Lawrence and Eastwood, David (eds), *A Union of Multiple Identities. The British Isles, c.1750–c.1850* (Manchester, 1997).

Brooke, John, *King George III* (1974 edn).

Brougham, Henry Peter, Lord, *Political Philosophy* (3 vols, 1853 edn).

Brown, Lucy, *The Board of Trade and the Free-Trade Movement, 1830–42* (Oxford, 1958).

Browning, Reed, *Political and Constitutional Ideas of the Court Whigs* (1983).

Bucholz, R. O., *The Augustan Court* (Stanford, 1993).

Burns, Arthur and Innes, Joanna (eds), *Rethinking the Age of Reform* (Cambridge, 2003).

Christie, I. R., *Crisis of Empire 1754–1783* (1966).

Christie, I. R., *British 'Non-Elite' MPs 1715–1820* (Oxford, 1995).

Chronological Table and Index of All the Statutes (2 vols, 1896).

Clark, D. M., *The Rise of the British Treasury. Colonial administration in the 18th century* (Yale, 1960).

Clark, J. C. D., *The Memoirs and Speeches of James, 2nd Earl Waldegrave, 1742–63* (Cambridge, 1988).

Clark, Peter, *British Clubs and Societies 1580–1800. The Origins of an Associational World* (Oxford, pb.edn, 2001).

Claydon, T., *William III and the Godly Revolution* (Cambridge, 1996).

Clifford, Frederick, *A History of Private Bill Legislation* (2 vols, 1885–7).

Coleman, Bruce, *Conservatism and the Conservative Party in nineteenth-century Britain* (1988).

Colley, Linda, *In Defiance of Oligarchy: The Tory Party, 1714–1760* (Cambridge, 1982).

Colley, Linda, *Britons* (Yale, 1992).

Collinge, J. M., *Foreign Office Officials* (1979).

Collini, Stefan, Winch, Donald and Burrow, John, *That Noble Science of Politics. A Study in Nineteenth-century Intellectual History* (Cambridge, 1983).

Colvin, H. M. (ed.), *The History of the King's Works* (6 vols, 1963–82).

Cook, Chris and Keith, Brendan, *British Historical Facts 1830–1900* (1975).

Cookson, J. E., *Lord Liverpool's Administration 1815–1822* (Edinburgh, 1975).

Cookson, J. E., *The British Armed Nation, 1793–1815* (Oxford, 1997).

Costin, W. C., and Watson J. Steven, *The Law and Working of the Constitution: Documents 1660–1914* (2 vols, 1952).

Coxe, Gary W., *The Efficient Secret. The Cabinet and the Development of Political Parties in Victorian England* (Cambridge, 1987).

Croker, J. W. (ed.), *Memoirs of the Reign of George II . . . . by Lord Hervey* (2 vols, 1848).

Daunton, Martin, *Trusting Leviathan. The Politics of Taxation in Britain, 1799–1914* (Cambridge, 2001).

Davis, R. W. (ed.), *Lords of Parliament* (Stanford, CA, 1995).

Davison, Lee, Keirn, Tim and Shoemaker, R. B. (eds), *Stilling the Grumbling Hive* (Stroud, 1992).

Dickinson, H. T., *Liberty and Property. Political Ideology in Eighteenth-Century Britain* (1979 edn).

Dickson, P. G. M., *The Financial Revolution in England* (1967).

Drescher, Seymour, *Capitalism and Antislavery* (1986).

Eccleshall, Robert, and Walker, Graham, *Biographical Dictionary of British Prime Ministers* (1998).

Ehrman, John, *The British Government and Commercial Negotiations with Europe, 1783–1793* (Cambridge, 1962).

Ehrman, John, *The Younger Pitt* (3 vols, 1969–96).

Esher, Viscount (ed.), *The Girlhood of Queen Victoria. A Selection from Her Majesty's Diaries…1832–1840* (2 vols, 1912).

Esher, Viscount and Benson, A. C. (eds), *The Letters of Queen Victoria* (1st series 1837–61, 3 vols, 1907).

Fry, Michael, *The Dundas Despotism* (Edinburgh, 1992).

Gambles, Anna, *Protection and Politics: Conservative Economic Discourse, 1815–1852* (Woodbridge, 1999).

Gardiner, Robert, *Frigates of the Napoleonic Wars* (2000).

Gash, Norman, *Mr Secretary Peel* (1961).

Gash, Norman, *Reaction and Reconstruction in English Politics, 1832–52* (Oxford, 1965).

Gash, Norman, *Lord Liverpool* (1984).

Gatrell, V. A. C., Lenman, Bruce and Parker, Geoffrey (eds), *Crime and the Law. The social history of crime in Western Europe since 1800* (1980).

Ginter, Donald E. (ed.), *Whig Organization in the General Election of 1790* (Berkeley, 1967).

Gray, Denis, *Spencer Perceval 1762–1812. The Evangelical Prime Minister* (Manchester, 1963).

Gray, Peter, *Famine, Land and Politics: British Government and Irish Society, 1843–50* (Dublin, 1999).

Gregg, E., *Queen Anne* (1980).

Grey Earl, Henry (ed.), *The Reform Act of 1832. The Correspondence of the late Earl Grey with His Majesty King William IV* (2 vols, 1867).

Hall, C. D., *British Strategy in the Napoleonic War, 1803–15* (Manchester, 1992).

Hamlin, C., *Public Health and Social Justice in the Age of Chadwick. Britain, 1800–1854* (Cambridge, 1998).

Harling, Philip, *The Waning of 'Old Corruption'. The Politics of Economical Reform in Britain, 1779–1846* (Oxford, 1996).

Harris, Bob, *Politics and the Nation* (Oxford, 2002).

Harris J. (ed.), *Civil Society in British History* (Oxford, 2003).

Hatton, R., *George I* (1978).

Hawkins, Angus, *British Party Politics, 1852–1886* (1998).

Hay, William Anthony, *The Whig Revival, 1808–1830* (2005).

Hayter, Tony (ed.), *An Eighteenth-Century Secretary at War. The Papers of William, Viscount Barrington* (1988).

Hayton, D. W., *The History of Parliament. The Commons 1690–1715* (5 vols, 2002).

Hayton, D. W., *Ruling Ireland, 1685–1742. Politics, Politicians and Parties* (Woodbridge, 2004).

Hibbert, Christopher, *George IV* (2 vols, 1972–73).

Hill, B. W., *British Parliamentary Parties, 1742–1832* (1985).

Hill, B. W., *Sir Robert Walpole. 'Sole and prime minister'* (1989).

Hilton, A. J. Boyd, *Corn, Cash, Commerce. The Economic Policies of the Tory Governments, 1815–1830* (Oxford, 1977).

Hilton, A. J. Boyd, *The Age of Atonement* (Oxford, 1991 edn).

Holmes, Geoffrey, *British Politics in the Age of Anne* (1967).

Holmes, Geoffrey and Szechi, Daniel, *The Age of Oligarchy. Pre-industrial Britain, 1723–1783* (1993).

Hoppen, K. Theodore, *Elections, Politics, and Society in Ireland 1832–1885* (Oxford, 1984).

Hoppit, Julian (ed.), *Failed Legislation 1660–1800* (1997).

Hoppit, Julian, *A Land of Liberty? England 1689–1727* (Oxford, 2000).

Hoppit, Julian (ed.), *Parliaments, Nations and Identities in Britain and Ireland, 1660–1850* (Manchester, 2003).

Inglis, Brian, *The Freedom of the Press in Ireland 1784–1841* (1954).

Inikori, Joseph E., *Africans and the Industrial Revolution in England: A Study in International Trade and Development* (Cambridge, 2003).

Jenkins, T. A., *The Liberal Ascendancy, 1830–1886* (1994).

Jones, Clyve (ed.), *Party and Management in Parliament, 1660–1784* (Leicester University Press, 1984).

Jupp, Peter, *Lord Grenville 1759–1834* (Oxford, 1985).

Jupp, Peter, *British Politics on the Eve of Reform. The Duke of Wellington's Administration, 1828–30* (1998).

King, Peter, *Crime, Justice and Discretion in England, 1740–1820* (Oxford, 2000).

Kriegel, Abraham D. (ed.), *The Holland House Diaries 1831–1840* (1977).

Lambert, Sheila, *House of Commons Sessional Papers of the Eighteenth Century* (2 vols, Wilmington, Delaware, 1975–6).

Langford, Paul, *The Excise Crisis* (Oxford, 1975).

Langford, Paul, *Modern British Foreign Policy. The Eighteenth Century, 1688–1815* (1976).

Langford, Paul, *A Polite and Commercial People. England 1727–1783* (Oxford, 1989).

Langford, Paul, *Public Life and the propertied Englishman* (Oxford, 1991).

Lawson, Philip, *George Grenville* (Oxford, 1984).

Lemmings, David (ed.), *The British and their Laws in the Eighteenth century* (Woodbridge, 2005).

Longford, Elizabeth, *Victoria R. I.* (1964).

LoPatin, Nancy D., *Political Unions, Popular Politics and the Great Reform Act of 1832* (London, 1999).

McCahill, Michael W., *Order and Equipoise. The Peerage and the House of Lords, 1783–1806* (1978).

MacDonagh, Oliver, *O'Connell. The Life of Daniel O'Connell 1775–1847* (1991edn).

Machin, G. I. T., *The Catholic Question in English Politics 1820 to 1830* (Oxford, 1964).

Malcomson, A. P. W., *Archbishop Charles Agar. Churchmanship and Politics in Ireland, 1760–1810* (Dublin, 2002).

Mandler, Peter, *Aristocratic government in the age of reform: whigs and liberals, 1830–1852* (Oxford, 1990).

Middleton, C. R., *The Bells of Victory* (Cambridge, 1985).

Mingay, G. E., *Parliamentary Enclosure in England. An Introduction to its Causes, Incidence and Impact 1750–1850* (1997).

Mitchell, Austin, *The Whigs in Opposition, 1815–30* (Oxford, 1967).

Mitchell, L. G., *Lord Melbourne* (Oxford, 1997).

Morris, Marilyn, *The British Monarchy and the French Revolution* (Yale, 1998).

Namier, Sir Lewis, *Crossroads of Power* (1962).

Namier, Sir Lewis and Brooke, John, *The Commons 1754–90* (3 vols, 1985 edn).

Newbould, Ian D. C., *Whiggery and reform, 1830–41: the politics of government* (1990).

Oldfield, J. R., *Popular Politics and British Anti-Slavery* (Manchester, 1995).

O'Gorman, Frank, *The Whig Party and the French Revolution* (1967).

O'Gorman, Frank, *The Rise of Party in England. The Rockingham Whigs 1760–82* (1975).

O'Gorman, Frank, *The Emergence of the British Two-Party System, 1760–1832* (1982).

O'Gorman, Frank, *Voters, Patrons, and Parties. The Unreformed Electoral System of Hanoverian England 1734–1832* (Oxford, 1989).

Pares, Richard, *Limited Monarchy in Great Britain in the Eighteenth Century* (Historical Association Pamphlet, G35, 6th edn 1967).

Pares, Richard, *King George III and the Politicians* (Oxford, 1967pb. edn).

Parris, Henry, *Constitutional Bureaucracy. The Development of British Central Administration since the Eighteenth Century* (1969).

Paz, D. G., *The Politics of Working-Class Education in Britain, 1830–50* (Manchester, 1980).

Peters, Marie, *Pitt and Popularity* (Oxford, 1980).

Phillips, J. A., *Electoral Behaviour in Unreformed England, 1761–1802* (Princeton, 1982).

Phillips, J. A., *The Great Reform Bill in the Boroughs. English Electoral Behaviour 1818–1841* (Oxford, 1992).

Philips, David and Storch, Robert D., *Policing Provincial England 1829–1856* (1999).

Platt, D. C. M., *Finance, Trade, and Politics in British Foreign Policy, 1815–1914* (Oxford, 1968).

Plumb, J., *Sir Robert Walpole. The King's Minister* (1960).

Prest, John, *Liberty and Locality. Parliament, Permissive Legislation and Ratepayers' Democracies in the Nineteenth Century* (Oxford, 1990).

Reeves-Smyth, Terence and Oram, Richard (eds), *Avenues to the Past. Essays presented to Sir Charles Brett* (Belfast, 2003).

Roberts, Michael, *The Whig Party 1807–12* (1939).

Roberts, R. and Kynaston, D., *The Bank of England. Money, Power and Influence 1694–1994* (Oxford, 1995).

Rodger, N. A. M., *The Wooden World: an anatomy of the Georgian navy* (1986).

Rogers, Nicholas, *Whigs and Cities: popular politics in the Age of Walpole and Pitt* (Oxford, 1989).

Roseveare, Henry, *The Treasury. The Evolution of a British Institution* (1969).

Roseveare, Henry, *The Treasury, 1660–1870. The Foundations of Control* (1973).

Royal Kalendar (1835–51).

Rule, John, *The Labouring Classes in Early Industrial England 1750–1850* (1986).

Russell, Lord John, *Essay on the English Constitution* (1821).

Sack, James J., *From Jacobite to Conservative. Reaction and orthodoxy in Britain, c.1760–1832* (Cambridge, 1993).

Sainty, J. C., *Treasury Officials, 1660–1870* (1972).

Sainty, J. C., *Officials of the Board of Trade, 1660–1870* (1974).

Sainty, J. C., *Admiralty Officials, 1660–1870* (1975).

Sainty, J. C., *Home Office Officials, 1782–1870* (1975).

Sainty, J. C., *Colonial Office Officials* (1976).

Salmon, Philip, *Electoral Reform at Work. Local Politics and National Parties, 1832–1841* (Woodbridge, 2002).

Schwoerer, Lois, G. (ed.), *Revolutions of 1688–9* (Cambridge, 1992).

Scott, H. M., *British Foreign Policy in the Age of the American Revolution* (Oxford, 1990).

Sedgwick, Romney, *The House of Commons 1715–54* (2 vols, 1970).

Smith, E. A., *Whig Principles and Party Politics. Earl Fitzwilliam and the Whig Party, 1748–1833* (Manchester, 1975).

Smith, E. A., *Lord Grey 1764–1845* (Oxford, 1990).

Smith, E. A., *The House of Lords in British Politics and Society 1815–1911* (1992).

Smith, E. A., *George IV* (Yale, 1999).

Smith, Henry Stooks, *The Parliaments of England*, vols. 1–3 (1844).

Spence, Peter, *The Birth of Romantic Radicalism: War, Popular Politics and English radical Reformism, 1780–1815* (Aldershot, 1996).

Sutherland, G. (ed.), *Studies in the Growth of Nineteenth-century Government* (1972).

Taylor, Sir Henry, *The Statesman* (1836).

Thomas, Peter, D. G., *The House of Commons in the Eighteenth Century* (Oxford, 1971).

Thomas, Peter, D. G., *Lord North* (1976).

Thompson, Noel W., *The People's Science. The Popular Political Economy of Exploitation and crisis 1816–34* (Cambridge, 1984).

Thomson, M. A., *The Secretaries of State 1681–1782* (Oxford, 1932).

Thorne, R. G., *The House of Commons 1790–1820* (5 vols, 1986).

Van Thal, H. (ed.), *The Prime Ministers*, vol. 1 (1974).

Vincent, J. R. *Pollbooks: How Victorians Voted* (Cambridge, 1967).

Vincent, J. R. and Stenton, M. (eds), *McCalmont's Parliamentary Poll Book of all Elections 1832–1918* (8th edn Brighton, 1971).

[Wade, John], *The Extraordinary Black Book* (1831).

[Wade, John], *History of the Middle & Working Classes* (1833, reprint, New York, 1966).

Wahrman, Dror, *Imagining the Middle Class. The Political Representation of Class in Britain, c.1780–1840* (Cambridge, 1995).

Walker, B. M. (ed.), *Parliamentary Election Results in Ireland, 1801–1922* (Dublin, 1978).

Waterman, A. M. C., *Revolution, Economics and Religion* (Cambridge, 1991).

Wellington, the Duke of (ed.), *Despatches, Correspondence, and Memoranda of…Arthur Duke of Wellington* (2nd series, 6 vols, 1867–77).

Williams, E. N, *The Eighteenth Century Constitution* (1977 edn).

Wilson, Kathleen, *The Sense of the People. Politics, Culture and Imperialism in England, 1715–1785* (Cambridge, 1998 pb. edn).

Woodham-Smith, Cecil, *Queen Victoria* (vol. 1, 1972).

Wyndham, H. P., *The Diary of the late George Bubb Dodington, Baron of Melcombe Regis* (1784).
Young, D. M., *The Colonial Office in the Early Nineteenth Century* (1961).
Ziegler, Philip, *William IV* (1971).
Ziegler, Philip, *Melbourne* (1976).

Articles, chapters in books and internet references

Alexander, J. L., 'Lord John Russell and the origins of the Committee of Council of Education', *HJ*, vol. 20 (1977).
Aspinall, A., 'The Cabinet Council 1783–1835', *Proceedings of the British Academy*, vol. 38 (1952).
Asquith, I., 'The Whig party and the press in the early nineteenth century', *HR*, vol. 49 (1976).
Aydelotte, W. O., 'The House of Commons in the 1840's', *BIHR* vol. 27 (1954).
Barrell, John, http://www.history.ac.uk/ 04/10/2000 at 20.38pm.
Bartrip, P. W. J., 'British Government Inspection, 1832–1875: some observations', *HJ*, vol. 25 (1982).
Beales, Derek, 'The Electorate before and after 1832: the Right to Vote, and the Opportunity', *PH*, vol. 11 (1992).
Beattie, J. M., 'The cabinet and the management of death at Tyburn after the Revolution of 1688–1689' in Schwoerer, Lois G. (ed.), *Revolutions of 1688–9* (Cambridge, 1992).
Beattie, John, 'London crime and the making of the 'Bloody Code', 1689–1718', in Davison, Lee, Keirn, Tim and Shoemaker, R. B. (eds), *Stilling the Grumbling Hive* (Stroud, 1992).
Beckett, J. V., 'Land Tax or Excise: the levying of taxation in seventeenth- and eighteenth-century England', *EHR*, vol. 100 (1985).
Black, Jeremy, 'Foreign Policy in the Age of Walpole' in Black, Jeremy (ed.), *Britain in the Age of Walpole* (1984).
Black, Jeremy, 'Fresh light on the fall of Townshend', *HJ*, vol. 29 (1986).
Black, Jeremy, 'Parliamentary Reporting in England in the early eighteenth century. An abortive attempt to influence the magazines in 1744', *Parliaments, Estates and Representation*, vol. 7 (1987).
Blanning, T. C. W., ' "That Horrid Electorate" or "Ma Patrie Germanique"? George III, Hanover and the *Fürstenbund* of 1785', *HJ*, vol. 20 (1977).
Blum, Jerome, 'English Parliamentary Enclosure', *Journal of Modern History*, vol. 53 (1981).
Bowen, Huw, V., ' "The Little Parliament": the general court of the East India company, 1750–1784', *HJ*, vol. 34 (1991).
Bowen, Huw, V., 'The Bank of England during the long eighteenth century, 1694–1820', in Roberts, R. and Kynaston, D. (eds), *The Bank of England. Money, Power and Influence 1694–1994* (Oxford, 1995).
Breihan, John, R., 'William Pitt and the Commission on Fees, 1785–1801', *HJ*, vol. 27 (1984).
Brent, Richard, 'The Whigs and Protestant Dissent in the decade of reform: the case of Church Rates, 1833–41', *EHR*, vol. 102 (1987).
Brent, Richard, 'New whigs in old bottles', *PH*, vol. 11 (1992).

Brett, Peter, 'Constituency organization, and the power of the electoral register: national perspectives and the Bristol battleground 1832–41', *Southern History*, vol. 18 (1996).

Broad, J., 'Parish economies of welfare, 1650–1834', *HJ*, vol. 42 (1999).

Brown, Desmond H., 'Abortive attempts to codify English criminal law' *PH*, vol. 11 (1992).

Brundage, A., 'Ministers, magistrates and reformers: the genesis of the rural Constabulary Act of 1839', *PH*, vol. 5 (1986).

Brundage, A., Eastwood, D. and Mandler, P., 'Debate: the making of the New Poor Law', *P&P*, vol. 127 (1990).

Buck, A. R., 'Property, aristocracy and the reform of the land law in early nineteenth century England', *Journal of Legal History*, vol. 16 (1995).

Bullen, R., 'Party politics and Foreign Policy: Whigs, Tories and Iberian Affairs, 1830–36', *BIHR*, vol. 51 (1978).

Cain, P. J. and Hopkins, A. G., 'The Political Economy of British Expansion Overseas, 1750–1914', *EconHR*, vol. 33 (1980).

Childs, John, 'The army and the state in Britain and Germany during the eighteenth century' in Brewer, J. and Hellmuth, E (eds), *Rethinking Leviathan. The Eighteenth-Century State in Britain and Germany* (Oxford, 1999).

Christie, I. R., 'The cabinet during the Grenville administration 1763–65', *EHR*, vol. 73 (1958).

Christie, I. R., 'Party Politics in the Age of Lord North's Administration', *PH*, vol. 6 (1987).

Christie, I. R., 'The anatomy of the opposition in the parliament of 1784', *PH*, vol. 9 (1990).

Clark, Peter, 'The "Mother Gin" controversy in the early eighteenth century', *TRHS* 5th series, vol. 38 (1988).

Collins, Michael, 'Monetary policy and the supply of trade credit, 1830–1844', *Economica*, vol. 45 (1978).

Connors, Richard, ' "The Grand Inquest of the Nation." Parliamentary committees and social policy in mid-eighteenth century England', *PH*, vol. 14 (1995).

Conway, S., 'Bentham and the nineteenth-century revolution in government' in Bellamy, R. (ed.), *Victorian Liberalism. Nineteenth-Century Political Thought and Practice* (1990).

Conway, Stephen, 'The politics of British military and naval mobilization, 1775–83', *EHR*, vol. 112 (1997).

Cruikshanks, E., 'The political management of Sir Robert Walpole' in Black, Jeremy (ed.), *Britain in the Age of Walpole* (1984).

Davis, Ralph., 'The rise of protection in England, 1689–1786', *EconHR*, vol. 19 (1966).

Davis, Richard, W., 'Whigs in the age of Fox and Grey', *PH*, vol. 12 (1993).

Davis, Richard, W., 'The Duke of Wellington and the resurgence of the House of Lords' in Davis, R. W. (ed.), *Lords of Parliament* (Stanford, CA, 1995).

Davison, Lee, 'Experiments in the social regulation of industry: gin legislation, 1729–51' in Davison, Lee *et al* (eds), *Stilling the Grumbling Hive* (Stroud, 1992).

Devereaux, Simon, 'The making of the Penitentiary Act, 1775–1779', *HJ*, vol. 42 (1999).

Dickinson, H. T., 'Popular politics in the Age of Walpole' in Black, Jeremy (ed.), *Britain in the Age of Walpole* (1984).

Dinwiddy, J. R., 'Early-nineteenth-century reactions to Benthamism' *TRHS* 5th series vol. 34 (1984).

Dinwiddy, J. R., 'The 'Influence of the Crown' in the early nineteenth century: a note on the Opposition case', *PH*, vol. 4 (1985).

Ditchfield, G. M., 'Parliament, the Quakers and the Tithe question 1750–1835', *PH*, vol. 4 (1985).

Ditchfield, G. M., 'Review of Donald E. Ginter's Voting Records of the British House of Commons, 1761–1820' *PH*, vol. 15 (1996).

Drescher, Seymour, 'Whose abolition? Pressure and the ending of the British slave Trade', *P&P*, vol. 143 (1994).

Dunkley, Peter, 'Emigration and the state, 1803–1842: the nineteenth-century revolution in government reconsidered', *HJ*, vol. 23 (1980).

Dunkley, Peter, 'Whigs and Paupers: the reform of the English Poor Law, 1830–1834', *JBS*, vol. 20 (1981).

Eastwood, David, ' "Amplifying the Province of the Legislature": the flow of information and the English state in the early nineteenth century', *HR*, vol. 62 (1989).

Eastwood, David, 'Men, morals and the machinery of social legislation, 1790–1840', *PH*, vol. 13 (1994).

Eastwood, David, ' "Recasting our Lot": Peel, the nation, and the politics of interest', in Brockliss, Lawrence and Eastwood, David (eds), *A Union of Multiple Identities. The British Isles, c.1750–c.1850* (Manchester, 1997).

Emsley, Clive, 'Repression, "terror" and the rule of law in England during the decade of the French Revolution', *EHR*, vol. 100 (1985).

Evans, Chris, 'Tories and colliers: the fate of the "Act for the Security of Collieries and Mines" of 1800', *PH*, vol. 10 (1991).

Farrell, Stephen, 'Division Lists and the nature of the Rockingham Whig Party in the House of Lords 1760–1785', *PH*, vol. 13 (1994).

Finer, S. E., 'The transmission of Benthamite ideas 1820–50' in Sutherland, G. (ed.), *Studies in the Growth of Nineteenth-century Government* (1972).

Foord, A. S., 'The Waning of the "Influence of the Crown" ', *EHR*, vol. 62 (1947).

Fraser, P., 'Public petitioning and Parliament before 1832', *History*, vol. 46 (1961).

Gambles, Anna, 'Rethinking the politics of protection and the Corn Laws, 1830–52', *EHR*, vol. 113 (1998).

Gash, Norman, 'The organization of the Conservative Party, 1832–1846' Pts. 1 and II, *PH*, (1982 and 1983).

Goldman, Lawrence, 'The origins of British "social science": political economy, natural science and statistics, 1830–35', *HJ*, vol. 26 (1983).

Gorsky, M., 'Mutual aid and civil society: friendly societies in nineteenth-century Bristol', *Urban History*, vol. 25 (1998).

Graham, A. H., 'The Parliamentary Candidate Society, 1831', in Bossy, John and Jupp, Peter, *Essays presented to Michael Roberts* (Belfast, 1976).

Gunn, J. A. W., 'Eighteenth-Century Britain: in search of the state and finding the quarter sessions' in Brewer, J. and Hellmuth, E. (eds), *Rethinking Leviathan. The Eighteenth-Century State in Britain and Germany* (Oxford, 1999).

Gwyn, J., 'British government spending and the North American Colonies, 1740–55', *JICH*, vol. 8 (1979–80).

Haakonssen, Knud, 'The science of a legislator in James Mackintosh's moral philosophy', *History of Political Thought*, vol. 5 (1984).

Handler, Phil, 'Forgery and the end of the "Bloody Code" in early nineteenth-century England', *HJ*, vol. 48 (2005).

Handley, Stuart, 'Local legislative initiatives in Lancashire', *PH*, vol. 9 (1990).

Harding, R. W., 'Sir Robert Walpole's ministry and the conduct of the war with Spain', *HR*, vol. 60 (1987).

Harling, Philip, 'The Power of Persuasion: Central Authority, Local Bureaucracy and the New Poor Law', *EHR*, vol. 97 (1992).

Harling, Philip, 'Robert Southey and the language of social discipline' *Albion*, vol. 30 (1998).

Harris Bob, 'Scotland's Newspapers, the French Revolution and Domestic Radicalism *c.*1789–1794', *The Scottish Historical Review*, vol. 34 (2005).

Harris, Ron, 'Political economy, interest groups, legal institutions, and the repeal of the Bubble Act in 1825', *EconHR*, vol. 50 (1997).

Hawkins, Angus, 'Lord Derby' in Davis, R. W. (ed.), *Lords of Parliament* (Stanford, Calif., 1995).

Hayton, D. W., 'Walpole and Ireland' in Black, Jeremy (ed.), *Age of Walpole* (1984).

Hilton, A. J. Boyd, 'Peel: a reappraisal', *HJ*, vol. 22 (1979).

Hilton, A. J. Boyd, 'Whiggery, religion and social reform: the case of Lord Morpeth', *HJ*, vol. 37 (1994).

Hilton, A. J. Boyd, 'Robert Peel' in Eccleshall, Robert and Walker, Graham (eds), *Biographical Dictionary of British Prime Ministers* (1998).

Hitchcock, Tim, 'Paupers and Preachers: the SPCK and the parochial workhouse movement' in Davison, Lee *et al* (eds), *Stilling the Grumbling Hive* (Stroud, 1992).

Hoppit, Julian, 'Reforming Britain's Weights and Measures, 1660–1824', *EHR*, vol. 108 (1993).

Hoppit, Julian, 'Patterns of Parliamentary Legislation, 1660–1800', *HJ*, vol. 39 (1996).

Hoppit, Julian, 'Political arithmetic in eighteenth-century England', *EconHR*, vol. 49 (1996).

Hyland, P. B. J., 'Liberty and Libel: Government and the Press during the succession crisis in Britain, 1712–1716' *EHR*, vol. 101 (1986).

Innes, Joanna, 'Parliament and the shaping of eighteenth-century English Social Policy', *TRHS* 5th series vol. 40 (1990).

Innes, Joanna, 'The local acts of a national parliament: parliament's role in sanctioning local action in eighteenth-century Britain', *PH*, vol. 17 (1998).

Innes, Joanna, 'Legislating for three kingdoms; how the Westminster parliament legislated for England, Scotland and Ireland, 1707–1830', in Hoppit, Julian (ed.) *Parliaments, nations and identities in Britain and Ireland, 1660–1850* (Manchester, 2003).

Innes, Joanna, 'Central government interference: changing conceptions, practices and concerns 1688–1840' in Harris, J. (ed.), *Civil Society in British History* (Oxford, 2003).

Innes, Joanna, 'Legislation and public participation: aspects of a changing relationship 1760–1830' in Lemmings, David (ed.), *The British and their Laws* (Woodbridge, 2005).

Jones, Clyve, 'William, First Earl Cowper, Country Whiggery, and the Leadership of the Opposition in the House of Lords, 1720–23' in Davis, R. W. (ed.), *Lords of Parliament* (Stanford, CA, 1995).

Jones, G.W., 'The Office of Prime Minister' in Van Thal, H. (ed.), *The Prime Ministers*, vol. 1 (1974).

Jubb, Michael, 'The Cabinet in the Reign of George I', *BIHR*, vol. 55 (1982).

Jubb, Michael, 'Economic policy and economic development', in Black, Jeremy (ed.), *Britain in the Age of Walpole* (1984).

Jupp, Peter, J., 'Irish parliamentary representation and the Catholic vote, 1801–20', *HJ*, vol. 10 (1967).

Jupp, Peter, 'Government, Parliament and Politics in Ireland, 1801–41' in Hoppit, Julian, *Parliaments, Nations and Identities in Britain and Ireland, 1660–1850* (Manchester, 2003).

Jupp, Peter, 'Pictorial Images of the First Duke of Wellington' in Reeves-Smyth, Terence and Oram, Richard (eds), *Avenues to the Past. Essays presented to Sir Charles Brett* (Belfast, 2003).

Jupp, Peter, J., Royle, Stephen A., 'The social geography of Cork City elections, 1801–30', *IHS*, vol. 29 (1994).

Keirn, Tim, 'Parliament, Legislation and the Regulation of the English Textile Industries, 1689–1714' in Davison, Lee *et al* (eds), *Stilling the Grumbling Hive* (Stroud, 1992).

Keith-Lucas, B., 'County Meetings', *The Law Quarterly Review*, vol. 70 (1954).

Kelly, Paul, ' "Constituents" instructions to Members of Parliament' in Jones, Clyve (ed.), *Party and Management in Parliament, 1660–1784* (Leicester University Press, 1984).

Kriegel, Abraham D., 'Liberty and Whiggery in early nineteenth-century England', *Journal of Modern History*, vol. 52 (1980).

Lambert, Andrew, 'Preparing for the long peace: the reconstruction of the Royal Navy 1815–1830', *The Mariners' Mirror*, vol. 82 (1996).

Lambert, Andrew, review of Gardiner, Robert, *Frigates of the Napoleonic Wars* (2000), reviews-list@ihr.sas.ac.uk, 04/10/00, 20.39.

Lawson, Philip, 'Further reflections on the Cabinet in the early years of George III's reign', *BIHR*, vol. 57 (1984).

Lawson, Philip, 'Parliament, the constitution and corn: the embargo crisis of 1766', *PH*, vol. 5 (1986).

Leys, Colin, 'Petitioning in the nineteenth and twentieth centuries', *Political Studies* vol. 3 (1955).

Lobban, Michael, ' "Old wine in new bottles": the concept and practice of law reform, *c*.1780–1830' in Burns, Arthur and Innes, Joanna (eds), *Rethinking the Age of Reform* (Cambridge, 2003).

Lowe, William C., 'Peers and Printers: the beginnings of sustained press coverage of the House of Lords in the 1770s', *PH*, vol. 7 (1998).

McCahill, Michael M., 'Peerage creations and the changing character of the British nobility, 1750–1830', *EHR*, vol. 96 (1981).

MacDonagh, Oliver, 'The Nineteenth-Century revolution in government: a reappraisal', *HJ*, vol. 1 (1958).

Marshall, Peter 'The Eighteenth-Century Empire' in Black, Jeremy (ed.), *British Politics and Society from Walpole to Pitt, 1742–1789* (1990).

Middleton, Cyrill R., 'Pitt, Anson and the Admiralty, 1756–1761', *History*, vol. 55 (1970).

Middleton, Cyrill R., 'The formation of Canning's ministry and the evolution of the British cabinet, February to August 1827', *Canadian Journal of History*, vol. 10 (1975).

Mitchell, L. G., 'Foxite politics and the Great Reform Bill', *EHR*, vol. 108 (1993).

Newbould, Ian, D. C., 'William IV and the dismissal of the Whigs, 1834', *Canadian Journal of History*, vol. 40 (1976).

Newbould, Ian, D. C., 'Whiggery and the Dilemma of reform: liberals, radicals and the Melbourne administration, 1835–9', *BIHR*, vol. 53 (1980).

Newbould, Ian, D. C., 'The emergence of a Two-Party system in England from 1830 to 1841: Roll Call and Reconsideration', *Parliaments, Estates and Representation*, vol. 5 (1985).

Newbould, Ian, D. C., 'Whiggery and the growth of party 1830–1841: organization and the challenge of Reform', *PH*, vol. 4 (1985).

Newbould, Ian, D. C., 'The Whigs, the Church, and education, 1839', *JBS*, vol. 26 (1987).

O'Brien, P. K., 'The political economy of British taxation, 1660–1815' *EconHR*, vol. 41 (1998).

O'Brien, P., Griffiths, T., and Hunt, P., 'Political components of the industrial revolution: Parliament and the English cotton textile industry, 1660–1774', *EconHR*, vol. 45 (1991).

O'Gorman, Frank, 'The Electorate before and after 1832', *PH*, vol. 12 (1993).

Olson, Alison, G., 'The Board of Trade and London-American interest groups in the eighteenth century', *JICH*, vol. 8 (1979–80).

Olson, Alison, G., 'The London Mercantile Lobby and the coming of the American Revolution', *Journal of American History*, vol. 69 (1982).

O'Shaughnessy, A. J., 'The Formation of a Commercial Lobby: The West India interest, British Colonial Policy and the American Revolution', *HJ*, vol. 40 (1997).

Peers, Douglas, M., 'The Duke of Wellington and British India during the Liverpool Administration', *JICH*, vol. 17 (1988–89).

Peters, Marie, 'The Myth of William Pitt, Earl of Chatham, Great Imperialist Part II: Chatham and Imperial Reorganisation, 1763–78', *JICH*, vol. 22 (1994).

Peters, Marie, 'William Pitt, lst Earl of Chatham' in Eccleshall, Robert and Walker, Graham (eds), *Biographical Dictionary of British Prime Ministers* (1998).

Philips, David, 'A new engine of power and authority: the institutionalization of law enforcement in England, 1780–1830' in Gatrell, V. A. C. Lenman, Bruce and Parker, Geoffrey (eds), *Crime and the Law. The social history of crime in Western Europe since 1800* (1980).

Philips, David and Storch, Robert, D., 'Whigs and Coppers: the Grey Ministry's National Police Scheme, 1832' *BIHR*, vol. 67 (1994).

Pickering, Paul, A., ' "And Your Petitioners &c": Chartist petitioning in popular politics 1838–48', *EHR*, vol. 116 (2001).

Plumb, J., 'The Organisation of the Cabinet in the Reign of Queen Anne', *TRHS*, 5th series, vol. 7 (1957).

Porter, B., 'British Foreign Policy in the nineteenth century', *HJ*, vol. 23 (1980).

Prest, W., 'Law reform in eighteenth-century England' in Birks, P. (ed.), *The Life of the Law* (1993).

Raudzens, George, 'The British Ordnance Department 1815–1855', *Journal of the Society of Army Historical Research*, vol. 57 (1979).

Richards, Paul, 'The state and early industrial capitalism: the case of the handloom weavers', *P&P*, vol. 83 (1979).

Sack, James J., 'The Memory of Burke and the Memory of Pitt. English Conservatism confronts its Past, 1806–1829', *HJ*, vol. 30 (1987).

Scott, H. M., 'British Foreign Policy in the Age of the American Revolution', *International History Review*, vol. 6 (1984).

Sedgwick, Romney, 'The Inner Cabinet from 1739–1741', *EHR*, vol. 34 (1919).

Sheehan, M., 'Balance of power intervention: Britain's decisions for or against war, 1733–56', *Diplomacy and Statecraft*, vol. 7 (1996).

Shoemaker, Robert B., 'Reforming the city: the reformation of manners campaign in London, 1690–1738', in Davison, Lee, Keirn, Tim and Shoemaker, R. B. (eds), *Stilling the Grumbling Hive* (Stroud, 1992).

Simms, Brendan, ' "An odd question enough": Charles James Fox, the Crown and British policy during the Hanoverian crisis of 1806', *HJ*, vol. 38 (1995).

Smith, Hannah, 'The Court in England, 1714–1760: a declining political institution?', *History*, vol. 90 (Jan.2005).

Smith, S. D., review of Ashworth, William J., *Customs and Excise: Trade, Production, and Consumption in England, 1640–1845* (Oxford, 2003) and referring to Inikori, Joseph E., *Africans and the Industrial Revolution in England: A Study in International Trade and Development* (Cambridge, 2003) at www.history.a..uk/reviews/paper/smithSD.html.21/03/04

Strachan, Hew, 'The early Victorian army and the nineteenth-century revolution in government', *EHR*, vol. 95 (1980).

Targett, S., 'Government and ideology during the age of the Whig Supremacy: the political argument of Sir Robert Walpole's newspaper propagandists' *HJ*, vol. 37 (1994).

Taylor, Miles, 'Colonial representation at Westminster, *c*.1800–65' in Hoppit, Julian (ed.), *Parliaments, nations and identities in Britain and Ireland, 1660–1850* (Manchester, 2003).

Taylor, Stephen, 'Robert Walpole' in Eccleshall, Robert and Walker, Graham (eds), *Biographical Dictionary of British Prime Ministers* (1998).

Torrance, J., 'Social class and bureaucratic innovation: the commission for examining the public accounts 1780–87', *P&P*, vol. 78 (1978).

Townend, G. M., 'Religious radicalism and conservatism in the Whig Party under George I: the repeal of the Occasional Conformity and Schism Acts', *PH*, vol. 7 (1988).

Webster, Anthony, 'The political economy of trade liberalisation: the East India Company Charter Act of 1813', *EconHR*, vol. 43 (1990).

Wilkinson, C., 'The Earl of Egmont and the Navy, 1763–66', *The Mariners' Mirror*, vol. 84 (1998).

Woodland, Patrick, 'Political atomization and regional interests in the 1761 Parliament: the impact of the cider debates, 1763–1766', *PH*, vol. 8 (1989).

Parliamentary papers

Comparative circulation of parliamentary papers issued 1833–38, 1840 (130). xv. 250.

Estimates…[of]…salaries and expenses of public departments, 1850 (256.II) xxxiv. 313.

General index to reports of public petitions, 1833–1852, 1854–5 (531). liv.1.

Registered documents, papers, and correspondence, 1852 (116). xxviii.571.

Return of number of days on which House of Commons sat in each month of sessions 1831–81. 1881 (445). lxxiv.109.

Return of the number of petitions printed and circulated with the Votes in 1839 and 1840, 1841 (281). xxvii. 33.

Unpublished theses and papers

Bailey, De Witt, 'The Board of Ordnance and small arms supply: the Ordnance system, 1714–83', University of London Ph.D., 1988.

Collinson, M. G., 'Law, the State and the control of labour in eighteenth-century England', University of Sheffield Ph.D., 1982.

Crowe, Brian D., 'The parliamentary experience of the Irish Members of the House of Commons 1833–41', Queen's University of Belfast. Ph.D., 1995.

Donajgrodski, A. P., 'The Home Office, 1822–48', University of Oxford D.Phil., 1974.

Fedorak, C. J., 'The Addington ministry and the interaction of Foreign Policy and Domestic Politics, 1800–1804', University of London Ph.D., 1990.

Gaunt, Richard, A., 'The political activities and opinions of the Fourth Duke of Newcastle (1785–1851)', University of Nottingham Ph.D., 2000.

Henry, Barbara, 'The Monarch's speeches: an examination of the opening speeches presented to Parliament by King George III and Queen Victoria during the 1780s and the 1840s', Queen's University of Belfast MA Dissertation Module, 2005.

Innes, Joanna, 'The early history of select committees of enquiry, *c.*1688–1844'.

Nicholas, J. D., 'Lord Bute's Ministry, 1762–1763', University of Wales Ph.D., 1987.

Rees, Anita J., 'The practice and procedure of the House of Lords, 1714–1784', University of Wales Ph.D., 1978.

Archival sources

B. L., Lansdowne Mss.

Durham Univ., Grey Mss., 3rd Earl Grey's Diary.

Herts. R. O., Panshanger Mss.

Kent Archives Service, Camden Mss.

Index

The Enlightenment World

Edited by Martin Fitzpatrick, Peter Jones, Christa Knellwolf and Iain McCalman

'It is simply the best study of the Enlightenment World ever produced'
H.T. Dickenson, *Sir Richard Lodge Professor of British History, University of Edinburgh*

'A fine team of contributors...The imaginative range of topics is particularly impressive...An Enlightenment project that definitely succeeds!'
John Hedley Brooke, *Andreas Idreos Professor of Science and Religion, University of Oxford*

'The rich scholarship on the Enlightenment is critically and constructively invoked throughout, making this a fine reference work'
Knud Haakonssen, *Boston University*

The Enlightenment World offers an informed, comprehensive and up-to-date analysis of the European Enlightenment (circa 1720–1800) as both an historical epoch and a cultural formation. This prestigious collection begins with the intellectual origins of the Enlightenment, and spans early formations up to both contemporary and modern critics of the Enlightenment. The chapters, written by leading international experts, represent the most cutting-edge research within the field and include:

- The High Enlightenment
- Polite Culture and the Arts
- Reforming the World
- Material and Pop Culture
- Transformations and Exploration.

Covering topics as diverse as government, fashion, craftsmen and artisans, philanthropy, cross-cultural encounters, feminism, censorship, science and education, this volume will provide essential reading for all students of the Enlightenment.

ISBN10: 0–415–21575–7 (pbk)
ISBN13: 978–0–415–21575–6 (pbk)

Available at all good bookshops
For ordering and further information please visit:
www.routledge.com

The Routledge Companion to Britain in the Eighteenth Century, 1688–1820

John Stevenson and Jeremy Gregory

The Routledge Companion to Britain in the Eighteenth Century is an invaluable compendium of facts, figures, lists and chronologies on all aspects of British life from 1688–1820. A vital resource for students and scholars of the era, this *Companion* is crammed with information on the monarchy and outlines of British military campaigns, and also includes key events in literature, science, philosophy, religion and the arts during the era. Complete with a section of biographies of key individuals, a glossary of key terms, an annotated bibliography to aid further research and a map section, it provides a one-stop shop for those with an interest in this fascinating period of British history.

ISBN10: 0–415–37882–6 (hbk)
ISBN10: 0–415–37883–4 (pbk)

ISBN13: 978–0–415–37882–6 (hbk)
ISBN13: 978–0–415–37883–3 (pbk)

The Island Race: Englishness, Empire and Gender in the Eighteenth Century

Kathleen Wilson

Rooted in a period of vigorous exploration and colonialism, *The Island Race: Englishness, Empire and Gender in the Eighteenth Century* is an innovative study of the issues of nation, gender and identity. Wilson bases her analysis on a wide range of case studies drawn both from Britain and across the Atlantic and Pacific worlds.

Creating a colourful and original colonial landscape, she considers topics such as:

- sodomy
- theatre
- masculinity
- the symbolism of Britannia
- the role of women in war.

Wilson shows the far-reaching implications that colonial power and expansion had upon the English people's sense of self, and argues that the vaunted singularity of English culture was in fact constituted by the bodies, practices and exchanges of peoples across the globe. Theoretically rigorous and highly readable, *The Island Race will* become a seminal text for understanding the pressing issues that it confronts.

ISBN10: 0–415–15895–8 (hbk)
ISBN10: 0–415–15896–6 (pbk)

ISBN13: 978–0–415–15895–4 (hbk)
ISBN13: 978–0–415–15896–1 (pbk)

Available at all good bookshops
For ordering and further information please visit:
www.routledge.com

Gladstone and Disraeli

Stephen J. Lee

Gladstone and Disraeli surveys and compares the careers of these two influential prime ministers. Stephen J. Lee examines how Gladstone and Disraeli emerged as leaders of the two leading parties and goes on to consider their time in power, analysing many different aspects of their careers.

Using a wide variety of sources and historiography, Stephen J. Lee compares and contrasts the beliefs of Gladstone and Disraeli, their effect on the economy, social reform, the Irish problem and parliamentary reform, and on foreign policy.

ISBN10: 0–415–32356–8 (hbk)
ISBN10: 0–415–32357–6 (pbk)

ISBN13: 978–0–415–32356–7 (hbk)
ISBN13: 978–0–415–32357–4 (pbk)